Msgr. Maurice V. O'Connell | Joseph Stoutzenberger

⚆Harcourt Religion Publishers

www.harcourtreligion.com

For permission to reprint copyrighted material, grateful acknowledgment is made to the following sources:

Center for Teaching Peace, Washington, D.C.: From "Undeclared War to Declared War," "Love is the Measure," and "The Scandal of the Works of Mercy" by Dorothy Day in *Solutions to Violence*, edited by Colman McCarthy.
Chicago Province of The Society of Jesus: Untitled prayer by Oscar Romero from *Peace Prayers*, edited by Carrie Leadingham, Joann E. Moschella, and Hilary M. Vartanian. Text copyright © 1992 by HarperCollins Publishers.
James Clarke and Co.: From "Ninety-Five Theses" in *The Reformation Writings of Martin Luther*, volume I, translated and edited by Bertram Lee Woolf.
Costello Publishing Company, Inc., Northport, NY: From *Vatican Council II: The Basic Sixteen Documents*, edited by Austin Flannery, O.P. Text copyright © 1996 by Costello Publishing Company, Inc.
Crown Publishers, a division of Random House, Inc.: From *Canterbury Tales* by Geoffrey Chaucer, translated by J. U. Nicolson. Translation copyright 1934 by Civici Friede, Inc.
Darton Longman Todd, Ltd., London: Untitled prayer by St. Augustine, translated by Robert Dodaro, OSA from *The Radical Tradition*, edited by Gilbert Márkus. Translation © 1992 by Robert Dodaro, OSA.
ICS Publications, 2131 Lincoln Road, N.E. Washington, D.C. 20002-1199: From *The Collected Works of St. John of the Cross*, translated by Kieran Kavanaugh and Otilio Rodriguez. Translation © 1979, 1991 by Washington Province of Discalced Carmelites.
International Commission on English in the Liturgy: From the English translation of *Rite of Baptism for Children*. Translation © 1969 by International Committee on English in the Liturgy, Inc. From the English translation of *Order of Christian Funerals*. Translation © 1985 by International Committee on English in the Liturgy, Inc.
International Consultation on English Texts: English translation of the Nicene Creed by the International Consultation on English Texts.
Liturgical Press, Collegeville, MN: From *Twentieth-Century Apostles* by Phyllis Zagano. Text copyright © 1999 by The Order of St. Benedict, Inc.
Orbis Books, Maryknoll, NY: From *St. Martin de Porres* by Alex García-Rivera. Text copyright © 1995 by Alex García-Rivera.
Pauline Books and Media: "Through Our Hands," "Making Love Practical," and "Lead Me" by Mother Teresa in *A World on Its Knees*, compiled by Madonna Therese Ratliff, FSP. Text copyright © 2001 by Daughters of St. Paul.
Paulist Press, New York/Mahwah, N.J., www.paulistpress.com: From *Francis and Clare: The Complete Works in The Classics of Western Spirituality*, translated by Regis J. Armstrong, O.F.M. CAP and Ignatius C. Brady, O.F.M. Translation copyright © 1982 by Paulist Press, Inc. From *Catherine of Siena: The Dialogue in The Classics of Western Spirituality*, translated by Suzanne Noffke, O.P. Translation copyright © 1980 by Paulist Press, Inc.
Religious Task Force on Central America and Mexico: From "Jean Donovan: Except for the Children." Text copyright © 2005 by RTFCAM.ORG.
Twenty-Third Publications: From *The Church Emerging from Vatican II* by Dennis M. Doyle. Text copyright © 1992 by Dennis Doyle.
United States Catholic Conference, Washington, D.C.: From the English translation of the *Catechism of the Catholic Church* for the United States of America. Translation copyright © 1994 by United States Catholic Conference, Inc. – Libreria Editrice Vaticana. From the English translation of the *Catechism of the Catholic Church: Modifications from the Editio Typica*. Translation copyright © 1997 by United States Catholic Conference, Inc. – Libreria Editrice Vaticana.
The Zondervan Corporation: Chart #25 "Arguments for the Existence of God – the Five Ways of Thomas Aquinas" from *Chronological and Background Charts of Church History* by Robert C. Walton. Copyright © 1986 by The Zondervan Corporation.

Printed in the United States of America
ISBN 0-15-901870-6

Contents

INTRODUCTION
**The Wonder of the Church: Christ's
Presence in the World**............................ vi

Who Needs the Church?

Church History—People with a Mission

A Closer Look: Bringing the Past to Life,
Recognizing Christ's Presence

CHAPTER 1
**Beginnings: The Church of
the Apostles**.. 2

Jewish Roots of the Church

Built on the Good News

A Closer Look: Youth News

A Closer Look: Saint Peter the Fisherman

The Beginnings of the Church

Images of the Church: An Apostolic Church

Christians Inspire Hope

A Closer Look: Mary—Mother of Christ,
Mother of the Church

A Closer Look: Saint Paul: The Apostle to
the Gentiles

Age to Age: Teen Retreats

CHAPTER 2
**Spreading the Message:
The Church Enters the Empire** 32

Persecution for the Faith

A Closer Look: Saints Perpetua and Felicity

A Closer Look: Deacon Laurence

Images of the Church: The Seed
of the Kingdom

The Church Formulates Essential Beliefs

The Church Refines the Way She Worships

One Body in Christ

Age to Age: Litany of the Saints

CHAPTER 3
**Church Victorious: The Age of
the Fathers**... 62

Christianity, Religion of the Empire

Images of the Church: Bride of Christ

The Western Roman Empire Falls

A Closer Look: Saint Leo the Great

The Fathers of the Church

Monasticism

A Closer Look: Saint Anthony of Egypt

Age to Age: Hermits and Monks

CHAPTER 4
**Expansion and Growth:
Creating a Christian European World** 90

Christianity East and West

Christianity, Judaism, and Islam

The Christian Experience

The Work of Missionaries

Images of the Church: The Universal
Church

A Closer Look: Saint Patrick and the
Conversion of Ireland

A Closer Look: Saint Hilda

Age to Age: Liturgical Music

CHAPTER 5

Church and World United: Toward the High Middle Ages 118

Christendom and the Middle Ages

Troubles and Triumphs

    A Closer Look: Liturgy of the Hours

    A Closer Look: Margaret of Scotland

    Images of the Church: Vine and Branches

The Medieval Christian Experience

Crusaders and Reformers

    A Closer Look: Saint Clare of Assisi

Age to Age: Saint Dominic and the Rosary

CHAPTER 6

From Disorder to Beauty and Hope: The Road to the Renaissance 156

Decline of Unity

    A Closer Look: Saint Catherine of Siena

Time of Tragedy and Intense Prayer

    Images of the Church: The Sacrament of Salvation

    A Closer Look: Saint Joan of Arc

The Ever-Changing Geography

The Renaissance

Age to Age: Holy Cards

CHAPTER 7

Challenge and Response: The Church in Disunity 182

The Protestant Reformation

    Images of the Church: Sacrament of Unity

Spread of Protestantism

    A Closer Look: Heroes of the Reformation

Differences in Teachings

    A Closer Look: Saint Margaret Clitherow

The Catholic Reformation

    A Closer Look: Saint Charles Borromeo

    A Closer Look: Two Catholic Visionaries

Age to Age: Forty Hours Devotion

CHAPTER 8

Sacred or Secular: Rationalism Confronts the Catholic Church 218

The Church and Science

    Images of the Church: A Holy People

An Age of Nation-States

    A Closer Look: Christina, Queen of Sweden

    A Closer Look: Cardinal Ercole Consalvi

Catholicism in England and Ireland

    A Closer Look: Three Leaders of the Church in England

A Changing World

    A Closer Look: Saint Paul Miki and Companions

Age to Age: New Religious Communities

CHAPTER 9

Mosaic of Unity and Diversity: The Church in the Americas 254

A Collision of Cultures
    A Closer Look: Our Lady of Guadalupe
    Images of the Church: A Pilgrim People
The French Presence
    A Closer Look: Blessed Kateri Tekakwitha
Catholicism in the Colonies
The Immigrant Church
    A Closer Look: Bishop John Hughes
    A Closer Look: Saint Elizabeth Ann Seton
Age to Age: A Multicultural Church

CHAPTER 10

A Spiritual and Moral Presence: The Church in the Modern World 290

The Industrial Revolution
    A Closer Look: Mother Jones
Political Controversies
    A Closer Look: James Cardinal Gibbons
    A Closer Look: Pope Saint Pius X
Catholic Spiritual Life
An Age of World Wars
    Images of the Church: Temple of the Holy Spirit
Age to Age: Catholic Relief Services

CHAPTER 11

The Church of Vatican Council II 326

Call for Renewal
Vatican II—Christ's Presence
The Impact of Vatican II
    Images of the Church: The People of God
    The Documents of Vatican Council II—Major
        Themes and Implications
Pope Paul VI
Age to Age: The Rite of Christian
    Initiation of Adults

CHAPTER 12

The Gospel of Life 354

The Church Enters a New Millenium
    Images of the Church: The Light of Christ
The Church in the World
The Church in the United States
    A Closer Look: Sister Thea Bowman
Present and Future
Age to Age: The Gospel of Life

Glossary 382

Index 387

INTRODUCTION

THE WONDER OF THE CHURCH

CHRIST'S PRESENCE IN THE WORLD

INTRODUCTION GOALS

In this introduction you will:

★ see that the Church is the assembly of people called to be the Body of Christ.

★ learn that the Church transcends history while still being a part of it.

★ explore Church history as it traces the impact of Christ in and through the lives of his people.

Who Needs the Church?

S torms travel quickly and fiercely across the Kansas plains. On this particular evening, the storm seemed especially fierce. Melissa saw the frightened look on the faces of the two children she was baby-sitting. She huddled them together on the couch and assured them, "It's fine. I'm here. Everything is going to be all right. How about if we sing songs and I tell you happy stories?"

Science class got Mick thinking . . . "The universe has been around such a long time and is so vast. In the big picture, life on earth has a brief history. The saga of human existence takes up only the slightest fraction of time. In the grand scheme of things, it's hard to take seriously the dignity and worth that we humans give our species. What makes us think that we're so special? Why would we possibly believe that anyone—besides ourselves—cares for the entire human race, not to mention any of us individually?"

"Here we go again," Rondell thought. "Ms. White is going to try to get us to volunteer for some service project. Operation Rice Bowl? That sounds like a great time! Why in the world would I cut back on money spent on lunch and give it to an organization that helps people who are poor whom I don't even know? I've got troubles enough of my own."

When Molly's grandfather died, her mother was devastated. Molly didn't know how her mother was going to get through those first days after she heard the news. Their neighbors came over, bringing food and flowers. Aunts, uncles, and cousins Molly didn't even know she had showed up at the house. Everyone told her stories about her grandfather. Some of the stories she knew, and some she had never heard before. Pictures of her grandfather at different stages of his life were strewn over the coffee table. When, at the funeral, the priest said, "This day you will be with me in paradise," Molly glanced over at her mom and noticed her nodding and smiling through her tears. Molly was glad that her family, her friends, and her faith gave her mother such comfort during this difficult time.

The devastation of September 11, 2001 had hit hard at Antonio's school. Altogether, ten families lost close relatives. The father of one of Antonio's best friends had died that day. Ever since then, Antonio has struggled trying to make sense of evil and how best to respond to it.

FIRST THOUGHTS

Imagine what the future might be like if everyone forgot about Christ and his message. Then imagine a future in which most people seek to know and follow Christ. Describe the differences in these two visions of the future.

★ Why is the Church necessary for a Christ-filled future?

★ How can the study of Church history help you better understand your vision of the future?

The Church—Our Doorway to Jesus Christ

Some experiences in life definitely lead us to wonder. Is Melissa lying to the children she is baby-sitting, or does she honestly believe that, despite threatening storms, in the end everything will be all right? Where does she get the insight and the courage to calm the fears of frightened children? For his part, Mick entered into the mysteries of science enough to wonder about the universe: Does it have meaning, is there a purpose to human existence, is a guiding hand at work even amidst the vast expanse of the unknown? Rondell appears to have decided that the fate of people outside of his immediate circle has little to do with him, but is he right about that? Are we connected to everyone else—the living, the dead, and those to come? If we are, what is the nature of that relationship? Is there a way to celebrate that relationship? Are there responsibilities that come with relationships?

And Molly comes face to face with that greatest of mysteries, death, when her grandfather dies. Through the songs and prayers of the funeral Mass she attends, Molly finds reassurance that death does not mean the end for her grandfather. Finally, the tragic events of September 11, 2001, caused an entire nation to wonder. The site of the former World Trade Center has become honored ground, much like the Vietnam Memorial in Washington, D.C. People who have visited the site after the death and destruction that took place there often have paused to say a prayer or to leave a prayerful message on a banner or poster. After September 11, 2001, the words "God bless America" suddenly took on deeper meaning for many of us.

Perhaps you, too, have had moments of wonder. But, it seems the modern world is not particularly suited to wonder. We can't wonder if we don't stop and listen. Going to bed with ear phones blaring music can keep us from wondering even during those otherwise quiet moments of solitude. When we do find ourselves wondering about things, we could certainly use some light. Here is where the Church comes in. God has not left us alone with our wonderings, our fears, and our confusion. Jesus Christ is the light through whom we encounter God the Father. For that reason, the Son of God is the central event in all history. In him we meet the loving God. But how do we meet Christ? The answer is: in and through the Holy Spirit and the Church.

The Church Is the Body of Christ "Church" is a concept that is very simple but also multi-faceted; it is indeed a mystery. Quite simply, the Church is people—like Melissa and Rondell. The origins of the word suggest that the Church is a gathering of people who have been called together for a special purpose. The Church, therefore, is a "convocation"—an assembly of people called together. We know for a fact that the Church is made up of Melissas and Rondells from all the ends of the earth. The Church is that gathering of people right around you who celebrate the liturgy together in your own school chapel or parish church, who pray together before classes, and who get involved in community projects to help others.

If the Church is made up of a gathering of people who have been called, then who is doing the calling? The answer to that question is Jesus Christ. But, the relationship between Christ and the Church is quite complex. The *Catechism of the Catholic Church* describes this complexity: "She [the Church] draws her life from the word and the Body of Christ and so herself becomes Christ's Body" (#752). The Church is both a visible reality—the people gathered into a community and organization, with different roles and functions—and a spiritual reality—the Body of Christ in the world. Like Jesus, the Church is both human and divine. The relationship between Jesus and his Church is much more intimate and a greater mystery than what we normally mean by being called by someone. No single description of the relationship captures what the Church is and how she is one with Christ.

Saint Paul uses the following analogy to explain the relationship between Christ and the Church. He says that Christ is to his Church as the head is to the body. (See *1 Corinthians 12*.) Perhaps Saint Paul is saying that the head provides the spark by which the various parts of the body are animated, come to life, know what to do, and are capable of functioning. At the same time, the head directs the various parts of the body to be active in the many ways necessary for a body to interact with the rest of the world.

Another story from Scripture that attempts to explain the relationship between Christ and the people who make up the Church is found in the Gospel according to John. Jesus tells a man named Nicodemus who has been meeting with him in secret: "no one can see the kingdom of God without being born from above." Nicodemus, who definitely misses the point, tries to imagine how he can "enter a second time into the mother's womb." Jesus clarifies for him that "no one can enter the kingdom of God without being born of water and Spirit" (*John 3:3–5*). In other words, people who have been reborn through the waters of Baptism and through the Holy Spirit become one with Christ and share in his divine life.

The Son of God comes from the Father and becomes human so that human beings can become one with the Father in Christ and through the Holy Spirit. Slow down and read that sentence again. It's bursting with amazing implications. The great theologian Saint Augustine suggested an appropriate response to this unique relationship that Christians have with their Lord and Savior—"Marvel and rejoice: we have become Christ.[1]" (*CCC*, #795). The Church, made up of human beings but filled with the Holy Spirit, is one with Christ who is one in being with the Father. Christ is the Son of God who became human so that we might become like God. Through the Church, we come into relationship with the Trinity, the three Persons in one God—God the Father, God the Son, and God the Holy Spirit. Through Jesus and his Church, we come to know each of the Persons of the Trinity and the central significance of the Trinity to our faith.

The Church as Sacrament—The "Both-And" Nature of the Church An implication of the intimate union that exists between Christ and his Church is that the Church is a sacrament—meaning that she is a sign and an instrument of God's continuing presence, of the unity of all humanity, and of our union with God. As sacrament, the Church is a *visible community* that manifests a *spiritual reality*. The community that is the Church is made up of real people and has an identifiable organizational structure with people fulfilling various roles within that community. Through this very human reality, Christ communicates truth and grace to everyone (See Documents of Vatican II, *Lumen Gentium*, 8). The sacramental nature of the Church means that it is:

- a structured and hierarchical society that is also the mystical Body of Christ,

- a visible society that is also a spiritual community,

- an earthly Church and a Church of heavenly riches.

As a sacramental community, the Church is holy because it is one with Christ who is "holy, innocent, and undefiled[2]" (*CCC*, #827). If you don't feel as though you belong in such a community, remember once again the "both-and" nature of the Church: "All members of the Church, including her ministers, must acknowledge that they are sinners.[3] In everyone, the weeds of sin will still be mixed with the good wheat of the Gospel until the end of time[4]" (*CCC*, #827).

Does the Church, then, address the concerns of Melissa, Mick, Rondell, Molly, and the post-September 11, 2001 world? Indeed, without an intimate connection with God, their concerns would remain fears and anxieties. Christ sheds light on their troubles. In the Church we have a visible manifestation of the light of Christ. Wouldn't it be worthwhile to discover how the light of Christ and the Holy Spirit who gives life to all humanity has been revealed from the time of Jesus to the present? This is the reason for our Church history course.

The Church is the assembly of people called by Christ that is...
universal (united under the leadership of the pope and the world's bishops).
local (in individual parishes and gatherings of believers).
visible most fully in the Eucharist; she is a worshiping community that celebrates an intimate relationship with Christ.

" The one mediator, Christ, established and constantly sustains here on earth his holy church, the community of faith, hope and charity, as a visible structure through which he communicates truth and grace to everyone.[5]

Documents of Vatican II, *Lumen Gentium*, 8

Church History— People with a Mission

The largest gathering of Catholic bishops in the history of the Catholic Church took place at the Second Vatican Council in the 1960s. The bishops said the following:

> Henceforward the church, equipped with the gifts of its founder and faithfully observing his precepts of charity, humility and self-denial, receives the mission of proclaiming and establishing among all peoples the kingdom of Christ and of God, and is, on earth, the seed and the beginning of that kingdom.

Documents of Vatican II, *Lumen Gentium*, 5

This statement says a lot about the nature of the Catholic Church. The Church is on a mission, the same mission begun by Jesus. However, here again we see the dual nature of the Church. In one sense, we can proclaim in Christ Jesus, "Mission accomplished!" Through his sacrifice on the cross and his Resurrection from the dead, salvation has already been achieved. On the other hand, the Church has the ongoing mission of reconciling people to God as Jesus did and working for the kingdom of God on earth. In other words, the Church is in history but also *beyond* history. Its center—Jesus Christ—and the continuing of his mission of proclaiming God's reign, has not changed. However, the Church's visible representation in the world has changed over time. "This 'family of God' is gradually formed and takes shape during the stages of human history . . ." (*CCC*, #759).

Church history is the ongoing story of God's offer of salvation, which he first offered to the first man and woman, then to Noah, later to Abraham and Moses, down through the prophets, and finally and ultimately in his Son. It is an account of God's plan of salvation since the coming of Christ, over time and in specific places and manifest in the lives of individual people. Church history is the story of how the Holy Spirit has guided the Church—at times through troubling circumstances. Through the Holy Spirit, the Church has kept intact the message of Jesus so that today we still see him in the workings of his Church. This course invites you to look at the history of the Church with eyes of faith, believing that the hand of God is at work even when we have difficulty understanding how. Melissa, Mick, Rondell, Molly, and the post-September 11, 2001 world desperately need eyes of faith to see God's loving presence within them and among them. We do also.

Bringing the Past to Life, Recognizing Christ's Presence

Sometimes words like "the Church," "Church history," and even "the Holy Spirit" can sound very abstract. It's important to remember that the Church is made up of real people. As you might expect, the Church has had more than her share of very colorful characters. When we look at the people of history who make up the Church we are looking at the Holy Spirit at work, one image for whom is "the hand of God" present in our world. We need good storytellers to help us recognize the Holy Spirit is alive in the world.

Every family should have a Nellie O'Brien. She was my grandfather's first cousin and my godmother. She attended school only through the sixth grade; and although she could read and write, it was her memory that was her greatest asset. She was the best story-teller I ever met. She was born in 1897 and knew all our family stories. From the time I was able to drive, it was my job to get her to and from family gatherings. I loved those times together when she would tell me the stories of my family, beginning with my great-grandparents. Without her, I would have known only their names. Nellie made them real for me. She told me about the times they lived in and about what they thought and did. She was the family historian.

History is more than "just the facts" about the past. History involves passing on stories and describing the personalities involved in those stories, all the while seeking to make sense of why people did what they did.

History opens up new worlds to us. In so doing, it also sheds new light on our own world. Because of Nellie, the historian, the past came alive for me and took on personal meaning. It involved learning about the people whose actions, whether I like it or not, shaped me and my current situation and would also influence my future. When the people of our past cease to be merely pictures in a family album, and we try to allow them to speak to us, then we truly appreciate and understand our family history.

Rev. Maurice V. O'Connell

FAITH ACTIVITY

Family History Recall an event you have heard about from your family's history. (If you have one, ask your family storyteller about the details of the event.)

1. Write about the event in short-story form.

2. Describe how this story might speak to you in some way—to understand yourself and your family better, to appreciate how today is similar to or different from yesterday, or to offer guidance about things you might do in the future.

History and Church History

History is a record of the human story. You already have had history courses and you will likely have more. We study Church history to discover what transpired in the last 2,000 years in the unfolding story of the community of the Catholic Church. We also study Church history because we believe that human history does not run its course separate from the workings of the Holy Spirit. The Holy Spirit has been present in the people and events of the history of the Church. Finally, we study Church history because it is an ongoing story, one of a living family. Through the power of the Holy Spirit, we are making our own stories, creating our own history, and shaping the world for future generations. In this ongoing process it is helpful—indeed, essential—that we learn from the past. We need to learn from people of the past who called themselves Christians so that we can contribute our own gifts and talents to Christ's presence now and into the future. This is where our study of Church history comes in.

Let's Get Started Now we have some idea of what we will be studying and why we are studying it. The story begins with a small group of people living in a section of the Middle East that we now call the Holy Land. From there the group spread the message of their encounter with God in Jesus Christ to Africa, Asia, and Europe, later to the Americas, and finally throughout the globe. This group of disciples of Jesus represents the beginning of the Catholic Church, which has continued as an instrument by which Christ's Spirit remains a living and loving presence in the world. Let us begin our journey.

▼ *The Disciples Attempt to Fish in Lake Tiberias without Success* by **Cristoforo de Predis**

A.D. 50
Saint Paul writes first epistle; beginning of New Testament writings

TIMELINE

A.D. 33
Death of Jesus

A.D. 34
Death of Stephen, first Christian martyr

A.D. 35-67
Paul's conversion and mission to the Gentiles

A.D. 50
Council of Jerusalem

CHAPTER 1

BEGINNINGS

THE CHURCH OF THE APOSTLES

A.D. 30-100

CHAPTER GOALS

In this chapter you will:

★ explore the early Church's Jewish roots.

★ learn that at Pentecost the Holy Spirit inspired the followers of Jesus to continue Jesus' work in the world.

★ consider why the Church proclaims trust in God, salvation through Jesus, and personal and social conversion.

★ discover how the Church grew into a diverse, hope-filled community centered on Christ.

A.D. 54	A.D. 64-67	A.D. 70	A.D. 70-100	A.D. 81	A.D. 100
First persecution of Christians under Herod Agrippa	Martyrdom of Peter and Paul during the first Roman persecution under Nero	Destruction of the Temple in Jerusalem	Gospels written	Domitian persecution begins	Traditional date given for the death of John, the last Apostle

Jewish Roots of the Church

In every chapter of this book you will find a description of an image used to describe the Church. No doubt you already have some experiences of the Church in your life. Before learning about the Church's story, take time to think about your own experience of the Church.

★ What images symbolize the Church for you?

★ What aspects of the Church are most meaningful to you?

★ What do you think the Church was like in its beginning stages?

★ Where does the Church fit into your life today?

Have you ever had something happen that completely turned your life around? Did you ever experience an event that filled you with great joy or that helped you make sense out of life? Are there people you have known who were able to forget their own problems and be genuinely concerned about others? Have you ever been part of a group where you felt accepted and cared for?

During his lifetime Jesus built a community in which people had experiences that changed their lives; experiences in which they encountered the living God. After Jesus' Ascension into heaven, the Holy Spirit remained with this community. The followers of Jesus grew in number and within decades took on a new and distinctive identity. The Christian community spread out from Jerusalem to Rome and to the civilized world. So strongly did they believe in their Lord's message that early missionaries gave up their lives to teach it. Even before the death of the last Apostle, this Church which Jesus instituted during his lifetime had been firmly implanted in the world. Through the power of the Holy Spirit, the Church was born.

> The Church is closely linked with the Jewish people, who first heard the word of God. Judaism is a response to the revelation of God and to the covenant. God's covenant with the Jews has never been revoked.
> See *Catechism of the Catholic Church*, #839.

Your story didn't begin when you were born. Fascinating people came before you who underwent hardships, made choices, and fashioned a family heritage. They helped to decide why you live in one country and not another, why you speak the language you do, many of your physical and personality traits, and even some of your values. The same can be said of the birth of the Church.

A People and a Culture

Historians today help us understand the importance of Jesus' Jewish heritage and the Jewish roots of his Church. We can't understand how people of Jesus' time viewed him without understanding the Jewish culture in which he lived. We can look all the way back to the early **Hebrew** patriarchs—Abraham, Isaac, and Jacob—for the beginning of the story of God's special relationship with his people as recorded in the Old Testament. We learn from the Old Testament that God made himself known slowly over time, through actions and words. Out of sheer love, God sought a relationship with those he had created.

Christ and his Church fulfill and continue the story of the relationship that God established first with the Jewish people. For instance, the beginning of the Old Testament describes God's creation of the world in seven days. Christ's Resurrection is the "eighth day" of creation since through it God's glory is manifest in a new creation. As Adam was the first human being, Jesus is the "new Adam." The Gospel according to Luke describes how Jesus used the words of the Hebrew prophet Isaiah to explain the meaning behind his mission:

When he came to Nazareth, where he had been brought up, he went to the synagogue on the Sabbath day, as was his custom. He stood up to read, and the scroll of the prophet Isaiah was given to him. He unrolled the scroll and found the place where it was written:

"The Spirit of the Lord is upon me,
because he has anointed me
to bring good news to the poor.
He has sent me to proclaim release to the captives
and recovery of sight to the blind,
to let the oppressed go free,
to proclaim the year of the Lord's favor."
And he rolled up the scroll, gave it back to the attendant, and sat down. The eyes of all in the synagogue were fixed on him. Then he began to say to them, "Today this scripture has been fulfilled in your hearing."

✠ Luke 4:18-21

What is the Church? Read each
of the following scripture verses:
Genesis 12:1-4
Genesis 32:22-32
Exodus 14:5-14
Isaiah 9:2-7
Jeremiah 1:4-10
Ezekiel 37:1-14
Explain how the messages contained
in each might help us understand
what the Church is, or is meant to be.

Jesus begins his ministry by clearly identifying himself as the One who can accomplish what the people have longed for and what God had promised. The Old Testament prophecies, longings, and stories reach their fulfillment in the life of Christ. Jesus was indeed the Messiah, the Anointed One of which Isaiah had spoken. He would save the people from their suffering and sin, just as his name Jesus (which means "God saves") implies.

Much of the early Christian Church understood Christ, his message, and the Church's mission in light of these scriptural themes and stories. You may have already studied the Bible, where much of our knowledge of early Jewish history comes from, but let's take a look at some important moments in Jewish history.

According to the Book of Genesis, long before Jesus, a man named Abram (renamed Abraham after a life-changing encounter with God) and his wife Sarai (later renamed Sarah) lived in Ur, in what is today the country of Iraq. God spoke to Abram and told him to believe in him alone, rather than in the many gods of his pagan people. God then made a covenant, or solemn, lasting agreement with him, saying: "I will make of you a great nation, and I will bless you, and make your name great, so that you will be a blessing . . . and in you all the families of the earth shall be blessed" (*Genesis 12:2–3*).

In response to God's direction, Abraham left Ur and settled near the Dead Sea in the land of modern-day Israel. Although it seemed impossible because of their age, he and his wife finally had a son, Isaac, whom they loved. However, God again spoke to Abraham. This time he told Abraham to offer his son, Isaac, as a sacrifice. Abraham trusted God despite his own feelings and began preparations to follow God's will. God did not require him to make the ultimate sacrifice of offering his son, but, because Abraham passed such a great test of faith, God again promised him that he would make his "offspring as numerous as the stars of heaven and as the sand that is on the seashore"(*Genesis 22:17*).

In harmony with its Jewish roots, Christianity professes a monotheistic faith—that is, the belief in the one true God—but we know that the one God has revealed himself as Father, Son, and Holy Spirit. The one God is three in one, the Trinity. Not only is this belief an article of faith, but also a teaching that has implications for the way we should live. For example, if there is one God of all people, then we should treat all people as brothers and sisters. Secondly, the covenant originally made with Abraham is fulfilled and made new in Christ and thus continues in the Church. Jesus makes explicit reference to his fulfillment of the covenant at the Last Supper when he says of the cup he shares with his Apostles: "Drink from it, all of you; for this is my blood of the covenant, which is poured out for many for the forgiveness of sins"(*Matthew 26:27–28*).

We also recognize that the sacrifice of Abraham's son Isaac, which in the end God did not require, prefigured the sacrifice of God the Father's own Son on the cross. Finally, Christianity teaches that Abraham does become a blessing to all the nations of the world (see *Genesis 22:18*) through the Church, which has indeed spread the message of the covenant throughout the world. Thus, knowing the story of Abraham helps us understand how early followers of Jesus understood who Jesus was and what it means to be the Church.

GROUP TALK

1. List and discuss some elements from the Jewish faith that apply to the Catholic Church today.

2. Debate the following statements. In terms of how people live their lives, it makes no difference whether or not they:

   ★ believe in God.
   ★ believe in many gods or one god.
   ★ believe that every tribe, nation, or ethnic group has its own god.

FAITH ACTIVITY

Pilgrim People The stories of Abraham and the Exodus are journey stories; the Church is on a journey, so we are "pilgrim people." In response to this image of the Church as pilgrim people, answer the following questions:

★ What should members of the Church today journey away from?

★ What should they journey toward?

★ What are some of the tasks in which the Church should be engaged if she is to reach her final goal?

The Exodus Reveals a Loving God

Another event in Jewish history that defines our understanding of Jesus is the **Exodus**. The biblical account of Abraham's descendant named Joseph tells how the Hebrew people, or Israelites, settled in Egypt. Initially the ruling powers of Egypt welcomed the Israelites. However, when power changed hands, the Israelites were enslaved. In their suffering, they cried out to their God for freedom from slavery. The Old Testament Book of Exodus describes how God intervened on their behalf by sending Moses to lead them. Despite Moses' negotiations with the pharaoh (the Egyptian ruler), God had to send a series of plagues upon the Egyptian people from which the Israelites were spared. The culmination of the plagues came when the first-born sons of all Egyptians died. Israelite households marked their doorposts with the blood of a lamb and were spared this catastrophe. Moses was then finally able to lead the Israelites out of slavery, through the desert, and into the Promised Land, the land called Palestine where Abraham had once lived. This journey of the Israelites from slavery in Egypt to freedom in the land of their ancestors is known as the Exodus.

Jews celebrate the Exodus each year during one of their holiest feasts known as **Passover**. They do not simply recall the historical event but also enter into it as participants. In other words, God didn't just free the ancient Israelites from slavery; he also frees their descendants from spiritual slavery today.

The Exodus and Passover are intimately connected to the story of Jesus' death and Resurrection. In fact, Catholics refer to Christ's suffering, death, Resurrection, and Ascension as the **Paschal Mystery**. (*Pasch* is Greek for "passover.") Throughout history the community of people who make up the Church proclaims that they have been set free from the slavery of sin through Jesus, as God set free the Israelites in the Exodus. Every time Catholics participate in the liturgy, we recall and commemorate these saving events from the past, and the Holy Spirit makes them present and real to us again.

> Christ is risen from the dead!
> Dying, he conquered death;
> To the dead, he has given life. [1]
> *Catechism of the Catholic Church*, #638

The Jews of Israel and the Hellenistic Jews

To understand conflicts that arose within Christianity in its earliest stages, we also need to look back into Jewish history immediately before the time of Christ. Christianity began during a time of **Hellenization**. In the Hellenistic—Greek-ruled—and Roman periods, the region around Jerusalem became known as Judah. Judah and the nearby regions of Samaria and Galilee were also called Palestine.

Prior to the Hellenistic period, the forces of Babylon destroyed the kingdom of Judah in 587 B.C. and took many of the Jewish elite, the educated, and craftsmen back to Babylon as slaves. The Babylonians destroyed the Temple in Jerusalem and took its treasures, the most important of which was the Ark of the Covenant. In so doing they destroyed the center of Jewish life and worship as well. Many of the Jewish prisoners held onto their faith during their captivity, a period that lasted about fifty years and is known in Jewish history as the **Babylonian Captivity**. In time, these Jews became members of Babylonian society. Because they could not worship at their Temple, they developed a system of synagogues, which were initially informal meeting rooms where they would pray together and discuss the beliefs of their faith.

In 539 B.C. Cyrus, king of Persia, defeated the Babylonians and allowed the Jews to return to their homeland. Many returned to Judah, but some stayed in Babylon or went to other parts of the world. The Jews who continued to live outside of Judah became known as the Jews of the **diaspora**. Just prior to the time of Jesus, there were probably about four million Jews in the diaspora, while only about a million lived in Palestine.

Alexander the Great conquered the Persian Empire in 331 B.C. Under Alexander, Greek culture became the dominant culture throughout the eastern Mediterranean area. Greek culture greatly influenced the Jews of the diaspora, some of whom even took Greek names. Jews who adapted their Judaism to Greek culture are known as "Hellenistic Jews" or Hellenists.

FAITH ACTIVITY

Hellenization Write a report on classical Greek culture, Hellenization, or differences between Greek culture and traditional Jewish culture.

EXPLORE THE LAND

A Violent Relocation This map shows the Kingdoms of Israel and Judah just prior to the Babylonian Captivity. Through their hardships, the Jews retained their religion and faithfully praised God. If you were forcefully moved away from your home, friends, family, and Church, how would you keep your faith?

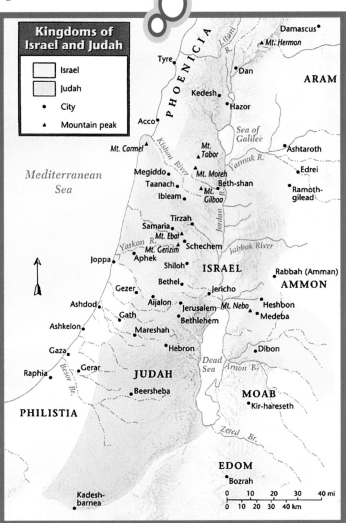

Kingdoms of Israel and Judah

- Israel
- Judah
- • City
- ▲ Mountain peak

By the time of Jesus, large Hellenistic communities existed in Rome, Alexandria, and Antioch. The Hellenistic Jews were frequently urban and wealthy, while those in Palestine were primarily rural and often poor. Those in Israel were isolated or "protected" from their non-Jewish neighbors. The Jews of the diaspora tended to interact in commerce and in social situations with their non-Jewish neighbors.

Most of the Jews of the diaspora read, wrote, spoke, and thought in Greek. They had so little contact with the Jews of Israel that around 200 b.c. Hebrew Scripture had to be translated into Greek so that people would be able to understand it when it was read in the synagogue. This translation was called the *Septuagint* because, according to tradition, seventy scholars—or seventy-two in some accounts—worked independently on the translation and yet all came up with the same text. It became the commonly used Scripture for the Jews of the diaspora.

As you might expect, the Judaism of the diaspora became different from the Judaism practiced in Palestine, especially in Jerusalem. Eventually some Jews of the diaspora moved back into Palestine and lived there, bringing with them the synagogue system and a more tolerant view toward non-Jews.

The Roman Empire spread throughout the region and in 63 b.c. Palestine came under Roman rule. Hellenistic culture continued during the Roman period, and at the time of Jesus, most diaspora Jews were Hellenists. Many of the first converts to "the Way" of Christianity came from among the Hellenistic Jewish population.

GROUP TALK

1 During the Hellenistic period, Greek rulers viewed their culture as superior to all others and attempted to spread their culture wherever they could. Hellenization led to conflicts with Jews and other cultural or religious groups. What are different ways that members of one religion might view other religions? How can this have an impact on what people believe or how they worship?

2 Make a case for or against the following statement: North American culture is the dominant culture throughout the world today, just as Greek culture was during the time of Jesus. To actively participate in international affairs, people in Asia, Africa, and elsewhere need to learn English, wear North American styles of clothing, and become familiar with aspects of North American culture.

Built on the Good News

Since the Church always seeks to be faithful to Jesus, we cannot know the Church unless we know Jesus and his message. We know tantalizingly little about the circumstances of his life. Most of what we know comes from the four New Testament books known as the **Gospels**, which focus on the life and teaching of Jesus. A carpenter by trade, Jesus lived in a town called Nazareth for most of his life. Nazareth was in Galilee, an area removed from Jerusalem, the center of Jewish life and power. In Jerusalem, people from Galilee were recognized by their accents, just as someone with a Southern accent would stand out in New England. Although Nazareth was a very small, poor village, it was also a few miles from a new and prosperous Roman town called Sepphorus. It's possible that Jesus did carpentry work for the wealthy people living in Sepphorus.

When Jesus was around thirty years old, his life completely changed. His cousin, John, was baptizing people in the Jordan River, calling upon them to "repent." At Jesus' request, John baptized Jesus even though Jesus was free from sin and did not need to repent. John knew he was the One for whom they had awaited. Soon after, Jesus gathered his own group of followers, saying: "The time is fulfilled, and the kingdom of God has come near; repent, and believe in the good news" (*Mark 1:14*). In this passage, we find three pivotal and intertwining themes in the teaching of Jesus: repentance, the "good news," and the kingdom of God.

Jesus called for repentance, a **conversion** of heart and mind, so that people could know and align themselves with God the Father. If people would accept the new way of being and acting that Jesus preached, they would participate in the **reign of God**. This term was already in use in the life and Scriptures of the Hebrew people, but Jesus described it in unique ways and made it the central theme of his message. He spoke about the kingdom of God as already present in him but as still to come in its fullness. He taught us that God is "Father," and showed us his unique relationship with the Father by calling on him while preaching, healing, and praying. In the most well-known and central Christian prayer, the Lord's Prayer, Jesus said to pray for God the Father's reign to come upon the earth as it already is in heaven.

FAITH ACTIVITY

Images of the Kingdom Look through the Gospels for references to the kingdom of God. You'll find many of them in Jesus' parables. Compose a poem or story illustrating one of the images used for the kingdom.

Sermon on the Mount by Albert Herbert.

FYI

Although we don't know definitively who wrote them, the four Gospels are named for the evangelists Matthew, Mark, Luke, and John. The author of the Gospel according to Luke is also the author of another New Testament book, the Acts of the Apostles. Since the Acts of the Apostles recounts the earliest events of Church history, it is an important source of information for our study of the Church during its fledgling period.

Jesus used intriguing images to give us a glimpse of what God's reign is like—including, a banquet to which people off the streets are invited because intended guests don't come, leaven added to bread to make it rise, a treasure hidden in a field, and seed planted among weeds. His preaching about the kingdom challenged those who were rich and comfortable but gave comfort and hope to those who were poor. (See *Luke 6:20–25*.) The Gospels according to Luke and Matthew contain the Beatitudes. They are Jesus' teachings about the blessings and true happiness that come from trusting in God and participating in the kingdom of God on earth so that we may know it in heaven. This is the divine life and happiness for which God made each of us.

Jesus' life is striking not only for what he said but also for what he did. He was a miracle worker. His miracles represent and reinforce his message of the coming of the kingdom of God. In other words, Jesus healed certain people, making them whole, just as all people will be made whole in the kingdom. Jesus forgave people's sins, just as the sins of those who enter the kingdom will be forgiven. Jesus healed Jews and non-Jews, the wealthy and the poor. His invitation to enter the kingdom went out to all people. The message he proclaimed in word and deed was one of love for all.

We know from the Gospels the result of Jesus' teachings and actions: he was condemned by the authorities and crucified. Just as the number of Jesus' followers was beginning to grow, Roman soldiers had him arrested. Some religious leaders and a number of other people—perhaps even some of Jesus' former followers—called for his crucifixion (the cruelest form of execution then practiced in the Roman Empire). The Son of God hung on a cross between two common thieves, suffering in agony for hours on a Friday afternoon until death mercilessly took him. His Roman executioners mockingly placed above him on the cross the insignia INRI, Latin letters for "Jesus of Nazareth, king of the Jews." His mother, a few women friends, and "the disciple whom he loved" looked on helplessly from a distance. Limp on the cross and emptied of life, he gave himself in an ultimate sacrifice for his message of God the Father's love.

Though Jesus, who was fully human and fully divine, truly experienced death, and, as the Apostles' Creed tells us, went down to the realm of the dead, his death was not the end. On the Sunday after his crucifixion, some of his women followers—among them Mary Magdalene, Joanna, and Mary the mother of James—visited his tomb to anoint the body. They found that the tomb was empty. Within the next few days, Jesus appeared to a number of his disciples in his glorified body. For instance, he appeared to Mary Magdalene, who initially mistook him for a gardener. (See *John 20:15*.) The disciples were overjoyed as they remembered that he had prophesied that he would rise from the dead. (See *Mark 8:31* and *Luke 24:6–7*.) Through this divine event, the bodily **Resurrection** of Jesus, he conquered sin and death and all that separates us from the love of God. Then he returned, body and soul, to the Father in heaven in his **Ascension**. By his Resurrection and Ascension, he opened the gates of heaven for all those who have died and will die in God's friendship. Before he ascended, Jesus told his Apostles to pray and to wait for the coming of the Holy Spirit. (See *Luke 24:49*.) The Holy Spirit came upon the Apostles during the first Christian **Pentecost**, and those who believe in Jesus have proclaimed and embodied his message ever since.

Pentecost

A most astonishing event occurred around the year a.d. 30 during *Shavu'ot*, the Jewish harvest Festival of Weeks, so called because it took place fifty days—or a week of weeks—after Passover. The Greek name for *Shavu'ot* was *Pentecost*, a word that means "fiftieth day." Many people gathered in Jerusalem for this feast. A small group of Jesus' Apostles and disciples were meeting in an upper room of a house there. While Jesus was still with them, they had received an almost unbelievable message of hope and saw him perform miraculous deeds of healing and power while proclaiming the reign of God.

As these followers gathered in the upper room, they tried to make sense of the preceding weeks, during which Jesus had been arrested, tortured, crucified, found missing from his tomb, appeared glorified and risen to a number of disciples, ascended into heaven, and then was no longer visibly present to them. We can hardly imagine the confusion and despair they were going through. They had experienced the kingdom of God in Jesus himself, and now he was gone. They had been filled with wonder at miraculous deeds one day, only to be baffled the next by puzzling things Jesus would say such as, "My kingdom is not from this world" (*John 18:36*) and people must be "born again" if they are to enter the kingdom. (See *John 3:3–5.*) Nonetheless, the crowd of followers had grown daily and then were left in despair by Jesus' death. To be sure, his Resurrection comforted them, but they soon felt left alone by his sudden departure. They were left with the question, "Now what?"

The Descent of the ▶ Holy Spirit, 15th Century.

We can read about what happened next in the second chapter of the Acts of the Apostles.

And suddenly from heaven there came a sound like the rush of a violent wind, and it filled the entire house where they were sitting. Divided tongues, as of fire, appeared among them, and a tongue rested on each of them. All of them were filled with the Holy Spirit and began to speak in other languages, as the Spirit gave them ability.

✝ Acts 2:2–4

As Jesus had promised, the Father had sent the Holy Spirit to be with his followers, to strengthen and guide them. The work of the Son and the Holy Spirit are intertwined, as we saw at Jesus' baptism when the Holy Spirit descended upon him, and at his Transfiguration when the Holy Spirit was present as symbolized by the cloud and light. Their missions to reconcile us to God the Father and make us one with him are joined.

This account of what happened during that first Christian Pentecost uses traditional Jewish images—fire and wind—to describe the Spirit of God that was seen and heard. God the Holy Spirit filled the Apostles, and they began to understand their new role—they were empowered by the Holy Spirit to manifest the Lord Jesus to the world.

The followers of Jesus in that upper room were not a gathering of community officials or leaders. Most of them were comfortable with hard physical work. They had done little public speaking. The Holy Spirit empowered them to do things that previously they would not have imagined. They spoke passionately to the crowd made up of people from across the Roman Empire. Those present heard the message in their own language. The leader of the group, a fisherman named Peter who had denied the Lord before his crucifixion, now stood his ground and preached a stirring sermon to the pilgrims. He told them that, "your young men shall see visions, and your old men shall dream dreams. Even upon my slaves, both men and women, in those days I will pour out my Spirit" (*Acts 2:17–18*). Inspired by the Holy Spirit, 3,000 new members were added in a single day to the newborn Church. (See *Acts 2:41*.)

No wonder Pentecost is often called the "birth of the Church"! Before his death, Resurrection, and Ascension, Jesus preached, healed, and gathered people together through his flesh and blood presence. He told people about God the Father, about what he wanted of them, and about what he had in store for them. Jesus had shared his work and mission in a special way with his Apostles, and he wanted them to continue his ministry. He gave them the power to act in his name, but they did not know what or how to do that. Now, thanks to the miraculous gift of the Holy Spirit, they were about to embark on a new journey. Christ would continue his presence in the world through them! They invited everyone to be baptized and to join them in proclaiming and living the Gospel.

A Closer Look

Youth News

Imagine a dynamic speaker in front of a crowd of thousands of people from a number of different countries. He speaks of hope, faith, love, and living a life directed toward building God's kingdom. You could be standing in the crowd at the first Christian Pentecost or you could be numbered among the youth at World Youth Day (WYD) with the pope. WYD is held every two to three years, at different places throughout the world. The first WYD was held in 1984 in Rome. More than 300,000 young people attended, and that number has increased with every WYD since. More than 150 countries were represented at the first WYD. Like those present at the first Pentecost, those present at WYD heard the same words of eternal life and celebrated their same faith, even though they were of different nationalities. Find out where and when the next WYD will be held and consider attending.

Saint Peter the Fisherman

We know little about Peter, the man identified in the Gospels as the original leader of Jesus' followers. Scripture indicates he made his living as a fisherman along with his brother Andrew, and the two brothers, James and John, known as the "sons of Zebedee." All would later become Apostles of Jesus. These business partners worked hard, fishing and caring for their small fleet of boats. We know that Peter was married since the Gospels mention his mother-in-law. The Gospels also portray him as having a fiery and strong personality.

His given name was not Peter but Shim'on or, in Greek, Simōn. We know him as Peter because Jesus gives him this name, which means "rock" in Aramaic. Why does Jesus call Peter the "rock"? The answer is found in Matthew 16:13-17: "Now when Jesus came into the district of Caesarea Philippi, he asked his disciples, 'Who do people say that the Son of Man is?' And they said, 'Some say John the Baptist, but others Elijah, and still others Jeremiah or one of the prophets.' He said to them, 'But who do you say that I am?' Simon Peter answered, 'You are the Messiah, the Son of the living God.' And Jesus answered him, 'Blessed are you, Simon, son of Jonah! For flesh and blood has not revealed this to you, but my Father in heaven.'" After Simon's inspired response, Jesus changed his name to Peter. He is the rock or foundation stone upon which Jesus will build his Church.

The Gospels portray a weak side to Peter as well. During Jesus' trial, the same Peter who earlier had proclaimed Jesus "Son of the living God" denied that he even knew him. (See *Matthew 26:69-74*.) Nonetheless, after Pentecost, Peter was clearly the head of the Christian Church. He performed miracles, and Scripture says that even people standing in his shadow were healed. (See *Acts 5:15*.)

After years of travel, Peter ended up in Rome, where, according to tradition, he was put to death in A.D. 64 during the persecutions under Nero. Considering himself unworthy to die as Jesus did, Peter asked to be crucified upside down. Buried on Vatican Hill, his tomb has become a place of pilgrimage. In the fourth century, a large church was built on the spot. Today St. Peter's Basilica rests on the spot where the original church was built. It is the central church for all Catholics. In 1950, excavations uncovered a tomb in the basilica believed to be that of Peter. The bones from this tomb now rest directly under the main altar of the basilica. The pope, the bishop of Rome, is Peter's successor and, therefore, head of the Church.

The Beginnings of the Church

" Christ accomplished God the Father's plan of salvation, which was the reason he was sent into the world. By preaching the good news of the reign of God, which had been promised in the Scriptures, Jesus inaugurated the Church. "

See *Catechism of the Catholic Church*, #763.

After Pentecost, the disciples of Jesus had a better understanding of their role to proclaim the reign of God and to call upon others to join them in living as Jesus intended them to. The Acts of the Apostles presents the link between Jesus and the Church. The author of Acts shows us that the Spirit at work in Jesus is the same Holy Spirit at work in the ongoing work of the Church.

Scripture scholars tell us that many early Christians believed that the "coming of the reign of God" would happen in their own lifetimes and that the world as they knew it would end. That is, Jesus would come again and take all believers with him to heaven. As time passed, however, Jesus' followers came to see that this was not going to happen immediately. They discerned that the Holy Spirit was calling them to participate in a more long-term plan. Once the followers of Jesus realized this, they relied on the Holy Spirit to help them establish ways by which Christ's presence would remain active in the world.

Over time, the Church clarified its structures so that the faith community had leaders and other members who served in a variety of roles. As a result, just as Jesus chose Peter and the Apostles to lead his fledgling community during its beginning stages, they chose others to follow them and continue the work of Jesus. So the successors of the Apostles—the pope and bishops of the Church—lead the Church acting in the person of Christ today. Throughout its history, therefore, the Catholic Church has continued to be an apostolic Church, that is, a Church rooted in the preaching and authority of Peter, the Apostles, and their successors. This is called apostolic succession, and it is the foundation of the Church being apostolic; apostolic is one of the four identifying characteristics or **marks of the Church**.

Architects of the Early Church

What inspired so many people to join the Church during its earliest days? Actually, we have little information about the first decades of the Church. Certainly, the formation and expansion of the Church were the work of the Holy Spirit, but how was the Spirit manifest at the time? Here are some aspects of the early Church that inspired people to join it:

- "Signs and wonders" that indicated the hand of God at work in the community.

- The prompting of the Holy Spirit drawing people to a new life of faith through grace and the work of the first followers of Christ.

- Radical trust in God, resulting from connecting oneself with those who were the least powerful.

- A new understanding of freedom, hope, and salvation.

- Personal and social conversion—viewing oneself and others as daughters and sons of one God, caring for and sharing with one another.

- The reign of God—recognition that God is present in the world and that people can experience God's presence and share that presence with others.

- A new, intense form of community composed of people from all social, ethnic, and economic backgrounds proclaiming Christ's message and carrying on his work.

People joined the Church community and worked to embody these values and beliefs. Isn't this as true today as it was then? The Church continues the work of the Holy Spirit begun in her earliest days. The Christian message is embodied in the members of the Church. Through them the Holy Spirit still inspires others to join the Church. The rest of this book tells about who became members of the Church, what challenges they faced, and what happened to them.

Gamaliel's Words of Wisdom We have already mentioned the Acts of the Apostles, the book of the Bible that contains the account of Pentecost and the beginning of the Church. This book gives us some idea about activities engaged in by the early Church. For instance, we know from Acts that tensions between the followers of Jesus and some of the Jewish authorities grew stronger after Jesus' death. We read that on one occasion Peter and John were arrested, imprisoned, and brought before the Sanhedrin, the Jewish high court. Before being released, Peter and John were threatened and told not to preach about Jesus ever again. They continued to preach even though it meant risking their lives. (See *Acts 4:1–22*.)

On another occasion, the Apostles were arrested and put in jail. During the night, however, an angel opened the gates and told them to go out into the temple area and preach to the people about the new life offered by Jesus. They did so. When the Sanhedrin became aware of the Apostles' escape from prison and of their preaching in the temple again, they wanted to kill them. But Gamaliel, a wise and respected member of the court, spoke up and saved their lives. He suggested waiting and leaving the Apostles alone saying, " . . . if this plan or this undertaking is of human origin, it will fail; but if it is of God, you will not be able to overthrow them—in that case you may be found fighting against God!" The Sanhedrin followed his advice. They had the Apostles flogged and then released. (See *Acts 5:17–42*.) Gamaliel's practical suggestion proved to be prophetic, for Christianity has withstood the test of time.

An Apostolic Church

In July Fourth celebrations across the United States, speakers talk of freedom and independence. In doing so, Americans want to make sure that the spirit, ideals, and principles of the first citizens still guide the nation and its people. Likewise, Catholics celebrate that the Church today is directly connected to and a continuation of the Church of the Apostles. What the earliest Christian community was, the Church today still strives to be. The Holy Spirit who inspired the Apostles continues to inspire the Church today. When a bishop is ordained, at least three other bishops perform a ritual of laying hands on the new bishop's head. Those bishops were previously ordained by bishops who laid hands on them. The ritual has been repeated down through the centuries and is part of the Sacrament of Holy Orders that bestows the authority and power given by Christ to Peter and the first Apostles and their successors, the bishops. Through their teaching, celebrating of the sacraments, and governing, the bishops present the truth passed down through the generations and are led by the Holy Spirit to help all of us understand and live the faith in our life and times.

Christians Inspire Hope

W e might be tempted to conclude from the New Testament that Christians were a clearly identifiable group from the beginning. In reality, the first followers of Jesus continued to see themselves as Jews. Being faithful Jews, they worshiped in the Temple, attended synagogue services, and followed the Law of Moses. They also met in one another's homes to share meals.

The Christian Jews, however, considered the sharing of a meal on Sunday a special event for it was the Lord's Day, the day of Christ's Resurrection. On Sundays, they gathered for the "breaking of bread"—the Eucharist—as Jesus had commanded them to do during his Last Supper. This was an essential part of their life together in Christ. Christ, Lord and Savior, was made present to them in their blessing of the bread and wine that became his Body and Blood. They did this in memory of Jesus just as members of the Church today gather and share in the Body and Blood of Christ in the Sunday Mass. Christ is present today in the Eucharist as he was when the first Christians gathered for the "breaking of the bread." These early Jewish Christians were held together by a dual bond, their Judaism and their belief in Christ. They didn't specify where their Judaism left off and their Christianity began. That was the work of later generations.

The Acts of the Apostles presents the image of Christians living closely together, awaiting Jesus, and growing in number. Chapter 2 of Acts tells us that "signs and wonders" accompanied the preaching of the Apostles, which led to a daily increase in the number of believers. Accounts of these signs and wonders describe miraculous, supernatural events, such as healing at the touch of a hand. Acts also reports that the early Christians sold their possessions and gave the proceeds to the Apostles for equal distribution. Food and goods were shared in common and distributed according to need. This new way of being together was one reason for the appeal of early Christianity.

GROUP TALK

According to the Acts of the Apostles, the early Christians "shared all things in common." It's easy to understand how those who were in need would find this practice worthwhile. However, people joined Christianity from all social and economic levels. How does the Church's equal treatment of rich and poor reveal the work of God from her earliest times through the present?

Mary—Mother of Christ, Mother of the Church

Mary, the Blessed Mother, has always been closely associated with the Church. From the moment that she said "yes" to bearing Christ in the Annunciation, she became the model of the Church and of all Christians. By agreeing to the Incarnation, Mary was participating in all the work that her Son would accomplish. As she bore Christ within her, so all Christians are called to be "Christ bearers" as well. From earliest times, Christians have been drawn to Mary and have cherished the tender care and compassion that she embodies. The Gospel according to John records that the first miracle that Jesus performed was at the request of his mother. Concerned that the wine supply at a wedding was running out, Mary asks her Son to help. Although the event obviously has deep symbolic significance, many of us have found comfort and hope that Mary would intercede with her Son for such a simple matter.

We honor Mary as the Mother of God because she is the mother of Jesus, the eternal Son of God. She is also Mother of the Church, the mother of those who believe in and follow Jesus. Paintings of the Blessed Mother and the child Jesus typically depict Mary as pointing to or looking at her son.

The Church looks to Mary to bring its members closer to Christ.

Christians also are drawn to Mary because of her steadfast dedication and hope even in times of great pain. On Calvary, she stands at the foot of the cross as her Son dies his slow and painful death. Before he dies, however, Jesus cements the relationship that is to exist between his mother and the Church. She will care for, as well as be cared for by, the beloved disciple. Thus, in time and eternity, Mary becomes the mystical mother of all Christ's disciples.

We see Mary for the last time in Scripture in Acts 1:14, which relates the events that happened between the Ascension and Pentecost: "All [the Apostles] were constantly devoting themselves to prayer, together with certain women, including Mary the mother of Jesus." What incredible sorrow must have been mingled with her joy in her prayers as she reflected on her life and that of her Son. The Church affirms that, at her death, Mary was taken body and soul into heaven. Once again, this last event of her life—the Assumption—gives us all hope. We hope that, at the end of time, we will follow Mary and the saints into heavenly bliss.

FAITH ACTIVITY

Mysteries of the Rosary Research the Joyful Mysteries of the Rosary. On a day when you are feeling great joy, share your joy with Mary in the recitation of the Joyful Mysteries. Her love and her compassion for our joy and sorrow have sustained Christians throughout the history of the Church.

Early Christian Communities: Unity out of Diversity

Jesus, the majority of his original disciples, and most of the earliest followers of Jesus were Jews born and raised in Palestine. Their Scriptures were written in traditional Hebrew, even though most of them probably spoke Aramaic. By A.D. 100, however, most Jews lived in other parts of the Roman Empire.

Alongside the Jewish diaspora communities (those living outside of Palestine), some Greek non-Jews, known as Gentiles, were also drawn to the monotheism and the strong sense of morality that Judaism possessed. These Gentiles often attached themselves to the synagogues and the Jewish communities in their particular cities without actually converting to Judaism; they were known as "God-fearers." Many God-fearers were compelled by Jesus' message and the witness of the Apostles and disciples.

The first century was a time of great religious searching. The official religion of the empire, a mixture of emperor worship and worship of many gods, did not meet the spiritual needs of many people. Christianity intrigued some of these people seeking a religious and spiritual connection. Among these people were some Gentiles, who also became "fellow travelers" with the growing Christian Church.

Saint Paul: The Apostle to the Gentiles

A young Jewish man named Saul radically opposed Christian belief. He agreed with the mob who stoned to death Stephen, a fellow Jew who was the first known martyr for the Christian faith. (See *Acts 7:54-60*.) Who was this Saul? He was a member of the Pharisees, a group of Jews known for their attempts to perfectly embody the Law in their lives. Saul studied in Jerusalem under the great rabbi Gamaliel. Many Pharisees and some of the people associated with them considered Christianity to be a threat to the Mosaic Law. Another significant fact about Saul is that he was born and raised in Tarsus, a city in modern-day Turkey. Therefore, while he was Jewish, he was also familiar with the culture of the Gentile world. In fact, Saul was a Roman citizen, which accorded him privileges that most people in the empire didn't possess.

Saul addressed the high priest in Jerusalem to obtain letters to the synagogues in Damascus empowering him to arrest and bring to trial any followers of Jesus. Then something amazing happened.

"Now as he was going along and approaching Damascus, suddenly a light from heaven flashed around him. He fell to the ground and heard a voice saying to him, 'Saul, Saul, why do you persecute me?' He asked, 'Who are you, Lord?' The reply came, 'I am Jesus, whom you are persecuting. But get up and enter the city, and you will be told what you are to do'" (*Acts 9:3-6*).

After this encounter with Jesus, Saul experienced a conversion and was baptized. He became an enthusiastic follower of Jesus and the Christian way. He preached the Gospel throughout the Roman Empire. He is known to us more by his Greek and Roman name, Paul. (See *Acts 13:9*.) During his travels he also wrote letters to the young Church communities that started to appear in various cities. These letters, also called epistles, are an essential part of the New Testament.

After almost a decade of spreading the Christian message, Paul returned to Jerusalem in A.D. 58. While he was there, the Jews with whom he had sided when he was persecuting Christians attempted to kill him. He was taken into protective custody by Roman authorities and sent for trial to the Roman procurator Felix in Caesarea. He spent two years in prison until the new procurator Porcius Festus arrived and wanted to send Paul to trial in Jerusalem on the charge of misrepresenting the true Jewish faith. Paul realized that he would be found guilty in Jerusalem. As a Roman citizen, he appealed to the emperor for a judgment and thus was taken to Rome in A.D. 61.

Under house arrest in Rome for about two years, Paul met with other Christians and wrote several of his epistles there. He may even have made a fourth missionary journey to Spain after his incarceration ended. During Nero's persecution of Christians, somewhere between A.D. 64 and 67, Paul was beheaded, a more honorable form of execution due to his Roman citizenship.

Through his missionary journeys, Paul added greatly to the numbers of Christians, especially from among the Gentile population. Therefore he is called "the Apostle to the Gentiles." In his writings, he reflected theologically about the place of Jesus in the divine plan and about what it means to believe in Jesus. Paul of Tarsus was indeed one of the most influential figures in the development of the Church at its beginning stages.

▼ **Stained Glass Window of the Conversion of Paul, Cathedral, Ho Chi Minh City.**

Gentile Converts We learn from the Acts of the Apostles that the various groups within the Christian Church got along well in some cases, and not so well in others. As with all new communities that are growing and establishing themselves, the Church experienced some growing pains. Even deciding who could join the Church community sometimes caused conflict. Early on, Christians debated whether—and if so, under what conditions—Gentiles could join the Christian community. Gentile beliefs and practices simply were not compatible with Judaism, and vice versa. Pious Jews couldn't sit down and share a meal with Gentiles because of strict dietary rules. An interesting story in Acts 10 speaks about this tension. With the help of the Holy Spirit, Peter and the other Apostles arrived at an important decision regarding Gentiles seeking to join the community. We read about Cornelius and Peter having visions. A man named Cornelius, a Roman centurion who is a God-fearer, is told by an angel to send for the Apostle Peter. Meanwhile, Peter is having a vision of his own. In a trance, he sees a sheet filled with all kinds of animals, including animals considered "unclean" by traditional Jewish standards. A voice says to him, "Take and eat." Peter replies that he has never eaten unclean food. He doesn't understand what the vision means.

Lunette with the Madonna ▶ and Child, 3rd century A.D.

The "Gentile Question" At the Council of Jerusalem, Paul was the leading advocate for accepting Gentiles into the Christian Church. Some of the elders associated with the Church of Jerusalem disagreed. The community listened to arguments put forth from both sides. In the end, they made a decision. Recreate the debate about the "Gentile question" as it might have taken place. Describe arguments for both positions and the decision that Peter and the elders finalized. Compare your debate with the one described in Acts 15.

When the messengers from Cornelius find Peter, Peter accompanies them back to their master's house. After hearing about the intense desire on the part of Cornelius to learn about the Lord, Peter realizes that his vision was telling him to offer God's word to people such as Roman centurions whom many other Jews would consider "unclean." Those who are gathered during this meeting feel the presence of the Holy Spirit, and Peter orders the Gentiles to be baptized. Since people joined the Christian community through Baptism, it also meant that they could now join in the community's meals during a time when sharing meals by Jews and Gentiles was taboo. Incidents such as this led Christians to realize God's will for the Church. It also resulted in the distinct separation between Christianity and Judaism that exists today.

Peter, as head of the Christian community, seems caught in the middle of the debate about Gentiles seeking Baptism. The Acts of the Apostles even suggests that some Jewish Christians refused to participate in the communal meal when Gentiles were present. Leaders of the Church addressed the issue directly during a meeting that took place in Jerusalem around the year A.D. 50.

An account of the meeting Peter had with other Christians, sometimes called the **Council of Jerusalem**, is found in Acts 15. This meeting came to pass when some Christian Jews taught at Antioch that Gentile converts had to be circumcised. Paul, Barnabas, and others traveled to Jerusalem to consider this matter with the Apostles and presbyters ("elders") there. The leaders of the Church announced the decision to free the Gentiles from this Jewish regulation and other Jewish dietary laws. (See *Acts 15:28–30*.)

As a result of this meeting, the Gentiles were welcomed as full and active members of the Christian Church, and they soon became the majority in the community. No longer was the Christian way strictly a Jewish way. Just as at Pentecost, the Holy Spirit had again guided the Church as its members discerned how Christ's will would best be served in light of new circumstances.

Teen Retreats

> "This retreat offers an opportunity to explore your relationship with yourself, your community, and God. Fellow students will help lead the retreat and make presentations about their faith life. There will be opportunities for prayer, conversation, and reflection. Come share your stories with others seeking the presence of God."

These words are from an invitation to students for a program called a "kairos retreat." During the retreat students leave campus for a few days and spend the time in intense reflection with one another, seeking to encounter Christ, to accept him more deeply into their lives, and to commit themselves to living in response to him.

No doubt, the disciples who gathered together at the first Pentecost were praying for guidance and inspiration before the Holy Spirit appeared to them as wind and fire. It's likely that they were also engaged in intense conversation and personal reflection as well. Surely they were preparing themselves for the Spirit who was to come. Today, you have opportunities through your school or parish to set aside time to ponder how you can better recognize and respond to the Holy Spirit's presence in your life. Retreat programs offer young people an opportunity to get away from the business of daily life and to contemplate what is most important in their lives. By attending a retreat you can deepen your relationship with the one who wants you to know how much you are loved, Jesus Christ. A retreat experience can become an important stepping stone in your faith journey. Through the retreat, just as at the first Pentecost, you might discover the Holy Spirit in your midst.

Teens gather to listen to Pope John Paul II during World Youth Day July 25, 2002 in Toronto ▶

Praying with the Church, Past and Present

Leader: God our loving Father, let us ponder the guidance offered us from the Apostles, those who first placed their faith and hope in your Son. May we be filled with the Holy Spirit and live lives that reflect our friendship with Jesus, who gave his own life for us. Amen.

Reader 1: "What good is it, my brothers and sisters, if you say you have faith but do not have works? Can faith save you? If a brother or sister is naked and lacks daily food, and one of you says to them, 'Go in peace; keep warm and eat your fill,' and yet you do not supply their bodily needs, what is the good of that? So faith by itself, if it has no works, is dead" (*James 2:14–17*). *Some ways I show my faith in my actions are . . .*

Reader 2: "But you are a chosen race, a royal priesthood, a holy nation, God's own people, in order that you may proclaim the mighty acts of him who called you out of darkness into his marvelous light" (*1 Peter 2:9*). *Some times when I saw God's light in my life were . . .*

Reader 3: "Beloved, let us love one another, because love is from God; everyone who loves is born of God and knows God. Whoever does not love does not know God, for God is love" (*1 John 4:7–8*). *My greatest challenge to loving others is . . .*

Reader 4: "But you, beloved, build yourselves up on your most holy faith; pray in the Holy Spirit; keep yourselves in the love of God; look forward to the mercy of our Lord Jesus Christ that leads to eternal life" (*Jude 1:20–21*). *Some ways my faith sustains me are . . .*

Leader: Lord Jesus Christ, through the Holy Spirit you inspired your first followers to preach your message of eternal life. May the legacy they have left continue to inspire us to live as your Church, so that we may share the love and joy you offer all your friends. Amen.

>Review

1. Why is it important that historians are emphasizing the Jewish background of Jesus more?

2. Name two Christian beliefs that flow from the story of Abraham.

3. Describe the major events that encompass the Exodus story.

4. What is the Paschal Mystery?

5. What distinguished Jews in Israel from Jews of the diaspora?

6. What is Hellenization?

7. Name the four Gospels.

8. Name two images Jesus used for the kingdom of God.

9. What accounted for the attitude of uncertainty among the followers of Jesus who gathered at Pentecost?

10. What two images indicated the presence of the Holy Spirit at Pentecost?

11. What new understanding came to the followers of Jesus as a result of the first Christian Pentecost?

12. Why is Peter referred to as the "rock" or foundation of the Church?

13. What position did Gamaliel take on the treatment of Jewish Christians?

14. What issue is illustrated in the story of Peter and Cornelius?

15. What resolution resulted from the Council of Jerusalem?

>Key Words

Acts of the Apostles (p. 12) The book of the New Testament that tells the story of the early Christian community.

Ascension (p. 13) The Risen Christ enters into heavenly glory.

Babylonian Captivity (p. 9) Period from 587 to 539 B.C. when the Jewish nation did not exist and Jewish leaders were exiled to Babylon.

conversion (p. 11) A radical reorientation of one's whole life away from sin and evil and toward God.

Council of Jerusalem (p. 27) The first Church council, which was called to resolve the growing controversy over whether or not Gentile Christians would have to observe Jewish law.

covenant (p. 6) Originally an agreement or contract between two parties. Came to be applied exclusively to the promise God made to the Jewish people and then through Christ to the Church.

diaspora (p. 9) Scattering of the Jewish people from their homeland.

Exodus (p. 8) God's saving intervention in history, as narrated in the Book of Exodus, by which he liberated the Hebrew people from slavery in Egypt and brought them into the Promised Land.

Gentiles (p. 23) Persons of non-Jewish faith or origin.

Gospels (p. 11) The four accounts of the life of Jesus in the New Testament. The word "Gospel" means "good news."

Hebrew (p. 5) The tribe of Abraham, later to be known as Israelites and then Jews.

Hellenization (p. 9) The spread of Greek culture, begun during the time of Alexander the Great.

marks of the Church (p. 18) There are four marks of the Church: the Church is one, holy, catholic, and apostolic. These are mentioned in the Nicene Creed.

Paschal Mystery (p. 8) The mystery of and events involved in our redemption: Jesus' suffering, death, Resurrection, and Ascension.

Passover (p. 8) Jewish feast commemorating the deliverance of the Jewish people from death by the blood of the lamb sprinkled on their doorposts in Egypt.

Pentecost (p. 13) The "fiftieth" day after Easter when the Holy Spirit was manifested, given, and communicated to the followers of Jesus, beginning the new "age of the Church," when Christ lives and acts in and through his Church.

reign of God (p. 11) Also known as the kingdom of God or kingdom of heaven, God's presence in the world through Christ. The Church "is the Reign of Christ already present in mystery" (*Catechism of the Catholic Church*, #763).

Resurrection (p. 13) "The bodily rising of Jesus from the dead on the third day after his death on the cross and burial in the tomb." (*Catechism of the Catholic Church*, Glossary)

▶Yesterday and Today

What do the first Christians have to say to us today? The early Church exemplifies the spark of excitement and enthusiasm that accompanies a radically new way of viewing one's relationship with God and of relating to others. Pentecost marked the beginning of the Church as a Spirit-filled community. It was not simply an event in time but an event for all time. The early Church consisted of members who walked and talked with Jesus. The glory of the Church is that it continues as the mystical Body of Christ just as much as it was during the time of the Apostles. Through our prayer, liturgy, teachings, and way of the life, the Church passes on all that we believe. The Church looks always to Jesus as a model and guide. The Church has the pope and bishops who connect us in a visible, concrete way with the Apostles and continue to guide the Church in being faithful to the message proclaimed by Jesus. Through the Church we can still touch and be touched by Jesus.

▼ A Baptism from a Spanish Manuscript.

A.D. **249–251**
Problem of the *lapsi*,
Christians who denied
faith under persecution

TIMELINE

A.D. C.**140–C.200**
First lists of some
New Testament writings
were made

A.D. **203**
Martyrdom of
Perpetua and Felicity

A.D. **248**
Cyprian is bishop of
Carthage

A.D. **249**
Decius begins
empire-wide
persecutions

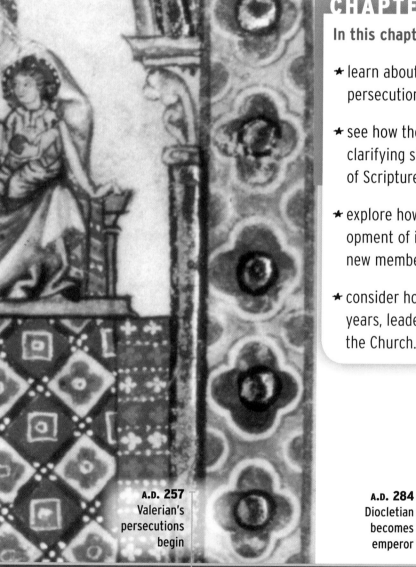

SPREADING THE MESSAGE

THE CHURCH ENTERS THE EMPIRE

A.D. 100-300

CHAPTER GOALS

In this chapter you will:

★ learn about the threat and experience of persecution early Christians endured.

★ see how the Holy Spirit guided the Church in clarifying statements of belief and the canon of Scripture.

★ explore how the Church took shape through development of its theology, liturgy, and initiation of new members.

★ consider how, during its first three hundred years, leaders emerged who guided and shaped the Church.

CHAPTER 2

A.D. 257
Valerian's persecutions begin

A.D. 284
Diocletian becomes emperor

A.D. 312
Battle of Milvian Bridge

A.D. c.251-356
Saint Anthony of Egypt, first Christian hermit

A.D. 258
Martyrdom of Saint Laurence

A.D. 260
Era of Peace

A.D. 303
The Great Persecution begins

A.D. 313
Emperor Constantine; Edict of Milan issued

Persecution for the Faith

FIRST THOUGHTS

The period of Church history covered in this chapter is filled with martyrs—that is, people who witnessed so strongly to their beliefs that they accepted torture and death rather than renounce their beliefs. Describe a situation in which you, or someone you know, personally gave witness on behalf of a person or belief. Explain what happened as a result of this witness.

Do you know anything about the most distant ancestors of your family—those who lived hundreds of years ago? Many probably faced great hardships to make life better for those who came after them. The way they handled the challenges and the joys they shared are a legacy handed down to you. More recently, did certain members of your family ever have a disagreement that led to months or years of no contact among them? Do some members of your family have a different spelling or pronunciation of the family's last name? How did that happen? Does one part of the family claim to have the "correct" spelling or pronunciation?

Our ancestors in faith—the followers of Jesus in the first three hundred years of the Church—faced challenges and joys, too. During that time Jesus' disciples grew from a small group of believers to a community encompassing a significant percentage of an empire that had tried to crush it. These early Christians may have endured persecutions and internal dissension, but included in their number were some of the most courageous people and greatest minds of the time. Slaves, peasants, artisans, philosophers, and politicians alike were called by Jesus and the message spread by his followers. These people formed the beginning of a Church that has profoundly affected the history of the world for over 2,000 years.

◄The Sermon of St. Stephen at Jerusalem, by Vittore Carpassio.

Inter-Jewish Conflicts

Martyrdom is the ultimate witness to a person's faith; a martyr bears witness by dying for the faith.

See *Catechism of the Catholic Church*, #2473.

At the time of Christ some of the Jews living in Jerusalem were descendents of Jews who had lived in foreign countries, not in the Promised Land. Among the earliest to join the "Way" or the "New Way," as the group of Jesus' followers was often called, were Hellenistic Jews. Some of these Hellenistic followers of the Way spoke Greek or Latin rather than the Aramaic or Hebrew of the Israeli Jews. In this and other ways, they felt "different" and estranged from the Christians who were Jews from Israel. They were worried that their widows were not being given their fair share of food: "Now during those days, when the disciples were increasing in number, the Hellenists complained against the Hebrews because their widows were being neglected in the daily distribution of food" (*Acts 6:1*). The Apostles decided to select seven assistants, or **deacons**, to take charge of this task. (See *Acts 6:1–7*.)

One of the first deacons was named Stephen. In addition to his duties of preaching and serving the needs of those who were poor, he also worked miracles among the people. People saw him as "a man full of grace and power," and he engaged in debates with other Greek-speaking Jews in their synagogues. Because Stephen "did great wonders and signs among the people," he was denounced as a blasphemer and brought before the Sanhedrin. During the debate that followed, Stephen traced for his listeners the history of Israel and showed how Jesus was the Messiah. He reproached them for their part in putting Jesus to death. The crowd that was gathered was furious. Some of them grabbed him, took him outside, and stoned him to death. He is considered the first Christian martyr. (See *Acts 6 — 7*.)

The first persecution of Christians centered mostly on the Hellenistic Jewish Christians. Before Stephen's death, the Hebrew-speaking followers of Jesus thought of themselves as Jews. They came to the Temple and followed Jewish dietary laws. They saw themselves as continuing in the line of Abraham and Moses along with other Jews. They believed that Jesus was the long-awaited Messiah and preached this message primarily to their fellow Jews. With the death of Stephen, many of the Hellenistic followers fled Jerusalem to avoid the persecutions led by Saul of Tarsus before his conversion to Christ. Some went to Antioch, the capital of Syria. There, the Hellenistic Christian Jews discovered another audience eager to hear the Gospel—Gentiles, or non-Jews. Gentile converts to Christianity grew in number.

!FYI

Jesus' followers were first called *Christians* in Antioch while Paul and Barnabus were present.

Modern Day Martyrs Since 1900, millions of Christians have been killed for their faith. Research a modern-day martyr and report your findings to the class. Examples of modern-day martyrs are the Filipino Jesuit Richie Fernando; the martyrs of El Salvador—Archbishop Oscar Romero, Jean Donovan, Sister Dorothy Kazel, Sister Maura Clarke, Sister Ita Ford; Sister Dorothy Stang; the Jesuit martyrs and their women workers; and Charles Lwanga of Uganda and his twenty-one companions.

GROUP TALK

The Church follows a liturgical calendar that contains major and minor feast days throughout the year that help us celebrate the saving events and mysteries of Jesus as well as the lives of the saints. The feast of Saint Stephen is the day after Christmas, the feast of the birth of Christ into the world. What symbolic significance does the juxtaposition of these two feasts have for Christianity?

The Roman Persecutions

The persecutions that most profoundly affected Christianity were the Roman persecutions. In the early days of the Church, leaders of the Roman Empire took little notice of the Christian community. This group seemed to be a small splinter group of Judaism. Usually when the Roman Empire occupied a country, they added the religious practices of the people to their own. Because of the monotheistic views of the Jews, this kind of transition had not been possible. The Romans had found the Jews difficult to conquer and to control. After many failed attempts to assume the Jewish practices, the Romans had decided to allow the Jewish people to practice their own religion. Considered a sect of Judaism, this attitude of tolerance or acceptance was extended to Christianity as well. However, Christian beliefs and practices later came into direct conflict with the purposes of the emperor, and persecutions began.

Factors That Made Christianity Susceptible to Persecution

After the Council of Jerusalem (A.D. 50), Gentiles were accepted into the Christian community without having to become Jewish.

Christianity became separate and distinct from Judaism.

Soon after being separated from Judaism, being Christian became illegal in the Roman Empire.

Christianity spread quickly throughout the empire.

Christianity rejected the worship of the emperor and the gods of the Romans.

Christians met in secret assemblies to avoid drawing attention to themselves.

Saints Perpetua and Felicity (died c. 202–203)

While so many other martyr's stories are shrouded in legend, a document from the early Church illustrates the faith and courage of other Christian martyrs. A twenty-two-year-old married woman named Perpetua lived during the third century in North Africa. She kept a diary. A later writer completed her story. Perpetua was of noble birth and had a slave named Felicity who served as her companion. When the Romans arrested Perpetua and Felicity, they were catechumens participating in the two- or three-year process of preparation for Baptism. Since they remained under house arrest, they were able to continue studying the faith and were baptized. Along with their instructor in the faith, Saturus, they were then moved to a prison in the city of Carthage.

In her diary, Perpetua details what it was like waiting for their deaths. Perpetua had an infant son whom she was breastfeeding. Her father, who was not a Christian, pleaded with her to think of her child and to "throw a little incense" over the statues of the non-Christian gods. Perpetua refused. Her companion, Felicity, was eight months pregnant when arrested. She feared that she would not be put to death with the other prisoners since Roman law forbade executing pregnant women. Three days before they were to be sent to the arena, she gave birth to a baby girl and gave her to a Christian woman to raise.

On the day of their deaths, Perpetua and Felicity were told to dress in the robes of non-Christian priest-esses, but they refused. Therefore they were tossed into the arena naked except for nets thrown over them. The two women stood next to each other and exchanged the Christian sign of peace as they met their deaths. These two women so well represented the strength and courage of the martyrs that their names are included in the first Eucharistic Prayer often recited during the Mass.

Fueled by Fire On July 19 in A.D. 64, a tremendous fire in Rome gutted entire districts of the city. This fire seemed to provide the impetus for Nero to begin his persecution of Christians. Some fifty years later, the Roman historian Tacitus wrote that the emperor himself had started the fire because he wanted to rebuild Rome. However, when he realized how angry the citizens were, Nero blamed the Christians and their God for the blaze. This burning of Rome began a full-scale persecution of Christians. Both Peter and Paul are believed to have died as a result of this period of persecution that lasted from A.D. 64 to 67.

The Emperor Domitian began the first empire-wide persecution (A.D. 81–96). However, we have mostly speculative accounts of Christians who died during this period. It appears that Domitian actually targeted all "atheists"—those who did not worship him as *Dominus et Deus* ("lord and god"). **Atheism**, as we understand it today, is the denial that God exists. He assessed a special tax on Jews, and he accused Christians of pretending not to be Jews in order to avoid paying the tax.

The Burning of Rome, by Robert Hubert. ▼

A letter from the early second century sent by a Roman governor named Pliny to his emperor, Trajan, asked what to do about Christians. The emperor replied that Christians should not be sought out. But, if they were reported and convicted, they were to be punished. If they repented and worshiped the gods, they should be set free. Later (in A.D. 250), Emperor Decius decreed that every citizen had to publicly worship the Roman gods, in which case they would receive a certificate indicating that they were loyal citizens. Anyone found not carrying this certificate could be tortured until agreeing to offer public worship.

Letter of Pliny, Roman Governor, to Emperor Trajan

" It is my practice, my Lord, to refer to you all matters concerning which I am in doubt. For who can better give guidance to my hesitation or inform my ignorance? I have never participated in trials of Christians. I therefore do not know what offenses it is the practice to punish or investigate, and to what extent. And I have been not a little hesitant as to whether there should be any distinction on account of age or no difference between the very young and the more mature; whether pardon is to be granted for repentance, or, if a man has once been a Christian, it does him no good to have ceased to be one; whether the name itself, even without offenses, or only the offenses associated with the name are to be punished.

Meanwhile, in the case of those who were denounced to me as Christians, I have observed the following procedure: I interrogated these as to whether they were Christians; those who confessed I interrogated a second and a third time, threatening them with punishment; those who persisted I ordered executed. For I had no doubt that, whatever the nature of their creed, stubbornness and inflexible obstinacy surely deserve to be punished. There were others possessed of the same folly; but because they were Roman citizens, I signed an order for them to be transferred to Rome.

. . . For the contagion of this superstition has spread not only to the cities but also to the villages and farms. But it seems possible to check and cure it. "

Imagine how difficult it must have been for Christians to hold fast to the faith when faced with the prospect of death if they didn't worship the Roman gods. However, many heroic Christians suffered and died rather than renounce their faith in Christ. Some of the stories we have about these early martyrs are embellished, but at the same time we can't dismiss the fact that martyrs suffered greatly and gave their lives so that the Christian faith could continue. For instance, according to popular custom, an African saint named Numidicus (d. 251) saw his wife executed. He was burned at the stake but somehow survived and was rescued by his children. He went on to be ordained a deacon and served the Christian Church in Carthage.

FAITH ACTIVITY

Mock Trial Pliny's letter suggests that many Roman officials sought sensible ways to deal with the Christians. Act out a mock trial of a group of Christians in the Roman Empire. Lawyers from each side should explain why Christians should or should not be punished.

Deacon Laurence
(died 258)

During persecutions in 258, one account says soldiers in Rome barged in upon Pope Sixtus II as he celebrated Mass and killed him and all those present. The local deacon, Laurence, was absent at the time, but a few days later he was also killed.

Because of their martyrdom, Christians venerated Pope Sixtus and Deacon Laurence, and stories developed about them. According to one such story, the Romans imprisoned Sixtus before killing him. Laurence went to see the pope and pleaded to be jailed with him. Instead, Sixtus directed him to go, give away all the money the Church had available, sell whatever possessions they had, and give the money to those in need. A government official overheard this request and ordered Laurence to return in three days with the treasury of the Church. When Laurence returned at the appointed time, he brought with him all those for whom the Church cared—widows, maidens, lepers, orphans, and persons who were disabled. He said to the official, "Behold the treasure of the Church."

The official was furious. He shouted that the empire would not be mocked. He assured Laurence that he would indeed get his request to die, but his death would be a slow and painful one. He ordered a large gridiron to be prepared and placed over hot coals. Deacon Laurence was stripped and slowly roasted on it. After a while Laurence cheerfully announced, "You may turn me now, this side is done." Laurence's story was told often after this and served as a source of encouragement to those still facing the possibility of torture and death. The Christian writer Tertullian said in reference to Laurence, "Crucify us; torture us; send us to death; wipe us out! Your injustice is the proof of our innocence! . . . The blood of the martyrs is the seed of the church." (Tertullian, "The Apology")

From Outsiders to Insiders

The middle decades of the third century proved to be a particularly corrupt period in Roman history. From a.d. 235 to 284, twenty-three different emperors ruled—some holding the office for only a month—leaving the empire on the brink of destruction. Diocletian came to the throne in 284 and, unlike his predecessors, demonstrated good management skills. He divided the empire into East and West and then further divided it into twelve areas that he called "dioceses," named after himself. He felt that by limiting people's freedom, he could better control things. One area he wanted control of was the gods the people worshiped. In 303, he began what later came to be called the Great Persecution by reinstating mandatory emperor worship for all citizens. He intended his new system to result in a peaceful transition of power instead of the conflicts that had been taking place before him.

However, when Diocletian stepped down, a power struggle again occurred. In 312, the armies of two generals met to determine who would be emperor of the West. One of these generals, Constantine, claimed to have had a vision in which he was told that under the symbol of the cross he would conquer. So he placed a Chi-Rho on his standards (helmets and other military garb). During battle on the Milvian Bridge, he indeed was victorious. Constantine became the undisputed emperor in the West.

The next year Constantine met with Licinius, the ruler of the Eastern Empire, and together they signed the **Edict of Milan** that instituted tolerance for all religions. Thus, the year 313 marks the beginning of a new era for the Christian Church. Persecutions did not entirely cease for Christians. For instance, to spite Constantine, Licinius later persecuted Christians. Constantine responded by defeating him in 324, and Constantine became the master of the entire Roman world.

The few hundred people who considered themselves Jesus' followers in a.d. 30, had grown by the fourth century, even after all the years of persecutions, to number about five million. On his deathbed, Emperor Constantine himself became a Christian.

FYI

A Chi-Rho is a cross symbol something like a monogram using the first two letters of the Greek word for Christ: Chi (x) and Rho (P).

GROUP TALK

1. How do you think the Edict of Milan affected the way Christians lived? Explain.

2. What words would you use to describe someone your age who stands up for their beliefs?

Heroes of the Church What do the tales of martyrs tell us about the early Christians? From them we discover how the Spirit of Christ was manifest during this difficult time. A great number of people felt strongly enough about their faith that they were willing to undergo horrible suffering and even death rather than renounce their faith. These early martyrs serve as a reminder of how precious faith is. There was no special desire on the part of Christians to die, but many found the courage to stand and proclaim their faith even if it cost their lives.

These martyrs came to hold a special place of honor and respect in the Church community. Throughout the year, the Church celebrates the deaths of martyrs as their "birthdays" into eternal life. In the early years after their deaths, their tombs became places where Christians gathered to pray and celebrate the Eucharist. Even today some altars in Catholic churches still contain stones with relics of martyrs—often small pieces of bones—to continue the custom of gathering around the martyrs' tombs to celebrate the Mass. The early martyrs are the great heroes of the Church.

Images of the Church

The Seed of the Kingdom

One way to look at the Church is to see it as "the seed and beginning of God's kingdom on earth" (Documents of Vatican II, *Lumen Gentium*, #5 and *CCC*, 541) The Christian martyrs during the time of persecutions certainly were seeds that, planted by their death, proclaimed God's kingdom is worth living and dying for. We know that the kingdom will be complete when Christ comes again at the end of time. The glorified Lord will reign forever–along with those he has judged to be just–and the world will be transformed. At the time, Christ will judge the living and the dead, based upon whether they have accepted his grace and how they have lived their lives and witnessed to the faith. Today members of the Church continue to witness to the faith by making decisions based upon Jesus' teachings and example. At school, at home, at work, and during community activities, Church members live out their faith–participating in the sacraments, giving of their time and energy for people in need, standing up for the rights of others, consoling those who are suffering, learning more about Church teachings, advocating for truth and just action in our government, engaging in daily prayer, and sharing Jesus' message in many other ways. Heroes of today's Church are living reminders that God's reign is marked by love and justice. While we hope for heaven and the true happiness and communion that will come from eternal life with God, we also rejoice that by Christ's first coming and the Church's continuation of his mission, we and others can experience the seed and beginning of the kingdom.

FAITH ACTIVITY

A Sign of the Kingdom What are some ways your family is a seed of God's kingdom by the way you act and live? What are some ways your school is? Make a list of these ways and discuss them with a partner. What can you do to help your family and school promote God's reign?

The Church Formulates Essential Beliefs

The Christian community of this era needed to address three areas of Church life:

- the way they expressed their beliefs
- the way they celebrated and ritualized these beliefs in the sacraments which Christ had given his followers
- the way the Church was structured

In other words, the Church during this time period took major steps toward clarifying her creed (essential beliefs), her rites (sacramental system), and her community organization (roles performed by various Church members).

Then, as now, the Christian faith was a lived experience. If, during the celebration of the Eucharist, a particular bishop used a prayer that people found to be especially meaningful, other bishops often adopted it. Eventually, only those prayers deemed most meaningful and most appropriate were used during liturgies. The same can be said of the Church's beliefs and organizational structures. Inspired by the Holy Spirit, the Church gained a greater understanding of the wonderful mystery of Jesus Christ that they were experiencing.

This deeper understanding did not always come easily or quickly. As we will see, great thinkers battled, sometimes for centuries, to determine what was "right thinking" in Christianity.

◀ Head of Plato, Musei Capitolini.

FAITH ACTIVITY

Identity Nations have constitutions and anthems. Organizations and associations have pledges or mottoes. Companies have vision and mission statements. When people gather together for a common reason, they share common beliefs and it's necessary to state those beliefs so that the identity that holds the group together is clear. In a small group, create a visual display of the important things that make your school a Catholic school. Present your display to the class.

Apologists Explain and Defend the Faith

FAITH ACTIVITY

Meeting a Challenge At Pentecost, through the Holy Spirit, Peter acted with courage and conviction in the face of a challenging situation. Write an essay describing a situation that would be a challenge to your courage and to your convictions. Describe what you think the experience would be like if you were not true to your convictions and then what it would be like if you *were* true to your convictions.

The early Christians had a powerful and wonderful sense that God was at work among them. They struggled to understand exactly what knowledge and insights set them apart from their Jewish brothers and sisters, as well as from the wider community. In response to this challenge, great leaders and theologians emerged in the Church to explain and defend the Christian faith in clear and convincing terms.

Christianity had begun in Jewish culture, but it soon moved into the Greek culture that dominated the Roman Empire of the time. This move profoundly affected how Christians viewed God and Jesus. Jews knew that God exists and lovingly cares for his people. They concentrated on how people should act in response to God. The primary focus in Judaism was on worshiping the one God, Yahweh, and right behavior as expressed in the Torah, or "the Law." Greek thought focused more on "being" than on "doing." It examined the nature of God, human nature, and other philosophical questions. By the time of the beginnings of Christianity, Greek thinkers had already developed sophisticated philosophies. When Christianity spread beyond Judaism, Christian thinkers applied philosophical reflection to their beliefs, which enriched their understanding of God.

Theology is "faith seeking understanding"—an enterprise in which the Church has engaged throughout her history. Early bishops and other Christian thinkers discussed and debated theological questions. During Constantine's time, Church leaders agreed on a statement of core Christian beliefs. That agreement did not come easily, however. Along the way intellectual battles raged. Those who clearly and effectively explained and defended Christian beliefs were called **apologists**.

Great scholars of Christianity formed their own school in Alexandria in Egypt, which had long been a center of learning for both Jewish and Gentile scholars. The Christians reflected on Jesus and his message. They wrote tracts or pamphlets that answered some of the criticisms being made against Christianity from philosophical and theological perspectives.

Sacrilege and treason Christians were accused of sacrilege and treason because they refused to worship the gods of the empire. Public celebrations of the time were not just political. They were also religious–typically involving worship of the emperor, which Christians refused to do.

Incarnation The Incarnation is the truth that the second Person of the Blessed Trinity, while remaining God, assumed a human nature and became man. It is "the mystery of the wonderful union of the divine and human natures" (*CCC*, #483) in Jesus, the Son of God. The idea that God would lower himself and become a man was incomprehensible to reason. As a result, some heresies developed that said Jesus was God, not truly human in a full sense (Apollinarianism and Gnosticism), while others said that Jesus was human, a created being not truly divine, less than God but greater than anything else God created. (Arianism).

Christian practices Christianity, which linked the human and the divine in its ritual celebrations such as the Eucharist and in its prayers and commemorations of those who had died, seemed unnatural and caused suspicion.

Social structure Non-Christian citizens found the Christian community to be disruptive and antisocial since its members did not follow all the norms of the established social order. For example, they called one another "brothers and sisters" regardless of their social status.

Orthodoxy and Heresy Establishing an accurate, authentic presentation of Christian faith in theological terms took time. Discussion, debate, and the sheer power of persuasion led to an affirmation and explanation of orthodoxy as opposed to heresy about Christian beliefs. **Orthodoxy** is a doctrine, belief, attitude, or teaching that is consistent with revealed truth and with the Church's doctrine of faith. **Heresy** is a belief, attitude, or teaching that is contrary to revealed truth and to the Church's doctrine of faith. Those thinkers who were baptized as Christians but denied officially defined teachings were known as **heretics**. In the process of refining Christian teaching, the Holy Spirit guided the Church in arriving at the understanding of the Trinity (three Persons in one God); the humanity, divinity, and redemptive work of Christ; and the human condition that we have today. Apologists, such as Justin Martyr (d. c.165), Tatian (d. 180), and Tertullian (d. c.230), to name a few, helped the early Church arrive at the formulation of essential Christian teachings that countered the heretics and have sustained the Church ever since.

GROUP TALK

In small groups, name a core Catholic belief, such as Christ's Resurrection. Make a list of ways the group could explain the belief and its importance for the way Catholics live their lives.

Setting the Canon—The Church Identifies Its Scriptures

The first followers of Jesus did not immediately sit down and write the books of the New Testament. Instead, the New Testament took shape as the Church did. By the end of the first century, the four Gospels that we find in the New Testament were written—the Gospels according to Matthew, Mark, Luke, and John. These Gospels developed in three stages.

Stages of Development Leading to the Gospels

The life and teaching of Jesus Jesus lived a life of public ministry for perhaps three years. During that time, he preached a message of love, taught about the kingdom of God, and performed miraculous deeds of healing. In all these ways he gave witness to his Father and fulfilled the covenant. Some of those who encountered Jesus became his followers–Apostles and disciples. They were the "living Gospels" who had seen, heard, and touched Jesus in the flesh.

The oral tradition This stage began after Pentecost as the Apostles and disciples who witnessed the life, death, and Resurrection of Jesus shared with others what they had heard and seen, with the fuller understanding provided through the enlightenment of the Holy Spirit. Eventually, others who had not witnessed the words and deeds of Jesus personally came to believe in him and share the good news as well. Preaching was then carried out by means of a combination of eyewitnesses and non-eyewitnesses and was adapted to the needs of different audiences. Oral tradition, then, refers to the spoken word, handed down from community to community, preacher to preacher, believer to believer.

The written Gospels As the Church spread, it was necessary to record the stories and truths of the faith so that all people could have access to Jesus' message. The Gospel according to Mark refers to itself as "the good news of Jesus Christ" (*Mark 1:1*). The word *gospel* literally means "good news." Under the guidance of the Holy Spirit, the Gospel writers made choices about which stories to tell, which words of Jesus to include, and which events to highlight. Of course, the writers intended to be faithful to Jesus, his life and message, but they also wanted to communicate through their writing how the Good News about Jesus speaks to their particular audience. Because the Gospels and all Scripture were inspired by the Holy Spirit, God is the author of Scripture. The Bible is God's word to us, a presentation of his saving truth.

We know that a number of writings about Jesus were circulating in the Christian community of the first century. Some of these writings came to be recognized as presenting the full and authentic message about Christ and make up the New Testament. These include: the four Gospels, the Acts of the Apostles, letters attributed to Paul and other Apostles, and a book known as "Revelation."

Late in the second century, the Muratonian canon listed writings of the Christian Scriptures that included practically all of the twenty-seven books now recognized as the New Testament. In the year 367, Saint Athanasius referenced this list when he listed the twenty-seven books of the New Testament as we have them today.

Why were certain writings considered "Scripture" and others not? The process by which the writings in the New Testament were recognized as inspired Scriptures is called "setting the canon." The **canon** is the official collection of inspired books that make up the Catholic Bible. The Greek word canon means "measuring rod," like a ruler or a yardstick used to measure length. A decision about what is and what is not Scripture did not take place all at once. Recognizing a particular writing as inspired Scripture was based on the following questions:

- Is the writing the work of someone with a direct connection to Jesus or to those who knew him?

- Did the writing accurately reflect the teachings of Jesus as commonly understood in the community?

- Had the piece of writing been consistently used in liturgical worship by Church communities for some time?

- Was there a general consensus that a particular writing was sacred and inspired by the Holy Spirit?

Two early works not included in the canon of the New Testament are writings that modern scholars have named "The Gospel of Thomas" (a.d. 50–140) and "The Gospel of Peter" (a.d. 70–160). While these "gospels" apparently circulated in early Christian communities, they are not named in any listing of New Testament writings. We also have letters and other writings from the time, usually attributed to one of the Apostles but of uncertain origin, not included in the canon of the New Testament.

FYI

Official Bibles of Catholics and Protestants include a slightly different number of books. The Catholic Bible includes 46 Old Testament books (seven of which were originally written in Greek and do not appear in non-Catholic Bibles) and 27 New Testament books. These are the books the Church has accepted as inspired by the Holy Spirit.

St. Luke, 13th Century Manuscript. ▼

The Bible is not the only way God makes himself and his will known to us. We know the beliefs, doctrines, and sacraments of the Church through Scripture and **Tradition**, which form the single source of God's revelation to us. As the process for setting of the canon indicates, these two sources of truth cannot be separated from each other. In a sense, the canon of the New Testament grew out of Church Tradition. On the other hand, Tradition must always remain faithful to Scripture. Together Scripture and Tradition make up the one source of the revelation of God. The *Catechism* teaches that Scripture and Tradition have the same source—God. They are bound together so closely that they are in some way one thing moving toward the same goal, making "present and fruitful in the Church the mystery of Christ" (*CCC*, #80.)

GROUP TALK

How is your parish a living witness to the faith? In what ways does your parish or school challenge the larger community to be true to Christ's values and teachings?

FAITH ACTIVITY

Scripture in Your Life Do any parables speak to you in a significant way? What teachings of Jesus or words of the Psalms might help you make important decisions or respond to a friend in need? Choose one book of the Bible. Say a short prayer to the Holy Spirit to help you be open to what you read, and then spend some time quietly reading through different passages.

We experience Christ's presence in many ways, but especially when we gather together for liturgy—the official public prayer of the Church. In the liturgy, we bless and praise God the Father as the source of all creation and our salvation. We give him thanks and praise for the greatest gift, his Son, through whom we can become the Father's adopted sons and daughters. In the liturgy we meet Christ, who is a sign and instrument of his grace. The work of the Holy Spirit makes all of this possible, bringing about the saving work of Christ, gathering us as an assembly and preparing us to meet Christ in the word proclaimed and the Body and Blood received. Because God's word is so important to Catholics, we proclaim it whenever we celebrate the Mass and other sacraments. God's truth is timeless; the insights of the Scripture stories speak to us today wherever we are in our lives. We meet God—loving Father, compassionate Son, and empowering Holy Spirit—in Scripture. So we reflect on what God's word means for us as a Church community living in the twenty-first century, relying upon one another as we discover our identity and faith. Scripture also has an important place in our personal prayer and reflection. When we know who Jesus was, how he acted, and what he taught, we can grow in our understanding of what it means to live as his disciple. God the Holy Spirit helps us understand what is being revealed to us in Scripture and helps us interpret the message and respond to it in our lives.

The Church Refines the Way She Worships

The sacraments have their origin and foundation in Christ. During his ministry, Jesus welcomed anyone and everyone to conversion. He helped people feel a sense of belonging to God the Father and one another. He fed people who had no food and shared meals with his followers. He healed the sick who had faith, forgave the sins of those who were truly sorry, and appointed Apostles to share in and continue his mission in a special way. He raised the dignity of marriage by responding to the needs of the newly wed couple by transforming jugs of water into wine. And, Jesus wanted his disciples to experience his welcoming, healing, life-giving presence when he was no longer with them. Jesus commanded the Apostles to baptize in the name of the Trinity, to bless and break bread in his memory, to heal and forgive sins in his name, and to continue his life-giving mission. In all of these ways Jesus is the origin and foundation of the **sacraments**, effective signs of grace, instituted by Christ and entrusted to the Church, by which we share in divine life through the work of the Holy Spirit.

Through the sacraments, Christians experience the new life won by Christ through his suffering, death, and Resurrection. The grace specific to each sacrament brings about what the sacrament signifies: new life, forgiveness, union with Christ, sealing in the Spirit, and so on. The seven sacraments celebrate important stages and moments of Christian life. Each one offers the opportunity of experiencing Christ's dying and rising in one's own life. The effectiveness of each sacrament in bringing about new life is rooted in the Father's love, the saving grace of Christ, and the Holy Spirit's presence in the Church. God takes the total initiative in the sacraments. They are free gifts from him so that we can share in divine life and be made holy. We do not earn or merit them. And our response is faith: belief in God who has been revealed to us as Father, Son, and Holy Spirit, and a commitment to live our lives based upon what God has made known to us through his words and actions.

Entering into the Mystery

Just as the New Testament was not written all at once, the way the Church celebrated the sacraments also underwent refinement during the early centuries of Church history. The word *sacrament* has pre-Christian origins. It first meant the initiation rite by which someone became a member of the Roman army. Latin-speaking Christians decided upon the term *sacramentum* to translate the Greek term *mysterion*. (See *Catechism of the Catholic Church*, #774.) In the Greek-speaking Church, mysterion referred to a person's entire life with Christ as well as to the specific ways he or she lived out that mystery. Latin-speaking Christians adopted the terms *mysterium* and *sacramentum* for these Christian mysteries. *Sacrament*, then, refers to the ways that Christians are invited into and celebrate the mystery of their life in Christ.

How did the sacraments become more consistently celebrated by various Church communities? Paul's first letter to the Church at Corinth hints at one possible explanation. In that letter, Paul refers to Corinthian Christians coming together to "eat the Lord's supper" (*1 Corinthians 11:20*). He complains of reports that "each of you goes ahead with your own supper, and one goes hungry and another becomes drunk" (*1 Corinthians 11:21*). Paul suggests that people should eat and drink at home in order to make sure that the solemnity of eating the bread and sharing the cup at the communal Eucharist is not lost. When one group performed Eucharist in a way that was particularly inspiring, other Christian communities adopted that formula for their own Eucharist. Different cities and sections of the empire devised ways of worship that became standard. For instance, in the area of Milan, a liturgy developed different in some ways from the liturgy of its sister Italian city, Rome. Saint John Chrysostom (c. 347–407) developed a liturgical form that became very popular around Constantinople and continues to be used by Byzantine Catholics today.

Christians recognized the Eucharist as a banquet in which they received the Body and Blood of Christ and experienced communion in the divine life and participation in the sacrifice of Christ's death and the glory of his Resurrection. Christ's message, "Do this in memory of me," has always been central to the Christian life. The Sacrament of the Eucharist is the "heart and the summit of the Church's life" (*CCC*, #1407).

Initiation into the Church

The Sacrament of Baptism is mentioned a number of times in Scripture, most notably in Jesus' commissioning of his Apostles to make disciples of all nations, baptizing them in the name of the Father, Son, and Holy Spirit. Then we read Saint Peter's sermon at Pentecost when he called upon the crowd to: "Repent, and be baptized" (*Acts 2:38*). The New Testament clearly presents the necessity of Baptism for the forgiveness, new life, and salvation that Christ offered.

The Greek word from which *baptism* comes means "to plunge or immerse" in water. The earliest form of Christian Baptism we know about involved immersion into a river or other body of water. Later, Christians built separate buildings for Baptisms—modeled after the Roman baths—where new members would be totally immersed in water.

It must have taken great faith to be baptized in the first centuries when it meant joining the ranks of the persecuted. Stories of people who did so—even soldiers and well-off citizens—attest to the faith, hope, and love that people experienced in Baptism. For instance, there is a story of an entire Roman legion, composed mainly of men from the Egyptian city of Thebes, who became Christian and refused to worship the Roman gods or massacre innocent local people. Another legion was sent off to kill the 6,600 Christian members of the Theban Legion (*Our Sunday Visitor's Encyclopedia of the Saints*, p. 415). One of the most famous early martyrs, Saint Cecilia (third century) was a member of an important Roman family who survived for three days after a botched attempt by a soldier to behead her (*Our Sunday Visitor's Encyclopedia of the Saints*, p. 159).

The Catechumenate At first, initiation into the Christian community was as simple as that described in Acts 8:35–38. The Apostle Philip comes upon an Ethiopian official riding in a chariot, explains the Good News of Jesus to him, and they both go down into a nearby body of water where the official is baptized. Within three hundred years, initiation into the Christian community became a lengthy process lasting two or three years. During the preparation period, those seeking initiation into the community would participate in a variety of activities to deepen and strengthen their growing faith. They would listen and respond to the Good News, go through a process of learning the essentials of the faith, and gradually be welcomed into full communion with the Church community and participation in the Eucharist.

Catechumens, those who were in the process of becoming initiated into the Church, went through a process of formation that helped them move from their previous way of life into the Church. Often this meant giving up associations and even occupations that were contrary to the Christian message. Mentors or catechists—also called sponsors and teachers, respectively—helped these individuals discern the changes they had to make and supported them with prayer and the teachings of Jesus. Generally the catechumens joined the community in worship on Sunday for the reading of Scripture and the initial prayers—or, what we call the Liturgy of the Word today. They were then dismissed, along with a catechist who guided them through a reflection on the Scriptures read that day and helped them apply the readings to their lives and decisions.

Before their initiation, the catechumens participated in a lengthy retreat-type experience. Some historians indicate that this final forty-day preparation period became what we now know as the season of Lent. When the community gathered for the all-night Easter vigil, those who had prepared for so long were immersed in a pool of water, anointed with oil, and welcomed at the table of the Lord. No longer catechumens, they were now full members of the community with a new family and a new home. These three sacraments—Baptism, Confirmation, and Eucharist—are called the Sacraments of Initiation. Today, as in the first centuries of the Church, these sacraments together make up full initiation into the Church. Baptism marks the beginning of new life, Confirmation strengthens it, and the Eucharist nourishes the disciple to live out that new life and to become more like Christ.

The formation of the new Christians continued after their initiation. This time, known as "mystagogy" since it further initiated people into the mystery of Christ, included more learning, much reflection, and assimilation into the community. Once initiated into the Church, the new Christians were able to help guide other catechumens on their journey into the Church.

!FYI

The Second Vatican Council brought about the restoration of an adult Catechumenate. The Rite of Christian Initiation for Adults (RCIA) was revised and restored in 1972 and mandated for use in the United States in 1988. The RCIA process models the initiation process for those received into the early Church communities.

Changes in the form used to celebrate all of the sacraments did not change their essential significance or the grace that they conveyed. We find that early Christian communities were filled with a sense of the mystery of Christ's life-giving presence among them. They engaged in many activities that were particularly effective in making that mystery real for them. While certain sacraments such as Baptism and the Eucharist clearly were always at the heart of the Christian life, in the beginning there was no set number of sacraments. However, since the beginning, the Church celebrated seven principal efficacious signs instituted by Christ and entrusted to the Church. In the thirteenth century, the Church taught more clearly how these seven were of a different order than all other Christian signs and celebrations: Baptism, Confirmation, Eucharist, Penance and Reconciliation, Anointing of the Sick, Holy Orders, and Matrimony. And while the way these sacraments have been celebrated throughout history may have varied, Christ's action in them has not.

FAITH ACTIVITY

Sacramental Life List the sacraments you have received and what you can remember (or what you've been told) about each. Share your experiences with a partner. Then work together to describe how your parishes celebrate the sacraments. Be sure to include anything you know about the preparation period before the celebration of the sacrament, when it takes place, who can receive it, and so on.

GROUP TALK

1 Why is it important for the Church to have a process for initiating new members into her community?

2 How does initiation into the Church differ from initiation into other groups or communities?

One Body in Christ

For as in one body we have many members, and not all the members have the same function, so we, who are many, are one body in Christ, and individually we are members one of another.

✝ Romans 12:4-5

Does the Church structure that exists today resemble the way the Church was structured in the beginning? Let's try to answer this question in light of developments that took place in the early centuries of Church history.

The above passage from the Letter to the Romans is key to understanding Church organization in both the past and the present. Christ alone is head of the body; the pope is his chief representative on earth. Different members of Christ's body, the Church, serve different functions. Among those in leadership roles are the bishops, priests, and deacons.

GROUP TALK

In small groups, discuss the qualities of a good leader. Then consider why good leaders are necessary for any community. As a class, talk about Church leaders you know or have learned about. Describe how they were good leaders for the community.

Leadership Roles

Jesus left us no exact blueprint for Church organization. However, Gospel accounts indicate that Jesus selected twelve Apostles for a leadership role among his followers. He also identified Peter as the leader of this group. Thus, we find in the Gospels that Jesus established Peter and the other Apostles as leaders of the Church.

In the Acts of the Apostles we find these leadership roles carried out. For instance, Acts 1:20 describes Peter telling a group of Christ's followers that since Judas betrayed Jesus and is no longer one of the Twelve: "Let another take his position of overseer." Two candidates were proposed, and the group selected a man named Matthias to join the ranks of the twelve Apostles. We also read that the Apostles prayed, laid hands on deacons chosen for service and ministry, and sent them out. (See *Acts 6:6, 13:3*.) We see that the Apostles served in leadership positions in the Church from her beginning.

If we read further in Acts, we discover that in some local churches leadership appears to be exercised by a group of elders, or **presbyters**. Acts contains ten references to these presbyters. For instance, the decision to spread the Gospel message to Gentiles at the Council of Jerusalem was made by "the apostles and the elders, with the consent of the whole church" (*Acts 15:22*). By the beginning of the second century, the model that exists in the Catholic Church today became the standard model of Church governance.

- An *episcopos* (or bishop) was appointed or elected to lead local communities, just as today bishops are regional leaders of their dioceses, under the authority of the pope, who is the supreme leader and pastor of the universal Church. The **bishops** succeed the Apostles in the role of governing, sanctifying (making holy through the celebration of the sacraments), and leading the Catholics in a regional, local Church known as a diocese.

- Deacons assisted these leaders, especially in the important work of caring for people with special needs in the community.

- Presbyters became representatives of the bishops as local communities expanded farther and farther. The title *priest* is related to the term *presbyter*, and priests are today's presbyters.

In summary, the early Christian Church recognized that she was to be "of one heart and soul" in embodying the Holy Spirit and in carrying out the message of Jesus. (See *Acts 4:32*.) She formed particular structures to help her in her task. Through her institutional structure, today's Catholic Church remains faithful to the model first developed as early as apostolic times.

FYI

There are two types of deacons in the Church today: transitional deacons—men preparing to become priests—and permanent deacons—men who may or may not be married and are not preparing for the ministry of the priesthood. The restoration of the permanent diaconate (meaning the ordination of permanent deacons) took place during Vatican II reforms. Both types of deacons help bishops and priests in the celebration of the sacraments, particularly in the Eucharist, visiting those who cannot participate in the Sunday liturgy and distributing Holy Communion, proclaiming the Gospel and preaching, presiding at funerals, and focusing on various ministries of outreach.

The Development of Church Structures Leadership positions existed in the earliest Christian community, and as the Church grew, clearly defined structures of authority grew with her. The model that exists in the Catholic Church today became standardized. The pope, bishops, priests, deacons, and the **laity**—baptized Catholics who share in Jesus' mission and continue his work in the workplace, in school, at home, and in the community, but are not ordained—have different functions serving a common purpose.

Women in the Early Church Determining what roles women had in the early Church requires some detective work. We know from the Gospels, for instance, that Jesus treated women in a way that was not typical in the culture of his time. For instance, he had women friends, such as Martha and Mary—the sisters of Lazarus. (See *Luke 10* and *John 11*.) Although Jesus chose twelve men as Apostles, there were a number of women among his regular followers—such as Mary his Mother, Mary of Magdala, Susanna, and Joanna. A number of women also helped Paul in his ministry.

I commend to you our sister Phoebe, a deacon of the church at Cenchreae, so that you may welcome her in the Lord as is fitting for the saints, and help her in whatever she may require from you, for she has been a benefactor of many and of myself as well.

Greet Prisca and Aquila, who work with me in Christ Jesus, and who risked their necks for my life, to whom not only I give thanks, but also all the churches of the Gentiles. Greet also the church in their house. Greet my beloved Epaenetus, who was the first convert in Asia for Christ. Greet Mary, who has worked very hard among you. Greet Andronicus and Junia, my relatives who were in prison with me; they are prominent among the apostles, and they were in Christ before I was.

✝ Romans 16:1-7

As Paul's letter indicates, both men and women played active roles in serving the Church. However, his use of the term *deacon* for Phoebe does not have the same meaning understood for those deacons ordained to ministry at that time or in the Church today. We are not certain the extent of duties performed by women in this leadership role, but indications are that they mainly engaged in ministry to widows, women, and children. Also, they assisted at the Baptisms of women converts. This function of women in the Church diminished around the sixth century in the Western Church and the eleventh century in the Eastern Church.

Pope John Paul II wrote about women in the Church:

> Unfortunately, a certain way of writing history has paid greater attention to extraordinary and sensational events than to the daily rhythm of life, and the resulting history is almost only concerned with the achievements of men. This tendency should be reversed. 'How much still needs to be said and written about man's enormous debt to woman in every other realm of social and cultural progress!'

("History Needs to Include Women's Contributions," *L'Osservatore Romano*, English edition, 31 May 1995, #6)

FAITH ACTIVITY

Roles of Women List the roles each of the following women played in the early Church:

Phoebe (Romans 16:1–2)

Priscilla (Prisca) (Acts 18:2, 18, 26; Romans 16:3; and 1 Corinthians 16:19)

Euodia and Syntyche (Philippians 4:2–3)

Nympha (Colossians 4:15)

Lydia of Philippi (Acts 16:14–15, 40)

Tabitha (Acts 9:36–42)

GROUP TALK

Of the various ministries that people in your parish perform, choose one and interview someone in that ministry. Report to the class on the activities involved in that ministry.

INTERPRET THE ART

Sorrow to Joy Mary Magdalene is among the most identifiable women in Scripture. Think of two instances in Scripture that show Mary was filled with sorrow and two where she was filled with joy.

The Magdalene by Piero di Cosimo

›Age to Age

Litany of the Saints

Throughout the history of Catholicism, many holy women and men have kept alive the faith through their exceptional lives of prayer, courage, fidelity, and virtue. A litany of the saints is a recitation of various saints' names, chanted or spoken during certain liturgies such as Baptisms, the liturgy of the Triduum (Holy Thursday, Good Friday, Easter Vigil, and Easter Sunday), and the ordination of deacons, priests, and bishops. The formula may vary, but the litany frequently reads something like this: 'Holy Mary, Mother of God . . . Pray for us. Saint Joseph . . . Pray for us. Saints Peter and Paul . . . Pray for us. All the holy martyrs . . . Pray for us.' We call on the saints of the past to help us because we believe that their saintly lives led to their being with God in heaven, where they can speak for us. Litanies were chanted in Christianity as early as the third century. You will hear a litany before the blessing of water at the Easter Vigil at your parish. Hearing the names of these great heroes of the past, one after another, reminds us that we are connected to a great community called the Church. We meet Christ in flesh and blood people, such as those who make up the Church. We even have a day, All Saints Day, when we celebrate the lives of many saints, both canonized and not canonized. It's another great occasion on which to sing a litany of the saints!

Praying with the Martyrs

Leader: Loving Father, so many of your son's first followers suffered because they believed in him and knew he was worth living and dying for. Grant that we not settle for what is comfortable and easy. Help us give of ourselves and work with the Holy Spirit in building your kingdom on earth as it is in heaven. Amen.

Reader: People are unreasonable, illogical and self-centered.
　　Love them anyway!
If you do good, people will accuse you of selfish ulterior motives.
　　Do good anyway!
If you are successful, you will win false friends and enemies.
　　Succeed anyway!
The good you do will be forgotten tomorrow.
　　Do good anyway!
Honesty and frankness make you vulnerable.
　　Be honest and frank anyway!
What you spend years building may be destroyed overnight.
　　Build anyway!
People really need help but may attack you if you help them.
　　Help them anyway!

(Dr. Kent M. Keith)

Leader: Lord Jesus, your holy martyr Saint Perpetua could have saved her life if she had renounced you. Instead, when asked if she was a Christian she replied, "I cannot be called anything else than what I am." May we be inspired by the martyrs to live the Christian life even during difficult times. Amen.

>Review

1. Who is the first known Christian martyr?
2. Which group of Christians was the primary target of persecution from their fellow Jews?
3. In what city were the followers of Jesus first called *Christians*?
4. List three reasons why Christians were particularly susceptible to Roman persecution.
5. What did the Edict of Milan grant?
6. Who was the first emperor to become Christian?
7. As applied to the Church, what do *creed*, *rite*, and *community* mean?
8. What function did apologists serve in the early Church?
9. What is the difference between orthodoxy and heresy?
10. What does "setting the canon" mean in regard to Scripture?
11. What does the Church use to determine Christian teachings? What is their single source?
12. What is the pre-Christian meaning of the term *sacramentum*?
13. How did Greek-speaking churches refer to what Latin churches called sacraments?
14. What does it mean to say that sacraments became more formalized?
15. Outline the basic transformation that took place in the early Church's institutional structure and describe how it relates to today's structure.

>Key Words

apologists (p. 44) Christian thinkers who defended and explained Christian beliefs.

atheism (p. 38) The denial that God exists.

bishops (p. 55) Means "overseers"; ordained Church leaders who are successors of the Apostles and have received the fullness of the Sacrament of Holy Orders.

canon (p. 47) The Church's complete list of sacred books of the Bible.

catechumens (p. 52) Unbaptized persons preparing for membership in the Church. A person becomes a catechumen after celebrating the Rite of Acceptance into the order of catechumens.

deacons (p. 35) Third degree of the Sacrament of Holy Orders; the man is ordained to assist the bishop and priests in a variety of ways; in the early Church, someone appointed to serve those who were poor or otherwise needy in the community.

Edict of Milan (p. 41) Declaration allowing religious freedom in the Roman Empire.

heresy (p. 45) A belief, attitude, or teaching that is contrary to revealed truth and to the Church's doctrine of faith.

heretic (p. 45) Someone baptized a Christian who obstinately holds a position on an article of faith that conflicts with officially defined Church teachings.

Incarnation (p. 45) The truth that the second Person of the Blessed Trinity, while remaining God, assumed a human nature and became man.

laity (p. 56) Baptized Catholics who share in Jesus' mission and continue his work on earth but are not ordained.

martyrs (p. 34) Persons who witness to the truth of the faith by enduring death to be faithful to Christ.

orthodoxy (p. 45) A doctrine, belief, attitude, or teaching that is consistent with revealed truth and with the Church's doctrine of faith.

presbyters (p. 55) Another name for elders or priests; in the early Church, presbyters were closely associated with the bishop in the exercising of leadership in some faith communities.

sacraments (p. 49) Effective signs of grace, instituted by Christ and entrusted to the Church, by which we share in divine life through the work of the Holy Spirit.

Tradition (p. 48) The living and authentic transmission of the teachings of Jesus in the Church.

>Yesterday and Today

For nearly three hundred years, members of the early Church encountered attacks and persecutions. However, they had the life and message of Jesus, who suffered and died but was raised to new life, to sustain them during these difficult first centuries. They discovered the meaning of Christ in their Scriptures, in their Tradition, and in one another. The witness given by the early martyrs can't help but inspire anyone who wonders whether there is anything worth living—and dying—for.

The Church also had its internal conflicts and controversies. Even people who share a common vision and purpose can disagree about what exactly the vision means and about how to achieve their goals. When people feel very strongly about something, as the early Christians did, then disagreements become even more heated. Today's world is not the first to address multiculturalism and various forms of diversity. Now, as then, Christians have Jesus to remind them that sharing resources and caring especially for people in particular need make God's presence real.

Finally, the Church gradually took on a definite shape. While differences remained from place to place, essentials of belief and practice became standard over these early centuries. Members of the Church today have a remarkable history. This history includes inspiring stories, statements of beliefs that great thinkers hammered out, established rituals for sacraments by which we encounter Christ, and an organization that connects them to fellow Church members down the street and around the globe. The early Christians gave their lives to be the Church through which Christ continues to be present. Their legacy, the wonderful unfolding of the Holy Spirit, remains with us today.

Madonna and Child with Justinian and Constantine, 6th Century.▼

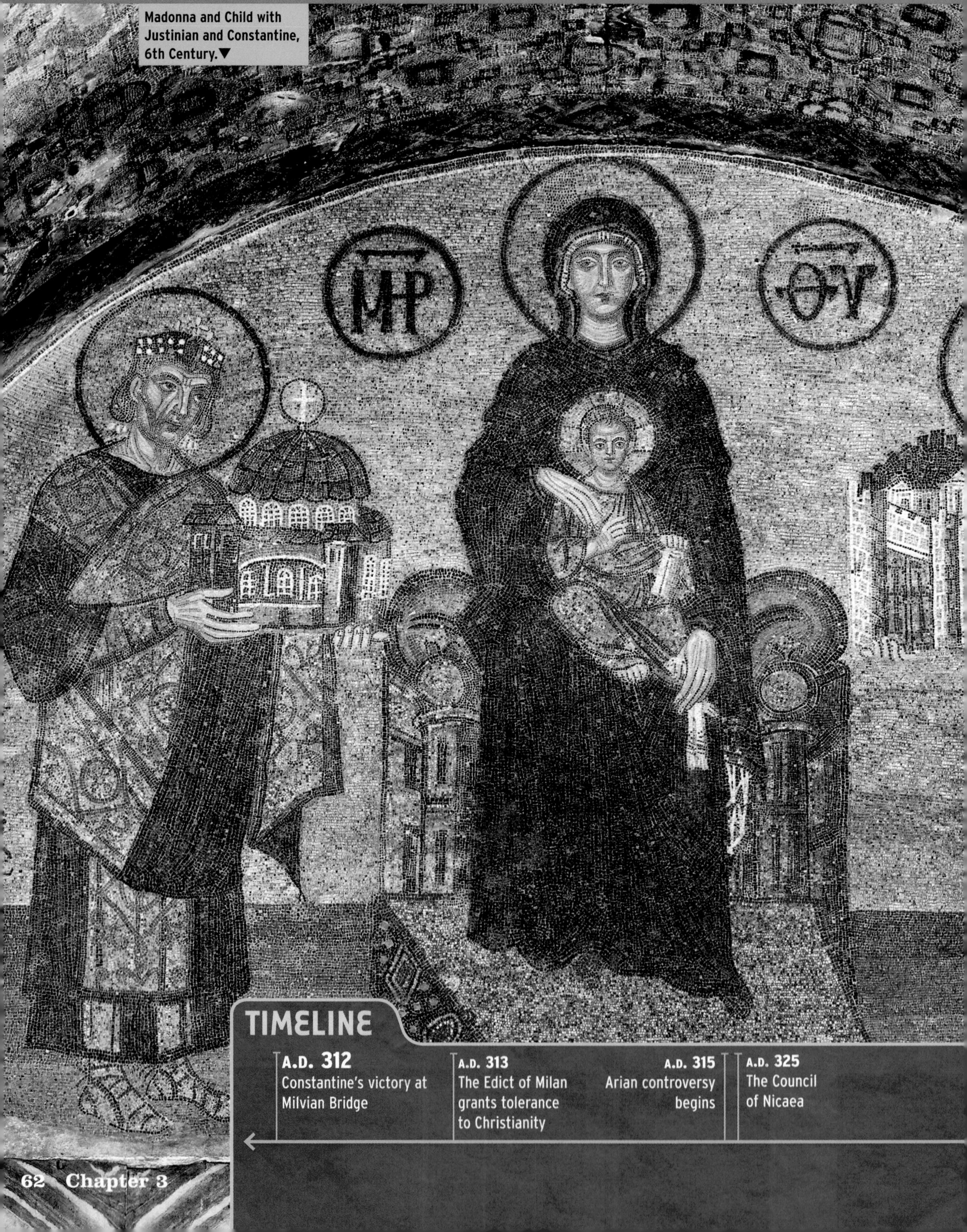

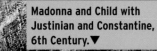

TIMELINE

A.D. 312 Constantine's victory at Milvian Bridge

A.D. 313 The Edict of Milan grants tolerance to Christianity

A.D. 315 Arian controversy begins

A.D. 325 The Council of Nicaea

CHAPTER 3

CHURCH VICTORIOUS

THE AGE OF THE FATHERS

A.D. 300-500

CHAPTER GOALS

In this chapter you will:

★ learn that under Emperor Constantine Christianity became the religion of the Roman Empire.

★ examine the fall of the Western Roman Empire.

★ explore the role of the Fathers of the Church who guided the early Church community through controversies and identified beliefs and practices that have sustained the Church.

★ discover how monastic spirituality developed after the age of the martyrs.

A.D. 381
THEODOSIUS I
"THE GREAT"
CREATES ORTHODOX
CHRISTIAN STATE

A.D. 431
The Council of
Ephesus

A.D. 451
The Council of Chalcedon

A.D. 381
First Council of
Constantinople

A.D. 387
The conversion
of Augustine

A.D. 398
John Chrysostom
becomes patriarch
of Constantinople

A.D. 432
Patrick returns
to Ireland
as bishop

A.D. 452
Pope Leo the
Great turns back
Attila from Rome

Christianity, Religion of the Empire

FIRST THOUGHTS

The prolific growth of the Church during its first five centuries was foremost the work of God in bringing people to the faith through grace in using the Church as his instrument in the proclamation of the truth of the faith. Read the list below and rank how these other factors may have contributed to the expansion and growth of the Church.

* the beauty and mystery of the liturgy and sacraments

* the sense of community and mutual concern among Church members

* the spirit of morality and justice advocated by the Church

* the profound depth of Christian beliefs and teachings

* the promise of eternal life that fills Church members with hope

* the inspiration of holy people living out their faith

Have you ever been on a team that went from last place one year to first place the next? Do you have a sense of what it sometimes feels like to be freshmen—outsiders, picked on, and considered unimportant, and then to be seniors—the people in leadership positions who set the standards for everyone else to follow?

A drastic turnabout such as this happened to Christianity. The Church begun by Jesus went from her humble origins to being the official religion of the Roman Empire three hundred years later. The wave of enthusiasm that had sustained the Church during its time of persecutions led to great expansion and growth when she found herself guiding Roman power rather than being under its attack. Church leaders provided leadership and kept civilization alive at a time when emperors were often weak, corrupt, or inept.

Debates about the true meaning of the faith didn't end when Christianity rose to power. Emperors themselves offered opinions about the relationship between God the Father, God the Son, and God the Holy Spirit. To sustain the spiritual vitality of the Church, a new form of living the Christian life emerged—monasticism.

During the period covered in this chapter, shifts in political and economic fortunes had a lasting impact on the Church. Civilization and Christianity flourished in the eastern part of the empire, leading to many remarkable developments in the Eastern Church. Western Europe during this period experienced both destruction and development. The one light flickering during these dark times was the light of Christ kept burning in his Church.

Constantine—From Roman General to Christian Ruler

You had a preview of the importance of Constantine in the previous chapter, and it stands to reason that Emperor Constantine deserves to be counted among the most influential persons in history. Born around the year 280, Constantine was the son of one of the generals of the Roman army that ruled the empire at the time. His mother Helena is known to have become a Christian. Constantine became the sole ruler of the Western empire after defeating a number of other generals who were seeking control of the region; later he also defeated Licinius, the emperor of the East, and became leader of the whole Roman world.

One of Constantine's first acts upon becoming emperor was to abandon Rome and build a new capital city along the straits of the Bosporus, the waters that divide Europe from Asia Minor. Formerly a small trading post called *Byzantium*, the city was renamed New Rome by Constantine. Most people, however, simply called it *Constantinople*—Constantine's city. Today the city is known as Istanbul, Turkey.

Because Constantine moved the empire's capital to Asia Minor, the center of civilization also moved from West to East. For many years, the majority of emperors and government leaders abandoned Rome and left the Romans to deal with the city's increasing decay. Roman leaders also had to deal with the steadily increasing threats of nomadic Germanic tribes from outside the empire who pillaged Roman frontier communities and eventually gained control of its western half. With civil power centered in the East, only Church leaders remained to care for the crumbling empire in the West.

Constantine favored Christianity, but he also allowed non-Christian customs to continue. He commissioned Christian churches to be built, but he kept the image of the sun god on the official coins of the empire and retained for himself the title *Pontifex Maximus*, a term meaning "the greatest bridge-builder." As during non-Christian times, emperors saw themselves in the priestly role of bridging the gap between the human and the divine. This title, held by the Roman emperors before Constantine, was later adopted by popes—the title today has been adapted to "pontiff." Even though Constantine turned to Christianity in 312, he was not baptized until just before his death in 337. The Byzantine Church considers Constantine to be a saint.

FAITH ACTIVITY

Life of Constantine Constantine's turn to Christianity came just before the Battle of the Milvian Bridge in the year 312. Research the life of Constantine, highlighting the Christian standards he legislated during his reign.

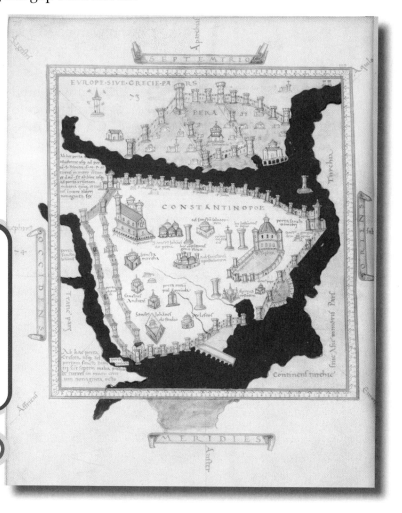

EXPLORE THE LAND

A New Capital Think of other major cities of the time—such as Rome, Alexandria, or Athens. Why was Constantinople an excellent choice to serve as the capital of the Roman Empire? Find out what you can about the history of this great city.

The Edict of Milan Grants Religious Freedom Truly one of the most significant events in Church history—indeed, one of the most important events in all of history—was the Roman Empire's embracing of Christianity during the reign of Constantine. As mentioned in the last chapter, under Constantine Christianity went from being a religion of outsiders to being a religion of insiders. After Constantine issued the Edict of Milan in 313, a Christian could sit amongst the powerful and well connected politically without fear or the need to hide his or her beliefs.

The rise to power did not dampen the spirit within the Church community. It did, however, cause that spirit to be channeled in different directions.

- Church leaders no longer guided isolated groups of Christians, providing for their religious and spiritual growth and keeping them on the right track. Now, Church leaders were called upon to provide guidance in secular affairs as well.

- The empire's leaders no longer persecuted or ignored Christianity. Instead they looked to the Church and its leadership to maintain and foster the well-being of the empire.

- Christians who wanted to give their all for Christ no longer lived under the threat of martyrdom. Now, those who wanted to sacrifice all the comforts of life in Christ's name had to make their way out to deserts or other isolated spots.

- Christian worship became a public ceremony, and places of worship openly represented Christ triumphant. Christian missionaries spread not only the Christian faith but also Roman civilization.

Lactantius Describes the Edict of Milan Lactantius, a Christian writer of the time, wrote about the "victory" of Christianity over its persecutors. In his essay he includes the following pronouncement from Constantine, emperor of the West, and Licinius, emperor of the East at the time. Their edict called for religious freedom for all, but Christianity is clearly the focus.

> When we, Constantine and Licinius, emperors, had an interview at Milan, and conferred together with respect to the good and security of the commonweal, it seemed to us that, amongst those things that are profitable to mankind in general, the reverence paid to the Divinity merited our first and chief attention, and that it was proper that the Christians and all others should have liberty to follow that mode of religion which to each of them appeared best; so that God, who is seated in heaven, might be benign and propitious to us, and to every one under our government. And therefore we judged it a salutary measure, and one highly consonant to right reason, that no man should be denied leave of attaching himself to the rites of the Christians, or to whatever other religion his mind directed him, that thus the supreme Divinity, to whose worship we freely devote ourselves, might continue to vouchsafe His favour and beneficence to us. And accordingly we give you to know that, without regard to any provisos in our former orders to you concerning the Christians, all who choose that religion are to be permitted, freely and absolutely, to remain in it, and not to be disturbed any ways, or molested.

"On the Deaths of the Persecutors," in Jean Comby,
How to Read Church History, Vol. 1, p. 45

Images of the Church

Bride of Christ

> The humanity of Christ is like the grape because it was crushed in the winepress of the Cross so that his blood flowed forth over all the earth . . . . How great is the love of the Bridegroom for his spouse, the Church.

Saint Anthony of Padua, *St. Anthony Messenger*, July 2005, inside cover.

What an unbelievable transformation the Edict of Milan brought about! Now the emperor himself felt compelled to be involved in Church affairs, and leaders of the Church became involved in affairs of state. However, the Church remained wedded to Christ because, from its beginning, Christ married himself to the Church and united himself to all things human. Saint Paul uses this image of the Church as "bride of Christ" in a number of his letters. The love that Christ has for the Church is like the love spouses have for each other; Christ is one with his Church as husband and wife are one. Although no marriage can measure up to the intimate relationship that Christ has with his Church, Paul finds the analogy of married love to be the best way to describe the relationship between Christ and Church. As in marriage, Christ and the Church "become one flesh." (See *Ephesians 5:31*.) This intimate union with Christ sustained the Church even as it became the religion of the empire. (See *Catechism of the Catholic Church*, #796.)

Councils Clarify Christian Beliefs

No sooner had peace and freedom come to the Church than a conflict about the Trinity arose that had been simmering for some time. A new heresy—called **Arianism**—begun by an Alexandrian priest caused much discord. A central Christian belief taught that God is one divine substance but three distinct Persons—Father, Son, and Holy Spirit. However, early in the fourth century, a priest in Egypt named Arius wrote a book of popular songs titled *Thalia* (*The Banquet*), in which he proclaimed that Jesus was not of the same substance as the Father. He proposed that only God the Father could be immortal. Arius's teaching stated, "There was once when he [the Son] was not." Therefore, Arius said, Jesus must have been created, and while Jesus is like the Father, he is not truly God. However, as the *Catechism* describes, this is not the case.

God is one in substance (essence, nature). The words *person* and *hypostasis* refer to the Father, Son, and Holy Spirit as they are distinct. The word *relation* refers to the fact that they are distinct in relation to each other. (See *Catechism of the Catholic Church*, #252.)

Many newly baptized Christians accepted the Arian view as it was more in line with their pre-Christian concepts. They could accept God as the perfection of all things, as described in Greek thought, and Jesus as a superhero, as was found in Greek and Roman mythology. Having previously believed these myths, some new Christians saw no problem in viewing Jesus this way. Arius's bishop, Alexander of Alexandria, however, knew this perspective was a rejection of the belief that Jesus was divine in the full sense of the word. He gathered local Church leaders who discussed the matter and condemned Arius and his teachings.

This condemnation did not settle the conflict, however. Arius was a very popular pastor who was skilled at com-

INTERPRET THE ART

Imagery in Art This image is a 16th century artist's interpretation of the Council of Nicaea. What specific images can you identify in this artwork, and how is it important? How is Scripture given prominence in this image?

Council of Nicaea by Cesare Nebbia.

posing catchy tunes through which he spread his teachings. Members of the Church were divided in the dispute. Riots even broke out in Egypt, where the debates were most intense. Eventually, the controversy began to affect the security of the empire itself.

Emperor Constantine was so concerned with the Arian controversy that in 325 he called for a meeting of all Church leaders to take place at a palace he had in the town of Nicaea, about fifty miles southeast of Constantinople. Constantine was not a baptized Christian at the time. He was acting out of the time-honored belief that the emperor had responsibility for religious affairs in the empire. This meeting Constantine called for is considered the first **ecumenical council**, or world-wide gathering of Catholic bishops.

The emperor himself opened the **Council of Nicaea** and insisted that the more than three hundred bishops in attendance must resolve this issue. He wanted a Church that had the same beliefs throughout his empire. "Division in the Church is worse than war," he declared, "because it involves souls." Arius presented his teachings. The bishops rejected the teachings and decided that they needed to formulate a creed that would describe clearly the relationship between God the Father and God the Son, Jesus Christ. All but two bishops signed the creed, and they were condemned and exiled along with Arius.

The creed the bishops created is called the **Nicene Creed**, or Niceno-Constantinopolitan Creed since a later council at Constantinople added to it. Catholic Churches all over the world proclaim this creed during Sunday Mass. In the creed, we profess our faith in Jesus as "true God from true God, begotten not made, one in Being with the Father." The key phrase is "one in Being." Arius called for wording that would mean "of similar being."

Even with the Council's decree, the Arian heresy was not stamped out for another sixty years. Disagreement about the relationship among the three Persons of the Blessed Trinity—God the Father, Son, and Holy Spirit—was continually debated and eventually figured into the split between the Eastern Orthodox and Western Churches. We will look at this split in chapter five.

GROUP TALK

In what ways can disagreements about core beliefs affect the ways a community acts and how its members interact with one another?

Lessons from the Arian Controversy and the Council of Nicaea

As we have seen, controversies over Christian teaching have been part of Church history for a long time. Councils have met to provide a procedure for the bishops of the Church, in union with the pope, to settle matters of conflict. In the midst of conflicts and adversity, wise leaders have emerged who clarify and keep alive the Christian message. This message is not just about eternal life but is also concerned about temporal affairs in light of eternity.

Council of Chalcedon

The Council of Nicaea and the Nicene Creed did not resolve all of the disputes about the place of Christ in the Christian perspective on reality. A series of councils took place over the next century or so. And the Council of Chalcedon, in 451, was a response to another misconception about Christ.

Eutyches, the head of a monastery near Constantinople, was a leading advocate of what came to be known as the heresy of **Monophysitism**. (*Mono* means "one," and *physis* means "nature.") According to Eutyches, the human nature of Jesus was lost in the divine, just as "a drop of honey, which falls into the sea, dissolves in it." This inaccurate teaching gained such support that a council at Ephesus in 449 endorsed it. However, later in 449 Pope Leo declared this council to be invalid. The emperor Marcian called for another council. Four hundred bishops attended the Council of Chalcedon and condemned Monophysitism. They declared that Christ is one person who possesses two natures—human and divine.

Faced with this heresy, the fourth ecumenical council, at Chalcedon in 451, confessed:

> . . .We confess that one and the same Christ, Lord, and only-begotten Son, is to be acknowledged in two natures without confusion, change, division, or separation. The distinction between the natures was never abolished by their union, but rather the character proper to each of the two natures was preserved as they came together in one person (*prosopon*) and one hypostasis.[1]
>
> *Catechism of the Catholic Church, #467*

The Ecumenical Councils of the Early Church

Location	Date	Emperor	Major Outcomes
Nicaea	325	Constantine	★declared Jesus, the Son of God, *homoousios* (coequal, consubstantial, and coeternal) with the Father ★condemned Arianism ★drafted original form of Nicene Creed
Constantinople	381	Theodosius	★confirmed teachings of Council of Nicaea ★affirmed deity of the Holy Spirit ★condemned Apollinarianism
Ephesus	431	Theodosius II	★declared Nestorianism a heresy ★condemned Pelagianism
Chalcedon	451	Marcian	★declared Christ's two natures unmixed, unchanged, undivided, inseparable ★condemned Monophysitism

Robert C. Walton, *Chronological and Background Charts of Church History*, #18.

We may think of theological controversies as debates between scholars that have little impact on ordinary people. Obviously, that was not the case with the debates over theological questions that took place in the early centuries of the Church. Today, if someone said to you, "I don't believe that Jesus is God," you may be puzzled by his or her words because for centuries we have professed that Jesus is human and divine. However, during these earlier times, people struggled to come to an accurate and precise understanding of core Christian beliefs.

FAITH ACTIVITY

Heresies In small groups research and report on these heresies: Appollinarianism, Nestorianism, Pelagianism. Discuss how the Church responded to these heresies.

Early Church leaders were guided by the Holy Spirit to formulate the core beliefs that have been passed on through the centuries. Clear summaries of the faith in creeds are so important because, in order to choose to believe, we need to know what we are saying "yes" to. In the celebration of the Sacrament of Baptism for infants and young children, the parents and godparents reject sin and renew their own baptismal vows in a profession of faith. After they have done so, the priest or deacon then says, "This is our faith. This is the faith of the Church" (*Rite of Baptism for Children,* 59). Then the child is baptized in the name of the Father, Son, and Holy Spirit.

This statement and its place in the sacrament is a very important reminder that our personal faith is also our communal faith. The faith of the Church makes our own faith possible, stirring it up in us, supporting and making it strong. But, as the questions to the parents and godparents also remind us, faith is always a personal choice—a free human act that comes from the dignity of being made in God's image with free will. The Holy Spirit helps us to be able to believe and live out that belief.

The Nicene Creed

We believe in one God,
   the Father, the Almighty,
   maker of heaven and earth,
   of all that is, seen and unseen.

We believe in the one Lord, Jesus Christ,
   the only Son of God,
   eternally begotten of the Father,
   God from God, Light from Light,
   true God from true God,
   begotten, not made, one in Being with the Father.
   Through him all things were made.

For us men and for our salvation
   he came down from heaven:
by the power of the Holy Spirit
   he was born of the Virgin Mary, and became man.

For our sake he was crucified under Pontius Pilate;
   he suffered, died, and was buried.
   On the third day he rose again
      in fulfillment of the Scriptures;
   he ascended into heaven
      and is seated at the right hand of the Father.
He will come again in glory to judge the living
   and the dead, and his kingdom will have no end.

We believe in the Holy Spirit, the Lord, the giver of life,
   who proceeds from the Father and the Son.
   With the Father and the Son he is worshiped and
      glorified.
   He has spoken through the Prophets.
   We believe in the one holy catholic and apostolic
      Church.
   We acknowledge one baptism for the
      forgiveness of sins.
   We look for the resurrection of the dead,
      and the life of the world to come.
   Amen.

The Western Roman Empire Falls

The time between the classical era and the Middle Ages, from the fifth century to Charlemagne's reign in 800, was in many ways a dark period for Western Europe. This period was marked by marauding tribes from the North, East, and West who fought against the people of the empire and among themselves, diminishing many of the accomplishments that marked earlier periods. These tribes, referred to collectively as barbarians, inhabited the territory beyond the northern, eastern, and western frontiers of the Roman Empire.

For the most part the tribes from the North and East had no established cities or communities and instead moved about so that their flocks could pasture. As Rome's control spread into their territory, the barbarian groups attacked those who lived on the edges of the empire. Eventually Roman soldiers could no longer control these invasions, and by the fifth century Rome itself was under attack. In 410, one of these invading groups, the **Visigoths**, actually captured Rome.

▲ *The Meeting of Pope Leo the Great and Attila* by Francesco Solimena.

With a depleted army and no effective defense against the invaders, authorities in the empire decided that one solution to the problem was to welcome the invaders as citizens. The first group to accept the offer was the Visigoths, the inhabitants of modern-day Spain, who had attacked and taken control of Rome. The **Vandals** were next. They gained control over much of the empire. Both groups adopted Christianity. However, they both also chose Arianism and ended up persecuting mainstream Christians in territories controlled by them.

The **Huns** came from the East, originally from the steppes of China. Their leader, Attila, received the nickname "the scourge of God" because of the havoc he wrought on the civilized towns and people that lay in his path. One group fleeing the Huns found themselves stopped by the sea in what is now northern Italy. To protect themselves from the Huns, they built islands on pilings and an elaborate series of canals that were separate from solid land. That watery settlement still exists as the city of Venice.

By the end of the fifth century, the empire in the West ceased to exist. It had become a collection of lands ruled by various barbarian tribes. As they settled into domestic life, leaders of the tribes saw Christianity as a unifying force that would allow their people to live peacefully with their neighbors. Although Arianism was the dominant religion in most of the West during the early stages of the Christian tribal period, the fidelity of the bishops of Rome and others kept Christianity alive so that it eventually came to dominate in Europe.

The Pope and the Empire

During the barbarian invasions, the position of the pope—as the bishop of Rome came to be called—grew in importance. While the rulers of the empire were living in Constantinople away from the fray, the bishop of Rome became, in effect, the political leader of the West while remaining the spiritual leader of the Church—having full, immediate, and universal power for the souls of those in their care. However, as we will see throughout this text, while the worldly (temporal) power of the pope may have varied, his spiritual authority remained constant.

Practically speaking, emperors and patriarchs in the East divided secular and spiritual rule. At times, emperors and patriarchs interfered with matters of concern to the other. In the West, the popes were the sole power overseeing the material and spiritual welfare of Western Europe. Without military power at their disposal, popes used faith and conviction to keep invaders from pillaging western territories.

Saint Damasus I, who was pope from 366–384, first used the term **Apostolic See** to refer to his office in order to strengthen in people's minds the connection between the papacy and Saint Peter the Apostle. Pope Damasus said that the early Church sent Peter and Paul, leaders among the Apostles, to Rome. Since they died in Rome, the city could claim them as citizens. Because of his personal holiness and his willingness to challenge heresy, Emperor Theodosius ordered all inhabitants of the empire to follow the form of religion advocated by Pope Damasus. Around the year 382, Pope Damasus asked Saint Jerome to translate the standard Bible from Greek into Latin and changed the language of the liturgy from Greek to Latin so that more people could understand it. These changes strengthened the position of the papacy but also added to the growing separation between the Western, Latin Church and the Eastern, Greek Church.

> **FYI**
>
> The word *see*, as in *Apostolic See*, is an abbreviation for the word seat—the chair designating an office of authority such as the chairperson of a committee or a county seat. Every bishop has a chair symbolizing his authority in a diocese.

> **GROUP TALK**
>
> Similar to the way the first four centuries of Roman rule are considered the glory days for Rome, some people refer to the twentieth century as the *American century* because U.S. ideals and culture came to dominate that century. Discuss what American ways of thinking and living became common world-wide during this time.

Saint Leo the Great (died 461)

Because of his strong defense of the role of the papacy, Pope Leo I, who served as pope from 440-461, is one of only three popes referred to as "the Great" (the others being Gregory I and Nicholas I). With no army behind him, Pope Leo was the sole authority representing Roman interests to the Huns, and then later to the Vandals. Pope Leo negotiated with Attila the Hun to spare the city and actually convinced him to do so. He also strengthened the papacy by stating that each pope succeeds Saint Peter rather than the previous pope. Each pope inherits the powers of Peter. Therefore, individual failings or vices of particular popes do not diminish the role of the papacy itself.

Two hundred years after his death, Pope Leo's body was exhumed and reburied near the tomb of Saint Peter in Saint Peter's Basilica; he was the first pope so honored. Pope Leo's strengthening of the power of the papacy was particularly important because the expectation at the time was that the emperor needed to approve whoever was to become pope. The distance between Rome and the East naturally limited the influence and control of the emperor over the papacy, and popes such as Leo the Great helped to make the papacy a powerful and independent force overseeing the Western Church. While in the East, the emperor continued to appoint the patriarch of Constantinople for some time.

▲St. Leo I the Great, Italian School.

The Fathers of the Church

What is the right way to think about the unique mission of God the Father, the Son, and the Holy Spirit in the life of the Church? What are good ways for Christians to practice their faith? During the years following Christianity's spread throughout the empire, such topics were discussed at all levels of social life in many parts of the empire. One writer of the time reported that when he went to the market, people were talking more about the nature of the Trinity than about the price of meat!

The writings and exemplary lives of many outstanding leaders of the time assisted Church members then and now in deciding matters of Christian beliefs and practice. These great thinkers are known collectively as the **Fathers of the Church**. Though the complete list numbers thirty-nine men from the Western Church and fifty-one from the Eastern Church, during this formative period a number of women also made important and essential contributions to Christian thought and practice. Because of social restrictions in existence at the time, the writings of the women are few.

FYI

Since the sixteenth century, the title "Doctor of the Church" has also been given by the Catholic Church in the West to canonized men and women who have been recognized by the Church as eminent teachers of the faith through the centuries. Some Doctors of the Church include Saints Teresa of Ávila, Anthony of Padua, Leo I, Thérèse of Lisieux, Catherine of Siena, and John Chrysostom.

A Few Fathers of the Church

West or Latin Church	East or Greek Church
Saint Ambrose, bishop of Milan (339-397)	Saint Athanasius, archbishop of Alexandria (296-373) Gregory of Nyssa, bishop of Sebaste (330-395)
Saint Augustine, bishop of Hippo (354-430)	Saint Basil, archbishop of Caesarea (330-379)
Saint Gregory the Great, pope (540-604)	Saint Gregory of Nazianzus, bishop of Sasima; patriarch of Constantinople (329-390)
Saint Jerome, priest; translated the Scriptures into Latin (the Vulgate) (331-420)	Saint John Chrysostom, patriarch of Constantinople (344-407)

The Patristic Period

The Church Fathers were people of courage, conviction, wisdom, and faith who sustained the Church during difficult times. Their influence has continued down through the centuries, impacting the Church of different eras. Because of the large number of men given the honor of being called a Father of the Church, we will limit our discussion here to three of the most prominent ones.

Saint Ambrose (339-397)   The son of an important Roman official, Ambrose used his family connections to become governor of northern Italy with its headquarters in Milan. This was a time when Arians were fighting mainstream Christians for control of church buildings and the Christian communities surrounding them. When Milan's bishop died in 374, Arians and Christians gathered in the cathedral to argue over who

would become the next bishop. When Ambrose heard about the commotion going on, he went to the cathedral to calm things down. Eventually someone shouted, "Ambrose for bishop." Soon the rest of the crowd joined in. Ambrose, who was not even baptized at the time, fled the building but was surrounded by the people and finally agreed to their wishes. Within a week he was baptized, confirmed, ordained a priest and then bishop.

As bishop, Ambrose applied his skills as a civil servant to being a servant of the Church. He trained his clergy and strengthened the process for those preparing for Baptism. He made sure that those in Milan who were poor were taken care of, and even gave away all of his own personal possessions. He studied the Bible so that he could deliver a thoughtful and inspiring sermon every Sunday. He wrote books on theology and commentaries on Scripture. Ambrose also needed his skills as a politician to address the Arian controversy as he had to defend the Church's doctrine against the Emperor Valentinian, who favored the Arians. When the emperor ordered that one of Ambrose's churches was to be given to the Arians, Ambrose refused. Troops arrived to take control of the church, but Ambrose stood in front of it and said, "The emperor is in the Church, not over it." The emperor backed down.

Of all the contributions that Ambrose made to the Church, however, his greatest perhaps was his role in inspiring Saint Augustine to become a Christian.

The Fathers of the Church challenged Christians to see a deeper, spiritual meaning in everything. In *City of God*, for instance, Saint Augustine applied this way of looking at things to the major crisis of his time—the conquest of Rome and the fall of the empire in the West. In this book, he

reassured his readers that while earthly kingdoms rise and fall, the City of God lasts forever. The history of nations is merely a ripple on the surface of reality. True history lies much deeper. It is the story of human souls that came from God making their way back to God. This perspective on reality, that the eternal is more important than the temporal and that everything should be looked at in light of eternity, became the dominant worldview of the medieval period. Certainly it sustained Roman citizens as they saw their empire crumbling in the face of barbarian invasions.

Saint Augustine of Hippo (354–430) Saint Augustine is well known for his many writings including *City of God, The Trinity,* and *Confessions*—considered by many to be the first true autobiography. He was born in northern Africa of a non-Christian father and a Christian mother, Monica. Augustine was very bright but he also engaged in a life of pleasure-seeking and self-indulgence. After he fathered a child out of wedlock, he turned to a religious cult known as the **Manicheans**, who believed that matter is evil, and was in a constant struggle with God, the source of all good. Around the age of thirty, Augustine went first to Rome and then to Milan. In Milan he met Ambrose, under whose influence Augustine turned toward Christianity.

In *Confessions,* Augustine states he had an experience of God when a voice said to him, "Take and read." He began reading the Bible and found the answers that he was seeking. Ambrose baptized Augustine in 387, and Augustine decided to return to Africa and live the remainder of his life as a monk. Four years later, however, the people of his local church asked him to be their priest and then their bishop. He served as bishop of Hippo for thirty-five years. Augustine's writings are numerous, and he is recognized by many as the greatest theologian of the Western Church.

Saint Jerome (331–420) A contemporary of Ambrose and Augustine, Jerome was from northern Italy but educated in Rome. He was particularly skilled in languages, and was one of the few people in the West who knew Hebrew and Greek. One night in a dream he heard God ask him how he saw himself. Jerome answered, "I am a Christian." God responded, "You are not a Christian. You are a Ciceronian. Where your treasure is, there is your heart." (Cicero was one of the greatest pre-Christian Latin writers.) As so many people of the time did, in response to a powerful religious experience, Jerome left the everyday world and became a monk. He dedicated himself to the study of the Scriptures. When Jerome was fifty years old, Pope Damasus asked him to return to Rome to become his secretary, which he did. Jerome made many enemies in Rome because he spoke out forcefully against the luxurious living and corruption that he found there. He had verbal skills to belittle the best opponent, and he didn't hesitate to use them.

Pope Damasus decided that he could use Jerome's skills with language to undertake an important task. The Greek translation of the Bible was in common use at the time. However, Latin had become the language of the people in the West. Some Latin translations had been made, but their quality was poor. Damasus asked Jerome to make a new Latin translation of the Bible, from the original Hebrew and Greek. Jerome left Rome for Bethlehem and spent most of the remainder of his life working on a Latin translation. His translation of the Bible is known as the *Vulgate* because it is in the language of the common people. It continues to be the authoritative text of Scripture in the Church.

Besides his Latin translation of the Bible, Jerome performed another service for the Church. He taught the Bible to women. Jerome found the wisdom and depth of understanding in his women companions to be of great assistance as he struggled to make sense of the Scriptures. Although he lived alone in a cave near the site of the birth of Jesus in Bethlehem, he and one of his women students established a number of monasteries in the area. These monasteries provided refuge for people who left their homes and came to the Holy Lands while Italy was under attack from the nomadic tribes.

One of Jerome's women companions, Saint Paula (347–404), was wealthy and a member of an influential Roman family. When Paula's husband died, she accompanied Jerome back to the Holy Land, taking one of her daughters with her. Paula mastered Hebrew and the Scriptures and helped Jerome in his work with the Bible. Paula founded a monastery for women in Bethlehem that also served as a hospice for pilgrims. She depleted her wealth in building churches and supporting good works. Saint Paula is the patron saint of widows.

FAITH ACTIVITY

Fathers of the Church Research the life and teachings of one of the Fathers of the Church. Report one of the teachings to the class, written as a homily that this person might give.

Saint Jerome ▼

The Influence of Women Many Christian women during this period went on pilgrimages to distant lands, studied the Scriptures, and established and ran monasteries for women and men. In addition, some women made their mark through their influence on sons and husbands.

- Saint Nonna's husband was a convert to Catholicism. Shorty afterward, he became a priest and later a bishop. He too is also recognized as a saint—Saint Gregory Nazianzen the Elder. Nonna and her husband had three children, all of whom lived such exemplary lives that they too are counted among the saints. The eldest, Saint Gregory Nazianzen the Theologian, became Patriarch of Constantinople and is known for his sermons explaining Christian beliefs in clear and precise terms. The other two children are Saint Gorgonia and Saint Caesarius.

- Emperor Constantine's mother, Saint Helena, visited the Holy Land where, according to legend, she found the cross on which Christ was crucified.

- Saint Monica, the mother of Saint Augustine of Hippo, prayed constantly for her son's conversion. He too became a saint.

- Arthusa, the widowed mother of Saint John Chrysostom, oversaw his education and training. He became perhaps the greatest preacher of the time.

These women and others influenced the Catholic Church tremendously through their faith, good works, and dedication.

◄Golgotha, the site of crucifixion.

Monasticism

Beginning in the third century, quite a few people went to great lengths to experience life with Christ. As society became increasingly Christian, more and more people felt the need to leave society. They determined that the best way to pursue life with Christ was to separate themselves from the comforts, temptations, and corrupting influences of society.

These people became *hermits*, a word derived from the Greek for "desert," since that is where they first found extreme solitude. A male hermit was also known as a **monk**, designating that he lived alone seeking prayer, meditation, and solitude. The Greek root of this term, *mono*, means "one." A woman living as a monk was known as a *nun*, although that term has come to mean any member of a religious order of sisters.

The first known monk was Saint Anthony of Egypt (250–355). According to a biography written by Saint Athanasius, Saint Anthony of Egypt spent more than eighty years living in the desert, providing for his needs with whatever food and shelter he could find there. He practiced great self-sacrifice, which became a characteristic of the monastic life. So many people imitated his lifestyle that he is known as the first of the **desert fathers**. He attracted a number of followers who wanted to live under his guidance. Although it might appear to be contrary to the meaning of the word monk, Anthony established a rule for *monks* who wished to live together.

GROUP TALK

Imagine you have the chance to talk to one of the desert fathers or mothers about his or her choice to retire from active society to solitude. What questions would you ask? Why? Share these questions with a partner, and have him or her answer them from the perspective of a desert father or mother.

Monasteries Established

Saint Pachomius is credited with establishing the first monastery around 320 in Egypt. A monastery is a place where monks live a communal life while still pursuing the goals of constant prayer, meditation, and solitude. His sister, Mary, established similar communities for women. Pachomius had been a member of the Roman Legion before converting to Christianity. No doubt his military service prepared him well for the rigors of monastic life.

FAITH ACTIVITY

Write a Letter Imagine that Saint Basil writes a letter to you containing the following message. Write a letter to Saint Basil in response.

"Things that merely improve this life have no true value for us; they are not what we call 'the real thing.' Good family, athletic valor, a handsome face, tall stature, men's esteem, dominion over others—none of these are important in our eyes or a petition fit for prayer; it is not our way to pay court to those who can boast them. Our ideals soar far above all that."
(Basil the Great, quoted by Jill Haak Adels, ed., *The Wisdom of the Saints*, p. 26)

Saint Anthony of Egypt
(251-356)

Let us not look back upon the world and fancy we have given up great things. For the whole of earth is a very little thing compared with the whole of heaven.

Saint Anthony of Egypt, quoted in Robert Ellsberg, *All Saints*, p. 34

We know about the founder of monasticism from the biography *Life of Saint Anthony* written by Athanasius, bishop of Alexandria in Egypt. Two passages from Scripture inspired Anthony to begin his life as a monk. His parents died and left him a large farm and care of a younger sister. One day he heard the words from the Gospels: "Go, sell all that you have and give it to the poor." Taking the passage to heart, he gave away all of his wealth except for enough to care for his sister. Later he heard another passage: "Be not concerned for tomorrow." In response to this message, he gave his sister into the care of religious women (the first time we have a recorded mention of convent life). Anthony began to live as a hermit in the desert of what is today Libya—in an abandoned tomb carved out of a mountain.

Saint Anthony possessed a brilliant mind, committing to memory much of Scripture. When his reputation for wisdom and holiness drew people to him, he moved farther and farther into the desert. After living alone in an abandoned fort for twenty years, he was persuaded to come out and begin a community of monks. He started the monks in their monastic life, left them, and then came back on occasion to see that they were living out his suggestions. Anthony preferred the solitary life. Athanasius reports that Anthony lived without any illness or bad health until his peaceful death at the age of 105.

In the East in 353, Saint Basil the Great receives credit for creating an effective system for monastic life. During the same time his sister, Saint Macrina, organized monasteries, or **convents**, for women.

In the Western Church, credit is given to Saint Benedict during the middle of the sixth century for shaping a style of monastic life that balanced work and prayer. His sister, Saint Scholastica, founded a convent directly across from Benedict's monastery on Monte Cassino in Italy.

In the fourth and fifth centuries, many men and women chose to live as monks—the population of some monasteries numbered in the thousands. One study found that in the seventh century more than thirty percent of monasteries were communities of women. Often these communities were known as double monasteries—communities of women and men near each other under common leadership. Monasteries following Saint Benedict's model came to be one of the most important social institutions of the Middle Ages in Europe.

The Consecrated Life   Women and men religious in monasteries today are part of a larger group of lay people, and some ordained priests, who have chosen the consecrated religious life. They take vows of poverty, chastity, and obedience and belong to a religious order or congregation—a community of women or men who've taken the same vows and are carrying out the Church's mission through their commitment to God and the good of the Church.

The founders of religious orders, such as Benedict, established an order or rule for all members to follow. Lay women religious are often called sisters. Lay men religious are called brothers. Priests who join religious orders are called fathers as all priests are.

Monks and nuns usually live a **cloistered** and contemplative religious life. They remain in the monastery or convent, dedicating their lives to prayer and to study of Scripture and other religious texts. Other religious live in active religious communities, where they go out to serve as missionaries, teachers, or hospital workers, and to do many other good works.

FYI

In Ireland, Christianity was spread by the monks. Unlike the enclosed monasteries where the monks rarely left the grounds, the monastic life introduced by Saint Patrick emphasized evangelization—going out to spread the Good News. This explains why Irish monasticism had outposts in Scotland, England, and on the European mainland as far south as Italy.

FAITH ACTIVITY

Retreats Many of the early Christians went to the desert for a while to find time to pray and grow spiritually; today many go on retreat. In a world where daily planners and cell phones are the norm, taking time to look at our relationship with Jesus and others, away from the hustle and bustle of daily living, is more important than ever. Seek out an opportunity through your church or school to participate in a retreat that is offered in your area, such as TEC (Teens Encounter Christ) for seniors or Search for younger students. Or plan on attending a larger gathering of the teen Church, such as the National Catholic Teen Conference.

>Age to Age

Hermits and Monks

Beginning early in the fourth century, some men and women chose a different way of life. They felt the best way to live the Christian life was to leave behind the comforts of society and family and instead to live in isolation and extreme simplicity.

This type of existence may sound odd and outdated to you. However, there are still men and women living as monks and nuns. You can find monasteries and convents in Wisconsin, Virginia, California, Washington, Oregon, Idaho, Utah, New York, and other states. In Philadelphia, groups of women live behind convent walls in the very midst of the city. Perhaps the most famous modern American monk was Thomas Merton, who died in 1968. He lived as a hermit on the grounds of Gethsemani Monastery in Kentucky. He described the monastic experience as detachment from "ordinary" and "secular" concerns of life. Living in solitude, turning inward, and working toward an experience of one's spiritual depth where God can be found were among his concerns. From his monastery, Merton kept abreast of current events and wrote forcefully about racism, social justice, and war. Being a monk afforded him a unique perspective on the issues of his day.

Praying with Saint Augustine

Leader: Lord Jesus Christ, you led Augustine from darkness to your light. May we also be engulfed in your love for us so that we may work passionately to transform the world into the city of God. Amen.

(Pause to reflect on Saint Augustine's words.)

- You, Lord, were with me, yet I was looking for You outside myself . . . You were with me, but I was not with You. (p. 102)

- Love alone distinguishes between the children of God and the children of the Devil. They may all sign themselves with the sign of the cross of Christ; they may all respond "Amen" to prayers and sing "Alleluia"; they may all be baptized, and come to church, and even build the church themselves. But we can discern the children of God from the children of the Devil by their love alone. (p. 135)

- For when there is a question as to whether a man is good, we don't ask what he believes, or what he hopes, but what he loves. (p. 85)

- God loves each of us as if there were only one of us. (p. 101)

- You have made us for Yourself, and our hearts are restless until they find their rest in You. (p. 191)

From Paul Thigpen, ed., *A Dictionary of Quotes from the Saints*

Leader: **Let us pray together:**

Lord God, who inspired Blessed Augustine to wrestle with your Word, through him you have given us many words: words of mercy, words of peace and truth. Through our speech and patient study, teach us words of mercy, that we may not judge; words of truth, that we may not be deceived by the propaganda of condemnation and war. Speak, Lord, your servants are listening.

Robert Dodaro, OSA, in Gilbert Markus, ed., *The Radical Tradition*, pp. 103–104

>Review

1. Why was the Edict of Milan one of the most important events in all of history?
2. Who was Arius, and what is the principal teaching of Arianism?
3. Who called for the Council of Nicaea? What does it mean to say that it was the first ecumenical council?
4. What is the Nicene Creed, and how does it describe the relationship between God the Father and Christ the Son?
5. What type of Christianity did the tribes from the North and East usually adopt when they became citizens of the Roman Empire?
6. Who was Attila, and what did Pope Leo the Great convince him not to do?
7. What does it mean to say that Rome meant more than a city or an empire?
8. What did Leo the Great do to shape the papacy?
9. What role did the Fathers of the Church perform?
10. What view of reality did Manicheans have?
11. What is the *Vulgate*?
12. What role did Saint Jerome play in helping Christians understand the Bible?
13. What crisis did Saint Augustine address in his book *City of God*?
14. Who was the first known Christian monk?
15. What contribution to Christianity was made by Saints Basil and Macrina in the East and Saints Benedict and Scholastica in the West?

>Key Words

Apostolic See (p. 75) A term used for the papacy, identifying the pope as successor to the Apostle Peter; also called the "Holy See."

Arianism (p. 68) A heresy denying that Jesus is truly God.

cloistered (p. 85) Literally, "behind walls"; women and men religious who choose to live within monasteries.

convents (p. 85) The residences of religious women who are bound together by vows to a religious life.

Council of Nicaea (p. 69) Meeting of bishops in 325 that condemned Arianism and formulated the Nicene Creed.

desert fathers (p. 83) Christian men who lived alone in desert territories of northern Africa and the Middle East in order to sacrifice their lives to Christ. Some women also choose this lifestyle.

ecumenical council (p. 69) A meeting to which all bishops of the world are invited to exercise their authority in union with the pope, the successor of Peter, in addressing concerns facing the worldwide Church.

Fathers of the Church (p. 77) A designation for Church leaders during the early centuries of Christianity whose teachings collectively helped to formulate Christian doctrine and practices.

Huns (p. 74) A tribe originating in China; one of the last barbarian groups to invade Western Europe.

Manicheans (p. 80) A religious cult that viewed reality as a constant struggle between spirit (good) and matter (evil).

monk (p. 83) A person who lives the monastic life, engaging in prayer, meditation, and solitude.

Monophysitism (p. 70) Belief that Jesus has only one nature, instead of the traditional Christian teaching that Jesus has two natures—human and divine.

Nicene Creed (p. 69) Summary of essential Christian beliefs written and approved at the Councils of Nicaea (325) and Constantinople (381).

***Pontifex Maximus* (p. 65)** The term means "the greatest bridge-builder"; title for emperors and, later, the pope.

Vandals (p. 74) One of the most destructive nomadic tribes; adopted Arianism when they converted to Christianity.

Visigoths (p. 74) A Germanic tribe who settled primarily in Spain; the first such group to lay siege to Rome.

***Vulgate* (p. 81)** Saint Jerome's Latin translation of the Bible; the word *vulgate* is derived from the same Latin root as *vulgar*, which originally simply meant "of the common people."

❯Yesterday and Today

After Constantine came to power, Church leaders became leaders in the broader community. During the era of the Fathers of the Church, Christian men and women clarified Christian teaching and practice so well that a uniform set of beliefs was established. Many of those who were involved in examining and clarifying Christian teachings reached an unprecedented level of intellectual achievement. Christianity also gave birth to a phenomenon that still nourishes the spiritual life of the Church—monasticism.

▼ Hagia Sophia, in present-day Istanbul.

TIMELINE

A.D. **529**
Benedict begins
his monastery at
Monte Cassino

A.D. **590**
Gregory I
(the Great)
becomes pope

A.D. **622**
Medina accepts Islam
as official religion

A.D. **664**
The Synod of
Whitby

EXPANSION AND GROWTH

CREATING A CHRISTIAN EUROPEAN WORLD

A.D. 500-800

CHAPTER 4

CHAPTER GOALS

In this chapter you will:

★ explore how the separation of the empire into East and West led to differences between Eastern Churches and the Western Church.

★ learn how the founding of Islam influenced the religious and political life of the time.

★ discover that as more people became Christian, all aspects of life became increasingly Christianized.

★ see how, through the efforts of courageous missionaries and determined popes, Europe became a predominantly Christian continent.

A.D. 716	A.D. 731	A.D. 732	A.D. 756	A.D. 800
Boniface begins his missionary work	The Venerable Bede writes *Ecclesiastical History of the English People*	The Battle of Tours	Pepin gives Pope Stephen the Papal States	Pope Leo III crowns Charlemagne emperor

Christianity East and West

FIRST THOUGHTS

Imagine that some young people come to you and make the following comments: "We're stuck. On the one hand, we feel a strong desire to experience God more in our lives. On the other hand, we also feel great spiritual emptiness. What do you suggest we do?"

★ If you were to design a set of practices that might help them develop their spiritual lives, what might it involve?

★ How are these practices similar to and different from the sacraments and other religious activities of the Catholic Church?

Think of a time you felt God's presence in your life. Did it happen during some kind of religious ceremony? Did the experience occur privately or in a community? What kind of community celebrations would best celebrate God's presence? The Church is a community in which God dwells, and the Church's celebrations, particularly the sacraments, invite us to celebrate and interact with God the Father, Son, and Holy Spirit.

By the year 500, large numbers of people in an expanding Christian world were experiencing God as manifested through Jesus Christ and witnessed to by Mary and an ever-growing community of saints. Christianity was firmly established in the empire, both East and West. Churches in the East flourished under relative stability during this period until the new religious movement, Islam, emerged out of the Arabian Desert in the seventh century. The Eastern Churches held on to their distinctive styles of church design and worship and became increasingly isolated from the struggles and developments occurring in the Western Church.

In the West, many groups of people had traveled from distant lands. They were not Christian or part of Roman society. Christian missionaries dedicated their lives to introduce these people to Christ's love for them. The courage, conviction, and sheer energy of these missionaries are a testament to the power of the Good News of Christ. As Christianity spread, the Church shaped each new culture, and the various cultures where it spread helped shape the Church. Those bent upon destroying the Church in earlier centuries had become her faithful sons and daughters. By the year 800, this transformation that had occurred earlier in the Roman Empire was being repeated in outlying lands.

The thousands of Christians who chose to live simple, austere lives in deserts, on remote mountaintops, or along rocky coasts of sea-swept islands represent only one portrait of the Church from the fourth to the ninth century. In Constantinople, the emperor continued to rule, and Church and state worked together as twin forces of authority. In 537, Emperor Justinian consecrated a great church lined with polished marble and modeled after the finest public buildings in the empire at the time. Some reported that he said about this building, "Solomon, I have surpassed you"—referring to King Solomon's Temple in Jerusalem. Justinian named the church in honor of Holy Wisdom—**Hagia Sophia**. Its grandeur makes a striking contrast with the simplicity of the monasteries that sprouted up from Ireland in the West to the Holy Land in the East. Hagia Sophia served as the central church of Eastern Christianity for over nine hundred years, after which it became a Muslim mosque. It still stands as a testament to the early days of imperial Christianity when people, including emperors, wanted to offer praise to God in whatever way they could.

Influence of Past Beliefs When persecution of Christians ceased in the fourth century, churches were built both as gathering places and as monuments representing faith in God. Church buildings carried over decorative styles from the non-Christian past. In some cases, Christians merely transformed temples into Christian churches. Church architecture was often used to convey what Christianity at the time stood for—protection and stability, a vision of the world, the dominance of eternal over temporal concerns, and the Church as the center of life.

As leaders of tribes from the North and East became Christian, their followers typically converted as well. Just as earlier Jewish and Gentile Christians added to Christian thought and practice from their own heritage, converts from the North and East brought new perspectives about what it meant to be Christian. In other words, the Irish added to the Christian worldview, as did people from what is

present-day France, Germany, and other places where Christianity spread. Often these new Christians accepted Baptism just because their ruler did. Christian leaders might have been pleased when entire groups were baptized all at once, but these mass "conversions" contained seeds for later problems. That is, the faith of the people often had little depth; their prior beliefs lay just below the surface ready to reappear at the smallest encouragement.

It is not surprising, therefore, that Church leaders increasingly felt the need to formalize beliefs and practices for Western Europe. The Church was to be a Church of Rome—following the rules set down by the pope, the successor to Peter. The Church recognized the need to be united and uniform.

GROUP TALK

1 Think about several different churches you may have visited or worshiped in. How were your experiences alike and different? Were some churches ornate and others more simple? How did the design of the church building impact the way you prayed or worshiped there? How did the design reflect what was important to the parish community when it was first built as well as in the present?

2 Imagine that you are a Christian missionary sent to a remote tribe of two hundred people who have had minimal contact with the rest of the world. The leader of the tribe tells you that he or she is ready to accept Baptism and that the rest of the tribe would therefore also accept Christianity. What would you do?

A Broadening Gap

Major population centers existed within the vast stretches of the Roman Empire. The largest cities became major Christian centers and greatly influenced the communities surrounding them. The leaders of the Christian communities in these cities held the title patriarch. Originally this term did not have a formal meaning but was used to recognize the bishops of major centers of influence in the Christian world.

Christians continued to view the head of the Church in Rome as head of the Western Church, but the patriarch of Constantinople rose to prominence in the East following two fifth-century doctrinal controversies involving the nature of the Trinity. Constantinople also held its place of prominence because it was the center of power in the empire. For one thing, Christian communities existed in Jerusalem, Antioch, and Alexandria at least as early as in Rome. Remember also that while Rome struggled under the threat of invasion, the Eastern Churches enjoyed a few centuries of peace and prosperity. That left Rome as the sole center of Christian authority in the West, often fighting for its life and traveling a course of development more and more distinct from that of the Eastern Churches.

From the fifth century, the gap between East and West continued to grow. Eastern Churches used Greek, which was the common language of the people living in the eastern part of the empire. Keep in mind that after Constantine became emperor, the emperor played an active role in Church matters through his power to install or remove the patriarch of Constantinople. The leaders of the various Christian Churches in the East gathered together to address common concerns. However, each patriarch or leader of a particular church had an autonomy greater than that of individual church leaders in the West.

The Western Church used its common language, Latin. As time went by, both civil and Church leaders from these two sections of the empire no longer understood each other's language. Thus language barriers contributed to the crisis that eventually resulted in the official split between the two Churches in 1054.

! FYI

The Eastern Church is sometimes called the "Greek Church" and the Western Church the "Latin Church" because of the dominant language spoken in each one.

Some Major Patriarchates (Cities with Patriarchs)

By the year 500, these patriarchates held prominence in Christianity:

- Rome in Europe
- Alexandria in Egypt
- Constantinople in Asia Minor
- Antioch in Asia Minor
- Jerusalem in the Middle East

EXPLORE THE LAND

Cities of Prominence Among the Major Patriarchates are some of the oldest cities in the world. What other reasons do you think there were for forming major Christian centers in these cities?

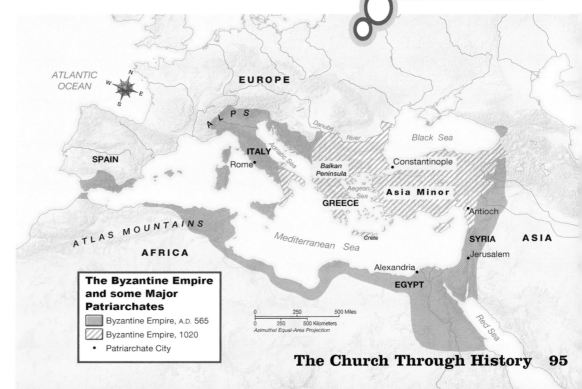

The Byzantine Empire and some Major Patriarchates
- Byzantine Empire, A.D. 565
- Byzantine Empire, 1020
- Patriarchate City

Christianity, Judaism, and Islam

How did Church leaders view the Jewish people during this period? Remember that according to Roman law, Jews were free to practice their religion. At the time of Christ, the Jewish people made up approximately ten percent of the population of the empire, and synagogues occupied prominent positions in many of the major towns and cities. When Christianity came to be the more dominant religion, some Church Fathers had harsh words to say about the Jewish people and Judaism. However, the words were generally not accompanied by persecutions of the Jewish people. Saint Augustine of Hippo spoke out against persecution of Jews. One reason he gave was that the Old Testament, to which Jews continue to witness, demonstrates that Christianity has deep and ancient roots.

In 591, Pope Gregory I had to deal with a situation in southern France where Christians were forcing Baptism upon the Jewish people living there. Pope Gregory admonished the Christians that people should be brought to conversion through "the sweetness of preaching" and not by force. A Jewish historian gives the following overall summary of Jewish-Christian relations during these early centuries of the Middle Ages:

▼ *A Preacher in the Ancient Ruins* by Giovanni Paolo Pannini.

"A recent study has concluded that of several hundred European rulers and sixty-seven popes over a period of four centuries in the early Middle Ages, only a dozen appear to have had an anti-Jewish policy. Many of them, recognizing the value of Jewish communities, followed a policy that was vigorously and consistently pro-Jewish. In their realms, Jews prospered, enjoying a legal status not materially different from that of their Christian neighbors.
"

Marc Saperstein, *Moments of Crisis in Jewish-Christian Relations*, p. 16.

As we will see in the next chapter, this overall atmosphere of tolerance for the Jewish people by the dominant Christian community would change drastically in a few centuries, in particular during a series of military actions known as the *Crusades*.

Christianity Meets Islam Early in the seventh century, a new religious movement began in Arabia that would have an impact on both Eastern and Western Christianity. At the time, Arabian society was tribal. Jews, Christians, other monotheists, and polytheistic tribes interacted with one another. Sometimes their exchanges were peaceful; at other times they battled over resources that were scarce in the harsh desert territory of Arabia.

Beginning in 610, a caravan driver from the centrally located town of Mecca told his wife, his acquaintances, and then anyone who would listen, that in caves outside of town the one, true God was speaking to him. The messages from God that the man, **Muhammad**, shared with his listeners were so compelling that large numbers of the townspeople of Mecca took them to heart. So many people joined him and became **Muslims**—people who submit to God's will—that the non-Muslims of Mecca felt threatened. In a migration called the *hijrah* (an Arabic word meaning "flight"), the Muslims secretly left Mecca and made their way to the city of Yathrib, which they renamed Medina. The citizens of Medina welcomed them and accepted **Islam**, the religion and way of life of the Muslims, as the law of the land. The *hijrah* occurred in 622, but, because this was the first year a Muslim community formally existed, Muslims identify it as year one of the Islamic calendar. Within one hundred years, Muslims controlled lands stretching from the Atlantic Ocean in the West to portions of India in the East.

FYI

The fundamental message of the Islamic holy book, the Koran, is one of peace achieved through faith in God and of justice for all people. From the beginning, Muslims recognized Jews and Christians as people who had received revelations from the one God, the same God who spoke to Muhammad. According to the Koran, Jewish and Christian places of worship were to be protected because, at least if the people who gathered there were true to their original beliefs, God is worshiped there.

FAITH ACTIVITY

Islamic Life Write a report on one of the following topics and share it with your class:

★ Islamic beliefs

★ Islamic perspectives on Jesus and Christianity

★ Christian perspectives on Islamic beliefs

★ The Battle of Tours

Muslims considered Jews and Christians to be "people of the book"—that is, people who had prophets who spoke for God and Scriptures that contained God's word. But they believed that Judaism and Christianity had corrupted the original message of the prophets. Many Christians converted to Islam in Muslim-controlled areas. For one thing, non-Muslims were required to pay taxes that Muslims did not have to pay. The majority of Christians who converted to Islam probably found the movement appealing because of its message, because of the enthusiasm of its followers, and because it was the religion of a spreading empire.

Just before the year 700, Muslims began a siege of Constantinople that lasted five years, but the city withstood the attacks. By the middle of the 700s, much of Spain came under Muslim rule, and it remained so until the late 1400s. At the Battle of Tours in 732, the Christian prince Charles Martel defeated a Muslim army that had invaded France. If not for this defeat, all of Europe might have fallen to the Muslim forces.

The Christian Experience

he movie *Gladiator* portrays a pre-Christian Roman general named Maximus praying devoutly before stone figures of his household gods. A few centuries later this same imaginary general would probably have offered his prayers to the Christian God. Is that the extent of the difference between pre-Christian Roman society and the experience of religion that most people had upon becoming Christian—the substitution of one image of god for another? In other words, what difference did Jesus and his Church make in the lives of average citizens between the years 300 and 800? We'll see the difference over the next few pages.

GROUP TALK

1 What difference does the Catholic faith make in your family life? In your school? In your friendships?

2 What are some ways you experience God's involvement in your life?

A World of Grace

You learned about Saint Augustine of Hippo in the last chapter. And although he died in 430, he was the most influential thinker in the Western Church from 500 to 800. Augustine and a number of theologians following him wrote extensively about the concept of **grace**, the participation in the life of God. Christians participate in the life of God because Jesus Christ, the Son of God, participated in human life.

We participate in the divine life because God the Holy Spirit lives within us through our Baptism and strengthens us in the various sacraments. Grace helps us respond to our call to become adopted sons and daughters of God.

As Christianity spread, Christians of the time found grace everywhere. Their lives were celebrated within the sacraments from birth to death. Christianity was adopted into the seasons of the year and into a **liturgical calendar**. This calendar was divided into the Seasons of Advent, Christmas, Lent, the Triduum, Easter, and Ordinary Time. The essentials of the Church year as we know it today were completed by the end of the sixth century.

> The liturgical year is the temporal structure within which the Church celebrates the holy mysteries of Christ: 'From the Incarnation and the Nativity to the Ascension, to Pentecost and to the wait in joyful hope for the Lord's coming.'
>
> Congregation for Divine Worship and the Discipline of the Sacraments, "Directory on popular piety and the liturgy: Principles and guidelines" (2001), #94

Popular Piety Near the end of the fifth century, some farmers in present-day France approached their local bishop with concerns about their harvest.

> Earthquake, fire, and inclement weather combined to cause crop failure and widespread hunger. Mamertus, the bishop of Vienne, called for penance and prayer on the three days preceding Ascension Thursday. The people responded to the call, and the Lord responded to the prayer.
>
> Throughout France, and ultimately beyond, word of this litany, this rogation, spread, finding a readiness in the hearts of believers. As the years went by, the same three days of penitential prayer were observed annually, and by the eighth century, universally.
>
> Rev. Peter Klein, *The Catholic Source Book*, p. 18

These days of prayer were known as **Rogation Days**. No aspects of life were beyond God's concern. Such practices reminded Christians that they were awash in a sea of God's grace.

According to Saint Augustine, Roman religion was a legalistic and superstitious affair. That is, performing rituals regularly and properly was the Roman way to appease the gods and avoid their anger. Certain aspects of the Roman view of the gods entered Christianity. Even though the image of Jesus as a suffering servant on the cross represented a complete reversal of the image of the mighty and vengeful Roman gods, Christians frequently continued to view God as

Life of Grace Grace is a participation in the life of God. In your notebook, make a day-long list of activities in which you experienced grace. Can you name any missed opportunities of grace?

a fearsome and threatening judge. Some people developed a level of comfort by seeking intercession through Mary and the saints who became the advocates before God, especially in the Eastern Church.

The Christian Calendar During this era, Christianity left a marked impression on the designation of years. In an attempt to establish the date for Easter, a Russian monk named Dionysius Exiguus decided that designating years starting with the founding of the city of Rome or in terms of the beginning of a particular emperor's reign was improper. In 525 he calculated as best he could when Jesus was born and designated years after that as a.d. (*anno Domini*, "the year of our Lord") and a.c. (*ante Christum*, "before Christ"), which later became b.c.—"before Christ." Within a few centuries, this new Christian calendar was adopted throughout Europe and eventually the world.

Developments in Church Practice

Not until the Second Council of Lyons in 1274 did a Church council officially identify the seven sacraments. Even if an official listing of seven sacraments did not exist before this time, the Church celebrated Christ's Paschal Mystery—his suffering, death, Resurrection, and Ascension—and our participation in the new life he won for us. The way these rituals were celebrated may have varied, but they were definitely a means of receiving grace.

Architecture For a period of time, two of the most important sacraments—Baptism and Eucharist—had buildings designed exclusively for their celebration. A **baptistery**, a smaller building located next to a church, was where Baptisms were held. It seems that baptistries were originally modeled after the Roman public baths, and reception of the Sacrament of Baptism by full immersion in a pool of water was standard practice. As infant Baptism became more common and full immersion less so, Baptisms were performed in small fonts in the churches themselves. However, separate baptistries were built in Italy well into the twelfth to fifteenth centuries. The cities of Pisa and Florence have such buildings.

INTERPRET THE ART

The Duomo In Florence, the Cathedral Santa Maria del Fiore—commonly known as the Duomo—has a detached baptistery, even though it was built in the 14th century. Why do you think a special building dedicated to the Sacrament of Baptism was, at one time, an important concept?

As in the case of Hagia Sophia, church design typically imitated that of public buildings popular at the time. A **basilica** was rectangular in shape with one rounded end. A bishop would sit at the rounded end. An altar would be between him and the people. Thus, the bishop and the rest of the congregation symbolically gathered around the altar. As the liturgy developed, an altar rail in the West and a screen in the East were introduced as a way to show special reverence for the consecrated Body and Blood of Christ. This resulted in the separation of priest from people during liturgies and led to a sense that the priest was offering the Eucharist *for* the people rather than together *with* them.

Music Another development that took place within the liturgy of the Western Church happened around the year 600. This was the introduction of a particular form of chant. **Gregorian chant** is named after Pope Gregory the Great, who served as pope from 590 to 604. It was probably modeled after an earlier form of Jewish chant. Before Gregory, it was used at solemn liturgies and in monasteries where monks and nuns regularly filled monastery chapels with the chanting of the psalms. Pope Gregory, who was a monk himself before becoming pope, popularized the chant and even wrote some chants for parts of the Mass. Although no longer used regularly during church services, you probably have heard Gregorian chant at some time. When a news program does a piece about Catholicism or a television commercial features a Catholic monk, frequently a Gregorian chant plays in the background. For almost fifteen hundred years, Gregorian chant was intimately associated with Catholic worship. To hear live Gregorian chant today, you probably would need to go to a monastery where monks or nuns continue to use it for singing their daily prayers.

Holy Orders As early as the fourth century, Church leaders were calling on priests to be celibate so that they would place spiritual fatherhood over physical fatherhood. However, as late as the tenth century some bishops and priests were still marrying. **Celibacy** became a standard practice for clergy in the West when an official policy was declared in 1123 at the First Lateran Council. This canon was renewed and strengthened in 1139 at the Second Lateran Council, which made the marriage of priests invalid. In the Eastern Churches, this policy took a different turn. Bishops must remain single, while priests and deacons may be married if they marry prior to ordination. If single when ordained, they must remain single. This is also true of deacons in the Western (Roman) Church who enter the permanent diaconate today.

Penance   When you read the Gospels, you can't help but be struck by the number of times Jesus tells people, "Your sins are forgiven." The Christian Church carried on this work of Jesus in what came to be known as the **Sacrament of Reconciliation**. During this time period, the manner in which sinners received God's forgiveness through the Church underwent a major change. Up until the seventh century, baptized Christians who had committed such a serious misdeed that they separated themselves from the Church underwent a reinitiation process. This process was public, overseen by the local bishop, and lasted for a period of years. Since being a public penitent meant performing acts of penance, many people put off requesting reconciliation until they felt they were near death. However, there are no records to indicate that private confession did not happen in some cases during this time period.

Reportedly, an Irish monk named Saint Columban (543–615) began in the West a practice of spiritual direction during which sins were privately confessed and the need for conversion was discussed. This practice was rooted in the process of spiritual direction engaged in by monks in Egypt and the Holy Land. Columban and other Irish monks spread private penance to mainland Europe where it became popular and eventually the officially recognized form of the Sacrament of Reconciliation, also called the Sacrament of Penance, Sacrament of Conversion, or Sacrament of Confession. For propriety, women confessed their sins behind a screen separating them from the priest, which later became common practice for both men and women. To this day, individual confession of serious sins and absolution by a priest are the only ordinary means of being reconciled with God and the Church.

Marriage During this time no specifically Christian wedding ceremony existed. This does not mean that Christians did not view marriage as a sacramental experience and a means of grace. Regardless of the form the ceremony took, Christians were "married in the Lord." The Fathers of the Church say little about marriage, and the early Church leaders left the regulations regarding marriages to civil authorities. As Church leadership became more stable than civil government, bishops and priests became more actively involved in performing wedding ceremonies and regulating marriages. Beginning in the fourth century, many Christian couples asked for a priest's blessing as part of their wedding ceremony. By the eighth century a priest's blessing of a marriage was accepted practice, and soon afterward it became the standard practice for Catholics.

GROUP TALK

1. What role did religion play in people's lives in the Christian West in the sixth to eighth centuries?

2. What aspects of the Christian message and practices do you think were most helpful to the people of the time?

The Work of Missionaries

"It is from God's love for all men that the Church in every age receives both the obligation and the vigor of her missionary dynamism.... Indeed, God 'desires all men to be saved and to come to the knowledge of the truth';[1] that is, God wills the salvation of everyone through the knowledge of the truth.... Because she believes in God's universal plan of salvation, the Church must be missionary."

Catechism of the Catholic Church, #851

The mission of the Church is to further God's reign in the world by sharing the Good News with those who have not heard it, and by helping people who have heard it respond in faith. Missionary activity goes back to the time of Jesus, who sent out his followers two by two to tell others of God's kingdom. (See *Luke 10:1–3*.) We all share in that mission through our Baptism, living it out in the everyday circumstances of our lives.

FAITH ACTIVITY

Volunteerism As members of the Church, we have a responsibility to evangelize, to share the good news of God's love with others. We can do this by our willingness to talk about our faith and to stand up for our belief in Jesus. We can also think about spending time as a member of a lay missionary or volunteer group. For more information, check out the Web sites of Maryknoll and Salesian Missions Online. Go to www.harcourtreligion.com for links to their Web sites.

▼ *Saint Augustine* ascribed to Jan Scorel.

Some people, however, dedicate their lives to this work as **missionaries**. In every era, missionaries work to introduce Jesus to others. This missionary work requires respect and a willingness to dialog with those who have not yet accepted the Gospel. It's necessary to appreciate the culture of those being evangelized, and acknowledge "those elements of truth and grace which are found among peoples, and which are, as it were, a secret presence of God[2]" (*CCC*, #856). Were it not for courageous missionaries, places such as Ireland, England, and Germany would not have known Christianity.

GROUP TALK

One way the Church is universal is by the way it welcomes all people to believe and participate. What are some signs of the universal Church? How do you see those signs in your parish community?

Images of the Church

The Universal Church

Christ sent his Church on a mission to the whole human race. The word *catholic* meaning "universal," as applied to the Church, expresses that she has the fullness of the means of salvation from Christ and that salvation is a gift meant for all people. The catholic nature of the Church is one of her four identifying marks. The call to universality inspired missionaries of the sixth to ninth centuries to risk many hardships in order to offer the gift of Christianity to the various groups of people throughout Europe. Charlemagne was crowned emperor in 800, of a kingdom later to be called a *Holy* Roman Empire. Still today, one of the greatest goals of recent popes has been that Christ's universal message of salvation would be heard and received by all people of the world.

Saint Patrick and the Conversion of Ireland (381-461)

Sanit Patrick, Apostle of Ireland, is one of the best known missionaries. He wrote an autobiography that provides some information about his personal life and missionary experience. He tells us that he was the grandson of a priest and the son of a deacon. He lived in Britain. At the age of sixteen, Irish pirates captured him, and he lived as a slave in Ireland for six years. While spending his time as a shepherd slave, he came to a greater appreciation of the faith that his parents had tried to impart to him. He managed to escape from Ireland to France, where he became a priest. Although he had wanted desperately to escape from Ireland and risked his life to do so, he found that he kept dreaming that the voices of Ireland were constantly calling to him, "We beseech thee, holy youth, to come and walk among us again."

After being made a bishop, Patrick returned to Ireland in 432. He spent his remaining thirty years crossing the length and breadth of the island. He met with great success, converting virtually all of Ireland to Christianity by the time of his death. He personally baptized tens of thousands of people. One of the keys to his success was his understanding and adaptation of Irish-Celtic culture to Christianity. He ordained hundreds of Irish priests and bishops and founded many monasteries. Many missionaries would depart from these monasteries and religious communities to the farthest parts of the world. The Irish monks also copied whatever writings they could acquire. Because of the zeal for Christianity among the Irish and their influence on Christianity in other lands, Ireland has gained the title, "Isle of Saints."

FAITH ACTIVITY

Culture Identify several different Catholic communities in your town or city. Record what you know about them with regard to cultural practices, languages spoken, and so on. Then find out more about the ways they worship and other activities they have. Make a presentation to the class on how the communities represent the universal Church.

The Conversion of England

Pope Gregory the Great was one of the most remarkable figures to serve as a bridge between ancient times and the Middle Ages. Although he counted two popes among his

ancestors, Gregory began his public life in civil, not religious, service. He served as prefect of Rome, meaning that his duties combined the roles of mayor, police chief, and treasurer. Rome at the time was in great need of repair, and Gregory restored the city. When his father died, Gregory sold his possessions and made his family home into a monastery. For four years he lived the simple life of a monk and established six monastic communities. Then Pope Pelagius II asked him to serve as the papal ambassador to Constantinople at a time when tensions between East and West were heating up. When the pope died in 590, the people of Rome called for Gregory to take his place. He asked the emperor not to approve their choice, but the emperor knew of Gregory's talents. Thus, Gregory became the first monk to become pope.

A story about Gregory asserts that he passed a slave auction in Rome one day and noticed a group of boys on the auction block. When he asked where the boys were from, he was told that they were Angles, that is, they were English. Gregory responded, "I will call them not *Angli* (Angles) but *angeli* (angels)." In another story he purchased the freedom of some Angles. These experiences inspired him to seek the conversion of the people of Angle-land, or England.

Pope Gregory had many accomplishments. He did a great deal to reform the Church from within. For example, he wrote guidelines for bishops to follow and took steps to straighten out the moral life of the clergy. He signed the many documents he wrote by referring to himself in a way that popes ever since have used: "Servant of the servants of God." He sent missionaries to numerous countries, spreading monastic spirituality throughout the Church. Pope Gregory asked a Roman monk named Augustine, known to history as Saint Augustine of Canterbury, to go to England with a group of forty monks to bring Christianity to the English.

Soon after Augustine's time, however, England returned to its pre-Christian ways. Christianity was reintroduced into the country through a Celtic priest, Saint Aidan, who followed some practices that were different from Roman practices. This caused tension and confusion until Celtic and Roman clergy met in 664 to resolve the issues between them. During this meeting, called the Synod of Whitby, the question was asked: Is the pope, the successor of Peter, appointed to head the Church? All agreed that he was. The king then decreed that England would follow Roman Church customs in all matters, such as the date when Easter is to be celebrated. This opened the way for the organization of the whole English Church to be united in doctrine and practice under one head.

The Church in England flourished, and monks from Rome brought many famous manuscripts from Rome to English monasteries, where they were copied and made available to many. One product of these monasteries is a work which some consider to be the first true book of history, the *Ecclesiastical History of the English People* (731), by a monk known as the Venerable Bede.

GROUP TALK

Why do you think Pope Gregory the Great signed his letters, "Servant of the servants of God"? In what ways have recent popes like Pope John Paul II and Pope Benedict XVI been servants? What impact has their role had on the faith of people all across the world?

Saint Hilda
(614-680)

The differences between the Celtic and Roman views of Christianity were largely based on underlying social differences in the two societies. While Roman society was primarily male-dominated, this was not necessarily the rule in Celtic society. In Ireland, a free woman held near-equality. For example, a woman was capable of:

- retaining her own property in marriage and sharing in joint property

- enjoying equal educational and professional opportunities

- holding equal status before the law

- occasionally being accepted as a warrior

Saint Hilda was descended from the Northumbrian line. She was the pupil of Saint Aidan who restored Christianity to Northumbria after its brief lapse into a non-Christian religion. Aidan put Hilda in charge of a religious house at Hartlepool. She later founded a double monastery for men and women at Whitby in 657. At the time, the country was divided between followers of Roman and Celtic Rites. In 663, the matter became more serious when King Oswy of the Celtic Rite realized that he would be celebrating Easter while his wife, who belonged to the Roman Rite, would be in the midst of Lent. Clearly, a solution was needed.

A synod was called in 664 at Whitby, under the supervision of the great Abbess Hilda. She was of the Celtic persuasion and sided with Colman, Bishop of Lindisfarne; they traced their tradition back to Saint Columban and Saint John. The opposition was represented by Saint Wilfred who looked to Rome and Saint Peter. After some discussion, the king gave judgment in favor of the Roman Rite, saying that he would rather be on good terms with the Keeper of Heaven's Gate than with Saint Columban.

Characteristically, Saint Hilda loyally accepted the decision for Rome, thus ending what might have been a serious Church crisis.

The Conversion of Europe

Some druid clerics became Christian priests during the early stages of the conversion of Ireland. In England, Pope Gregory advised Augustine of Canterbury to let the older temples remain standing and to transform them into Christian churches. "Thus the people, seeing that their places of worship have not been destroyed, will forget their errors and, having attained knowledge of the true God, will come to worship him in the very places where their ancestors assembled" (Saint Gregory the Great, quoted in Jean Comby, *How to Read Church History*, Vol. 1 p. 123).

As legend tells us, Saint Boniface (d. 754), known as the Apostle to Germany, used a very different missionary approach than Patrick and Augustine. Boniface heard about a sacred tree dedicated to the god Thor. He went to the tree and immediately chopped it down and used the wood to build a chapel. When the people who observed this spectacle realized that Boniface wasn't struck dead as a result of this assault on their god, they accepted Christianity.

The incident with Saint Boniface and the tree is thought to have happened in 723, which means that he didn't simply set foot in non-Christian lands and bring people to Christianity without a struggle. One historian describes the message by which missionaries gained success in attracting new members:

> The arguments which the missionaries used to combat pagan beliefs were simplistic but, given the limited literacy of many of the converts, compelling. God created the universe. There is only one God. The pagan gods and goddesses are mere sticks and stones. God sent his son Jesus Christ to offer salvation to all those who believe in his name; and for those who do not, there awaits the vivid pains of hell. Those who believe will receive their due reward, possibly in this life and certainly in the next.

> Vivian Green, *A New History of Christianity*, pp. 51-52

One of the last of the independent Germanic tribes was the Franks. Even before they embraced Christianity, however, they enjoyed a relationship with the empire that was known as *foederati*, which means that they were recognized as partners and not enemies of Rome. King Clovis was the first leader of the Franks to become Christian. First, in 492 he married a Christian woman named Clotilde. Then, four years later, Clovis won a critical battle and proclaimed that he gained victory through the intercession of God. He was baptized by Saint Remy, for whom Reims, France, is named. Clovis announced that "those who do not present themselves with me at the river tomorrow for baptism will incur my displeasure." Thus began a Christian kingdom that would rule Europe into the modern era.

FYI

Vatican City is still a city-state separate from Italy. For that reason, countries such as the United States have ambassadors to the Vatican.

Clovis's sons and heirs were generally weak rulers. Some two hundred years after Clovis, the Merovingian dynasty came to an end when a palace official who was strong enough to unite the kingdom again rose to power. The official, whose name was Charles Martel, defeated the forces of Islam in 732 at the Battle of Tours. Charles Martel's son and grandson have had a very strong and lasting influence upon the Church. His son, Pepin the Short, was crowned King of the Franks in 751 by Saint Boniface—the same Boniface who had converted the Germans. Thus began the Carolingian dynasty. Since Boniface was acting as the pope's representative, Pepin rewarded Pope Stephen III five years later by declaring him to be ruler of the middle section of Italy. This **Donation of Pepin** created the **Papal States** and made the pope a secular as well as a spiritual leader. It may be hard for us to imagine the pope as both the head of a nation and the head of the Church, but in fact the Papal States continued to exist until 1870. On Christmas day in the year 800, Pepin's son Charles was crowned emperor by Pope Leo III. He is known to history as **Charlemagne**—Charles the Great.

▼ *The Coronation of Emperor Charlemagne by Pope St. Leo III on Christmas Eve A.D. 800 by David Aubert.*

The ongoing Christianization of Europe meant not only getting people to accept Christianity. It also meant making sure that people understood that Jesus Christ was not just one god among many, but the second Person of the Blessed Trinity, the one true God. The task of spreading the Good News of Jesus and the Church continued, and still continues. During the Middle Ages, Church leaders and secular leaders would design a Christian worldview that would sustain Europe until the Renaissance.

Entanglements of Church and State The series of events that took place during the second half of the eighth century needs to be examined in light of circumstances at the time. When Pepin gave Pope Stephen III control over a large portion of Italy, he was essentially making official what already existed. The Roman emperor was supposed to protect the Church and citizens of the empire wherever they were. Instead, the pope was trying to do what he could to hold off attacks on Rome by the Lombards from Germany and from the Muslims known as Saracens.

When Pope Leo III crowned Charlemagne emperor, it was viewed as an insult to the emperor in Constantinople. However, the pope was again formalizing what already existed. The Frankish kings, not the emperors in Constantinople, really held power in Europe. The pope could communicate with and work with the Frankish kings much more readily than he could with the previously existing emperor. Once Charlemagne was crowned emperor, he was committed to protecting the Church and making sure that Church laws and practices were enforced throughout his empire. However, he also would oversee the appointment of various Church leaders, as the emperor had been doing in the Eastern Church. These entanglements of Church and state would create problems throughout the Middle Ages and into the modern era.

GROUP TALK

In what ways does the United States uphold the separation of Church and state today? Is this important? Why or why not?

Age to Age

Liturgical Music

> (Pope Saint Gregory the Great) gave wise directives to ensure that the conversion of new nations did not happen without regard for their own cultural traditions. Indeed, the Liturgy itself could be enriched by new legitimate cultic expressions and the noble expressions of artistic genius harmonized with more humble popular sensibilities.
>
> Congregation for Divine Worship and the Discipline of the Sacraments, *Directory on popular piety and the liturgy: Principles and guidelines* (2001), #27.

Pope Saint Gregory the Great made Gregorian chant the standard form of music used in liturgies up until Vatican Council II in the 1960s. During ceremonies marking the death of Pope John Paul II and the installation of Pope Benedict XVI in 2005, television viewers from around the world were treated to the glorious sounds of the ancient chants. However, Gregorian chant no doubt was borrowed from earlier forms of music, and Pope Gregory himself advocated using local artistic expressions in liturgical celebrations.

Many of the world's greatest composers wrote music to express their devotion to the great mysteries of the Christian faith. For instance, Handel's *Messiah*, although written with Lent and Easter in mind, has become closely associated with the Christmas season.

Since Vatican Council II, many Catholic composers have written music that has enriched liturgical celebrations. Sometimes their compositions reflect a particular culture, such as the Hispanic or African-American traditions. Many songs used at liturgies today reflect American popular music and folk music traditions. Unlike Gregorian chant, which does not need instrumental accompaniment, church music today is often enhanced with the sound of organs, guitars, flutes, and other instruments. Surely Pope Saint Gregory the Great would be pleased to know that today Catholics continue to worship God with music and song that rises from the heart and touches the soul.

Prayer

Praying with Alcuin
Pause and Ponder the Words of Alcuin of York (735-804):

Almighty God grant all go well with thee.
Be an honour to the church, follow Christ's word,
Clear in thy task and careful in thy speech.

Be thine an open hand, a merry heart,
Christ in thy mouth, life that all men may know
A lover of righteousness and compassion.
Let none come to thee and go sad away.

Hope of poor men, and solace to the sad,
Go thou before God's people to God's realm,
That he who follows thee may come to the stars.

Sow living seeds, words that are quick with life,
That faith may be the harvest in men's hearts.
In word and in example let thy light
Shine in the black dark like the morning star.

Let not the wealth of the world nor its dominion
Flatter thee into silence as to truth,
Nor king, nor judge, yea, nor thy dearest friend
Muzzle thy lips from righteousness.

Alcuin of York (735-804) in George Appleton, ed., *The Oxford Book of Prayer,*
pp. 82-83

Let Us Pray:

Eternal Light, shine into our hearts,
Eternal Goodness, deliver us from evil,
Eternal Power, be our support,
Eternal Wisdom, scatter the darkness of our ignorance,
Eternal Pity, have mercy upon us;
that with all our heart and mind and soul and strength
we may seek thy face and be brought by thine infinite mercy
to thy holy presence; through Jesus Christ our Lord.
Amen.

Alcuin of York, *The Oxford Book of Prayer,* p. 70

Review

1. What is Hagia Sophia?
2. Why did Christians build magnificent church buildings?
3. What role did patriarchs play in the early Church?
4. What was the overall atmosphere in Jewish-Christian relations in the early Middle Ages?
5. Who was the founder of the Muslim faith?
6. What significance does the hijrah have for Muslims?
7. How did Muslims view Jews and Christians?
8. Name two reasons why many Christians converted to Islam.
9. Why is the Battle of Tours important?
10. What did missionaries do for Christianity?
11. Briefly sketch the outline of Saint Patrick's life.
12. What Roman monk headed the missionary activities in England?
13. What controversy did the Synod of Whitby solve?
14. What is Saint Boniface reported to have done to convince the Germans of the power of the Christian God?
15. What did Saint Boniface do for Pepin the Short, and what gift did Pepin give the pope in return?

Key Words

baptistery (p. 101) The place where Baptisms are celebrated; originally a separate building and now typically a section of a church.

basilica (p. 102) A Greek word meaning "king's hall"; currently the term is used to designate a certain church of historical significance that continues to play an important part in the religious life of a particular region.

celibacy (p. 102) "The state or condition of those who have chosen to remain unmarried for the sake of the kingdom of heaven in order to give themselves entirely to God and to the service of his people" (*CCC*, Glossary).

Charlemagne (p. 112) King of the Franks who was crowned Roman Emperor by the pope in 800.

Donation of Pepin (p. 112) King Pepin's designation of the central part of Italy to be governed by the pope.

grace (p. 99) Our participation in the life of God. "Grace is *favor*, the *free and undeserved help* that God gives us to respond to his call to become children of God, adoptive sons, partakers of the divine nature and of eternal life"[3] (*CCC*, #1996).

Gregorian chant (p. 102) Follows a simple melody. It is chanted in monophonic ritualistic pattern in plainsong.

Hagia Sophia (p. 93) Church of the Holy Wisdom built in Constantinople and currently serving as a museum in Istanbul, Turkey.

hijrah (p. 97) The flight of Muslims from Mecca to Medina in 622; event marks the beginning of the Muslim calendar.

Islam (p. 97) A monotheistic religion based on submission to God's will, believed to have been revealed to Muhammed in the early seventh century.

liturgical calendar (p. 100) Seasons and feasts of the Church year to mark events in the life and Paschal Mystery of Christ as well as the lives of Mary and the saints.

missionaries (p. 106) People who spread the Christian message to other people, usually in other lands.

Muhammad (p. 97) Founder of the Islamic religion.

Muslims (p. 97) Members of the religion of Islam.

Papal States (p. 112) Part of Italy the pope ruled until 1870.

patriarch (p. 94) A Christian bishop of the early Church in certain major cities of the Roman Empire. This title is still in use in Eastern Churches today.

Rogation Days (p. 100) Three days of prayer and penance before the Solemnity of the Ascension to ask God's blessing on the harvest.

Sacrament of Reconciliation (p. 103) One of the Church's Sacraments of Healing and Forgiveness; the sacrament through which those who sin are reconciled with God and the Church.

>Yesterday and Today

The Church that became entwined with the Roman Empire under Constantine faced external challenges from Germanic tribes in the West and, later, Muslims in the East. Gradually Christianity won over the tribes, but Christianity's relations with Islam remained a significant concern of the Church throughout the Middle Ages. By the time of Charlemagne, political boundaries in Europe, northern Africa, and western Asia were established, and they would remain in place until the modern era. During this period of great expansion and growth, the Church drew in many people from a wide variety of cultures. Some members of the Church were leaders in the great political and economic transformations taking place, especially in Europe. Others separated themselves from worldly affairs altogether. When the once frightened disciples of a Jewish teacher started preaching his message at the first Christian Pentecost—the beginning of the Church—few could have predicted that 800 years later, most of Europe and portions of the Middle East would be converted by their spiritual descendants.

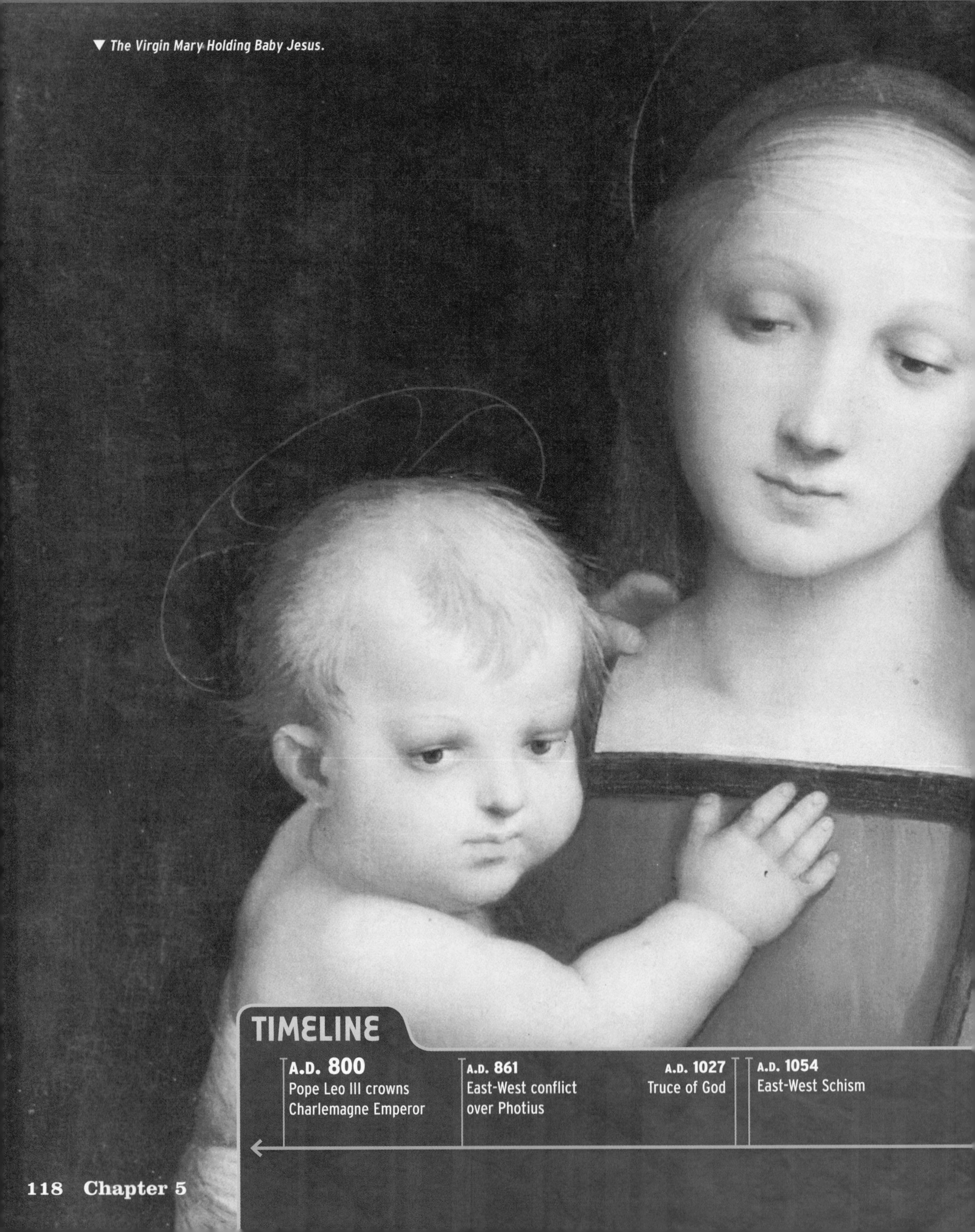

▼ *The Virgin Mary Holding Baby Jesus.*

TIMELINE

A.D. 800	A.D. 861	A.D. 1027	A.D. 1054
Pope Leo III crowns Charlemagne Emperor	East-West conflict over Photius	Truce of God	East-West Schism

CHURCH AND WORLD UNITED

TOWARD THE HIGH MIDDLE AGES

A.D. 800-1300

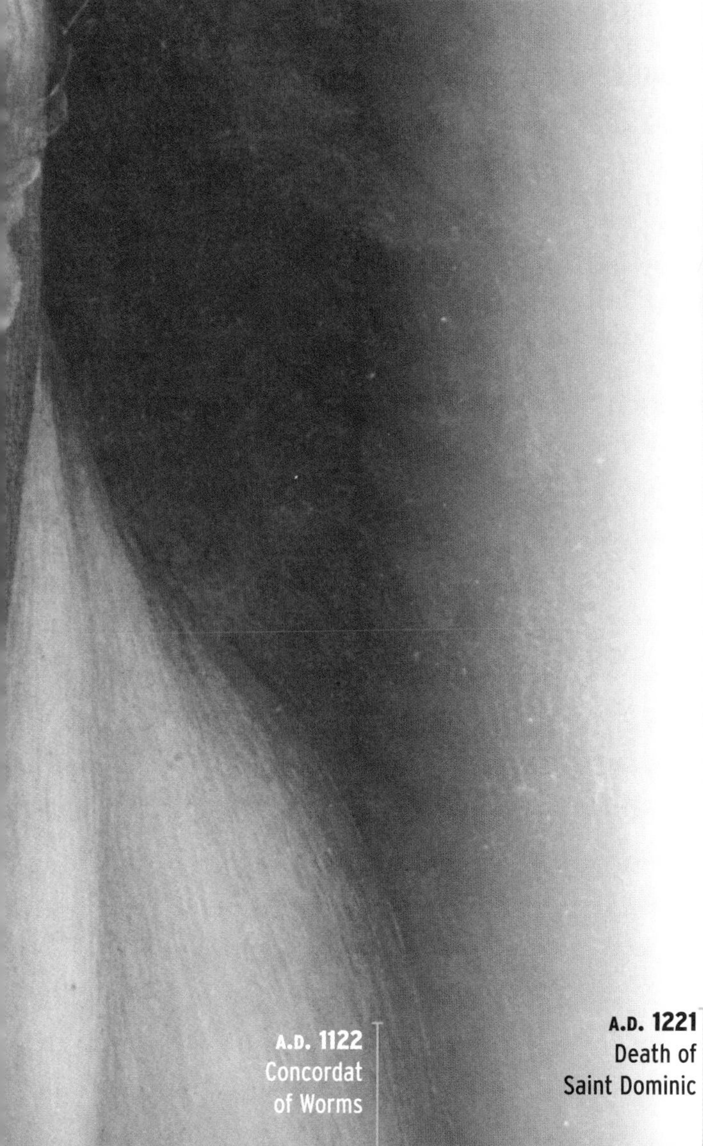

CHAPTER GOALS

In this chapter you will:

★ learn how feudalism provided a structure for society and Church to meet the needs of Western Europe.

★ explore reforms initiated by Church leaders and other Church members to counteract corrupting practices and what led up to the official split of the Western and Eastern Churches.

★ discover how people of the Middle Ages expressed their faith, and learn about key theologians such as Thomas Aquinas.

★ see how Christian-Muslim tensions and renewed heresies led to a series of crusades and an inquisition.

A.D. 1226
Death of
Francis of Assisi

A.D. 1221
Death of
Saint Dominic

A.D. 1232
Pope Gregory IX
appoints
inquisitors

A.D. 1122
Concordat
of Worms

A.D. 1270
Eighth and last Crusade

A.D. 1096
First Crusade

A.D. 1123
First
Lateran
Council

A.D. 1170
Death of
Thomas Becket

A.D. 1253
Death of
Clare
of Assisi

A.D. 1274
Death of Thomas
Aquinas

Christendom and the Middle Ages

FIRST THOUGHTS

Before reading this chapter, go to a library and research the period of European history called the Middle Ages. Name at least five things associated with the period. Then respond to the following questions:

★ What do you think would have been the advantages and disadvantages about living during the Middle Ages?

★ What roles did the Church play during the Middle Ages?

At the height of the Middle Ages, the Christian worldview was taken for granted. It marked the seasons and cycles of people's lives. Springtime was not just the time for planting; it was the season of Lent and then Easter. Death may have been the end of earthly life, but it was also the entrance into eternal life. Rulers who made laws or made war appealed to Christian teachings to explain their decisions. Education was done by and for the Church. During the Middle Ages, it was impossible to separate the Church from everything else. Although the pope, bishops, priests, monks, and nuns were most directly identified with the Church, all Christians measured their lives in terms of Church beliefs and practices.

Western Europe united as **Christendom**—a Holy Roman Empire—adopted a system of organization called feudalism that became the accepted way that people viewed both Church and society. During this period, the tension between Eastern and Western Christianity finally resulted in an official split between the two. Europe attempted to contend with a pre-existing religion and a later religion—Judaism and Islam. In the end of this time period, holy men and women emerged to revitalize the spirit of Christ for their time.

Meeting of Ruth and Boaz (The Summer) by Nicolas Poussin.▼

You may already have formed some impressions about the medieval world. Knights rode about on horseback, dressed in heavy armor, while ladies in flowing gowns waited for them back at the castle. Kings and queens lived in splendor and ruled with an iron hand. Lower-class people worked away in surrounding fields all day, barely ever looking up to notice what the lords, ladies, and knights were doing. Monks or friars were harmless, sometimes even pictured as comical characters who lived on the fringes of the social world of the Middle Ages. Many bishops dressed like princes and lived princely lifestyles, paying little attention to the sufferings of the lowly people surrounding their grand cathedrals.

As is true with any stereotype of the past, these images are partial truths at best. Since through the ages the Church and society have never been so closely united as they were during the medieval period, it is important for us to look more attentively at the images that make up the myth of the Middle Ages. In response to circumstances at the time, unique religious, political, social, and economic structures developed. We will see that in some cases the message of Jesus, and the Church conveying that message, blended into the medieval stereotypes of warring knights, overworked serfs, ladies of the manor, and wandering monks.

Be forewarned: we will discover in our study that Christian Europe of the time was made up of both saints and sinners, and even of people who, at times, were a combination of both. The first dominant figure of the Middle Ages—Charlemagne—is one such complex person. His dedication to the Church and to his faith cannot be doubted. However, his ways of expressing his fidelity to the faith can certainly be questioned.

GROUP TALK

Using specific examples, respond to the statement: Religion should guide and direct all aspects of one's life.

Charlemagne and the Holy Roman Empire

The crowning of Charlemagne in 800 marks an important turning point for Western Europe and the Church. Before looking at Charlemagne and Europe as it emerged from his coronation, we need to analyze the very concept of the "Middle Ages." When exactly were they? The broadest time span is 476 to 1450. In 476, the classical Roman Empire in the West ended. By the year 1450, radically new viewpoints formed which pointed to the modern era. So the Middle Ages, broadly speaking, span European history from the end of the classical period to the beginnings of the modern era. The period from about 1050 to 1300, often called the High Middle Ages, and the centuries just prior to that—from around 800—will be the focus of this chapter.

The Middle Ages saw thriving intellectual life, set standards for church architecture, and established political and economic arrangements that complemented the classical Roman system with influences from other sources. In particular, the Middle Ages were a time when people believed that Christianity provided guiding principles governing all aspects of life. In other words, Europe of the Middle Ages was Christendom, when Christian rulers and Church leaders attempted to create the world as they believed God intended it to be.

Medieval Christendom had to respond to the breakdown of centralized power and continuing attacks from outside the Christian world. The Church itself continued to be intertwined with the political, social, economic, and even military activity of the day. Christianity provided the primary lens through which all of reality was viewed.

EXPLORE THE LAND

Growth of an Empire This map shows the growth of Charlemagne's Holy Roman Empire over the course of nearly 50 years. Which modern-day countries did Charlemagne's rule cover? Choose one of the countries and find out three things about the Church in that country over the past 1,200 years.

The Rise of Charlemagne

The Rise of Charlemagne In the late Eighth century one group dominated—the Franks centered in modern-day France. Their leader was Charlemagne, or "Charles the Great." He had both the power and the charisma to create a unified, peaceful Europe. The emperor in Constantinople certainly exercised no control over Western Europe. In 771, Charlemagne began a thirty-year project to enlarge his kingdom by getting all the various Christian tribes to accept him as their leader. By 800, most of the European people formerly known as barbarians had become Christian.

By 800, Charlemagne, King of the Franks, was accepted as ruler by all the peoples of Western Europe from the Baltic to the Mediterranean Sea. With a strong military force behind him, he secured the borders surrounding these lands. Therefore, when Pope Leo III crowned Charlemagne Emperor, he was merely making official what already existed in fact—Charlemagne was emperor of the West.

History reports that in 800, when Pope Leo III crowned Charlemagne "Emperor of the Western Empire," it was a spontaneous gesture. Planned or not, the pope's action that Christmas day was an attempt to bring back the peace and stability of the earlier glory days of the Roman Empire in the West. Pope Leo saw in Charlemagne a man who could make life better for Europe. By crowning him, the pope was asserting that this emperor was to be a holy emperor; Charlemagne's empire was to be a holy empire. From that day on, Charlemagne signed all his official documents, "Charles, by the will of God, Roman Emperor." He took the Christian nature of his position seriously.

The pope's crowning of an emperor on Christmas day in the year 800 symbolized the union of Church and state in Western Europe, a union that would remain strong but tense throughout the medieval period. Charlemagne, therefore, is often called the "second Constantine" because he formed all of Europe into one family of faith.

The emperor in the East was furious when he heard about this crowning of Charlemagne. In his mind, he alone was emperor of all the lands that were the Roman Empire. However, he was powerless to challenge Charlemagne's claim. The crowning of Charlemagne added to the growing breach between Rome and Constantinople. In time the political division between East and West would also lead to a split between Eastern and Western Christianity.

Who Was Charlemagne?

- A biographer describes him as strong and athletic, a skilled hunter, and an avid swimmer. Of course, like all the competing princes of his day, he was a warrior.

- Although he could barely read, he recognized the importance of learning and education. He decreed that every monastery must have a school where young men could be educated.

- He brought the most learned monk of the time, Alcuin, to his capital and commissioned him to establish the finest school in the empire. He arranged for manuscripts to be brought to the school from all over the empire to be copied by the monks. A new form of writing called *script* was developed so that manuscripts would be transcribed in a uniform fashion. Some of the greatest written treasures of the ancient world were saved because of the monastery libraries of Charlemagne's time.

Charlemagne believed that he ruled the empire in God's name. Although he was crowned by the pope, he was determined not to be subservient to the pope. Charlemagne felt that it was his responsibility as Christian emperor to promote the welfare of the Church. As a result, he established a policy of involvement in Church affairs by lay rulers that would cause problems later on. He arranged for the manner of worship used in Rome to be followed throughout the empire. As a result, Western Christianity took on a uniformity that never existed in the Eastern Churches.

Charlemagne also attempted to establish a procedure by which the canons (priests) of a cathedral would choose the bishop, and monks or nuns of an abbey (monastery) would select their leader, called the *abbot* or *abbess*. In this way he hoped to ensure that holy and worthy people would hold positions of power in the Church. Charlemagne also instituted a set of rules for members of the clergy designed to make sure that they were living a religious life. Finally, he enacted laws against heresy and fought against the Saxons who were not yet Christian, offering them either Baptism or death.

Chaos Reigns Upon his death in 814, Charlemagne's empire fell into disunity until Otto the Great gained control of all Western Europe in 962. The years between Charlemagne and Otto were a time of much chaos in Western Europe. Charlemagne's successors—Louis the Pious, Louis the Stammerer, Louis the Child, Charles the Bald, Charles the Fat, and Charles the Simple—couldn't hold the empire together. The empire disintegrated into small territories with largely independent rulers who often fought one another. During most of these years, Western Europe had no emperor. Armies of nomadic Muslims, called Saracens, took advantage of the weakened empire and attacked southern Italy. Since there was little to prevent them, the Saracens even succeeded in overtaking Rome. The pope had to build a wall around Rome and provide for its protection as best he could. Another group called the Magyars raided throughout Western Europe before eventually settling in modern-day Hungary.

Most destructive of all were the Vikings, who raided seacoast villages during the eighth and ninth centuries. They met little resistance as they sailed up rivers into the mainland to take whatever they wanted. They soon discovered that monasteries were particularly defenseless and contained some of the best riches and stores of food supplies available.

Irish monasteries, which had assembled fine libraries containing manuscripts of both Christian and pre-Christian writings, were constantly attacked and ravaged by Vikings. At first the monks built towers without ground-level entrances to try to hide their precious objects. This did not deter Vikings who wanted, not the manuscripts, but the fine jewels that often adorned them. The *Book of Kells*, one of the few manuscripts to survive from this time, survived because it was sent further inland and hidden away.

FAITH ACTIVITY

Basis for Laws Historically, the United States has had laws, called "blue laws," based solely on religious beliefs. One such law in many areas of the country restricts the sale of alcohol on Sundays. Research "blue laws" of the United States and then explain how these laws relate to Charlemagne and his understanding of Christian principles as the basis for laws in his empire.

Feudalism

During the Middle Ages in Europe, religious matters were not separate from the rest of life. As nomadic pagan groups became Christian, they replaced their gods with the Triune God—God the Father, Son, and Holy Spirit. They adapted their style of life to fit the Roman system. The nomads were accustomed to living off the land, moving about from place to place in order to meet their needs. Fighting among themselves and against Roman settlers was simply a part of their lifestyle. The move to Christianity and to Roman civilization led to a different economic, social, and political arrangement for the nomadic tribes and the people they encountered. This new structure for society came to be known as feudalism.

Some historians have summed up the division of society under feudalism in these words: Some pray, some fight, some work, and a few rule. Feudalism was a system of contracts among groups of people designed to make productive use of the land while offering protection for those who worked it. This may have developed, in part, because with the collapse of the empire, the army was no longer available for protection. To be able to provide this service, the lord of an area forced or paid soldiers and knights to fight for him, if needed. The lord in turn would offer himself as a vassal to a stronger lord or king. He would promise respect and obedience to this overlord and would pay taxes in return for protection.

In Western Europe, the king ruled over all the landlords of his kingdom. These lords rented land to vassals through allegiances that were usually for military purposes. Even these vassals were considered "noble," and employed serfs, the lowest class of people, to till the fields, plant and harvest crops, and tend to the livestock. As determined by those in power above them, serfs retained a portion of the produce for themselves and the rest went to the lord of the land. Until late in the medieval period, over ninety percent of the people in Western Europe were serfs.

While medieval kings theoretically held absolute power, in reality they were dependent on those below them for peace and prosperity. Feudalism, therefore, represented a pyramid of power and responsibilities, most of which were based on force and necessity.

Troubles and Triumphs

Today we take for granted that the pope's supreme rule of the Church is not to be interfered with by the state. Charlemagne, however, had a different understanding. He exercised influence over bishops in his country who voted for the pope. The pope thus had some dependence upon the emperor for political power. However, when Charlemagne's descendants proved to be weak rulers, the popes grew more powerful in the daily affairs of the Church.

After Pope Leo III died in 816, the wealthy families of Rome began to consider the papacy to be a personal prize passed among them. These very families decided who would be chosen even though, by law, only clergy elected the pope. About forty-five years after the death of Charlemagne, Pope Nicholas I (858–867) stated that the pope governed the Church and the emperor's role was to protect it. However, most of the popes over the next two hundred years were good men but weak rulers, an example of the type of challenge that the Church has faced and overcome during its history thanks to the guidance of the Holy Spirit.

FYI

Even as late as 1903, Emperor Franz Joseph of the Holy Roman Empire threatened to veto the election of the pope. After being elected pope in 1903, Pius X immediately declared illegal any secular interference in future elections of popes.

The Church of the Middle Ages faced three significant challenges. To restore her spiritual leadership, she had to address these three problems.

Three Main Challenges the Church Faced during the Middle Ages

Lay investiture	Besides being spiritual leaders, bishops and abbots were also vassals to a king in the feudal system. The practice of kings or lords naming Church leaders is known as **lay investiture**. Lay rulers who invested authority in bishops and abbots expected favors in return. The pope, bishops, and abbots had to combine and balance their roles as secular rulers who did not act autonomously and as spiritual leaders.
Simony	**Simony** was the payment for appointment to a Church office. For example, a wealthy lord could purchase for one of his sons the position of bishop of an important diocese or abbot of a local monastery. The son might or might not have an interest in his spiritual role or carry out his duties responsibly.
Celibacy	During this time, a disregard for celibacy existed among some members of the clergy.

GROUP TALK

Discuss whether or not the following policies could have helped the Church during the Middle Ages. Explain.

* Church leaders divesting themselves of all lands and property except for church buildings and monasteries.
* Church leaders forbidding any members of noble families from becoming pope, bishops, or abbots.
* Church leaders removing from ministry all bishops and priests who disobeyed the rule of celibacy.
* The pope appointing all bishops without approval from secular rulers.
* Monks of a monastery electing their abbot.

A Time of Reform

Cluny and the Reform of Monastic Life In 909 in France, a local duke and a holy monk instituted reforms to monastic life that transformed the whole Church. Duke William of Aquitaine gave responsibility for a tract of land in Cluny, in southeastern France, to a monk named Berno so that he could establish a monastery there. William deeded the land directly "to Saint Peter and Saint Paul." The pope was to act on behalf of the Apostles but not to possess that which belonged only to the Apostles. In this way William placed the monastery directly under the authority of the pope, but the monks themselves were to select their abbot.

William wanted this monastery to be an example of spiritual life that counteracted the immorality he saw around him. He observed that some monastic communities had become corrupt after their destruction and plundering at the hands of Vikings and other groups. This corruption also resulted from power-hungry lords appointing immoral men to positions of leadership. William intended this monastery to be a place of authentic prayer and spiritual life. Abbot Berno used the rule of Saint Benedict, who had introduced monasticism to the West, to set up strict guidelines for the monastery. Monks at Cluny lived simply. Instead of the emphasis on prayer and work that marked the monastic system of the time, the monks of Cluny emphasized prayer. Together five or six times a day they recited the Divine Office or the Liturgy of the Hours.

A Closer Look

Liturgy of the Hours

God continually calls his children to know him and be close to him in prayer. Throughout the history of God's interaction with humans, prayer has been a call from him and a response by humans. The Church calls us to pray always. By the Middle Ages, a series of prayers were in place that coincided with the rhythms of the day. Taking time out five, six, or seven times a day was meant for everyone. Bells would toll, inviting local people to come to chapel for prayer. This series of prayers, called the Liturgy of the Hours, is still the mainstay of monastic practice in the Church. Parishes today often hold Morning or Evening Prayer in which all can participate. If you visited a Catholic monastery, you could join the monks or nuns in chanting the psalms throughout the day, or you could join in this universal prayer of the Church wherever you are.

The monks renewed the spiritual life of others in a number of ways.

- As artists they contributed to the inspiring art of the Middle Ages.

- They joined local diocesan councils to bring about change in the moral life of the clergy, particularly in terms of celibacy.

- They were instrumental in a movement called the **Truce of God**, which called on Christian warriors to abstain from doing battle during Christmas, Lent, special saints' feast days, and other times.

In time other monasteries followed in the footsteps of Cluny. Monks from the Cluny system became advisors to kings, bishops, and even popes. Abuses, such as simony, were greatly diminished.

Reforming Popes Despite its political involvement, the Church was viewed as greater than politics. Christians were concerned about salvation, and they recognized that the Church was the means of salvation and the vehicle for God's presence in their lives. In 1057, Pope Nicholas II took steps to stop the election of popes by the emperor or families of Rome by restricting the papal electorate to cardinals, instead of all bishops. Two centuries later, this would officialy develop into elections within a secret meeting called a **conclave** (*con* meaning "with," and *clave* meaning "key"). Only cardinals, who were locked behind closed doors during this time, could vote for the pope. Election of the pope by conclave of cardinals continues to this day.

Several popes following Nicholas II continued to improve structures within the Church. The most noted was Hildebrand, who in 1073 became Pope Gregory VII. Hildebrand had worked for a number of popes before being chosen himself. In fact, he was instrumental in designing the procedure of electing the pope in conclave. During his twelve years as pope, Gregory initiated so many measures to help Church governance run more smoothly that these changes came to be known as the **Gregorian Reforms**. Each Lent he would gather together Church leaders and invoke new legislation.

◄Cardinals entering the Sistine Chapel, at the beginning of the conclave.

Pope Gregory fiercely attacked two of the serious problems already mentioned—simony and lay investiture. He wanted secular powers to have no control or influence over the Church. Emperor Henry IV challenged Pope Gregory over control of Church offices by attacking Rome and forcing Pope Gregory to leave. Pope Gregory lived in exile until his death in 1085. As he lay dying Pope Gregory said, "I have loved justice and therefore die in exile." The reforms that he began would continue with succeeding popes.

Pope Gregory's successor, Callistus II, arrived at an agreement with Emperor Henry V, son of Henry IV. The pope would have the power to choose bishops and abbots and invest them with spiritual power, while the emperor would invest them with symbols of their temporal power. This compromise agreement is known as the *Concordat of Worms*.

Further Christian Expansion

During the Middle Ages, not all of Europe was Christian. Part of Spain remained Muslim until the end of the fifteenth century. The Scandinavian countries and Eastern Europe turned to Christianity by the eleventh century. Early missionary attempts to convert the "dreaded Norsemen"—the Vikings of Northern Europe—had ended in martyrdom for the missionaries. Even after a monk named Anskar (801–865) had succeeded in getting permission from the Swedish king to build a church in 832, his success was short-lived—at his death, the people of the area returned to their previous religious practices.

Interestingly, Christianity became rooted in Scandinavia not through missionaries but through the kings. In 1015, Olaf I became king of Norway. He had been educated in England, where he became a Christian. On becoming king he directed his subjects to accept Christianity and sent missionaries to Iceland and Greenland. Two other kings, Eric IX of Sweden (c.1120–1160) and Canute of Denmark (994–1035), were instrumental in bringing Christianity to their countries. They may have done so partially in order to have good relations with the rest of Europe and to make trade easier. Regardless of the reasons, by the twelfth century northern Europe had joined the Christian world.

In 899, King Stephen of Hungary became Christian, as did the Magyars who had previously invaded Rome and Northern Italy. Around 992, the people of Poland converted to Latin Christianity as well. The conversion of Ukraine and Russia to Christianity had a unique twist to it. In 988, Prince Vladimir of Rus, whose capital city was Kiev in modern-day Ukraine, decided that it was time to join one of the major religions bordering his territory. He sent envoys to Western Christianity, Byzantine Christianity, Islam, and Judaism.

FAITH ACTIVITY

Gregorian Reforms Research one of the Gregorian reforms and write a brief essay on its influence on the Church.

FAITH ACTIVITY

Appointment of Bishops and Abbots Role-play a debate between Emperor Henry IV and Pope Gregory VII over who should decide the appointment of bishops and abbots. Include in the debate the history of this practice during Constantine's and Charlemagne's time. Also, describe how the issue might be addressed today.

Margaret of Scotland (1045–1093)

An English princess is credited with bringing Christianity to Scotland in the British Isles. Margaret and her mother sailed to Scotland to escape the king who had conquered their land. King Malcolm of Scotland welcomed them and before long asked for Margaret's hand in marriage. As queen, Margaret influenced her husband and the country for the better. Prominent among Margaret's activities was religious reform. She encouraged abstaining from work on Sundays, observance of the Seasons of Advent and Lent, and the reception of Eucharist on Easter. She founded several missionary groups and frequently visited and cared for those who were sick. On a larger scale, she had hostels constructed for those who were poor.

Margaret was declared a saint in 1250, particularly for her work for religious reform and her charitable works. In 1673 she was declared patroness of Scotland.

Cyril and Methodius (d. 869 and 885)

A move toward Christianity was also taking place in Eastern Europe. Two brothers, Cyril and Methodius, figure prominently in the conversion of the Slavic people of the area. Methodius had been a governor in a Slavic territory, and both he and his brother knew the Slavic language. The Byzantine emperor commissioned them to spread Christianity to the Khazars in Russia and then to the Slavic people. To assist them in their work, the brothers wrote an alphabet for the Slavic language, known as the *Cyrillic alphabet*. Thanks to Cyril and Methodius, Slavic became a written as well as a spoken language. The brothers also used the Slavic language in the liturgy. Many Church leaders, especially German bishops, questioned this practice. The Eastern Church used Greek in its liturgy; in the West, Latin was standard. Cyril and Methodius had to go to Rome to defend their teachings and their practices. In 878, Methodius received the pope's permission to use Slavic in the liturgy. In 1980, Pope John Paul II proclaimed Cyril and Methodius copatron saints (along with Saint Benedict) of Europe.

When the envoys to Constantinople came back with reports of the beauty and majesty of Hagia Sophia and of the lavish liturgies celebrated there, Prince Vladimir adopted Eastern Christianity for himself and his people. Vladimir cemented the relationship between the people of Rus and the Eastern Empire when he married the sister of the Byzantine emperor the next year. With the conversion of Russia, Poland, and the Slavic people of Eastern Europe, the Christian world now extended from the northwest tip of Spain to the Baltic Sea in the West and to Russia and Constantinople in the East.

GROUP TALK

1 Why is it important for worship and liturgies to incorporate different languages, styles, and practices to reflect those who are participating in the celebration?

2 If you wanted to introduce someone from a different religion to the beauty and meaningfulness of Catholic worship, to what type of service would you bring him or her? Why?

The East–West Schism

The tenth and eleventh centuries should be known as the time when Christianity welcomed many European peoples into the fold. However, in 1054 a problem that had been brewing for some time cast a shadow over the spread of the Good News. Even before Christianity had become the religion of the Roman Empire, differences between East and West had caused problems. As the Eastern and Western sections of the Empire grew apart, so did the Eastern and Western Churches.

For a thousand years the Eastern Church held on to its Hellenistic tradition and Greek language. Little had changed in Eastern Church practice, and few people saw the need for dramatic change. The Western Church, on the other hand, had faced different challenges that required adaptation. For instance, the Romans, Irish, English, French, and Germans made their mark on the Western Church. The need for a pope to be a strong secular and religious leader affected the role of the papacy in a way unknown to the Eastern Church, where the emperor oversaw secular matters. Thus the two sections of the one Church—East and West—had grown apart. The distance and differences between them led to tensions as well.

The **East-West Schism** officially happened in 1054. A schism is a breaking of a relationship between two groups who still hold essential beliefs in common. As we will see, the leader of each section of the Church excommunicated the other. This mutual **excommunication**, however, was merely the culmination of a series of problems and misunderstandings between leaders of the Eastern and Western Churches. Here are highlights of events leading up to and following the East-West Schism.

The *Filioque* and Iconoclast Controversies We read about the Nicene Creed in chapter 3. The bishops at the Council of Nicaea (a.d. 325) wrote that the Holy Spirit proceeds "from the Father." Later, in order to make the teaching clearer and to counteract some heretical views then popular in the West, the Church in the West added the phrase "from the Father *and the Son*." The emperor Charlemagne, who desired uniformity in worship, allowed the change to be used by the entire Western Church. In time the pope affirmed this wording of the creed. This is known as the *filioque controversy*.

Church leaders in the East were angry, not only because they disagreed with the change in wording, but also because they were not consulted about the change and because secular rather than Church authority imposed it. This controversy illustrates the type of problems that consistently plagued relations between Eastern and Western Churches. Conflicts were not only about theology and teachings but also about governance and the two groups getting along.

The **iconoclast controversy** is another example of how the way in which issues were dealt with caused problems. Icon, or *ikon*, is a Greek word meaning "image." While Judaism and Islam either discouraged or even condemned the use of images for the sacred, Christianity encouraged the use of pictures to portray parts of the liturgy, stories from the Bible and from the life of Christ, and the lives of the saints. These paintings inspired the faithful and helped a largely illiterate community to better understand their faith. The Church Father, Gregory of Nyssa, explained the use of icons by saying that, "The silent painting speaks on the walls and does much good."

While both the Eastern and Western Churches made use of sacred images, icons held special significance for Eastern Christians, where an icon artist created a painting according to very specific guidelines.

In 726, the Eastern emperor Leo the Isaurian forbade the use of icons because he felt it was idolatry, the worship of false gods or of an image of God. Backed by the patriarch of Constantinople, Leo had thousands of icons destroyed. The common people, supported by monks, held an uprising in support of icons. The pope, Gregory II, agreed with the use of icons in liturgy. However, this issue for the pope may not have been solely about how Eastern Christians viewed icons, but rather about upholding the principle that civil authority—Leo the Isaurian—had no right to intervene in Church matters. The iconoclast controversy continued for more than fifty years and caused many bloody confrontations. In 787, the Second Council of Nicaea upheld the use of icons and condemned as heresy the calling of their veneration or use "worshiping false idols." This practice is based upon the fact that God became man to reveal himself to us, and thus the practice does not conflict with the First Commandment to have no false gods. One of the questions that arose about East-West relations during this controversy was: Does the pope have jurisdiction over the patriarch of Constantinople, and does the emperor have jurisdiction over the Church?

Sicily—East or West? Events such as the *filioque* and iconoclast controversies demonstrated that relations between the Eastern and Western Churches needed only a spark to ignite tension and distrust between them. This spark occurred in 1043 and started the two Churches on the road to the schism that remains in effect today. Sicily, an island off the coast of southwest Italy, had for a long time been under the control of the Eastern Empire. The patriarch of Constantinople had responsibility for the Church there, which followed Eastern practices.

In 1043, the Normans captured Sicily, and the Eastern emperor was powerless to try to regain control of it. With Sicily now ruled by the West, who was to oversee its churches there? The patriarch of Constantinople, Michael Cerularius, declared that he had jurisdiction over Sicily, and the Eastern Emperor supported his claim. The pope, however, appointed a new archbishop of Sicily to bring Western practices to the churches there.

Patriarch Michael Cerularius called together Eastern bishops and condemned the pope for not supporting the patriarch's responsibility for Sicily. The patriarch also brought up charges that Eastern Church leaders had made before against the Western Church. In retaliation for the pope's actions in Sicily, the patriarch closed all Western Christian churches in his jurisdiction and removed the name of the pope from

FAITH ACTIVITY

Icons For an introduction to icons and an explanation on how they are painted, check in an encyclopedia or another resource for information that describes the creation process. Write a report on one aspect of this art or try your own hand at painting an icon with the directions given.

prayers said during the liturgy. Although attempts were made to resolve the dispute, it dragged on. Finally, in 1053 Pope Leo IX sent a special envoy to attempt a reconciliation.

Part of the problem at this time was that leaders on both sides did not really understand the language or culture of the other. The envoy, Cardinal Humbert, was a man of high moral character, but he could be unbending and uncompromising. Although well educated, he knew little of the Greek culture and none of the language. It seems in his mind he was going to Constantinople to have the Greek Church submit to the authority of the pope. For a period of time Patriarch Michael Cerularius refused to meet with Cardinal Humbert. Incensed at this inhospitable treatment, Humbert placed on the altar of Hagia Sophia a proclamation from Pope Leo, which declared that the patriarch of the Greek Church was excommunicated. In retaliation, the patriarch excommunicated the pope.

At first, leaders of other Eastern Churches didn't take this mutual excommunication seriously. They viewed it as a squabble between two feuding brothers, such as had happened before in the life of the Church. However, this time those involved in the split would resist efforts at reconciliation, especially as the animosity between the Eastern and Western Church was fueled by the fires of the Crusades beginning some fifty years later.

FYI

In 1965 Pope Paul VI and Patriarch Athenagoras of Constantinople rescinded the mutual excommunication. However, the Eastern Orthodox Churches remain officially separate from the Catholic Church centered in Rome.

Eastern Orthodox and Eastern Rite Catholics The Eastern Churches no longer in union with Rome came to be known as the Orthodox Churches. To complicate things even further, some of the Eastern Churches decided that they wished to stay in union with Rome by accepting the supremacy of the pope over the entire Church. Therefore, today there are **Eastern Orthodox Churches** and **Eastern Rite Catholic Churches**. The vast majority of Eastern Christians are Orthodox and are not officially in union with the Church centered in Rome.

Pope Paul VI and Patriarch Athenagoras ▶ embrace in Jerusalem.

Eastern Catholics accept the pope as head of the Church, but continue to follow the styles of worship and Church practices of the Eastern Churches. Although different from Western and Latin Catholics in this way, they are nonetheless fully Catholic. The diversity within the Church does not take away from the unity that comes from accepting and following the Tradition of the Church. Both Eastern and Western Catholics are under the spiritual leadership of the pope, are also united by the Creed we all profess, the apostolic succession of bishops who guide and lead us, and the seven sacraments through which we celebrate the same mystery of Christ. This oneness is a mark of the Church; the Church is one because she believes in one Lord, celebrates one Baptism, and is united by the same Holy Spirit to be the one Body of Christ. The *Catechism of the Catholic Church* reminds us that:

> The sole Church of Christ which in the Creed we profess to be one, holy, catholic, and apostolic, . . . subsists in the Catholic Church, which is governed by the successor of Peter and by the bishops in communion with him. Nevertheless, many elements of sanctification and of truth are found outside its visible confines.[1]

Catechism of the Catholic Church, #870

FAITH ACTIVITY

A Different Experience Under the direction of your teacher and pastor, attend a liturgy in either a Latin Catholic church if you are a member of an Eastern Catholic Church, or an Eastern Catholic church if you are a member of a Latin Catholic Church. Describe in writing how the experience differs from the Mass as you know it.

Images of the Church

Vine and Branches

In 1995 Pope John Paul II wrote an Apostolic Letter called "Light of the East," in which he spoke of the beauties of the Eastern Churches. He pointed out that: "The development of different experiences of ecclesial life did not prevent Christians, through mutual relations, from continuing to feel certain that they were at home in any Church, because praise of the one Father, through Christ in the Holy Spirit, rose from them all, in a marvelous variety of languages and melodies" (*Light of the East*, #18). Pope John Paul's affirmation of the different ways of being Church, Eastern and Western, reminds us of an image used by Jesus himself when he said: "I am the vine, you are the branches" (*John 15:5*). In other words, the Church has one source—Jesus. This same Church of Jesus Christ has many branches—with unique points of emphasis, styles of worship, and cultural trappings. The pope's letter asks us to look back to Jesus as our common source and also to look forward to the day when all Christians are united, many branches of the one true vine.

The people of the Middle Ages found a variety of ways to express their faith. In fact, they viewed all that they did as an expression of their faith, whether it was farming, fighting, ruling, or praying. In this section, we will look at some of the ways that medieval people experienced and expressed their Christianity.

The Pilgrim

> A pilgrimage is a religiously motivated journey to a sacred shrine or holy place. The medieval pilgrimage became a metaphor for the journey of the human person searching for salvation and eternal life with God in the next world while traveling through this world.
>
> Thomas D. McGonigle and James F. Quigley,
> *A History of the Christian Tradition*, p. 148

We are all on a journey from God seeking to make our way back to God. We are religious by our very nature, and we are called to be with our Maker. This is what God created us for, to find happiness and communion with him. That is, whether we ever leave our hometown or not, we are all pilgrims. From a religious understanding and experience, a pilgrimage is not simply about the destination. The journey itself has religious significance. Christians went on pilgrimage fairly early in Church history, usually to the Holy Land to visit the places where Jesus lived and preached. History indicates that for many people during the Middle Ages, going on a pilgrimage was a major expression of their religious faith. Pilgrimages were highly regulated. Pilgrims received special papers from their local religious leaders, wore special clothing identifying them as pilgrims, and generally visited specific holy sites.

Among the most important and common destinations for pilgrims were the Holy Land, Rome, and the tombs of the early martyrs—such as Compostela in Spain, where the Apostle James the Greater is said to be buried, and Canterbury in England, where Saint Thomas Becket was martyred.

Of course, going on pilgrimage was also an adventure, just as traveling is today. And, as you can imagine, maintaining a popular pilgrimage spot was also good business. However, none of this takes away from pilgrimage as a deeply religious experience. Later in the medieval period, Geoffrey Chaucer (1342–1400) catalogued the pilgrimage experiences of some travelers in his work *The Canterbury Tales*. Although Chaucer's Wife of Bath is a fictional character, she mentions the most popular pilgrimage destinations during the Middle Ages:

Three times she'd journeyed to Jerusalem;
And many a foreign stream she had to stem;
At Rome she'd been, and she'd been in Boulogne,
In Spain at Santiago, and at Cologne.
She could tell much of wandering by the way.

Prologue to *The Canterbury Tales*, tr. J.U. Nicholson , p. 15

Two prominent figures of the Reformation era—the sixteenth century—criticized people for going on pilgrimage since in their eyes it meant neglecting what they considered to be the true work of Christians. The great Catholic thinker Erasmus remarked regarding pilgrimage that: "You could run off to Rome or Compostela and buy up a million indulgences, but in the last analysis there is no better way of reconciling yourself with God than reconciling yourself with your brother" (Lawrence Cunningham, *The Catholic Heritage*, p. 58). Martin Luther gave this advice to someone who planned to go on a pilgrimage: " . . . apply the money and effort required for the pilgrimage to fulfilling God's commandments, and to doing works a thousand times better than a pilgrimage, namely, meeting the needs of his family and his poor neighbors" (Cunningham, *The Catholic Heritage*, p. 59).

Criticisms aside, pilgrimage provides a window into the Christian mindset of the Middle Ages. Jesus Christ is both divine and human. He was born, lived, and died in actual places that one could visit. The Apostles and the saints, especially the martyrs, were also flesh-and-blood people. Their physical remains and objects associated with them—relics —their graves, and the places where they spent time were sacred. The medieval pilgrim went on pilgrimage to absorb the special aura that surrounded the holy places. Both the journey and the destination had symbolic, spiritual significance. Pilgrimages remain a significant part of Catholic popular piety and devotions today.

The Cathedral

> The Catholic tradition has always been sympathetic to, and supportive of, artistic activity. Catholicism as a historical tradition is unthinkable apart from its churches, paintings, sculptures, works of literature, musical compositions, and finely crafted items of religious and liturgical usage.

Lawrence Cunningham, *The Catholic Heritage*, p. 128

If you walk into a museum that features art of the Middle Ages, you can't help but notice that religious themes are part of practically every art piece. The art form in which medieval Europe excelled was architecture. While the Greek Church had its icons, the Western Church of the Middle Ages had its great Gothic cathedrals to help the faithful raise their hearts and minds to God and revel in his glory. A *cathedral*, from the Latin word *cathedra* meaning "chair," is officially the church of the bishop of a diocese. In popular usage, a cathedral has incorrectly come to mean a particularly large church. Before the twelfth century, the style of large churches was Romanesque. This style mimicked ancient Roman architecture. In a Romanesque church, walls were thick and openings for light were small, creating a dark, fortress-like atmosphere.

In 1124, Abbot Suger wanted to rebuild his abbey church in Paris in a way that would introduce more light into the building. He came up with a combination of innovations that would allow walls to be higher and lighter, allowing much more space for windows. The larger window spaces resulted

▲ Cathedral in Milan

in an interior bathed in light. Abbot Suger used stained glass to depict scenes of the Christian story while creating a rainbow of light within the church. This style became known as Gothic architecture.

Just as the medieval pilgrimage had symbolic as well as physical meaning, the shape and design of Gothic cathedrals also had symbolic, spiritual significance as well. Both from the outside and the inside, the lines of a cathedral seem to be pointing ever upward. By design, the architecture directs the eyes to the awesome mystery of God. The medieval pilgrim who stepped inside a cathedral and was bathed in the light from the stained glass windows could relate that light to Christ, the Light of the World. To emphasize the connection between the light and Christ, artisans typically built cathedrals facing east so that the assembly, facing the altar on which the Son of God was made present, was also facing the rising sun.

The Theologian

After a new translation of Aristotle from the original Greek appeared, his philosophy and that of his teacher Plato became the philosophical basis for much of medieval theology. Theologians of the day placed great emphasis on using reason to investigate the teachings of Christianity.

The first medieval theologian to attempt a rigorous study of Christian thought was Saint Anselm, who defined theology as "faith seeking understanding." This approach to theology, using philosophical tools to understand and organize Christian teaching, came to be known as *scholasticism*. Schools of theology flowered into great universities. The university system of education that exists throughout the world today can trace its origins back to this movement during the Middle Ages.

The most renowned of the medieval theologians was Saint Thomas Aquinas (1225–1274). A Dominican priest, Aquinas succeeded in writing a complete and rigorous investigation of Christian thought. His monumental *Summa Theologica* makes a strong case for the reasonableness of Christian teaching. After Aquinas, if any thinker attempted to dispute that Christianity rests on solid philosophical foundations, he or she would need to confront the logical presentation of Christian teachings in Aquinas's summary of theology. In the sixteenth century, Protestantism moved away from Aquinas because they perceived his teaching as being unbiblical, whereas Catholic theology emphasized the scholastic approach well into the modern era. Thus Catholicism sees faith and reason as complementary and never contradictory. In 1880, Aquinas was named patron saint of Catholic schools, colleges, and universities.

FAITH ACTIVITY

Reason and Faith Describe the relationship between reason and faith in the life of someone you admire. Then think about the connection between the two in your own life. How can reason be a help in experiencing and living your faith?

Arguments for the Existence of God—The Five Ways of Thomas Aquinas			
Argument	Oberservation	Implications	Conclusion
From motion	Motion cannot start itself but must be started by something already in motion.	An infinite chain of movers is impossible, for then there would be no first mover and therefore no motion at all. The chain must have a beginning.	The unmoved mover is the one whom we call God.
From causation of existence	Certain events are caused by other events, which are themselves caused by prior events, and so on.	As above, the causal chain cannot be infinite.	The uncaused first cause is the one whom we call God.
From possibility	Certain things are temporary, their existence unoriginal. Their existence is possible rather than necessary.	The chain of unoriginal existence cannot be infinite but must find its source in a self-existent necessary being.	This self-existent necessary being is the one whom we call God.
From imperfection	We judge certain things to have a lesser degree of perfection than others.	Relative assessments require an absolute standard of perfection.	This absolute standard, God, must exist.
From design	Inanimate things function together to accomplish an ordered purpose.	This cannot occur by chance but requires an intelligent designer.	The designer is the one whom we call God.

Adapted from Robert C. Walton, *Chronological and Background Charts of Church History*.

The Knight

Saint George is usually depicted as a medieval knight on horseback, slaying a dragon. The true Saint George died a martyr around 300. Beyond that, we know very little about him. However, we do know that devotion to Saint George was very popular during the Middle Ages. He was a model for Christian knights because he selflessly went out to do battle against evil—symbolized by the dragon—and protected women and others who needed him. His symbol, a red cross on a white background, became the banner for the knights who fought in the Crusades. Saint George is the patron saint of a number of countries, including England, which incorporates his red cross on white background as part of its flag.

During the Middle Ages, many came to view knighthood as an ideal expression of the Christian life. The European groups who joined Christianity had a history of engaging in warfare. Rather than eradicating this instinct, Christian leaders of the Middle Ages channeled it into a form of service: knights were to uphold morality and fight for the good. The ceremony by which someone received the title of knight reveals that the profession had religious significance. Before becoming a knight, a young man spent a night in prayer in a chapel. In the morning, he took a ritual bath, had his weapons blessed by a priest, and received his knight's garb in a religious ceremony. Knights were expected to be persons of strong moral character, ready to give their lives for others. In the eyes of the Church, the greatest act of heroism that a knight could perform was to fight in defense of the faith. This belief contributed to the start of the Crusades.

FAITH ACTIVITY

Religious Symbolism Two popular sets of stories about medieval knighthood were the stories about King Arthur and the Knights of the Round Table and the story about the search for the Holy Grail. Read a summary of one such story, or if you have previously read a story, recall specific details. Describe possible religious symbolism or meaning that it might have.

Knight on horseback with armor, banner and shield, 15th Century. ▶

Crusaders and Reformers

The Middle Ages were a time of both crusaders and reformers. On the one hand, Christian knights of the period engaged in the killing of non-Christians and Christians alike as part of the Crusades. At the same time, a young Italian man from Assisi chose to reject war and instead live a life of simplicity. His story continues to inspire Christians and people of other religions to this day. Also in this time period another type of religious community emerged, and its members were instrumental in addressing new heresies confronting the Church.

> Let us pray that each one of us, looking to the Lord Jesus, meek and humble of heart, will recognize that even men of the church, in the name of faith and morals, have sometimes used methods not in keeping with the Gospel in the solemn duty of defending the truth.
>
> Pope John Paul II, "Service Requesting Pardon," *Origins 29:40* (March 23, 2000): 647

The Christian Attempt to Win Back the Holy Land

Islam gained control of much of the Middle East, including the Holy Land, in the seventh century. It was difficult for Christian leaders to accept that the places where Jesus lived were controlled by non-Christians. From the time of Charlemagne, an uneasy peace prevailed between Muslims and Christians who lived in this area. Christians did travel to the Holy Land on pilgrimage, and some settled there and lived as neighbors to Muslims.

The peace came to an end in 1071 when Seljuk Turks conquered Jerusalem and prevented Christians from living in or coming in pilgrimage to the Holy Land. When, a few years later, Muslims began to attack Constantinople, the Eastern Emperor sent an urgent message to the pope asking that Western Christians come to the aid of their fellow Christians. Pope Urban II convened a council in Clermont in 1095. At the council the pope called on the nobility of Europe to take up the sword and to free the Holy Land. The cry went up, *"Deus vult"*—"God wills it!" Those who accepted this mission wore on their chests a cross of red fabric called *crociati* and thus became known as *crusaders*.

GROUP TALK

Discuss why you think it was important to Christians to have access to the holy places of our faith.

- The First Crusade lasted from 1096 to 1099 and resulted in the recapturing of Jerusalem. After Turks recaptured some of the conquered territory, the Second Crusade commenced in 1147.

- The monk Saint Bernard of Clairvaux (1090–1153) preached strongly in favor of the Second Crusade; but, because of conflicts between the German and French kings who were leading it, the Second Crusade was a dismal failure.

- The Third Crusade, in 1190, also encountered difficulty and only managed, thanks to the leadership of Richard the Lionhearted of England, to take the city of Jaffa and to arrange for safe passage for Christian pilgrims to Jerusalem.

- The Fourth Crusade (1200–1204) marked a turning point in the Crusades, as the recovery of the Holy Land for spiritual reasons seemed to become a secondary motive to the economic advantages of having control of the Holy Land. The crusaders attacked and plundered Constantinople. Thousands of Eastern Christians were massacred, and many important religious artifacts were taken.

Two unofficial crusades took place, both of which also resulted in disaster. Even before the actual armies of the First Crusade arrived in the Holy Land, a *People's Crusade* set out. An eccentric but eloquent preacher named Peter the Hermit called on the average citizens of Europe to go on a crusade of their own. He gathered together a poorly armed and disorganized band who intended to make their way to Jerusalem and set it free. Peter led the people through Asia Minor and into Constantinople. From there, those who had survived the arduous journey went to the Holy Land, where most of them were massacred. Later, in 1212, there was a so-called *Children's Crusade*. Caught up in crusader fever, some people called on children to mount their own crusade. Thousands of youth from all over Western Europe gathered together, believing that with God's help they would simply walk to Jerusalem without resistance. Many children died of starvation and disease as they marched to the sea. Before reaching the Holy Land, many were sold into slavery and were never seen again.

In total, there were eight crusades between 1096 and 1270. They did little to achieve their original objective, which was the return of Christian control of the Holy Land. In fact, the wanton killing that took place during the Crusades—of Muslims, Jews, and Eastern Christians alike—caused many people from those traditions to distrust Western Christians and the Latin Church. The popes and other Church leaders who called for crusades never intended the crusaders to massacre people as they did, and they certainly didn't want the churches and religious objects of their fellow Christians to be destroyed.

In May of 2001 while visiting Greece, Pope John Paul II apologized to Orthodox Christians for the "sins of action and omission" by Western Christians including the sacking of Constantinople by crusaders in 1204 that contributed to the collapse of the Byzantine Empire about three centuries later.

The Mendicant Orders— Franciscans and Dominicans

▼ *Stories of the life of Saint Francis: The trial by fire before the Sultan by Benozzo Gozzoli.*

In 1219 during the time of the Fifth Crusade, a young man and his companion asked permission of the cardinal overseeing the crusading forces in Egypt to go to the Muslim leader Sultan Malik-al-Kamil to seek his conversion to Christianity. Even though the cardinal had doubts about this endeavour, he yielded to the young man's persistence; the cardinal allowed the man and his companion to set out for unfriendly territory. The two men, Francis of Assisi and Brother Illuminato, were members of a new kind of religious order. They were soon captured and tortured by Muslim forces; but their strange appearance— unarmed, unafraid, and dressed in beggar's robes—piqued the curiosity of the sultan. Francis and the sultan met daily for a month discussing religion. Neither converted the other, but the sultan was so impressed with Francis that he granted Francis and Illuminato a passport to travel safely to the Holy Land. Francis and the sultan departed from each other as brothers.

Who was this Francis who approached the so-called enemies of Christianity in a spirit so different from that of the crusaders? For centuries, living the religious life meant living as a monk in a specially designated community within a monastery. During the Middle Ages, most monasteries functioned within the feudal system in existence at the time.

However, several religious orders emerged that presented a new system. Instead of living apart from the rest of people, the members of these orders lived among the people in towns and cities. Instead of being independent, they attempted to be totally dependent on God's providence. Instead of being self-sufficient like monasteries were, these groups lived on whatever people chose to give them. Therefore, these new religious orders are called mendicant, a word that means "to beg." The two men who founded the largest of the **mendicant** orders were Saint Francis of Assisi and Saint Dominic. Both systems of religious communities continue to flourish and benefit the Church today.

Saint Francis of Assisi Francis was born in 1182, the son of a wealthy Italian cloth merchant. Most accounts tell us that Francis grew up spoiled and self-indulgent. He was carefree and popular with the other youth of the city, always ready to spend his family's wealth. When he was in his twenties, he took part in a battle against a rival city and was captured and imprisoned. On his return to Assisi, he remained ill for about a year and then had his "conversion."

Praying in the rundown chapel of San Damiano outside of Assisi, Francis heard a command from the chapel's crucifix, "Repair my church, which has fallen into disrepair." Francis took the command literally, and set about restoring the little chapel, stone by stone. To get supplies, he sold material and clothing from his father's storehouse. His father was furious and beat him and locked him in a room. Francis escaped and went to the local bishop. When his father came to demand repayment, Francis stripped himself and gave back to his father everything that his father had given him, including his name. The bishop covered Francis in a coarse cloth. He continued to wear this robe as a sign of his new life and his new commitment to living free of all earthly possessions. This event took place in 1206 or 1208. Thus we have had the mendicant style of religious life in the Church for 800 years.

Caring for Creation Saint Francis took the common vocation we all have to be caretakers of God's creation very seriously. To be made in God's image and likeness means, among other things, being called to cooperate with God in the care of his creation. This means to appreciate the beauty and wonder of nature, to protect and preserve the environment, and to respect human life, to work in partnership with God in building up not only our world but the kingdom of God. One way to do this is to make a special commitment to help the environment. Another way is to work with Right to Life organizations.

▼ *Life of St. Francis. St. Francis Preaching to the Birds* by Giotto di Bondone.

As Francis continued his rebuilding of San Damiano, other young men from the town joined him in the project. They formed a community called the Friars Minor. A young woman friend, Clare, following Francis's spirit and teachings, founded a convent of women. Francis wanted his community to be totally dependent upon God's providence, living in complete poverty and simplicity. By doing so, he radically challenged the growing materialism of his time. For instance, on one occasion he and some of the members of his community were living in an abandoned monastery. A young member of the community came to Francis and said, "I looked for you in your cell, and you were not there." Francis replied, "I have no cell of my own," and never returned to that room again.

Francis and his followers owned nothing and found food and shelter by begging from the people in the towns through which they traveled. In 1210, Francis appealed in person to the pope, who approved the rule of the group that has come to be called the Franciscans.

One of the messages that Francis taught was the unity of all creation. He referred to the sun as "Brother Sun" and the moon as "Sister Moon." This is why people in the ecology movement often look to Francis for inspiration.

In 1224, Francis received the *stigmata*, visible wounds on his body similar to those of Jesus on the cross. Francis died in 1226, requesting to be laid on the earthen floor, dressed in the habit his bishop had given him. Two years after his death Francis was declared a saint. The pope said that in Francis we find the most perfect example of a true follower of Jesus. His feast day is October 4.

GROUP TALK

1 In groups discuss how living a simple life free from preoccupation with material things could help spread the Good News during the Middle Ages.

2 What are some ways simplifying your life could help you focus on following Jesus' example and being the person he calls you to be?

Saint Clare of Assisi (1194–1253)

Clare was born in Assisi on July 16, 1194. She was the cofoundress of the Order of Poor Ladies, or Poor Clares. She was from a wealthy family who owned a large castle in Assisi. Even as a young girl she was known for her devotion to prayer and for her desire to grow spiritually. She was eighteen when she heard Francis preach. Inspired by his message, she set out to follow his simple way of life.

Believing God was calling her to be a nun, she ran away from home and, with Francis's help, entered a Benedictine convent. Eventually Francis established a convent for Clare and others who had chosen to join her. Within a few years monasteries of Clare's followers were located in Italy, France, and Germany. The order adopted Francis's way of life—sleeping on the ground, eating only vegetables, and not speaking unless an act of charity necessitated it.

The story is told that in 1234 as the army of Frederick II was attacking Assisi, Clare arose from her sickbed and carried the ciborium containing the Blessed Sacrament to the window of the abbey. She raised the ciborium just as the soldiers were ready to attack the monastery, and the soldiers retreated. It is with reference to this incident that Saint Clare is often portrayed in art bearing a ciborium.

Clare died in 1253, twenty-seven years after the death of the man who had inspired her. Her feast day is August 11.

FAITH ACTIVITY

Saintly Lives Research more about Saints Francis of Assisi and Dominic. Name three themes associated with their movements. Describe ways that you could reflect these themes in your own life.

Saint Dominic Domingo de Guzman, now known as Dominic, was born in Spain in 1170. He became a priest and served as a canon of the cathedral in the town of Osma. Well-liked by the community, Dominic was asked to assume many leadership roles. At the time, a major problem facing the Church in Spain and around the city of Albi in France was the resurgence of an old heresy that saw matter as evil and spirit as good. The group who held this belief came to be known as Albigensians. The most adamant of the followers of Albigensianism were called the *perfects*. They practiced severe mortification, even to the point of starvation and suicide. The less extreme members, called *believers*, did not engage in these practices but sometimes would help the perfects to accomplish the state they sought by murdering them.

Pope Innocent III asked Dominic's bishop to preach to the Albigensians. Dominic, known for his preaching, accompanied the bishop and had some success. However, when the pope's representative was murdered, a crusade against the Albigensians took place and much bloodshed resulted. Dominic attempted to restore peace but eventually withdrew.

With the help of a wealthy benefactor, Dominic received a castle to which he invited those who wanted to join a community dedicated to the conversion of heretics. Like Francis, he wanted his followers to be out on the road, but Dominic's primary objective was to have his followers preach against heresy. After much opposition, Dominic received permission to found the Order of Preachers—the Dominicans. Dominic died in 1221 and was canonized in 1234. His feast day is August 8.

The Inquisition

As part of the campaign against the Albigensians, the pope called for trials during which the beliefs of the heresy were to be examined and shown to be in error. If heretics persisted in error, they were to be excommunicated from the Church. This process was known as the **Inquisition**.

At the time, heresy was seen as an attack against the state. In 1252, in keeping with standards of the time, Pope Innocent IV permitted the use of punishment to seek out truth. Punishment could include public penance and imprisonment. Those who were unyielding were handed over to civil authorities who killed the supposed heretics. By the end of the fourteenth century the use of inquisition against heretics declined. We will encounter the term *inquisition* again in the late fifteenth century, after Christian rule was restored in Spain.

FYI

During a special Mass at the Vatican on March 12, 2000, designated the Day of Pardon, Pope John Paul II took an unprecedented step. As the leader of the Catholic faith, he publicly asked God's forgiveness for the sins committed by Catholics over the past 2,000 years—including their treatment of Jews, heretics, women, and native peoples.

>Age to Age

Saint Dominic and the Rosary

From the earliest days of monasticism, monks had knotted cords to keep count of their prayers. Non-ordained brother monks who couldn't read used their cords to note the number of *Pater Nosters* (Our Fathers) they said. When a monk from another monastery died, priest monks would offer a Mass for the soul of the deceased, while the brothers recited 50 or 150 *Pater Nosters*. Each day when the monks gathered to recite psalms together, those who couldn't read instead counted off one hundred and fifty *Pater Nosters* on their cords.

In the eleventh century the prayer we call the Hail Mary developed as a full-fledged prayer and began to be used with the Our Father and the Doxology ("Glory to the Father, and to the Son, and to the Holy Spirit: as it was in the beginning, is now, and will be forever. Amen.") A garland (rosary) of prayers consisting of an Our Father, ten Hail Marys, and a Glory to the Father was used as a primary form of prayer by illiterate monks. Each set of ten Hail Marys was combined with a meditation on one of the great mysteries in the lives of Jesus and Mary. There were five sorrowful, five joyful, and five glorious mysteries on which to reflect. When all three sets of mysteries were used, the monks would have said over 150 prayers, just like the 150 psalms of the Liturgy of the Hours.

One account has the Rosary being given by the Blessed Mother to Saint Dominic in response to his request for help in combating the Albigensian heresy. During Dominic's time it served as a powerful prayer that helped people (especially former heretics) lift their minds and hearts to God. The Dominicans gave the Rosary its definitive form. In 2002, Pope John Paul II added an optional set of mysteries called the Mysteries of Light (the Luminous Mysteries). Now through the Rosary we can follow the mysteries of Christian faith from the Annunciation to the Crowning of Mary as Queen of the Universe.

Praying with Francis of Assisi

Let us praise God for all his creatures and with his creatures, our brothers and sisters, in the words of Francis: .

Most high, all powerful, all good Lord!
　All praise is yours, all glory, all honor, and all blessing.
To you alone, Most High, do they belong.
　No mortal lips are worthy to pronounce your name.
All praise be yours, my Lord, through all that you have made.
　And first, my Lord, Brother Sun,
　Who brings the day; and light you give to us through him.
How beautiful is he, how radiant in all his splendor!
　Of you, Most High, he bears the likeness.
All praise be yours, my Lord, through Sisters Moon and Stars;
　In the heavens you have made them, bright and precious and fair.
All praise be yours, my Lord, through Brothers Wind and Air,
　And fair and stormy, all the weather's moods,
　By which you cherish all that you have made.
All praise be yours, my Lord, through Sister Water,
　So useful, lowly, precious, and pure.
All praise be yours, my Lord, through Brother Fire,
　Through whom you brighten up the night.
　How beautiful is he, how gay! Full of power and strength.
All praise be yours, my Lord, through Sister Earth, our mother,
　Who feeds us in her sovereignty and produces
　Various fruits with colored flowers and herbs.
All praise be yours, my Lord, through those who grant pardon
　For love of you; through those who endure sickness and trial.
Happy those who endure in peace,
　By you, Most High, they will be crowned.
All praise be yours, my Lord, through Sister Death,
　From whose embrace no mortal can escape.
Woe to those who die in mortal sin!
　Happy those she finds doing your will!
　The second death can do no harm to them.
Praise and bless my Lord, and give him thanks,
　And serve him with great humility.

Amen.

>Review

1. Why are the Middle Ages in Europe also known as the time of Christendom?

2. What does it mean to say that Charlemagne was a "holy emperor" and the "second Constantine"?

3. Name two ways that Charlemagne attempted to serve the Church as Holy Roman Emperor.

4. How did the feudal system function?

5. Name three problems that the Church had to face during the early Middle Ages.

6. How did the Cluny movement help reform Church practices?

7. Describe the name for and some of the changes that Pope Gregory VII introduced into the Church.

8. Explain the iconoclast controversy.

9. What is the difference between Eastern Orthodox and Eastern Rite Catholic Churches?

10. Describe the difference between Romanesque and Gothic architecture.

11. What is scholasticism?

12. Whose *Summa Theologica* examined Christian beliefs in light of Greek philosophy?

13. What two actions by the Seljuk Turks helped spark the Crusades?

14. What was the intended outcome of the Crusades? How successful were the Crusades in meeting their objective?

15. How were the mendicant religious communities different from monastic communities?

>Key Words

Christendom (p. 120) Christian-dominated Western Europe of the Middle Ages.

conclave (p. 130) A meeting of cardinals to elect a pope.

Eastern Orthodox Churches (p. 136) Christian Churches with origins in the Eastern Roman Empire that are not in union with the pope and Church centered in Rome.

Eastern Rite Catholic Churches (p. 136) Catholic Churches whose origins were in the Eastern Roman Empire that are in union with the pope and Church centered in Rome.

East-West Schism (p. 134) The official separation of the Eastern (Orthodox) Church and the Western Church; also referred to as the Great Schism.

excommunication (p. 134) A severe ecclesiastical penalty that excludes the offender from taking part in the Eucharist or other sacraments.

filioque **(p. 134)** Latin term meaning "and from the Son."

Gregorian Reforms (p. 130) A series of Church reforms under Pope Gregory VII.

iconoclast controversy (p. 134) Conflict caused by the Eastern emperor's decision to condemn the use of icons in worship.

Inquisition (p. 151) Trials established to help curb the spread of heretical doctrines.

lay investiture (p. 128) The practice of lay persons (such as kings) appointing bishops, priests, abbots, and abbesses.

mendicant (p. 147) Religious communities whose members live among people and rely on the charity of others.

simony (p. 128) The payment of money to be appointed to a Church office.

Summa Theologica **(p. 141)** Saint Thomas Aquinas's comprehensive systematic examination of Christian theology.

Truce of God (p. 130) A rule enacted by the medieval Church forbidding warfare during certain holy days of the year.

❯Yesterday and Today

During the Middle Ages in Europe, Christianity touched every aspect of life. The Church was intimately connected with society and political decision-making. While it was a time of the involvement of Church leaders in secular affairs, it was also a time of exceptional saintliness. The beautiful and the holy blended together during the Middle Ages, and great cathedrals and great works of art resulted. Christianity expanded to include almost all of Europe, but for the first time we find an official, large-scale division within Christianity as Churches of the East and the West severed their ties. Life was hard for the medieval Christian, but the Church continued to carry the message of hope offered by Jesus. Because of the Church, people saw that beyond their temporal trials, eternal life awaited them.

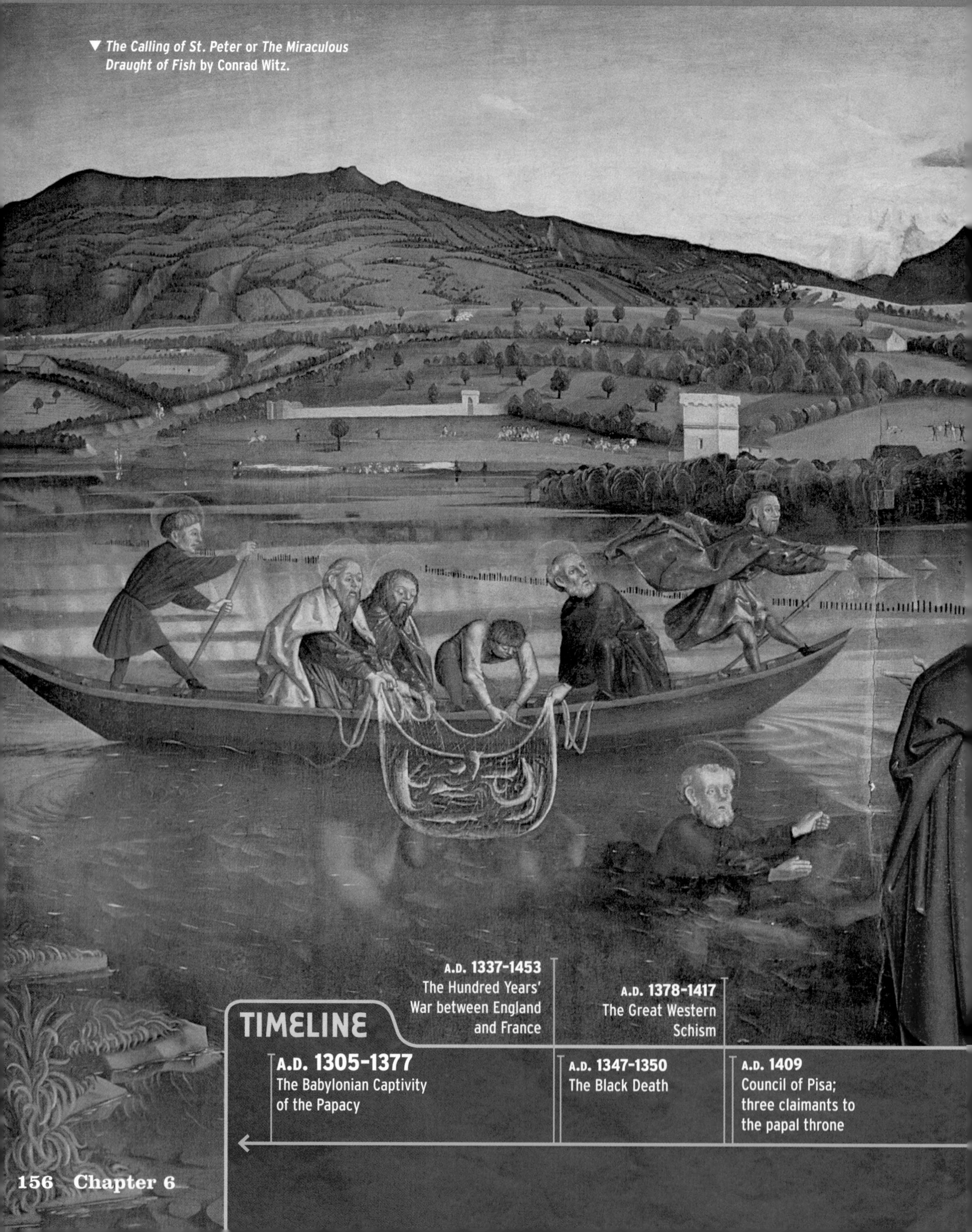

▼ *The Calling of St. Peter* or *The Miraculous Draught of Fish* by Conrad Witz.

TIMELINE

A.D. 1305–1377
The Babylonian Captivity of the Papacy

A.D. 1337–1453
The Hundred Years' War between England and France

A.D. 1347–1350
The Black Death

A.D. 1378–1417
The Great Western Schism

A.D. 1409
Council of Pisa; three claimants to the papal throne

FROM DISORDER TO BEAUTY AND HOPE

CHAPTER 6

THE ROAD TO THE RENAISSANCE

A.D. 1300-1500

CHAPTER GOALS

In this chapter you will:

★ see how the secular power of the papacy was weakened during the period of the Avignon popes and the Great Western Schism.

★ explore how the Black Death devastated Europe and discover how medieval mystics fostered spirituality based on their experiences of God's love.

★ consider how the fall of Constantinople led to a power shift in the Eastern Church and why Spanish rulers reclaimed their country for Catholicism and introduced the religion to new lands.

★ learn about the Renaissance with its renewed creative and artistic activity.

A.D. 1469
Queen Isabella and King Ferdinand of Spain unite their kingdoms

A.D. 1492
Expulsion of Muslims and Jews from Spain

A.D. 1431
Death of Joan of Arc

A.D. 1455
Invention of the printing press

A.D. 1498
Death of Savonarola

A.D. 1415
Council of Constance ends the Great Western Schism

A.D. 1453
Fall of Constantinople

A.D. 1478
Establishment of the Spanish Inquisition

A.D. 1492
Columbus discovers America

A.D. 1498
Missionaries arrive in India

Decline of Unity

FIRST THOUGHTS

Think about the ways you identify with your nation. Then think about the ways you identify with your faith.

★ What possible conflicts might there be between the values and interests of your nation and those of your faith?

★ How would you address such conflicts?

Have you ever had a day when everything seemed to go wrong? Europe went through such a period beginning in the fourteenth century. During this time the ideal of a unified Christendom, in which the pope would preside over all the people of Europe and would guide them in living the Christian life, disintegrated into nation fighting nation, or one city fighting another. One war, between England and France, actually lasted nearly a hundred years. As we will see, the papacy itself came to be caught up in conflicts.

Even more devastating than the power struggles of the time was the **Black Death**—the bubonic plague—which ravaged Europe. One-third of the population of the continent died because of it. Imagine what your school would be like if a third of everyone, including teachers and staff, were suddenly gone. Nonetheless, the Church and the papacy weathered the difficulties they faced. They continued to be the sign of Christ's loving presence when that awareness was sorely needed. In fact, during this period a number of women and men attained levels of spiritual experience that have helped shape Catholic spirituality. Also toward the end of this period, a flowering of artistic creativity emerged from which we have some of the finest religious works of art ever produced.

▼ Teen pilgrims gather at the Vatican.

Church and State Conflicts

If you are ever fortunate enough to travel to Rome, you would marvel at the magnificent churches and works of art found there. Some of that artwork was created for a special celebration held in 1300 when Pope Boniface VIII called for the first **jubilee year**, a special year of prayer and pilgrimage in the Catholic Church that takes place every fifty years. All during 1300, thousands of pilgrims went to Rome to receive the special graces associated with the celebration and also to enjoy the beauty and grandeur that the city had to offer. But even in the midst of this display of Rome's glory and papal power, forces were at work aimed at diminishing the authority of the pope, at least in secular matters.

In the historical sense, the division of the world into separate nation-states is a fairly recent occurrence. Recall that under Constantine, and later under Charlemagne, there was an empire which spread across many ethnic and language groups. Although often in tension, leaders of Church and state ruled the empire together, following their understanding of Christian principles.

Late in the thirteenth century, however, rulers of specific nations started to see themselves as solely responsible for what happened in their respective countries. For instance, the kings of France and England decided that members of the clergy were obligated to pay taxes to the crown. The English king said the clergy would have no protection of law until they paid taxes. The pope responded that secular princes could not tax members of the clergy. In 1302, Pope Boniface VIII issued a **papal bull**, or formal decree, called *Unam Sanctam* (literally "one holy"), stating that all rulers are subject to the pope and that it was "necessary for salvation" for every human to be subject to the pope. The two kings were not pleased with the pope's pronouncement. King Philip IV of France sent soldiers to arrest him. Although some people from his hometown in Anagni rescued Pope Boniface, he died a month later. Pope Boniface's successor served as pope for only eight months, and then no one was chosen for almost a year. Of the sixteen cardinals at the time, none of them wanted to elect someone who would continue the conflict with the French and English kings.

> Therefore, of the one and only Church there is one body and one head, not two heads like a monster; that is, Christ and the Vicar of Christ, Peter and the successor of Peter . . . [One power] ought to be subordinated to the other and temporal authority, subjected to spiritual power . . . This authority, however, (though it has been given to man and is exercised by man), is not human but rather divine, granted to Peter by a divine word and reaffirmed to him (Peter) and his successors by the One Whom Peter confessed . . . Furthermore, we declare, we proclaim, we define that it is absolutely necessary for salvation that every human creature be subject to the Roman Pontiff.
>
> *Unam Sanctam*, Boniface VIII

FYI

A jubilee year is a biblical concept. (See *Leviticus 25:1–11*.) The Sabbath, the "seventh day," is a day of prayer. The fiftieth year is the year after seven times seven years.

FAITH ACTIVITY

Jubilee Year 2000 At the threshold of the new millennium, Pope John Paul II called for a jubilee year to celebrate 2,000 years of Christianity. Research Jubilee Year 2000 and the first jubilee year in 1300. Describe the differences and similarities between the two jubilee years.

The Avignon Papacy The cardinals reached a compromise that they hoped would appease both the English and the French. In June 1305 they chose Bertrand de Got, the Archbishop of Bordeaux, as pope. Since Bordeaux was under the control of the English, that made Bertrand a subject of the English king; but he had been born a Frenchman and had been a personal friend of the French king since childhood. He agreed to be crowned at Lyons in France. However, Bertrand did not want to settle in French territory. Suffering from cancer at the time, he accepted the hospitality of Dominican friars in the town of Avignon in the kingdom of Naples. His decision had an important effect on the Church because his successors also decided to stay in Avignon. For the next seventy years the pope, the Bishop of Rome, would not live in Rome. Instead, a series of seven popes lived in Avignon. Rome, which had been the physical and spiritual center of the Church, lost its political and moral clout.

The Italian poet Petrarch referred to the period from 1309 to 1377 as the **Babylonian Captivity of the Papacy**, equating it to the years, described in the Bible, when the Israelites had been forced to live in exile in Babylon. In time, one of the Avignon popes purchased land in Avignon and built a papal palace. Most of the popes during this period did good works and continued reforming Church structures. Some made major improvements to the city of Rome, even though they never went there. During his office from 1334–1342, Pope Benedict XII ordered all bishops and priests who were

▼ Polais de Papes by Pierre Poissan in Avignon, France.

"hangers on" at the papal court to go home and serve their people. He called for religious communities to meet every three years to examine their lifestyle.

Although most people of the time believed that the pope belonged in Rome, having the pope residing in Avignon was not such a bad idea.

- First, Avignon was a more peaceful place than the bustling city of Rome.

- Second, Avignon was, or at least became, papal territory.

- Third, it was closer than Rome was to many of the major centers of Catholicism in Western Europe.

- Fourth, the popes of the time and the majority of cardinals were French.

On occasion, the issue of the pope's return to Rome was discussed, but nothing permanent came of it. Two women of the time who were recognized for their holiness, Saints Bridget of Sweden and Catherine of Siena, implored the pope to return to Rome. Perhaps due to their influence, in 1377 the newly elected Pope Gregory XI did move to Rome. He died shortly after his return—a mere three months later.

Saint Catherine of Siena (1347–1380)

We know that after a thirty-year-old Italian woman met with Pope Gregory XI in Avignon, he returned the papacy to Rome in 1377. Who was this person who could convince a pope to move from the place that had been home to the papacy for seventy years? Catherine of Siena was one of twenty-five children of the Benincasa family. As early as five years old, she had profound spiritual experiences. Such experiences continued throughout her life. The road to holiness, however, was not an easy one for Catherine. For three years she struggled with doubts and demonic visions. This dry spell ended with the help of, in her words, laughter. She experienced a profound sense of union with Christ.

Catherine worked with those who were sick, including plague victims and condemned prisoners. She also gave her attention to broader affairs. She wrote hundreds of letters to the pope and other religious and secular leaders offering them advice. Given her reputation for holiness, her advice was not easily dismissed. Toward the end of her life, she wrote about her religious experiences. Because of the impact that her writings have had on the Church, Catherine was declared a Doctor of the Church in 1970. She is also the patroness of Italy.

The Great Western Schism

Of the sixteen cardinals who gathered in Rome to elect the pope after the brief reign of Gregory XI, nine were French. The continued French dominance incensed the people of Rome. Marching around the building where the cardinals were meeting, the people demanded a Roman, or at least an Italian, pope. The cardinals chose an Italian archbishop who lived in Bari, which was a distance from Rome. Since he couldn't get to the city quickly, the cardinals dressed one of their own as pope and presented him to the people to calm the crowd. Then the cardinals fled the city.

When the elected pope arrived in Rome in April 1378, he took the name Urban VI. The people of Rome accepted him, and in time the cardinals of the Church returned to Rome and pledged their obedience to him. At first, the new pope seemed to be a good choice. He had a great deal of experience in Church and state affairs, was a capable administrator, and was recognized as an honest man. However, in a few weeks it became clear that he made quick decisions and would not listen to advice from the cardinals. He criticized the decisions of others, especially those of the cardinals. Many would describe his style as volatile.

All the cardinals except one left Rome and met in northern Italy. They announced that, since they were under duress when they had chosen Urban as pope, his election was unlawful. The cardinals "elected" another man, a French cardinal named Robert of Geneva, to be "pope." He attempted to take the papal throne by force but was repelled by the people of Rome. Robert then took up residence in Avignon and claimed to be the rightful pope.

Many people, including Saint Catherine of Siena, pointed out that the cardinals had accepted Urban VI as pope, had celebrated Holy Week liturgy with him as pope, and had pledged their obedience to him. Therefore, there was no question that he was the validly elected pope. However, the cardinals who supported Robert would not back down. So Pope Urban VI named new cardinals and excommunicated the old ones, including the cardinal claiming to be pope and living in Avignon. The Avignon "pope" in turn excommunicated Pope Urban and his followers. Thus the world found itself with two claimants to the papal throne. Secular leaders and the common people began to take sides with one or the other. This situation, in which two men claimed to be pope at the same time, lasted thirty-eight years and is called the **Great Western Schism**.

GROUP TALK

The Catholic Church continues to be a community that transcends national loyalties. Apart from its religious value, why is it beneficial to belong to an organization that spans the globe?

Resolving the Schism The first attempt to end the Great Western Schism took place in 1409 when leaders of both Church and state called for a council to be held in Pisa, Italy. The council deposed both claimants to the papal throne and elected Peter of Candia to be pope. He lived only a short time thereafter, but the cardinals he had named chose the next "pope," who took the name John XXIII. Neither of the two previous claimants to the papacy recognized the right of a council to be convened without papal approval, and so they did not resign. As a result, *three* people claimed to be pope: Gregory XII in Rome, the claimant Benedict XIII in Avignon, and now John XXIII.

Finally in 1414, the Holy Roman Emperor at the time forced John XXIII to convene a council at Constance, Italy. This council was well attended and lasted for more than three years. During this time, the legitimate pope, Gregory XII in Rome, offered his resignation but soon after died. Benedict XIII in Avignon refused to resign. He was denounced by the council, accused of heresy and schism, and went into exile still believing he was pope. The man who went by "Pope John XXIII" tried to flee but was stopped and forced to resign. He then retired quietly and served as a bishop in Italy. In November of 1417, the council declared the papal throne to be empty. Cardinals met and elected one of their own, who took the name Pope Martin V. For the first time in forty years, one person was universally recognized as the pope and as the rightful successor to Peter. The Great Western Schism was over.

It took two Church councils to straighten out the Great Western Schism. Some of the leaders gathered at these meetings proposed that councils therefore had more authority in the Church than the pope and that councils be held on a regular basis. This incorrect position is known as **conciliarism**. A council did meet a number of years after the schism ended, but it dragged on without settling anything. Conciliarism proved to be so chaotic that after this period, Church leaders hesitated to call another council. In the next century, the Reformation progressed beyond any hope of reconciliation before Church leaders called for a full council—the Council of Trent—to address the issues.

▼ The Council of Trent, Italian School.

Church-Recognized Popes During the Great Western Schism	
Urban VI	April 8, 1378–October 15, 1389
Boniface IX	November 2, 1389–October 1, 1404
Innocent VII	October 17, 1404–November 6, 1406
Gregory XII	November 30, 1406–July 4, 1415
Martin V	November 11, 1417–February 20, 1431

Popes and Anti-Popes The pope is the successor to Saint Peter and visible head of the Church. Historically there have been a number of methods used to select the pope. Today, the cardinals of the Church elect him, a practice begun in the eleventh century. However, during the time of the Great Western Schism there were two and then briefly three men who claimed to be pope. One was the actual pope; the others were anti-popes. An **anti-pope** is someone who falsely claims to be pope. The first anti-pope in history was Hippolytus, a priest who in A.D. 218 did not approve of the man chosen to be pope. A band of his followers proclaimed Hippolytus pope instead. Hippolytus eventually reconciled with the Church and died a martyr and saint. In all, there have been thirty recognized anti-popes, the last of whom was Felix V in the 1400s.

The popes who served in Rome continued as the true popes during the thirty-eight years of the schism. Those who called themselves pope but resided in Avignon during this period are not recognized as valid popes and are therefore known as anti-popes. However, into the modern era it was not completely clear whether the two popes selected by the Council of Pisa were valid. As you recall, one of those two men took the name "Pope John XXIII." In 1958 when Cardinal Giuseppe Roncalli, who had been a history teacher, was elected pope, he announced that he would take the name John. The cardinal-deacon said to him, "You will be John XXIV." The pope-elect corrected him, "No, I will be John XXIII." Thus ended any question about the status of the fifteenth-century John XXIII. He was an anti-pope.

Time of Tragedy and Intense Prayer

During the time of the Avignon papacy, a disaster struck Europe that would leave its mark for years to come. The bubonic plague, also known as the Black Death, began in 1347. The first outbreak lasted for three years. During that time, one-third of Europe's population died. The plague, probably carried by rats aboard ships, first appeared in the Italian seaport of Genoa. Fleas on the rats carried the plague to humans. When it spread to Venice and Florence, 100,000 people died in each city. Siena lost 80,000 people, four-fifths of its population. The French city of Marseilles lost 57,000 people, including its bishop and most of its clergy. In Paris, 80,000 people died in less than four months.

Although the plague abated during the winter of 1350, it surfaced again in England and France between 1361 and 1400. Each time, large portions of the population died. European life was never the same.

The Impact of the Plague on Religious Life Church leaders attempted to mandate sanitation policies, and many religious communities took charge of tending those who were sick and burying those who died. However, so many towns were left without any priests that large numbers of people received no consolation of the sacraments in their time of greatest need.

Saint Louis of France prays ▶ for the end of the Plague by Carlo Bonone.

Even before the plague, there had been no buildings or formal processes set aside for the training of priests. Some men did prepare for the priesthood in monasteries and later in universities. If a priest knew someone he thought would make a good priest, he invited the young man to learn from him. The young man might be a student or just a member of the village. The priest taught the younger man some Latin, whatever other academic subjects he thought would be helpful, how to celebrate Mass, and how to administer the other sacraments. The man was ordained a priest in the Sacrament of Holy Orders, and when the older priest became ill or died, the younger priest took his place.

With the sudden death of so many clergy during the time of the plague, many students of the priesthood who knew only the basic parts of the Mass and the other sacraments were left without mentors. The people desperately wanted to participate in the sacraments, so it didn't seem to matter how knowledgeable or trained the priests were. The young priests might celebrate the Mass with a combination of poor Latin and gestures, and the people received little faith formation that dealt with a loving God and the heart of the Christian message.

When the plague spread to England, many abbeys and monasteries lost large numbers of monks. Because they needed numerous people to function, many monasteries fell into disrepair. Monasticism would never again return to the level it had reached during the earlier Middle Ages.

In an attempt to grasp the situation, many people tended to have two responses to the plague: a search for scapegoats and a search for miracle cures. All kinds of explanations were put forward for the plague, from claims that the end of the world was coming to claims that enemies were poisoning the well water. As has unfortunately happened a number of times in history, some people blamed Jews. Prior to this time, laws had been enacted that restricted Jews from working the land and required them to wear distinctive clothing. Jews, therefore, generally lived apart from their Christian neighbors as a separate and distinct group. When Jews in the Avignon area were accused of spreading the plague and were persecuted, the pope opened up safe havens for Jews living in the area. The pope also extended sanctuary in Germany to Jews blamed for the plague there. Nonetheless, hundreds of Jewish communities were destroyed by people who suspected Jews of spreading the plague.

People of the Middle Ages saw power in the holiness exhibited by the saints, and they wanted to tap into that holiness. Anything associated with a saint was treated with great reverence and was also viewed as possessing special power. These items, called relics, have played a role in Christianity from the time of the martyrs.

FAITH ACTIVITY

Relics Write a report on the use of relics in Catholic spirituality. As part of your report, address the following questions:

★ What would you describe as an appropriate attitude toward relics?

★ What would you consider to be a misuse of relics?

★ Is there still a place for relics in today's spirituality?

★ What is current Church teaching regarding relics?

During the plague, religion focused on death and the afterlife. Frightening images of hell and purgatory abounded. Many people wanted to ensure that Masses and prayers would be offered for them after they died so that they would be spared the torments of purgatory and enter heaven quickly.

Even today we do not know why the plague stopped, but we do know that it caused great disruption to Church life and European society. That disruption also helped set the stage for the Reformation, which we will study in the next chapter.

The Sacrament of Salvation

You may have heard the saying, "There are no atheists in foxholes." It implies that people in desperate, life or death situations call upon God no matter how strongly they had previously believed in God. The years of the plague were certainly a foxhole situation for Europe. People encountered death constantly; didn't know why, when, or whom it would strike; and felt powerless to do anything about it. Many people turned to their faith. The Church could assure people that there is more than earthly life for them, with all its inevitable sufferings. Faith and belief in God are the sources of salvation; in fact, they are necessary to experience the fullness of eternal life with God. Just as she does now, the Church provided the way to this salvation. She is a sign of our communion with God, and a visible reminder of the heavenly Jerusalem, the place of eternal peace that awaits when suffering has ended.

Medieval Mysticism

Even in the midst of the horrible devastation caused by the plague, many Catholics were certain that in the end all would be well. Where did their confidence come from? The answer is: the Church and its message of salvation. Catholics of the time were immersed in the Church, their essential link to God. Some even experienced a strong, tangible sense of communion with God. Such intense experiences are known as **mysticism**. Mysticism often becomes more prevalent during particularly desperate times. According to Saint Thomas Aquinas, *Mysticism is the knowledge of God through experience.* That is, while theology attempts to *know about* God, mysticism seeks an *experience of* God. By way of analogy, mysticism is like directly experiencing a beautiful sunset as opposed to understanding a scientific explanation of a sunset.

The late Middle Ages produced a number of Christian mystics. Some of them wrote about their experiences in a way that gives us a hint of how they perceived God. One popular preacher of the time who also wrote about mysticism was the German Dominican friar Meister Eckhart (1260–1328). One of the most important contributions that Eckhart made to our understanding of God is sometimes called **negative theology**. Eckhart reminds us that God completely surpasses any image or concept that we might have of him. For instance, the Bible says that "God is love." Eckhart would point out that God's love actually goes beyond any notion of love that we might have. While we may constantly attempt to describe him, Eckhart wants us to remember that the mystery of God cannot be confined to or contained by our limited capacity to comprehend the mystery. Eckhart challenges us not to settle for a God that we can "know about" and pushes us to be open to an "experience of" God who is an indescribable mystery.

Eckhart's ideas certainly stretched the Christian imagination. Some people questioned whether Eckhart's ideas were heresy. Eckhart denied that any of his teachings were heresy, but he was summoned to the papal court in Avignon to explain his ideas. He died before he had a chance to state his case. Even so, the papal court did rule that some of his teachings were in fact heretical. A number of Dominicans, in good standing with the Church, followed Eckhart and continued to advocate the importance of experiencing God's presence within them and around them.

A Mystic Describes God's Love Mysticism is open to everyone, not just monks, nuns, or people who are educated. One mystic, an Englishwoman who lived alone in a room attached to her parish church, had mystical experiences that she called simply **showings**. We know her as Julian of Norwich (1342–1424). As is typical of mystics, she spoke of being overwhelmed by God's love. The language she used was not intellectual but rather emotional; it was the language of love. She referred to God in feminine terms and even called Jesus "our true mother who carries us in the womb and nourishes us like a mother." Here is her account of a "showing" that she received during one of her mystical experiences.

> I saw that he [Jesus] is to us everything which is good and comforting for our help. He is our clothing, who wraps and enfolds us for love, embraces us and shelters us, surrounds us for his love, which is so tender that he may never desert us. And so in this sight I saw that he is everything which is good, as I understood. And in this he showed me something small, no bigger than a hazelnut, lying in the palm of my hand, as it seemed to me, and it was round like a ball. I looked at it with the eye of my understanding and thought: What can this be? I was amazed that it could last, for I thought that because of its littleness it would suddenly have fallen into nothing. And I was answered in my understanding: It lasts and always will, because God loves it; and thus everything has being through the love of God.
>
> In this little thing I saw three properties. The first is that God made it, the second is that God loves it, the third is that God preserves it. But what did I see in it? It is that God is the Creator and the protector and the lover.

Patrick V. Reid, *Readings in Western Religious Thought*, Vol. II, pp. 270–271

The words that Julian uses for her encounter with Christ are words of love: He wraps around us, enfolds us, embraces us, and shelters us tenderly. She sees herself as very small and insignificant, practically nothing—like a hazelnut. And yet, even in her littleness, she experiences herself as created and loved by God. She sees that she will also be preserved forever by God. The message expressed in this passage is basic Christian theology. However, to actually *experience* the message is a special gift from God. Such is the gift of the mystics.

FAITH ACTIVITY

Experiencing God When have you felt God's presence in your life in a particularly strong way? Using a creative form of your choice, describe something of the experience.

GROUP TALK

What are some ways that members of the Church today can experience Christ as the mystics did?

Saint Joan of Arc (1412–1431)

A person from this time period who fascinates Catholics and others is Saint Joan of Arc. Born in the small village of Domremy in 1412, Joan worked on her family's farm. Although she could neither read nor write, Joan knew all her prayers by heart. As a child she loved to hear stories of the saints.

One day, at the age of thirteen, she heard bells ringing and saw a bright light descend upon her in the garden. She knelt down, and a voice told her not to be afraid. The voice identified itself as that of the archangel Michael. The angel told her that soon Saint Catherine of Alexandria and Saint Margaret of Antioch would visit her and guide her on what she was to do. Over the next five years, these saints appeared to Joan about three times a week and encouraged her in her spiritual life. Joan vowed to be like them—to remain a virgin and to be open to whatever God wanted her to do. The local priests, with whom she shared these visions, encouraged her in her spiritual development.

In time Joan came to learn that three tasks were being entrusted to her: She was to save the city of Orleans from its siege by the English; she was to arrange for the crowning of the dauphin, Charles, as king of France at the cathedral in Reims; and she was to drive the English from French soil.

Just a teenager at the time, Joan went to Chinon where the dauphin lived and said simply, "I have been sent from God to bring help to the kingdom and to yourself." After many delays and examinations, Charles gave Joan permission to lead his troops in an attempt to seize Orleans back for the French. When she was successful, Charles agreed to go to Reims and be crowned as king. On the way Joan led the troops in a series of victories. She then asked Charles to allow her to drive out the English, but Charles was hesitant. Instead of going to Paris, the capital, he took his court to Gien. There Joan was forced to await the king's decision. While waiting, she was told in a vision that the enemy would capture her. On May 23, 1430, she fell into the hands of the Burgundians, who later sold her to the English.

Joan's captors wanted to kill her but were afraid to do so. Instead, they turned her over to an ecclesiastical (Church) court. There she could be tried as a heretic for claiming to hear saints speaking to her. Joan resisted abuse and torture for several months. At last, exhausted and abandoned by her friends, she "submitted to the Church" and denied her voices. She was condemned to life in prison. Within days, she retracted her submission, whereupon she was handed over to the secular leaders as a relapsed heretic. On May 30, 1431, she was burned at the stake in Rouen. Almost immediately, many people began to question the validity of the trial, and in 1456 the trial and its verdict were annulled. In 1920, Joan was declared Saint Joan of Arc, the Maid of Orleans and patroness of France.

The Ever-Changing Geography

The fifteenth century saw the beginning of more transformations in the geography of Christianity. One event, the discovery of the Americas by Europeans, introduced whole new continents to Christianity. During this time the fate of Christianity in many areas was linked to the fortunes of Islam. In the East, Muslim Turks brought an end to the Roman Empire. In the West, Christian rulers regained control over all of Spain after nearly eight hundred years of an Islamic presence there.

The Fall of Constantinople

One issue that arose again after the Great Western Schism ended was the relationship between the Western and Eastern Churches. By 1386, Ottoman Turks had encircled and conquered all but a small area around Constantinople in the Eastern Roman Empire. Finally, in 1439 a delegation from the East, including the emperor himself, came to Florence to meet with the pope and other Church leaders. The emperor believed that the pope was still in a position to call for a crusade and to come to his aid against the Turks. Desperate for help, the Eastern delegates agreed to all matters that had been in dispute between the two groups, including the *filioque* clause in the creed and the supremacy of the pope. All participants signed a statement called the **Union of Florence**, which would have officially ended the split between Eastern and Western Christianity.

However, when the Eastern delegates returned home, their members condemned their giving in to the Latins. A mob attacked Hagia Sophia, the great church in Constantinople, and rejected the clergy who had signed the Union. When the head of the Russian Church arrived home wearing a Roman cross, he was imprisoned. His fellow bishops condemned his action as treason and elected a new patriarch. This was the beginning of a separate Russian Orthodox Church.

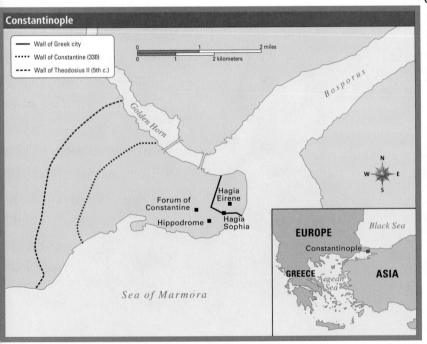

Constantinople

- Wall of Greek city
- Wall of Constantine (330)
- Wall of Theodosius II (5th c.)

0   1   2 miles
0   1   2 kilometers

Golden Horn
Bosporus
Forum of Constantine
Hagia Eirene
Hippodrome
Hagia Sophia
Sea of Marmora

EUROPE
Black Sea
Constantinople
GREECE
Aegean Sea
ASIA

Thus, the union between East and West failed, and the Eastern Empire was left to its own resources in combating the Turks. In 1453, the final siege of Constantinople began. There were only 7,000 defenders against an army of 80,000. The siege lasted eight weeks. On May 29, the city fell, marking the end of the Roman Empire. Soon after the fall of Constantinople, Russian rulers began to look upon their capital, Moscow, as the third Rome. The rulers even began to refer to themselves as *czars*, referring to the title "Caesar." From 1500 on, the Russian Orthodox Church became a leading voice in the world for Eastern or Orthodox Christianity. The rich tradition of Eastern Christian spirituality remained strong in Russia until the Communist takeover of the country in the twentieth century.

Christianity in Spain and the New World

Spain had been a divided country ever since Muslims took control of it in the eighth century. In the fifteenth century that control was limited and growing weaker. In 1469, two Christian rulers of sections of Christian-controlled Spain were married—Isabella and Ferdinand. They were determined to rid Spain of heretics and of anyone who was not a Christian. Keep in mind that they viewed heresy as a crime against their newly established state as well as a crime against the faith. Leaders of Church and state viewed being Christian and being a loyal subject as one and the same. In 1478, Queen Isabella and King Ferdinand asked the pope to reinstitute the Inquisition in order to investigate the sincerity of people who had converted to Christianity from Judaism or Islam.

Although the pope issued strict guidelines about how to conduct these trials, many abuses occurred and many people were tortured and killed in Spain in the late fifteenth century. This was the **Spanish Inquisition**. To correct abuses, in 1483 the pope appointed the Dominican Tomás de Torquemada as Grand Inquisitor to oversee all inquisitions in Spain. It is estimated that under Torquemada perhaps as many as two thousand Jews died, and frequently, their property was confiscated by their accusers.

In 1492, Isabella and Ferdinand gained control of all of Spain, ending Muslim rule in the southern part of the country. In the same year, they expelled all Jews from Spain. Actually, Jews had a choice: they could either convert to Catholicism or leave the country. Dangers and suffering accompanied either option. Of those who left the country, many died on the way to Morocco or elsewhere. Some ended up being sold into slavery.

Convert or Leave If you were given the choice today to convert to another faith other than Catholicism or leave the country, what would you do? Write a short essay describing the choice and what your faith means to you.

Jews and Muslims who converted to Christianity were called *conversos*. Once people are baptized and become members of the Church, they should be welcomed into the fold and treated as brothers and sisters in Christ. However, in the atmosphere of distrust that existed in Spain at the time, some older Christians suspected that the new converts were not sincere in their motives for entering the Church. Some newly converted Jews were accused of "Judaizing" Christianity and of trying to subvert the Church, now from within. Thus, some of the *conversos* were subject to the trials and tortures of the Inquisition. Although in time its implementation subsided, the Spanish Inquisition did not officially end until 1834.

As part of Jubilee Year 2000 activities, Pope John Paul II asked forgiveness for mistreatment of Jews throughout history:

> God of our fathers, you chose Abraham and his descendants to bring your name to the nations: We are deeply saddened by the behavior of those who in the course of history have caused these children of yours to suffer, and asking your forgiveness, we wish to commit ourselves to genuine brotherhood with the people of the covenant. We ask this through Christ our Lord. Amen.
>
> Pope John Paul II during "Service Requesting Pardon" as part of Jubilee Year 2000 (*Origins 29:40*): 647

As you know, 1492 is significant for another reason. The Spanish rulers commissioned an Italian sailor to seek a western passage to India and the East. When Christopher Columbus arrived instead in the Americas, a whole new chapter in the story of Christianity began. We will look at that story in depth in chapter 9.

The Renaissance

The Renaissance was more than a movement; it was a happening. From the birth of the poet Petrarch in 1304 to the death of Titian in 1576, Italy experienced a flowering of artistic expression that left an indelible mark on that country and the world. That the Renaissance began in what is now Italy is understandable because the area had relative political stability. There was no nation of Italy until 1870; instead, it was a collection of city-states. These city-states vied with one another for economic superiority, but at the time of the Renaissance each was having great success. For this reason, they had the resources to endow the arts. Scholars, poets, craftsmen, and artists were supported by patrons such as the Medici family of Florence, the doges (mayors) of Venice, the Storza family of Milan, and the popes of Rome.

The word *renaissance* means "rebirth" or "revival." It has come to mean the humanistic revival of classical art, architecture, literature, and learning that originated in Italy in the fourteenth century and spread from there to the rest of Europe.

While spiritual matters were the point of focus in the earlier Middle Ages, the Renaissance emphasized broader human endeavors. For this reason the Renaissance is known as a time of **humanism**. Sculpture and art glorified the human form, much as classical Greek art had done. However, the Renaissance did not reject the spiritual dimension of human life. Just as Aquinas had used Greek thought to help people understand Christianity better, Renaissance artists and thinkers used styles inspired by the classical period to bring people closer to God. Renaissance poets and artists recognized that the source of all beauty was God, and they used their talents to create beauty that evoked a sense of the sacred. Through their art, they attempted to enter into the depths of the human heart and to exalt the soul, leading people into the mystery of God. The Renaissance fostered an overall sense of human creativity and ingenuity as a means to praise God and to serve the Church.

FAITH ACTIVITY

Works of Art Find a book by Sister Wendy Beckett, or watch a portion of one of her PBS videos about art. Write about a work of art that she believes conveys a sense of the sacred. Explain her reasons.

▼ *Portrait of Bianca Cappello Wife of Francesco de Medici by Alessandro Allori.*

FAITH ACTIVITY

Sense of the Sacred Design your own work of art or choose the work of another that you believe conveys a sense of the sacred. In writing, explain why.

Leonardo da Vinci (1452–1519) was a model "Renaissance man"—an artist, scientist, inventor, and all-around scholar. For instance, da Vinci envisioned flying machines long before the invention of the airplane. Michelangelo (1475–1564), who was also a fine poet, showed his great abilities as a sculptor in the statue of young David that he did for the city of Florence. Later, in 1499 he signed a contract in which he promised to create "the most beautiful work in marble that exists today in Rome." The result was **La Pietà**—a magnificent and moving statue of the dead Jesus lying in the arms of his mother. This beautiful work stands today inside Saint Peter's Basilica in Rome.

Pope Julius II also called upon Michelangelo to paint his private chapel, the Sistine Chapel, in the Vatican. At first Michelangelo refused because he saw himself as a sculptor, not a painter. However, he finally agreed and spent almost four years seventy feet above the chapel floor painting the ceiling. His painting remains one of the most magnificent frescoes ever produced.

FYI

A few days after the completion of *La Pietà*, Michelangelo moved among the visitors to hear their comments. He overheard one person saying that the sculpture was the work of a rival of Michelangelo's. Later that night, Michelangelo returned and chiseled his name on the statue. It is the only work that he ever signed.

GROUP TALK

Leonardo da Vinci was considered a "Renaissance Man." This title is often used today to describe persons who exhibit many talents. Do the Renaissance men and women in today's society resemble those of the Renaissance period? Why or why not?

INTERPRET THE ART

Comparing Two Masters The artist responsible for this version of *The Pieta* was based in Venice, and is credited with making the city a center of Renaissance art that rivaled the other major cities of Italy. Using an art history textbook or another source, compare this piece to Michelangelo's *La Pietà*. What similarities do you see? What differences?

The Pieta by Giovanni Bellini.

Dissenting Opinions during the Renaissance

The controversies over the papacy and the flourishing artistic expression that took place during the Renaissance influenced people's attitudes toward Christianity and the Church as well. For instance, some people began to question structures and beliefs that had been at the center of European society. This questioning reached a high point during the period of the Reformation. However, more than one hundred years before the Reformation certain thinkers posed viewpoints that would take hold among Protestants. John Wyclif, an English theologian (1324–1384), proposed that Scripture is more important than Tradition for Church teaching. However, Catholics know that these two cannot be separated for they are the one deposit of God's word and revelation to us. Both are of equal importance. Perhaps in response to the battles going on among Church leaders, Wyclif also taught that all Christians together were the Church and that the Church has no head except Christ. Therefore, the Church and state do not have the right to rule others.

Later a theologian from Prague followed along the same line of thinking. John Hus (1369–1415) criticized conditions in the Church and called on it to return to the poverty and simplicity of the Gospels. His sermons were passionate and well received by many, but some—for instance, wealthy clergy in his native Czechoslovakia—attacked him. Hus was called upon to defend his ideas before the Council of Constance, the same council that settled the Great Western Schism. The council condemned his ideas. Hus was executed, but this action sparked dissension in his native country for decades.

A third person who anticipated the controversies that would erupt in the Reformation was Savonarola (1452–1498), a fiery Dominican preacher who succeeded in bringing great moral reform to the city of Florence. However, when he ended up attacking the pope of the time, the pope responded by placing an **interdict** on Florence. An interdict meant that no Masses or other sacraments would be allowed to be celebrated and people would be refused a Christian burial. The people of Florence turned against Savonarola, and he was tortured and burned at the stake as a heretic in 1498.

Age to Age

Holy Cards

Catholic pictorial art may have reached its zenith during the Renaissance, but Catholicism continues to appreciate beautiful art. When celebrating your First Communion or the Sacrament of Eucharist, you might have received a small card with a picture of Jesus, Mary, or one of the saints on it. If you attend a Catholic funeral, chances are that you will receive a similar card that may give the deceased person's name and dates of birth and death on the back. Members of the Hispanic community frequently distribute cards with a saint's picture on it to mark a child's Baptism. Such cards, called simply "holy cards," have been popular in Catholicism for centuries. The earliest holy card we know of dates from 1423. It depicted Saint Christopher on paper lace made from a wood block print. Holy cards were popular throughout France and Germany during the fifteenth century.

Holy cards became extremely popular throughout the Catholic world with the invention of lithography by the German Alois Senefelder in 1798. They are still given as little gifts for special occasions. Often along with the picture they include an accompanying prayer. Holy cards depicting Saint Francis of Assisi on one side and the Prayer of Saint Francis on the back are particularly popular. Catholics hold onto these holy cards, often using them as bookmarks in a favorite Bible or prayer book. They serve as keepsakes and reminders of reception of the sacraments, of special occasions, and of family and friends who have died.

John the Baptist Baptizing Jesus. ▶

Praying with Saint Catherine of Siena

Reader 1: O immeasurable love!
O gentle love!
Eternal fire!
You are that fire ever blazing,
O high, eternal Trinity!
You are direct
without any twisting,
genuine
without any duplicity,
open
without any pretense.
Turn the eye of your mercy on your creatures.
(pp. 61-62)

Leader: Let us pause and ponder the fire of God's love . . .

Reader 2: Eternal goodness,
you want me to gaze into you
and see that you love me,
to see that you love me gratuitously,
so that I may love everyone
with the very same love.
You want me, then,
to love and serve my neighbors gratuitously,
by helping them
spiritually and materially
as much as I can. (p. 71)

Leader: Let us pause and ponder the fire of our love for others . . .

Reader 3: You want us to serve you
in your way,
eternal Father,
and you guide your servants in different ways
along different paths.
And so today you show us
that we neither may nor can in any way judge
what is within a person
by the actions we see. (p. 62)

Leader: Let us pause and ponder the unique beauty of all people . . .

Excerpted from Mary O'Driscoll, OP, ed. *Catherine of Siena: Selected Spiritual Writings.*

▶Review

1. What is a jubilee year? When was the first jubilee year held?

2. To what does the term *Babylonian Captivity of the Papacy* refer?

3. What action by the majority of cardinals at the time brought on the Great Western Schism? How was the Great Western Schism resolved?

4. What position on Church authority is held by conciliarism?

5. What was the impact of the plague on Church structures and religious life?

6. What role does mysticism play in religion?

7. Describe Meister Eckhart's negative theology.

8. How did Julian use the image of a hazelnut to describe her relationship with God?

9. What was the Union of Florence? Why did it fail to hold?

10. How and when did the Roman Empire end?

11. How did Isabella and Ferdinand go about ensuring the Christianization of their nation?

12. What and when was the Renaissance?

13. Who is the model for the "Renaissance man"?

14. What two positions did John Wyclif hold that would later be advocated by Protestants?

15. What was the focus of the sermons of John Hus?

▶Key Words

anti-pope (p. 165) Someone who falsely claims to be pope.

Babylonian Captivity of the Papacy (p. 160) Period during which the pope resided in Avignon in the Kingdom of Naples.

Black Death (p. 158) Popular name for the bubonic plague, so named because body parts turned black from lack of blood.

conciliarism (p. 164) Belief that Church councils have greater authority than the pope.

conversos **(p. 174)** Jews and Muslims who converted to Christianity, either willingly or unwillingly, following the Christian takeover of Spain.

Great Western Schism (p. 163) The period from 1378 to 1417 during which two and then three rival people claimed papal authority.

humanism (p. 175) During the Renaissance, an emphasis on the human in intellectual and artistic activity.

interdict (p. 177) Prohibition against celebrating sacraments in a particular area.

jubilee year (p. 158) A special year of prayer and pilgrimage in the Catholic Church that takes place every fifty years; also called a holy year.

La Pietà **(p. 176)** Michelangelo's statue of Mary holding the crucified Jesus.

mysticism (p. 168) Knowledge of God through experience; an intense experience of communion with God.

negative theology (p. 169) Belief that God can never be known by the intellect alone.

papal bull (p. 159) A formal decree by a pope sealed with a round leaden seal (in Latin, *bulla*).

showings (p. 170) Julian of Norwich's term for her mystical encounters with Christ.

Spanish Inquisition (p. 173) The process in Spain for identifying and punishing suspicious non-Christians and those said to be heretics.

Union of Florence (p. 172) A short-lived agreement between leaders of Eastern and Western Christianity on certain doctrines of faith.

Yesterday and Today

As the Church moved out of the Middle Ages, it faced many political challenges—including challenges to the papacy itself. The center of power in Eastern Christianity shifted northward to Russia. In the West, people were identifying more and more with their particular national group. Meanwhile, Church leaders and many members did what they could to help the people of Europe as they suffered through the onslaught of the plague. Some Christians provided solace to others by conveying a message of God's loving concern, which they received during mystical encounters with Christ.

Finally, Europe underwent a Renaissance that combined Christian themes with classical Greek concepts in a marriage that gave birth to some of the greatest artistic masterpieces ever produced. The Renaissance offered a vision of beauty and hope. The Church was a major advocate of that vision. However, Christianity in the West was entering another phase. As has always been the case, new situations call for new responses. The question now before the Church was: Would the response be reform or revolt?

TIMELINE

A.D. 1521
Emperor Charles V
and Diet of Worms find
Luther guilty of heresy

A.D. 1509
Henry VIII becomes king
of England

A.D. 1517
Martin Luther issues
his *Ninety-Five Theses*

A.D. 1521
Pope Leo X
excommunicates
Luther

A.D. 1525-1526
Peasants' Revolt
takes place

CHAPTER 7

CHALLENGE AND RESPONSE

THE CHURCH IN DISUNITY

A.D. 1500-1600

CHAPTER GOALS

In this chapter you will:

★ see how controversy led to a split within Western Christianity.

★ consider the Protestant theology that emerged, which differed from traditional Catholic beliefs and teachings.

★ learn that the Council of Trent clarified Catholic teaching and initiated reforms.

★ explore how new religious orders and the dedication of many Catholics helped set new directions for the Catholic Church.

A.D. 1533
English parliament declares King Henry VIII head of the Church in England

A.D. 1545-1563
Council of Trent brings reform

A.D. 1562
Saint Teresa of Ávila establishes Discalced Carmelites

A.D. 1529
Second Diet of Speyer reverses earlier concessions

A.D. 1540
Pope approves Society of Jesus (the Jesuits)

A.D. 1541
John Calvin institutes Presbyterian theocracy in Geneva, Switzerland

A.D. 1555
Peace of Augsburg

A.D. 1598
Edict of Nantes grants Protestants some rights in France

The Protestant Reformation

FIRST THOUGHTS

Consider what you would do if you disagreed strongly with certain policies and practices of your school or an organization or team to which you belong.

★ What actions would you take?

★ Can you imagine feeling so strongly about policies that you would take actions that could lead to your being expelled or dismissed?

★ Explain why you would or would not take such actions.

Have you ever been in a relationship in which tensions simmered for a long time? If your bad feelings toward someone lingered and then you actually confronted the person, you might have ended up saying things and doing things that went far beyond your original intent. Your words most likely would have caused the two of you to harbor anger and distrust afterward. Sometimes others might get involved in the disagreement, and make matters even worse.

The sixteenth century brought this type of severing of relationships within Christianity. A number of conditions existed that caused the Protestant Reformation. Once sparks were ignited, the fire spread throughout Western Europe. By mid-century, a united Christianity no longer existed. At this time, being Catholic meant not being Protestant; however, the majority of Europeans remained in the Catholic Church. In response to the Protestant Reformation, the Catholic Church clarified her own principles of belief and established her own agenda for reform. By the end of the century, Catholicism was a renewed Church. However, the anguish of a divided Christianity remains to this day.

Protestantism Develops

The **Reformation** refers to a series of events that took place primarily during the first half of the sixteenth century. The outcome of these events was, in fact, more than a reform. It was a completely different political and religious landscape of Western Europe. At the beginning of the century, all people in Western Europe who called themselves Christian belonged to the same Church: the Catholic Church. Indeed, they couldn't imagine things being otherwise. But by mid-century, some Christians disagreed with numerous fundamentals of the faith. In time, they were named Protestants and their religious practices, Protestantism.

At the beginning of the century, an emperor—at least in name—ruled much of Western Europe. By mid-century, Europe had become deeply divided politically and religiously. At the beginning of the century, Church-affiliated groups owned over half of the land on the continent. By mid-century most of that land had been taken over by non-religious leaders. What precipitated this remarkable transformation? It began with a longstanding debate over indulgences, but also included dissent over the Church's core theological teachings, such as the nature of Christ's presence in the sacraments, especially the Eucharist.

Luther's Ninety-Five Theses On October 31, 1517, a German Augustinian friar wrote a local archbishop outlining his position on a number of theological issues. He never envisioned that his action would lead to a division in Christianity that has yet to be healed. Father Martin Luther included **ninety-five theses** in his letter to Archbishop Albrecht of Mainz. Luther sent copies to a number of other bishops as well.

Luther was a university professor and a priest. His immediate concern was what he considered a scandalous practice then occurring in his area. Archbishop Albrecht owed the pope a good deal of money because he sought appointment to head a third diocese. Albrecht already served as the head of two dioceses. (At the time a bishop was considered a secular leader, responsible for collecting taxes and for other secular matters, as well as a spiritual leader.) As was customary at the time, Albrecht's appointment to a third diocese would cost

!FYI

Popular legend has it that Luther posted his theses on the door of his church in Wittenberg. Although no solid historical evidence exists that he actually did this, today the doors of the church have Martin Luther's theses permanently inscribed in them.

money, since he stood to gain from revenues collected in the diocese. The pope granted the archbishop's representatives permission to collect money in exchange for **indulgences**—the reduction or elimination of temporal punishment for sins confessed and forgiven in the Sacrament of Penance and Reconcilitation—with the understanding that half of the money collected would be used for the construction of Saint Peter's Basilica in Rome.

This campaign needs to be understood in light of Catholic teaching on sin, the Sacrament of Penance and Reconciliation, and indulgences. In the Sacrament of Penance and Reconciliation, God forgives the truly sorry and contrite sinner for sins confessed. The forgiveness of grave or mortal sin brings the person back into communion and friendship with God, remitting the eternal punishment—separation from God forever—had the sin not been forgiven. However, mortal and venial sin reflects or results from an unhealthy attachment that needs to be purified while here on earth or in purgatory. This purification frees the person from the temporal punishment of sin. Purification through performing the Works of Mercy, prayer, and other charitable acts can help the person become more like Christ.

Purgatory, the root meaning of which is "cleansing," is a state of purification in which those who die in God's friendship can be cleansed or purified in order to enter the happiness of eternal life with God in heaven. Indulgences reduce or eliminate the time a person spends in purgatory as a result of sins committed. But indulgences do not stand alone. They are connected to the edicts of the Sacrament of Penance; sins have to be forgiven before a person can obtain an indulgence. One way to gain an indulgence, for oneself or for the souls in purgatory, is by contributing to a good cause.

During Luther's time, the campaign to help build Saint Peter's, the great basilica in Rome, was a good work in which preachers were encouraging people to participate. People who contributed financially to this cause then received certification from the pope himself that they gained a plenary (full) indulgence, that is, removal of all temporal punishment due to sin.

Luther was not the first person to recognize that some preachers misinterpreted, misunderstood, or misused the theology behind indulgences. However, the misunderstandings of some Church members did not diminish the validity of the Church's teaching on indulgences. A number of factors inflamed the controversy instigated by Archbishop Albrecht's campaign.

- Money and taxation (as opposed to land) were growing in importance. This campaign meant taking money out of Germany and sending it to Rome at a time when people were beginning to identify more and more with their own nation.

- Many were irritated that the money was going to leaders in Rome whom they perceived to be corrupt.

- And thanks to the printing press, an invention at the time only decades old, Luther's message questioning the spread of indulgences throughout Europe proliferated. It resonated with the misconceptions that many people had.

Archbishop Albrecht wrote the pope about Luther and his teachings. In August of 1518, the pope sent a representative to meet with Luther in Augsburg, Germany. The representative had public meetings with Luther, but Luther did not retract his teachings on indulgences or the Church's sacramental system. The pope's representative had no interest in debating Luther. Instead, he simply condemned Luther for questioning the pope's authority.

FAITH ACTIVITY

Conversion Christ continues to call each of us to conversion, to turn from what keeps us from following him and to be transformed by grace. Jesus calls for a conversion of heart. Write about some things you need to change or "cleanse" in your own life—priorities, thoughts, actions, feelings, relationships—so that you can better accept and share God's love.

Luther on Indulgences Luther believed that if the pope knew how Church teaching on indulgences was being manipulated and abused, the pope would condemn the money-raising campaign then underway. Here are some of the ninety-five theses that explain Luther's position.

> 21. Hence those who preach indulgences are in error when they say that a man is absolved and saved from every penalty by the pope's indulgences.
>
> 24. It must therefore be the case that the major part of the people are deceived by that indiscriminate and high-sounding promise of relief from penalty.
>
> 27. There is no divine authority for preaching that the soul flies out of purgatory immediately when the money clinks in the bottom of the chest.
>
> 28. It is certainly possible that when the money clinks in the bottom of the chest, avarice and greed increase; but when the church offers intercession, all depends on the will of God.
>
> 32. All those who believe themselves certain of their own salvation by means of letters of indulgence will be eternally damned, together with their teachers.
>
> 36. Any Christian whatsoever, who is truly repentant, enjoys plenary remission from penalty and guilt, and this is given him without letters of indulgence.
>
> 38. Yet the pope's remission and dispensation are in no way to be despised, for, as already said, they proclaim the divine remission.
>
> 42. Christians should be taught that the pope does not at all intend that the purchase of indulgences should be understood as at all comparable with works of mercy.
>
> 43. Christians should be taught that one who gives to the poor, or lends to the needy, does a better action than if he purchases indulgences.
>
> 91. If, therefore, indulgences were preached in accordance with the spirit and mind of the pope, all these difficulties would be easily overcome, and, indeed, cease to exist.

John Dillenberger, Martin Luther: Selections from His Writings,
pp. 492–500

Church Teaching on Indulgences Church teaching on indulgences must be considered in connection with the Sacrament of Penance and in light of another Catholic teaching—the **communion of saints**, all the faithful Church members on earth, in heaven, and in purgatory; the term refers to communion in holy things and among holy people.

> In the communion of saints, 'a perennial link of charity exists between the faithful who have already reached their heavenly home, those who are expiating their sins in purgatory and those who are still pilgrims on earth. Between them there is, too, an abundant exchange of all good things.'[1] In this wonderful exchange, the holiness of one profits others, well beyond the harm that the sin of one could cause others. Thus recourse to the communion of saints lets the contrite sinner be more promptly and efficaciously purified of the punishments for sin.

Catechism of the Catholic Church, #1475

▼ *Virgin and Saints* by Bartholomeus Bruyn the Elder.

In other words, Catholic teaching about indulgences rests upon the connections that exist between the faithful of the past and present and that these connections are dynamic and beneficial. We might wonder: How can we ever make amends for harm we have done? The concept of indulgences points out that Jesus' saving work has endless value and merit for us before God the Father. What Christ accomplished for us makes it possible for us to have the hope of new life. And this "treasury of merit" also includes the prayers and good works of Mary, the greatest among the saints, and all the other saints whose holiness can benefit us. This treasury is available through the Church to those of us who are seeking to make good, having in the Sacrament of Penance and Reconciliation admitted our wrongdoing and expressed sincere sorrow for our sins. Church teaching on indulgences is not meant to let us off the hook when it comes to straightening out our lives. However, it does remind us that we are not alone in our quest to turn our lives around. The work of Christ and holiness of Mary and the saints brings us untold benefits.

GROUP TALK

1. What are some ways Church members connect to the holy people who have gone before us?

2. Why do you think it's important to pray for those who have died?

3. What "holy things" do you hope to be remembered for once you are gone?

The Break with Catholicism

While the pope and Church leaders focused on other matters after this initial condemnation of Luther's ideas, Luther spent the next few years refining his theological position. His ideas grew in popularity. Generally, Vatican officials saw the matter as a debate between two religious orders—the Augustinians (Luther) and the Dominicans (Fr. John Tetzel being one of the main preachers of indulgences). Many German peasants believed that Luther and his ideas supported their cause against oppressive land-owners. As you can see, many people turned to Luther not necessarily for religious reasons, but for political ones. Finally, in 1520 Pope Leo X issued a papal bull, *Exsurge Domine*, excommunicating Luther unless he retracted his beliefs, which countered key Catholic principles on the primacy of Tradition, free will, and the ministerial priesthood. On December 10, 1520, Luther gathered together students from the University of Wittenberg where he taught, built a bonfire outside of the town, and burned the papal letter. On January 3, 1521, in the papal bull *Decet Romanum Pontificem*, Pope Leo formally excommunicated Luther.

The next step after excommunication was for secular authorities, in this case Emperor Charles V, to deal with Luther as an outlaw. Luther appeared before the emperor at a gathering called the **Diet of Worms**, but he would not recant his heretical teachings.

The emperor signed the Edict of Worms in May 1521, declaring Luther a heretic who could be punished by death. However, before Luther could be arrested, Duke Frederick had Luther "kidnapped" and taken to his castle in Wartburg to protect him from harm. Luther stayed there for over a year, working on a translation of the Bible into German and refining his theology. Meanwhile, other people were using Luther's ideas to back up their grievances, taking his ideas in directions that Luther himself would consider heretical.

FAITH ACTIVITY

Theological Debate Luther initially wanted to debate teachings *within* the Church—not to *dissent from* Church teachings.

★ Identify one practice or teaching currently being debated within the Catholic Church.

★ Describe your understanding of the teaching and the questions you have about the teaching.

★ Find out what the official Church teaching is by researching official documents and then talk about why you think the Church holds this teaching.

Peasants' Revolt A number of revolts by peasants had taken place before Luther's time, but now German peasants saw an opportunity to use religious backing in their call for justice. At first Luther supported the peasants. But after the German princes killed thousands of their number, the peasants retaliated by murdering and plundering in indiscriminate fashion. Luther rejected these actions of the peasants and encouraged the princes to use whatever means necessary to restore order. In all, more than 130,000 German peasants were killed during this period of the **Peasants' Revolt**. After this rejection by Luther, most peasants either rejoined the Catholic Church or joined one of the more radical Protestant groups.

The first Diet of Speyer, in 1526, allowed each prince of the Holy Roman Empire to determine the religion of his territory. Some German princes ended up aligning themselves with Luther, while others aligned themselves with Catholicism. In 1529 the emperor called the second Diet of Speyer, which led to the reversal of earlier concessions. Some of the Catholic representatives also called for carrying out the earlier prosecution of Luther as a heretic. Lutheran princes protested these decisions, thus receiving the name *Protestants*. This name became the popular designation for those groups in Europe who rejected Catholicism, though often non-Lutherans are called Reformed Churches.

▼ *Martin Luther* by Lucas Cranach the Elder.

Sacrament of Unity

The separation of Christians into Catholics and Protestants in the sixteenth century was a shocking development in the Church. The Catholic Church teaches that non-Catholic Christians who have been baptized are in "a certain, although imperfect, communion with the Catholic Church" (*CCC*, #838). As we will see, Vatican Council II in the 1960s expressed the continued desire among Catholic leaders for unity among all Christians. In the *Constitution on the Church*, the Council stated: "All those, who in faith look towards Jesus, the author of salvation and the principle of unity and peace, God has gathered together and established as the Church, that it may be for each and everyone the visible sacrament of this saving unity" (#9). Since the Council, animosity between Catholicism and most Protestant groups has significantly diminished. In 1993, Pope John Paul II met with Billy Graham, the most famous Protestant evangelical pastor in the world at the time, and called him a "brother." When John Paul II died in 2005, Billy Graham praised him as "the greatest Christian witness of the second half of the twentieth century."

Over the next few decades, a number of attempts at reunion were made and failed. Finally, in 1555 the emperor reluctantly approved a decision made by the imperial assembly, a decision called the **Peace of Augsburg**. According to this decree, the prince or king of each state could select either Catholicism or Lutheranism as the official religion for his territory. It forbade all sects of Protestantism other than Lutheranism and ordered all Catholic bishops to give up their property if they turned Lutheran. This agreement is known in Latin as *cuius regio, eius religio*. That is, the ruler under which people live determines their religion. People who didn't want to join the local official religion could move to a state where their religion was approved. In less than forty years, Luther's dismissal of Church teaching had become the basis for a state-supported religion separate from Catholicism.

Spread of Protestantism

To appreciate conflicts that the Church will face later, we need to understand the Reformation, the spread of Protestantism, and the differences and similarities between Protestantism and Catholicism.

The Reformation in France and Spain

During the sixteenth century, France had the same problems that other countries did. However, Protestantism never made the inroads into France that it made in the northern European countries.

- Ever since the Avignon papacy in 1378, France had maintained greater control over internal Church affairs than other countries had.

- Another reason for the weak Protestant stance was that Catholic scholars at France's great universities negated Protestant ideas early on.

French Protestants, known as **Huguenots** (meaning "oath comrades" asserting their independence from the Church), did gather strength over the course of the sixteenth century. And even the first Bourbon king of France, Henry IV (1589–1619), flirted with Protestantism for a while until he realized that the lower classes had mostly remained staunchly Catholic and that he needed their support. Henry then reconverted to Catholicism saying, "Paris is worth a Mass." But it's important to keep these politically based faith decisions in perspective; many French chose to practice Catholicism based upon what they truly believed and wanted to practice.

In 1598, Henry promulgated the **Edict of Nantes**, by which Huguenots were allowed to build churches and hold religious services in specified villages in France. This edict ended a series of religious wars between Catholics and Protestants that had ravaged France from 1562 to 1598. Although the Protestant movement diminished greatly in France, the Protestant-Catholic conflicts created among many French people a critical attitude toward Church leaders, an attitude that has remained strong into modern times.

GROUP TALK

Henry IV of France allowed the Huguenots to build churches of their own in France.

1 In small groups, list one country today where groups of different religious or ethnic backgrounds are having difficulty living together as one nation.

2 Give the history of the problems as you know them and discuss possible solutions.

For the most part, Spain also avoided Protestant influence. This was due largely to three factors.

- First, in the late 1400s, Queen Isabella herself instigated reforms in the Church. These reforms were not related to Church teaching but to corruption and abuses by Church leaders.

- Second, the Inquisition held heresy in check with the threat of force.

- Third, a number of exceptional figures who emerged in Spain and Portugal during the Reformation helped restore the Church to a more intense spiritual life.

King Henry VIII and the Anglican Church

The position of King of England fell to Henry VIII only after his older brother died. Barely a teenager, Henry was betrothed to his brother's eighteen-year-old widow, Catherine of Aragon. They were married a few years later. Henry became king in 1509 at the age of eighteen. A devoted Catholic, Henry in 1521 wrote a pamphlet against Luther and Protestantism. In response the pope gave Henry the special title, "Defender of the Faith."

FYI

The Church of England, also known as the Anglican Church, or in the United States as the Episcopal Church, does not accept the oversight of the pope. Some branches of the Anglican or Episcopal Church have in time become more Protestant in spirit and practice. However, many similarities remain between the worship and creeds of the Catholics and Anglicans.

Although Henry and Catherine had a number of children, only one, a daughter named Mary, lived past infancy. Mary became betrothed to the heir to the French throne. Since Henry did not believe a woman could rule, if Henry had no other children and had this wedding taken place, the king of France (Mary's husband) might become king of England as well. Such a state of affairs would be totally unacceptable to the English. Henry petitioned the pope to have his marriage to Catherine annulled so that he could, hopefully, have male children with another wife. For a number of reasons, some of which could be interpreted as political, the pope's representative refused to grant the annulment. In 1533, Henry called upon the English parliament to declare that he was not responsible to any foreign powers. In effect, parliament proclaimed the king head of the Church in England. This constituted a break with the pope and the Catholic Church.

Initially, the English Reformation was based largely upon the Church's teachings on the dignity of marriage and ultimately its stance on divorce and annulments. Henry did not see this separation from Rome as a move in the direction of Protestantism. For the most part he wanted to keep Church practices as they had been, but not under the leadership of the pope in Rome.

Once he declared himself head of the Church in England, Henry VIII took over all monastery lands and divided the lands up among his most loyal subjects. During the reign of Henry VIII's second daughter, Queen Elizabeth I, the Church of England became more Protestant. Many English people who remained Catholic were killed or persecuted during Elizabeth's reign. One group of English Protestants wanted to "purify" the English Church even further by ridding the Church of all Catholic trappings. However, they, too, were suppressed and eventually made their way to America where we know them as the Puritans.

FAITH ACTIVITY

Protestant Groups Write a report on one of the following groups who emerged during or shortly after the Reformation period: Anabaptists, Methodists, Quakers, or Presbyterians. Give some examples of how they are similiar to and different from Catholics.

◀ *Henry VIII* by Joos van Cleve.

Heroes of the Reformation

During any time of crisis, heroes emerge. They can be people who hold to their principles in the face of personal risk or who seek common ground among conflicting parties. Depending on your point of view, many leaders who held a variety of positions on the debates of the time would qualify as heroes. Here are two prominent figures from the time who deserve consideration.

▼ Thomas More

Erasmus—The Great Humanist (1466-1536)

Erasmus was a Dutch monk who was perhaps the greatest humanist thinker of his time. Erasmus remained a faithful Catholic while constantly calling for reform. He wanted a reformation without violence and debate without animosity. He constantly called upon people to conduct themselves toward others as Christ would want them to do: How can you say "Our" Father if you plunge steel into the guts of your brother?

Thomas More—Martyr of Conscience (1478-1535)

A Catholic layman and a friend of Erasmus, Thomas More was appointed chancellor of England in the midst of King Henry VIII's battle with the pope over seeking to have his first marriage annulled. After Henry declared himself head of the Church in England, he called upon significant English subjects to sign a statement to that effect. Thomas refused to sign the oath and was imprisoned. After a trial in which he was falsely accused, More was sentenced to be beheaded. Once he was condemned, More explained that a temporal ruler had no right to declare himself head of the Church. For remaining true to his beliefs, More was beheaded. His dying words were, "I die as the king's true servant, but God's first." Thomas More is a saint of the Catholic Church and patron of lawyers.

Two Protestant Reformers

In many ways Luther had more in common theologically with Catholicism than with many of the other Protestant leaders during the Reformation period. Ulrich Zwingli (1484–1531) had introduced Reformation ideas into Switzerland even before Luther issued his ninety-five theses in Germany. Zwingli advocated Scripture as the sole source of truth and denied that Church leaders had special authority to interpret Scripture. He also criticized corruption among Church leaders and asked for the right of priests to marry. Based in Zurich and with the support of a council of elders, Zwingli came to rule both Church and state in Switzerland. Switzerland became a **theocracy** in which Church and state were united. More specifically, in a theocracy, the religious leaders make the rules governing all aspects of society because they are seen as divinely guided.

In Switzerland, Zwingli decided what beliefs were acceptable and what beliefs were not. His rejection of traditional Catholic teachings went beyond Luther's. For instance, in 1529 he and Luther met to discuss their theologies. Zwingli suggested that the Eucharistic words, "This is my body," should be interpreted spiritually. Luther pointed out that the biblical text states clearly and precisely that Jesus said, "This is my body." Luther believed that the meaning of this phrase should not be spiritualized. Although he understood it somewhat differently than Catholicism did, Luther held to a belief in the real presence of Christ in the Eucharist; Catholic teaching upholds that Jesus is truly, really, and physically present in the Eucharist. Thus, Zwingli and others took the Protestant movement further away from Catholicism than Luther intended or wanted. Their more radical expression of Protestantism came to be known as Reformed Christianity.

The leader of the Reformed movement who had the greatest impact on Protestantism was John Calvin (1509–1564). French by birth but drawn to the Reformed expression of Christianity in Switzerland, Calvin made his way to Geneva where his writings served as a model for governance of the city. A group of elders, or presbyters, decided all matters, both religious and secular. This **Presbyterian** form of Church leadership continues to be followed by many Protestant communities today. Calvin based all laws on the Bible. However, people were not to interpret the Bible for themselves, but were required to accept what the clergy and the ruling presbyters decreed the Bible to mean. Calvin and his successors in Geneva focused on discipline as a mark of the Presbyterian Church.

FAITH ACTIVITY

Image of God Calvin viewed God primarily as a judge. Our Catholic heritage, from Scripture forward, gives us a rich variety of images for God. Draw or write a description of your image of God when you were younger and your image now.

One belief that Calvin held was **predestination**. That is, people are destined by God for either eternal salvation or eternal damnation. Only a select few are saved. A person doesn't know whether he or she is counted among the saved, but good indications are that the person lives a morally upright life and is an industrious member of society. As we will see, this concept is not based in the Catholic Tradition nor is it a belief that Catholics profess. Calvin's message appealed to the growing middle class of northern Europe. John Knox introduced Presbyterianism to Scotland, where it became the dominant version of Christianity.

Differences in Teachings

Political and economic factors contributed greatly to the Reformation. However, Protestantism opposed major truths of the faith that had been part of Church belief and practices for centuries. While the message and life of faith have not changed, how the Church expresses her message and responds to the cultures of the time have evolved. Protestant dissent tended to focus on three theological principles addressed in the following sections.

Scripture and Tradition or Scripture Alone?

As the documents of Vatican II remind us, "Sacred Tradition and Sacred Scripture make up a single deposit of the Word of God" (*Dei Verbum*, 10). Both Scripture and Tradition find their source in God, thus being one sacred deposit coming from and pointing toward the same God. Both are to be accepted and honored equally as the word of God. The Holy Spirit did not abandon the Christian Church after Pentecost. Catholicism recognizes that the Bible plays a central role in determining truth for Christians—it is the inspired word of God. However, it is also important to see that the Church itself is divinely inspired. Therefore, under the continuing guidance of the Holy Spirit, the Church has interpreted and applied God's word in the ever-changing historical circumstances in which the Church has found itself. This living and authentic transmission of Jesus' teachings in the Church is evidenced in our creeds, liturgy, institutions, councils, and more.

Luther rejected this fundamental teaching for *sola scriptura*—that Scripture alone is the source of divine revelation and truth. In this view, the Bible alone is the infallible, divinely inspired source of truth. Christians must always return only to Scripture for guidance in the spiritual life. In Luther's perspective—and that of most reformers—Scripture alone is the authority for the Christian life.

However, as our study has indicated, the life of the Church did not happen outside of particular times and circumstance. The Church has never existed apart from historical realities within and around her. The living witness of the Church is that she passes down to each generation all that she believes through doctrines, liturgy, and life. The Church has always faced conflicts, and Church leaders have always made decisions in response to those conflicts. Recall that as early as twenty years after the death of Jesus, Church leaders hotly debated whether or not to accept non-Jews into the Christian community. Had Peter and the Apostles rejected the Holy Spirit's guidance and decided differently, it would have had a great impact on how the Church developed. Recall also that Church leaders even determined what was to be accepted as divinely inspired Scripture and what was not. In other words, the very instrument that Protestants look to as source of truth and divine revelation—Scripture—cannot be separated from the divinely inspired Church.

Therefore, *Scripture and Tradition together are the basis for truth*. From the earliest years of the Church, leaders and believers have relied on the Holy Spirit's divine inspiration in proclaiming and following Christ's message.

GROUP TALK

1 What are some ways Tradition helps us understand Scripture better?

2 What are some ways that the living Tradition of the Church helps us respond to what's happening in our personal lives as well as in our communities and the world?

Faith and Good Works or Faith Alone?

For Luther, God gives, and humans receive. Luther's perspective is that on their own, humans can do nothing to bring about their salvation. Being saved is a totally free gift from God, merited by Jesus Christ's sacrifice on the cross. If humans could do anything to merit this gift, it would no longer be a gift. Therefore, humans can do nothing but have faith in God. Even faith itself is a gift. This complete trust that God takes sinful humans and makes them righteous, or just, in his eyes is known as **justification by faith**. By refusing to acknowledge the human response to faith and acceptance of grace, the principle tenet of free will is undermined. The issue of justification and righteousness has been at the heart of Christianity since Saint Paul wrote his numerous letters to the early Church communities, letters that later became part of the New Testament.

Luther's viewpoint could be interpreted to mean that human beings should do nothing but passively accept God's grace. For instance, by wrongly interpreting Luther, one could suggest that it doesn't matter that one person commits horrible sins while another leads an outstanding life. Both are "justified," or cleansed from sin, returned to the original state of holiness for which humans were created. The Catholic teaching on justification is that Christ earned it for us through his suffering, death, and Resurrection, and by justification we are offered the gift of eternal life. While it is a free gift totally unmerited by anything we can do, we must respond in faith, turning away from sin and toward God. And, while faith is a gift from God, it is also a free, human act; so, we are prompted by the grace of the Holy Spirit to accept that gift, but we still must make the choice, believe, and respond. So, we are not passive recipients of God's grace but instead participate in the action of salvation.

Also, faith is not just a matter between an individual and God. Rather, people stand before God as members of a community. The Church and sacraments play a vital role in the faith life of Catholics, including our justification, for it is through Baptism that we are joined to Christ's death and Resurrection and thus are justified. So, we do not merit this initial gift of grace, but we do cooperate with it by the way we live our lives. If we respond to God's grace and prompting, we can then earn (merit) the grace needed to continue to be holy and to achieve eternal life with God.

Recently, Lutheran and Catholic scholars examined the teachings on justification in their two traditions and determined that the differences need not divide them. Furthermore, the Roman Catholic Church and the Lutheran World Federation released a solemn agreed statement known as the *Joint Declaration on the Doctrine of Justification* on October 31, 1999.

FAITH ACTIVITY

Justification by Faith Draw a set of scales. On one side of the scales, write "The suffering and death of Christ on the cross." On the other side of the scales, write "All the wrongdoing and sinfulness that exist in the world." Which side carries more weight? Why?

GROUP TALK

How would you describe the relationship between faith and good works?

Saint Margaret Clitherow (1555–1586)

During the Reformation, debates about religion became so heated that people representing every expression of Christianity died for their beliefs. For instance, in 1570 the pope declared that Queen Elizabeth, who sided with Protestantism, was not the rightful ruler of England and excommunicated her. Fearing a Catholic uprising in response to this proclamation, Elizabeth called for persecution of Catholics. Priests especially were targeted. The city of York had a particularly strong Catholic population. One woman, a butcher's wife named Margaret Clitherow, became a Catholic in 1574. Even though her husband attended the established Anglican Church, the couple built a "priest hole" in their home to hide priests who came to celebrate Mass in secret. The couple also sent their son to France to learn Catholicism in the English Catholic community in exile there.

In 1585, Margaret's husband, John, was questioned about the Catholic activities of his wife and son. The sheriff of York raided the home and discovered the secret room, Mass vestments, and sacred vessels hidden there. Margaret was arrested, and the court decided to make an example of her. Margaret refused to enter a plea, saying, "Having made no offense, I need no trial." By her silence she kept secret any information she had about the members of the Catholic community in York.

The judge tried to convince her to think of her husband and children. He warned her that her death would be slow and painful. Margaret remained silent. The judge ordered her to be "pressed to death." That is, a board was to be placed upon her and weights would be added over a period of three days after which a sharp stone would be placed behind her until the weight would cause the stone to pierce her heart. When Margaret still would make no plea, the judge decided to put the sharp stone under her on the first day. Margaret died within fifteen minutes. She was declared a saint and martyr in 1970.

The Ministerial Priesthood or the Priesthood of All Believers?

The Church herself is a sign and instrument of God's grace and work in the world. To be sacramental is to be a vehicle through which God acts, through which his presence is experienced, and through which his grace is granted. Thus, the Church is sacramental and our lives are sacramental, and we celebrate the seven sacraments given to us by Christ using material realities to convey God's presence and receive a share in his life.

Traditionally, Catholic churches would be more likely to have statues and paintings, candles and vigil lights, bells and incense, priests in vestments, and elaborate rituals than their Protestant neighbors' churches would. During the sixteenth century, Protestants took over church buildings and vastly simplified the décor inside them. They often destroyed statues and replaced elaborate altars with simple wooden tables. In fact, altars became less significant and pulpits, from which preachers preached, became much more significant. In general, Protestantism emphasized "word" and denied the sacrificial nature of the Eucharist. The written word (the Bible), the spoken word (the sermon), and the sung word (hymn singing) play a more prominent role in most Protestant services.

Most Protestant denominations celebrate only the two sacraments which they see as having clear Gospel mandates—Baptism and Eucharist. Catholicism continues to celebrate all of the sacraments and to emphasize the sacramental character of symbols and rituals in its liturgy. The words of the sacraments are as important as the actions and the elements—the bread, wine, water, and oil.

This sacramental understanding of Church relies on the role of the ordained priesthood. Luther, who was a priest, eventually married and had a number of children. He praised the Christian family as the ideal and minimized the need for a separate group of ordained priests. For Luther, a separate priesthood took away from the priesthood of all Christians. However, Catholicism clearly recognizes the significance of both the ministerial (ordained) priesthood and the common priesthood of the faithful, and the sharing of all baptized in the mission of Christ as priest, prophet, and king. Through the Sacrament of Holy Orders, baptized men are ordained to "serve in the name and in the person of Christ the Head in the midst of the community" (*CCC*, #1591). With regard to the liturgy, it is the whole Body of Christ—assembly, ordained priest, and Christ himself—who celebrate, for the liturgy is the participation of the people of God in the work of God.

FYI

While many differences exist in the ways Protestants and Catholics pray, the Lord's Prayer remains the quintessential Christian prayer of all those baptized in Christ. It summarizes the whole of Christ's Good News and reminds us that we can call God Father because Jesus revealed him to us as Father. With only minor differences, Christian communities around the world pray this prayer when they gather.

FAITH ACTIVITY

Representing Christ List the priests who have been part of the sacramental celebrations of your life. Find their addresses through a diocesan directory and send them a thank-you note for representing Christ to you through the sacraments.

In Catholicism, ordained priests serve an important function within the sacramental system and represent Christ to the people and the people before God the Father. In other words, those who are consecrated into ordained priesthood have the task "not only of representing Christ—Head of the Church—before the assembly of the faithful, but also of acting in the name of the whole Church when presenting to God the prayer of the Church, and above all when offering the Eucharistic sacrifice"[2] (*CCC*, #1552).

GROUP TALK

The *Catechism of the Catholic Church* states that "On entering the People of God through faith and Baptism, one receives a share in this people's unique, *priestly* vocation" (*CCC*, #784).

What are some ways Church members your age can exercise their priestly vocation?

A priest extnds his hands in ▶ the Sacrament of Penance and Reconciliation.

The Catholic Reformation

The second half of the sixteenth century was a period for reform within the Catholic Church herself. The event most closely associated with Catholic reform is the **Council of Trent**, which lasted off and on from 1545 to 1563 because of some military conflicts going on at the time. Over the course of these eighteen years, Church leaders clarified Catholic theological positions and also established norms for Church practices to curb real or perceived abuses among some of its members. In addition to the council, a second expression of Catholic reform was manifest through new religious orders and renewed spiritual life among Catholics.

The Council of Trent

Emperor Charles V proposed that a council be held on German soil in response to the Protestant Reformation. At the end of 1545, Pope Paul III convened a council in Trent, just over the Italian border in German territory. Many Church leaders were not exactly sure how to go about reforming the Church. Some wanted to address abuses; others wanted to clarify Catholic Church teaching to meet the Protestant challenges. Over the course of the eighteen years that the council was in session, both goals would be met.

One of the major reforms brought about by the council was the revitalization of the life of priests on all levels.

- The council instructed the pope to take special care in selecting cardinals since they performed such important functions within the Church. During the time of Trent, a number of cardinals were appointed who took active roles in Church reform.

- Bishops were instructed to reside in their diocese, to meet with their clergy regularly, and to visit the parishes in their diocese. Although this change did not occur immediately, over time Catholic bishops came to view their role more clearly as pastors of the people in their particular diocese.

- The council reaffirmed celibacy for priests in the West and notified priests not living a celibate life that they would lose their positions.

- Priests were also to wear distinctive garb so that they could be distinguished from lay people. Seminaries were to be instituted for the education and training of priests. If possible, candidates for priesthood were to begin seminary training at a very early age.

Regarding Church teaching, the council restated and clarified what had been longstanding Catholic teachings on all major doctrines. Clarifying authentic teachings in this way was itself a reforming step. As pointed out earlier, problems often arose because beliefs were misunderstood or misrepresented. For example, Luther found that some people viewed grace as something they gained as a result of actions they performed rather than as a free, unmerited gift from God. The idea of "gaining grace" is a misinterpretation of traditional teaching on the subject. Similarly, Christ's Real Presence in the Eucharist had always been a fact of Church teaching. As mentioned earlier, medieval theologians used concepts borrowed from Greek philosophy to explain this teaching. In doing so, some popular preachers described Christ's presence in the Eucharist in ways that were inaccurate, which led to reactions in opposite directions by other preachers.

The Council of Trent stated teachings in orderly and precise terms in order to correct misinterpretations of Catholic doctrine. For instance, since Protestants rejected private confession of sins, the Council of Trent specified rules for confession to a degree that had not existed previously. As recommended by the council, a catechism stating fundamental Catholic beliefs in precise terms was published in 1566. It was called the *Catechism of the Council of Trent*. It served as the official catechism of the Catholic Church until the *Catechism of the Catholic Church* was released in 1992.

In 1570, an official Roman Missal was published. A missal contains the words to be said and the gestures to be followed by the priest at Mass. Eventually, words to be said by the priest were written in black while directions for actions to be taken during Mass were printed in red and thus came to be known as *rubrics*, from the Latin word for red.

The council stated teachings in terms that made it clear it was responding to inaccuracies in teaching. For example, most Protestants accepted only two sacraments, Baptism and Eucharist, as having a firm basis in Scripture. By way of contrast the council said:

> If anyone says that the sacraments of the new law were not all instituted by Jesus Christ, or that there are more or less than seven, or that any of the seven is not truly and strictly speaking a sacrament, let them be anathema [cursed, banned].

Quoted in Jean Comby and Diarmaid MacCulloch,
How to Read Church History, Vol. 2, p. 27

GROUP TALK

Discuss the pros and cons of each of the following.

1 Religious brothers, nuns, and priests wearing distinctive clothing.

2 Boys who express an interest in becoming priests entering a seminary program as early as ninth grade.

3 Members of the assembly having a missalette in hand in order to follow along with the words and actions of the liturgy.

4 Catholic schools using a catechism in their religious education stating core Catholic beliefs.

Saint Charles Borromeo
(1538–1584)

Charles Borromeo was in his early twenties and not even a priest when his uncle, Pope Pius IV, made him a cardinal of the Church. Borromeo served his uncle as Secretary of State at the Vatican, was ordained a priest, and then spearheaded the call for reform during the last sessions of the Council of Trent—all while still in his twenties. During this time Borromeo was wounded by an assassin who was angry at his reform proposals. After the council, as bishop of Milan, Borromeo worked diligently to transform his diocese into the ideal that the council wanted the Church to be. When a famine struck the city, he oversaw the feeding of thousands of people every day. An outbreak of the plague also took place in Milan during his time as its bishop. He personally cared for plague victims and instructed all priests and religious of the region to do likewise.

Four hundred years later, during Vatican Council II, Pope Paul VI gave all the participating bishops a copy of the life of Charles Borromeo. Paul VI hoped that after Vatican II each bishop would return to his diocese to put into practice on a local level the vision of the council, just as Borromeo had done after Trent.

Catholic Spirituality

Even as Christianity was being torn apart by the Reformation, Catholicism was actually enjoying a golden age of spirituality. There were the Jesuits, and there were the mystics.

The Society of Jesus In 1521, while Luther was gaining followers in Germany, a young soldier from the Basque region of Spain lay recuperating in a castle after a cannonball had shattered his leg. He spent more than a year in the castle. His constant companions were two books—one on the life of Christ and the other a book on the lives of the saints. As a soldier, he was impressed with the courage and dedication of the saints that he read about. He decided that if and when he recovered, he would live the life of a saint himself.

Thus began the journey of a man, and a group of men, who would help prevent the further expansion of Protestantism in Europe, introduce Catholicism to people in distant lands, educate many of the best minds in Europe and eventually around the world, and greatly renew the spiritual life of Catholics on all levels.

Ignatius Loyola left the castle and began to live a life of extreme poverty and self-denial. During this time, he devised a system of **spiritual exercises** designed to help people overcome self-centeredness, encounter Christ on a personal level, and discern God's will for them. After this period of spiritual cleansing, Ignatius believed that his task was to go to the Holy Land and seek the conversion of Muslims to Christianity. After an initial trip to Jerusalem, he realized that he needed more education to accomplish his goal.

Ignatius spent the next eleven years in various universities. A group of young men gathered around him. Together they journeyed to Rome, intending to travel again to Muslim territory to seek converts. Once in Rome they realized that missionary work in the Holy Land was impossible. Therefore, Ignatius presented himself and his companions to the pope, intending to do whatever menial tasks the pope would choose for them. They presumed that the pope would want them to work among those who were poor and care for those who were sick in Rome, which they immediately began to do. However, the pope saw a different potential in this group who would dedicate themselves to carrying out his directives. He saw the group as a response to the Protestants, who were going about rejecting the pope and Church leadership at every turn. In 1540 the pope designated Ignatius's group to be not just another religious order but a new society—the Society of Jesus, or Jesuits.

FAITH ACTIVITY

Early Jesuits Write a report on one of the following early Jesuits: Francis Xavier, Peter Faber, Peter Canisius, Francis Borgia, Edmund Campion, or Aloysius Gonzaga. Be sure to include how the Jesuit is inspiring for Catholics today. Share your findings with your class.

Jesuit Meditation Read one of the following Gospel passages and imagine yourself actually present at the event. Describe the event in your own words and suggest possible questions or meanings that the passage presents to you. This activity is in the spirit of Jesuit meditation.

* John 3:1-21
* John 9:1-41
* Luke 4:14-21
* Matthew 15:21-28
* Matthew 26:26-30
* Luke 23:39-43
* John 13:1-15

Ignatius founded the Gregorian University in Rome and a German college designed to train priests to combat Protestantism. Within twenty-five years, more than a thousand Jesuits ran one hundred colleges in Europe and the New World. Their rigorous program of study, coupled with the Ignatian program of spiritual exercises, created an educated group of Catholics who could challenge the best Protestant minds and thus maintain authentic Catholic understanding and practice in other parts of Europe. Zeal for the faith among Jesuits led to many of them making their way to other continents where they spread the Catholic faith. Jesuits soon became outlawed in a number of countries, but they carried on their work in secret and continued to grow in numbers. The Jesuits played a major role in the Catholic Reformation and in making Catholicism a dynamic faith as it entered the modern world.

Jesuit Spirituality Based on the Spiritual Exercises

1. **Christ centered** – an ever-deepening relationship with Jesus in all parts of life

2. **Apostolic** – service in collaboration with God for the well-being of others

3. **Discerning** – individual and communal experiences which aid in choosing options that support and collaborate with God's action in the world

4. **Generous** – offering fairness and charity in response to others

5. **Fraternal** – companionship in service

6. **Spiritual integration** – finding God in all things

Richard P. McBrien, ed., *Encyclopedia of Catholicism*, p. 694

Two Catholic Visionaries

Saint Philip Neri—The "Second Apostle of Rome" (1515-1595)

Talk of the corruption that existed in Church circles during the Reformation can give the impression that such problems represented the entire life of the Church at the time. But this is far from the case. Quite a few models of saintliness lived an active spiritual life during this time. Someone who exemplified a unique expression of spirituality was Philip Neri. In his late teens, Philip left his uncle's business and went to Rome to dedicate himself to God's service. He formed a community of young men who met to discuss religious matters and to care for those who were sick or on pilgrimage to the city.

When people sought out this famous holy man, Philip would often respond in very playful ways. Once he greeted a group of guests while wearing a hat that was many sizes too small for his head. Another time he shaved off half of his beard. On one occasion, he was hearing confessions when a man came to him and confessed a long list of minor offenses. Philip said to the man that he was taking himself much too seriously and told him for his penance that he should walk around Rome for the day with a live chicken on his head. Philip's spirituality of playfulness and his celebration of God who delights in people, even in their foibles, make a pleasant contrast to the seriousness of the conflicts going on throughout the Christian world of the time.

Saint Angela Merici (c. 1470-1540)

Up until this time, religious life for women essentially meant entering a cloistered convent and living the monastic life. Angela Merici had the vision to create a whole new way for women to live the Christian life. In her hometown, she saw many poor girls in need of help. She felt that she was called to care for them and educate them. As often happens when good work is being done, other women joined Angela in her endeavors. Although they took the name "Ursulines," Angela didn't see her group as a new religious order. They didn't wear distinctive clothing, take vows, or live in convents. They were simply a group of women doing God's work.

Many people questioned this new way for women to live. However, Angela received approval for her community from the pope. Today, we are familiar with many religious communities of women and men who dedicate their lives to education, health care, and social work. It is important to remember that these communities exist because people like Angela Merici had the foresight to respond in creative ways to the needs of people they saw around them.

The Mystics The Catholic mystical tradition flourished during the Reformation period. Indeed, two of the greatest Catholic mystics of all time were the Spaniards Teresa of Ávila (1515–1582) and John of the Cross (1542–1591).

Teresa entered a bustling convent, only to find that the sisters there were not working diligently at pursuing spiritual development. She decided to found another convent where a simpler life and a more rigid expression of spiritual discipline would be the rule. To distinguish her group from a religious order known as the Carmelites she named them *discalced* Carmelites (meaning "without shoes"). Many women joined Teresa, and she traveled about founding many convents. She attained such a depth of spiritual experience that she was called before the Inquisition to explain her "visions." To answer their questions, Teresa wrote about her experiences. Her writings on the levels of spiritual development continue to inspire people today, and she is numbered among the Doctors of the Church for her contribution to explaining the Christian life.

Like Philip Neri, Teresa also exhibited a lighter side to her spirituality. One day, when the sisters were gathered for their community recreation, she entered the room dancing and playing castanets. She remarked, "God deliver us from sullen saints."

Under the guidance of Teresa, John of the Cross led the reform of the Carmelite order for men. His attempts at reforming the order met with such resistance that one group of monks locked him in a cell for months. His friend Teresa appealed to the king to have him released. Eventually, John managed to escape. Like Teresa, John reached the heights of mystical experience. Although no words can capture what exactly a mystical experience is like, John wrote with such inspiration about his experiences that his Spanish poems are recognized as some of the best ever written. John used sensual imagery to describe the relationship that occurs between the mystic and God. For example, in the following passage to explain his experience of God, he uses the image of a bride and groom united in marriage.

> Oh, how sweet Your presence will be to me. You Who are the supreme good! I must draw near You in silence and uncover my feet before You that You may be pleased to unite me to You in marriage (Ruth 3:7), and I will not rest until I rejoice in Your arms.

Alphonse Ruiz OCD, ed.,
The Prayers of John of the Cross, p. 20

For his exceptional writings, John of the Cross is also recognized as a Doctor of the Church.

FAITH ACTIVITY

God's Presence Slowly and meditatively read the following poem written by John of the Cross:

How gently and lovingly
You wake in my heart,
Where in secret You dwell alone;
And by Your sweet breathing,
Filled with good and glory,
How tenderly You swell my
heart with love!

The Prayers of John of the Cross, p. 38

Think about experiencing God's presence in your life. Write a paragraph, a poem, or song that expresses that experience.

Forty Hours Devotion

In reaction to the challenge to Catholic teaching of Christ's Real Presence in the Eucharist, in 1527 Saint Antonio Maria Zaccharia of Milan introduced a practice called Forty Hours devotion. A custom already existed that when a city faced a disaster, such as the plague or an attack by an enemy, the Blessed Sacrament would be taken from the tabernacle where it was kept for the sick and placed in a special container called a monstrance. People could then go to their church and pray before the exposed Host and petition God's help in their time of need. It was called Forty Hours because, in the Church of the Holy Sepulcher in Jerusalem, it was customary to place the Blessed Sacrament in a "tomb" from three o'clock in the afternoon on Good Friday until seven o'clock on Easter Sunday morning—forty hours. The faithful would spend that time in prayer before the tomb.

Many parishes continue this practice today. For forty hours the Blessed Sacrament is displayed on the altar, special services are held, and people come and pray in the church whenever they can during that period. Some parishes now even have a small chapel where the Blessed Sacrament is visibly displayed twenty-four hours a day, seven days a week. Individuals and groups commit themselves to spend an hour each week in the chapel so that the total time is covered. This practice is called Perpetual Adoration. Some Catholic schools also have designated times when the Blessed Sacrament is displayed in the school chapel, and students can sign up for a period of time to visit or simply stop in for prayer.

Gilded Copper Monstrance, c. 1460. ▶

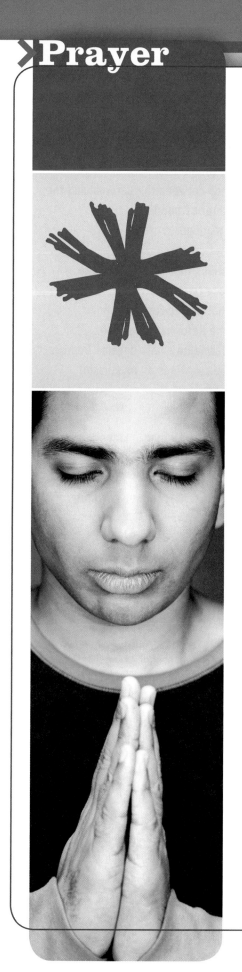

Praying with Saint Ignatius of Loyola

Leader: Let us pray together Saint Ignatius's prayer called the *Suscipe*:

All: Take, Lord, and receive all my liberty,

my memory, my understanding
and my entire will,
All I have and call my own.

You have given all to me.
To you, Lord, I return it.

Everything is yours; do with it what you will.
Give me only your love and your grace.
That is enough for me.

(Pause to reflect on God's gifts to you…)

Leader: Let us pray together Saint Ignatius's Prayer for Generosity:

All: Lord, teach me to be generous.
Teach me to serve you as you deserve;
to give and not to count the cost,
to fight and not to heed the wounds,
to toil and not to seek for rest,
to labor and not to ask for reward,
save that of knowing that I do your will.

(Pause to reflect on the virtue of generosity…)

Amen.

>Review

1. What happened at the Diet of Worms?
2. What decision was reached at the Peace of Augsburg assembly?
3. What action by Martin Luther led the way to the Reformation? What was he protesting?
4. Name three factors that helped inflame Luther's protest.
5. What is a Presbyterian form of leadership?
6. Give two reasons why Protestantism did not become strong in France.
7. Name three factors that helped keep Spain Catholic.
8. What title did the pope give King Henry VIII of England? Why?
9. What does the Protestant principle *sola scriptura* mean? What is the Catholic position on this principle?
10. Explain what justification by faith means in Catholicism and in Lutheranism.
11. What is the difference between the Catholic and the Lutheran position on priesthood?
12. What were the two main goals of the Council of Trent?
13. Name four contributions that Ignatius and the Society of Jesus made to Catholicism.
14. Name two groups that helped foster Catholic spirituality during the Reformation period.
15. What two Spanish Carmelite saints became Doctors of the Church for their writings on mysticism?

>Key Words

communion of saints (p. 189) All the faithful Church members on earth, in heaven, and in purgatory.

Council of Trent (p. 205) Post-Reformation meeting of the world's Catholic bishops to reform the Church and clarify Catholic teaching.

Diet of Worms (p. 190) Meeting of the leadership of the Holy Roman Empire during which Luther refused to recant his beliefs.

Edict of Nantes (p. 194) Document granting some rights to Huguenots.

***Exsurge Domine* and *Decet Romanum Pontificem* (p. 190)** Papal decrees excommunicating Martin Luther.

Huguenots (p. 193) Members of the French Reformed community.

indulgences (p. 186) The remission of temporal punishment resulting from sin for oneself and also for the souls in purgatory.

justification by faith (p. 200) God's gracious act of rendering a sinful human to be holy and endowed with grace (in Catholic and Orthodox doctrines) or as acceptable to God (Lutheran).

ninety-five theses (p. 185) Martin Luther's statement of principles regarding penance and the abuse of indulgences.

Peace of Augsburg (p. 192) Allowed each prince to decide the religion of his subjects.

Peasants' Revolt (p. 191) A series of uprisings by German peasants against their landowners.

predestination (p. 198) Belief that God has selected some people for hell and others for heaven regardless of any personal actions or merit.

Presbyterian (p. 197) A Protestant Christian religion characterized by governance by a group of elders and traditionally Calvinistic in doctrine.

Reformation (p. 185) A series of political and religious events beginning in the sixteenth century that resulted in the division of Western Christianity into Catholic and Protestant communities.

sola scriptura (p. 199) Belief that the Bible is the sole source of religious truth.

spiritual exercises (p. 209) A thirty-day program of spiritual practices developed by Saint Ignatius Loyola.

theocracy (p. 197) Form of government in which religious leaders are the secular leaders as well.

Yesterday and Today

Even though in 1500 many people in Europe saw the need for changes in Church practices, no one would have predicted the extent of change that was to take place over the next one hundred years. No one would have predicted that by the end of the century, groups of European Christians would no longer view themselves as members of the one, holy, catholic Church. During the middle and latter half of the century the Catholic Church did reform herself and clarified her teachings. Following this unfortunate split in Christianity, Catholics continued to find ways to experience Christ and to live out their relationship with Christ. Unfortunately, as we will see, both Catholics and Protestants suffered because of their battles with each other. After the period of the Reformation, many people in Europe would decide that they no longer needed any religion to guide their lives or to give their lives meaning. In other words, once again the Church would find herself seeking to remain faithful to Christ on a new battleground.

▼ *Adoration of the Trinity*
by Francesco Bassano.

TIMELINE

A.D. 1615
Roman Inquisition
condemns Galileo

A.D. 1618
Thirty Years' War
begins

A.D. 1648
Peace of
Westphalia ends
Thirty Years' War

A.D. 1650
Death of
Descartes

A.D. 1682
King Louis XIV issues
Gallican Articles

CHAPTER 8

SACRED OR SECULAR

RATIONALISM CONFRONTS THE CATHOLIC CHURCH

A.D. 1600-1870

CHAPTER GOALS

In this chapter you will:

★ see how the Enlightenment presented new challenges for members of the Catholic Church.

★ explore how political changes in Europe affected the way Catholics viewed the role of their Church.

★ consider the changing role of the Church in England and Ireland.

★ learn about dedicated Catholics who gave themselves to new ways of living the Christian life.

| A.D. **1793** Reign of Terror begins | | A.D. **1833** Oxford Movement in England | | A.D. **1858** Bernadette of Lourdes | A.D. **1869-1870** Vatican Council I |

| A.D. **1773** Suppression of the Jesuits | A.D. **1789** French Revolution | A.D. **1804** Reign of Napoleon begins | A.D. **1814** Congress of Vienna | A.D. **1846** Election of Pope Pius IX | A.D. **1870** End of the Papal States |

The Church and Science

FIRST THOUGHTS

Imagine that your school is sponsoring a panel discussion with Church leaders and renowned scientists who will address the following questions: What can the Catholic Church offer science? What can science offer the Catholic Church?

★ If you were the moderator of the panel, what questions would you ask of the various panel members?

★ If you were one of the scientists, what points about the topic would you want to make?

★ If you were a Catholic Church leader, what points about the topic would you want to make?

If, on the evening news you heard that a new galaxy had been discovered or that a cure had been found for a deadly disease, would you be surprised? Probably not. You were born during a century when over three-quarters of the machines now in use were invented. You may accept that new discoveries are part of life and that things go out of fashion and become obsolete quickly. Change is the one constant.

However, for seventeenth-century people, their world did not change much. They accepted the structures and beliefs passed on to them by previous generations. Then, during the Reformation, time-honored truths were challenged and fought over.

During this period of European history, the Christian worldview itself would be challenged. A transformation known as the **Enlightenment** would lead to questioning Church, religion, and the existence of God. The Enlightenment in many ways glorified the rational mind over all other sources of truth. For the first time since before Constantine, the Catholic Church found herself on the outside of major political conflicts and intellectual developments. Nonetheless, great numbers of people stayed with the Church or joined her as their life-giving link to Christ.

Galileo and the Church

"Science and technology are precious resources when placed at the service of man and promote his integral development for the benefit of all. By themselves however they cannot disclose the meaning of existence and of human progress."

Catechism of the Catholic Church, #2293

The Italian scientist Galileo Galilei (1564–1642) wanted to test longstanding notions by using direct observation. For instance, most scholars of the time believed that two objects of different weights would fall at different speeds. Galileo, a native of Pisa, climbed its famous tower and demonstrated this viewpoint false. His findings contradicted what the Greek philosopher Aristotle had said on the matter. Therefore, many Aristotelians, who believed their master to be the final word on scientific truth, rejected Galileo's results. Galileo had to leave town, but he received teaching positions in mathematics, first at Padua and then at Florence.

Later, Galileo heard about a Dutch optician who produced an instrument that magnified distant objects. Galileo immediately understood the theory behind this discovery and worked through the night to create his own such instrument, the telescope. Galileo used his telescope to support a theory that had previously been proposed by the Polish astronomer Copernicus—namely, that the earth and other planets revolve around the sun. Copernicus had proposed a heliocentric solar system almost seventy-five years before Galileo did. Copernicus received support from a local cardinal and a bishop, and even dedicated his work to the pope of the time.

Galileo published his opinions proposing a **heliocentric** system—as opposed to the commonly accepted **geocentric** system—the belief that the sun revolves around the earth. He was again going against commonly held beliefs, and much controversy followed. Because a number of people denounced his ideas as heresy, Galileo went to Rome in 1615 and appeared before the court of the Inquisition. The court raised essentially three objections against Galileo's heliocentric theory:

1. Galileo offered no firm proof for it.

2. It appeared to contradict certain statements in the Bible.

3. It could present a danger to the faith of the common people if it circulated beyond the scientific community itself.

Galileo left the Inquisition promising not to speak or write about this particular topic. Nonetheless, when he returned to Florence, he upheld his heliocentric teachings and taught about them on many occasions. Galileo again appeared before the Inquisition and denied his belief in the Copernican system. This time, however, the judges did not accept his denial, and Galileo spent the rest of his life officially under arrest—but living comfortably with various friends in and around Rome.

The time of Galileo marks another transition period in the history of

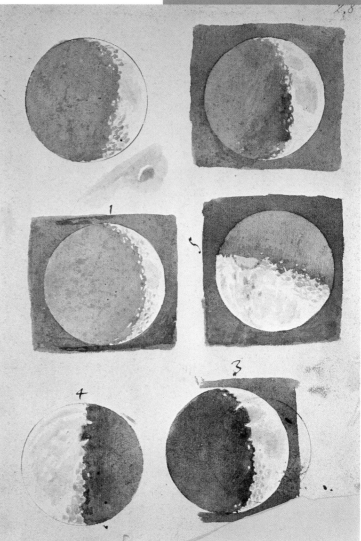

▼Illustrations of phases of the moon by Galileo Galilei.

the world. As they have always had to do, Church leaders had to meet the challenges posed by new ideas and new perspectives. The worldview that emerged after the Reformation period had intellectual, moral, and political implications. Galileo's story points out a number of issues Catholics faced as they entered into the dramatically changed world of the seventeenth and eighteenth centuries.

First, since the time of the great medieval thinkers, Catholicism had sided with scholastic philosophy as its window into the truths of the natural world. **Scholasticism** is rooted primarily in revelation and uses other philosophical sources, especially Aristotle, to help shed light on God's work of salvation. Thomas Aquinas and other medieval scholars used human reason in a particular way to determine truth. Essentially, scholasticism used deductive reasoning in its approach. Deductive reasoning poses general principles, raises questions about those principles, and then uses logic to draw conclusions "deduced" from the principles. Recall that Aquinas deduced the existence of God using this approach.

In contrast, Galileo was using an inductive approach in the search for truth. Inductive reasoning draws a generalized conclusion from particular instances. Over the next few centuries, Christianity, both Catholic and Protestant, would face challenges posed by a developing modern science. Until well into the twentieth century, most Catholic thinkers continued to rely on scholasticism as their primary approach to truth seeking. Some Protestant groups came to be reconciled with modern scientific thought as early as the nineteenth century.

FAITH ACTIVITY

Mission of the Church Write a paragraph describing how science and technology can either enhance or inhibit the mission of the Church.

Second, at the time many people considered the Bible to be literally true. For instance, the Book of Joshua reports that during a battle the sun stood still for an entire day. (See *Joshua 10:12–13*.) If the earth revolves around the sun, how could that passage from the Bible be true? Since this era of Enlightenment, many Catholics have come to a better understanding of the Catholic interpretation of Scripture. As God's word, the Bible contains the truths of faith and salvation that God wanted to convey to us. The issue is not necessarily literal fact, but truths of faith. That is, we misread the Bible if we treat it only as a scientific text, for it has different literary styles and senses. However, determining the correct relationship between the Bible and science would remain a challenge for centuries. Some Protestant communities still hold that we must choose between literal biblical truths and scientific truths and that the two are irreconcilable.

Third, Galileo's story represents a shift in the role Catholic Church authorities would play in the pursuit of truth. For centuries the most learned people in the Christian world were affiliated with the Church in some way. Universities were viewed as extensions of the teaching mission of the Church. As already mentioned, in the mid-1500s Copernicus received sponsorship from Church leaders; and at the beginning of the 1600s Galileo subjected his theories to investigation by Church courts. Asking representatives of the Church to scrutinize new theories was customary. After this time, science and religion would go their separate ways for the most part. Most scientists would no longer view their work as a function of the Church searching for truth or as one piece of a total, interrelated system of truth. In fact, many scientists would consider the Church and religion itself to be an obstacle to authentic truth seeking. The medieval synthesis of the sacred and the secular was unraveling.

Characteristics of the New Age of Science

An early proponent of the new age of science was the French mathematician and philosopher Rene Descartes (1596–1650). Take note of his fundamental point of view, and imagine how it might have been received by Christian thinkers of the time. Descartes believed that nothing should be accepted unquestioningly. In fact, it is our very ability to question that proves our existence. You are probably familiar with his famous maxim, "I think; therefore, I am." Descartes could have substituted the words "I doubt" or "I question; therefore, I am." In effect, Descartes believed that reason was the key source of human truth. Leading thinkers during and after the time of Descartes posed new challenges for the Catholic Church. For instance, Francis Bacon (1561–1626) proposed that nothing should be accepted solely on the basis of authority. Tradition was an obstacle to truth. The scholastic approach to truth-seeking was too abstract. Inductive reasoning, beginning with observable phenomena, was for Bacon far superior to deductive reasoning. That is, knowledge comes from using the senses to observe the natural world.

This period during which many people elevated science to being the exclusive source of truth is known as the Enlightenment. When asked, "What is the Enlightenment?" philosopher Immanuel Kant replied that it meant "Courage to use the mind without the guidance of another. Dare to know! Have the courage to use your own understanding!" (Quoted in Jaroslav Pelikan, *The Melody of Theology*, p. 69.) The Enlightenment encouraged innovations in science and technology and promoted charitable standards of tolerance, equality, and freedom in social reforms. The challenges of the Enlightenment struck at the heart of the Catholic Church even more than the Reformation did. The Reformation split Western Christianity, but in many ways the Enlightenment undermined Christianity itself.

Actually, most Enlightenment thinkers did not reject Christianity. Instead they interpreted Christianity as being in agreement with their viewpoints. For Enlightenment thinkers, belief in reason was the one true religion. In their view, human beings are good and powerful by nature. People should concentrate on this world and not on the next. The natural world holds out the possibility of things being known and controlled; the supernatural should be left in God's hands. The more people live and act according to reason, the better the world will be. Superstitions, prejudices, and preconceived notions hold people back. Once these are let go, humans will have created a paradise on earth. Most Enlightenment thinkers did not distinguish between what was superstitious in religion and what was authentic religious practice.

The belief in unbounded human progress achievable through ever-increasing knowledge of the natural world has been called **rationalism**. Rationalist thinkers stood in opposition to religion based on mystery or revealed truth. To them, a religious teaching was true only insofar as it was reasonable.

Another view of God and religion that rejected revealed truth also surfaced during this period—**deism**. This view looks at God and religion as being about the past; deism's focus is the future. God was neither a positive nor a negative force. The God of the deists is a passive, uninvolved God. He created the world but no longer interferes in its workings. God is like a watchmaker. He made the world and sent it off into history with all its inner workings in place that keep it running on its own. Humans—using reason, experimenting with science, and observing the natural world—can come to know the inner workings of nature without needing to refer to divine revelation.

FAITH ACTIVITY

Scientific Debate Make a list of activities or practices that are being debated in various scientific fields today. Next to each item, state what the Catholic Church has said, if anything, about these issues.

FYI

Two of the most famous advocates of deism were the French thinkers F.M.A. de Voltaire (1694–1778) and J.J. Rousseau (1712–1778). In America, the writings of Ethan Allen, Thomas Paine, Benjamin Franklin, and Thomas Jefferson all reflect some deist views.

Key Theories of Deism
God exists.
God created the world.
Once it was created, God left the world alone.
The world operates by definite natural laws.
Humans can discover these laws through the use of reason.
Human reason should be used to scrutinize all truth claims.
Human reason should guide all human endeavors.

The Catholic Response to Rationalism and Deism

> "Reason and human science often lead you into error because they are too weak and limited to penetrate to the knowledge of the things of God, which are infinite and incomprehensible."
>
> Saint John Eudes as quoted in Jill Haak Adels,
> *The Wisdom of the Saints*, p. 176

Prior to his Ascension, the risen Christ let his Apostles know that they were to engage the whole world with his message of redemption and new life. Inspired by the Holy Spirit at Pentecost, from its very beginning the Church had the strength and guidance to carry out her mission. A Spirit-inspired Church was not to stand still but was to grow and develop as it encountered the various cultures in which its representatives found themselves. Early on, Christianity was able to explain itself to proponents of reason—the great philosophical thinkers of the classical world—in their own terms. Saint Paul made a case for the reasonableness of Christianity to the people of Athens. Christianity was such a vibrant movement partially because it was able to synthesize Jewish thought with the insights of classical philosophy.

The seventeenth and eighteenth centuries brought new intellectual challenges to Catholic thought. By making reason their universal starting point, Descartes and Bacon attempted to start fresh in making sense of the world. They believed that as Europe had recently discovered new lands across the seas, so European minds could discover new truths. Enlightenment thinkers came to believe in unbounded human progress gained through the use of human reason. The free and unfettered investigation of nature and the application of the principles of nature to human problems would improve the common lot of humanity. Just as Catholicism in the Reformation held onto its essential beliefs and practices, so it rejected the basic tenets of rationalism and deism that seemed to contradict those beliefs and practices. For centuries, the Catholic Church stood firm against both even while many in the Western world were embracing them.

What was the nature of the Catholic Church's response to rationalism and deism? Essentially, there were three levels of response.

Entrenchment of Scholasticism

For one, Catholic scholars held onto scholasticism as their principal method for seeking truth. The scholastic approach was based in particular on the medieval theologian Saint Thomas Aquinas. This approach predates the challenges of modern science, but these two approaches—scholasticism and modern science—are not mutually exclusive. Vatican Council II in the 1960s encouraged Catholic scholars to continue to engage in dialogue with modern science and the intellectual currents coming out of the Enlightenment while maintaining the truths of faith.

Popular Devotions

A second level of response to rationalism took place among the Catholic faithful. Whereas deism painted the picture of a distant, removed, impersonal God, popular Catholic piety reminded believers that God the Father was present and active in their lives, sustaining them through the power of his Son and the Holy Spirit. Popular piety offered many personal images of God the Father, his Son Jesus, and the Holy Spirit; Mary; and the other saints. For instance, in the seventeenth century, devotion to the Sacred Heart of Jesus became very popular. This representation of Jesus, with his heart externally visible, provided an image of warmth, care, compassion, and love that the God of deism did not offer. A similar image of the Immaculate Heart of Mary became popular at the same time.

Other events that generated popular piety were the apparitions of Mary. In 1858, the Virgin Mary appeared to a young teenage French girl named Bernadette Soubirous in a cave near Lourdes. Although authorities tried to suppress this apparition, the spot became one of the most frequented pilgrimage sites in Europe. A spring emerged from the cave soon after Bernadette's vision. The spring continues to produce water on a regular basis, and many people have found the water to have miraculous healing powers.

The Moral and Spiritual Authority of the Pope A third reaction to rationalism was the strengthening of the role of the pope as a moral and spiritual leader. Some popes of the Middle Ages and the Reformation saw themselves as the secular ruler of the Papal States first and the spiritual head of Christianity second. As the secular power of the popes declined, they tended to speak out more forcefully on moral and spiritual matters. The strongest pronouncement about papal authority in the area of faith and morals came at the First Vatican Council, in 1870. The bishops gathered in Rome declared the pope to be **infallible** (incapable of error) when, under the influence of the Holy Spirit, he makes an official definitive statement about faith or morals. It is the responsibility of the pope and bishops to make statements on moral issues that deal with natural law and reason as well as to teach the faithful how to apply moral teachings to their lives.

▼*Apparition of Our Lady of Lourdes*, engraved by Bouasse-Lebel.

Bouasse-Lebel imp Edit.   29 rue St Sulpice, Paris
JE SUIS L'IMMACULÉE CONCEPTION
U. L. FRAU VON LOURDES

A Holy People

"The Church, then, is 'the holy People of God'[1]... and her members are called 'saints'[2] (*Catechism of the Catholic Church,* #823). The Enlightenment tended to split the world into "the sacred" and "the secular." In this view, science and politics are secular affairs, while God, spirituality, and the Church are sacred or religious affairs. For Christianity, life is not meant to be compartmentalized in this way. Science and politics are intended to be holy enterprises; they are ways to encounter God and to manifest him in the world. Because of its relationship with Christ, the Church is a holy people. Members of the Church, even those engaged in so-called "secular" matters such as science and politics, are called to be saints.

> We teach and declare as a divinely revealed dogma that when the Roman pontiff speaks *ex cathedra*, that is, when, in the exercise of his office as shepherd and teacher of all Christians, in virtue of his supreme apostolic teaching, he defines a doctrine concerning faith or morals to be held by the whole Church, he possesses, by the divine assistance promised to him in blessed Peter, that infallibility which the divine Redeemer willed his Church to enjoy in defining doctrine concerning faith or morals.

Vatican Council I as quoted in Alfred McBride O. Praem., *The Story of the Church*, p. 153

!FYI

A pronouncement made *ex cathedra*—"from the chair" of Peter—identified a papal statement as infallible. In 1950, Pope Pius XII declared *ex cathedra* that the Virgin Mary was bodily assumed into heaven. Therefore, Mary's Assumption is an infallible Catholic doctrine.

The Catholic doctrine of infallibility reflects the relationship that exists between Christ and his Church. The Gospels proclaim Christ as the Truth. Christ conferred upon the Church a share in his truth. Thus, when the bishops of Vatican Council I declared the doctrine of infallibility, they were stating in precise terms how the Church has always viewed herself.

An Age of Nation-States

Besides its emphasis on science, the post-Reformation period in Europe was characterized by the formation of clearly distinct nation-states. Europe had kings before this time, but during feudalism they functioned as the first among equals. Also, the emperor at least theoretically held authority over all local rulers. In the seventeenth century the concept of a **monarch**, someone who was the one and only ruler of a nation, began to develop. People saw themselves not as Bavarians or Normans (people who spoke a particular dialect and lived in a specific section of a country) but as German or French. While we take for granted that the world is divided into separate and distinct nation-states, this concept is a relatively recent one. Monarchs who saw themselves as possessing absolute power were the embodiment of unified nations. On the one hand, monarchs lessened the power of nobles under them. On the other hand, they also greatly diminished the power of transnational entities, such as the emperor and the pope.

EXPLORE THE LAND

The Formation of Countries Count how many nation-states you can identify in the map below. Then, look at a modern map of Europe. How many of those nation-states still exist today? What are the five most recent countries to gain independence in Europe?

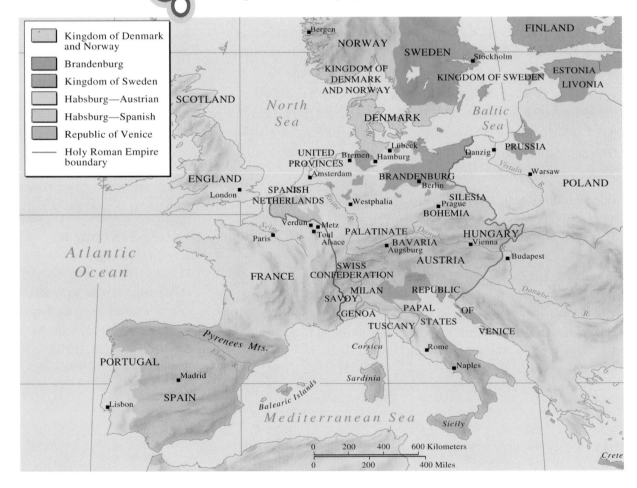

Legend:
- Kingdom of Denmark and Norway
- Brandenburg
- Kingdom of Sweden
- Habsburg—Austrian
- Habsburg—Spanish
- Republic of Venice
- Holy Roman Empire boundary

The **Thirty Years' War** did much to establish in Europe a system of nation-states ruled by monarchs. The war lasted from 1618 to 1648, leaving Germany in ruins and the Holy Roman Empire politically doomed. The war initially began with the rebellion of the Bohemians against King Ferdinand II. When the Peace of Westphalia ended the conflict, three outcomes strengthened the modern nation-state system of Europe.

Outcomes of Thirty Years' War

First, the Holy Roman Empire was reduced to being one nation among many. The emperor ruled Germany as its monarch but could no longer lay claim to exercising power over other European countries. Germany became simply one more nation-state of Europe.

Second, the pope became a minor voice in European politics. He spoke out against anti-Catholic wording in the Peace of Westphalia, but his comments went unheeded.

Third, religious lines were sharply drawn in Europe. The Lutherans were mainly located in Scandinavia, Prussia, and parts of southern Germany; most Calvinists lived in Switzerland, much of Holland, and Scotland; England had its own Church; and all the rest of Europe was predominantly Catholic. Therefore, in future political conflicts, religion became less important than national identity.

GROUP TALK

1 Discuss the impact of the following on our sense of nationalism and globalism: business, religion, television, the Internet, the military, and natural resources.

2 Based on your discussion, is the world moving away from emphasizing separate nation-states? Explain.

Christina, Queen of Sweden (1676–1689)

At the battle of Lutzen in 1632 during the Thirty Years' War, King Gustavus Adolphus Wasa of Sweden was killed. His daughter and heir Christina was only six years old at the time, so a council of regents ran the country until she became an adult. When she turned eighteen in 1644, Christina took the throne and used her influence to end the war and bring about the Treaty of Westphalia. According to the terms of the treaty, every nation would take the religion of its ruler. Christina was a Protestant, as was Sweden. However, she was drawn to Catholicism and considered converting. Her advisers attempted to arrange a marriage for her with a number of Protestant rulers, but she declined their offers. Ten years after assuming the throne,

Christina decided to begin receiving instruction on the Catholic faith. She abdicated to her cousin, joined the Catholic Church in 1655, and moved to Rome. Although she twice attempted to regain her throne, she instead lived out her life in Rome doing acts of charity for those who were poor. She died in 1689 and is buried in St. Peter's Basilica, the only woman accorded this privilege.

Christina of Sweden ▶
by Sebastien Bourdon.

National Churches and the Universal Church

France is the best example of a nation-state that was ruled by a powerful monarch following the Thirty Years' War. Its greatest king, Louis XIV, attempted to wrestle control of the Catholic Church in France away from Rome. He advocated what came to be known as **Gallicanism**—control of Church affairs by the nation and not by the pope. King Louis XIV issued the *Four Gallican Articles* in 1682 and called upon all French clergy to agree to them. The articles stated that:

- Neither the pope nor the Church has power over temporal civil matters.
- The power of Church councils is greater than that of the pope.
- The pope's power is limited by the customs and privileges of national churches.
- The pope's decisions require the consent of the Church.

The king insisted that the Gallican Articles be taught in French seminaries, and he recommended as bishops only those priests who agreed to the articles. However, Pope Innocent XI rejected the articles and refused to assign bishops to French dioceses when they became vacant. Finally, after thirty dioceses were without bishops, the pope agreed to appoint as bishops the priests chosen by the king but only if they renounced the articles. However, the bishops in France were more loyal to the state than they were to the Catholic Church, even though they had renounced the articles. A similar conflict between papal oversight and national control of the Catholic Church emerged in Germany and Austria.

Many European monarchs applied Enlightenment concepts to themselves and thought of themselves as "enlightened despots." That is, they saw themselves as being the person best suited to be in charge of every aspect of life in their nation. Curbing the power of the papacy over the Church in their countries was part of their attempt to exercise complete control over the nations. In order to ensure that the pope was weak, monarchs influenced their cardinals to elect popes who were not strong leaders. For a period of time, the men chosen to be pope were old and in poor health. Between 1585 to 1605, six popes were elected—an average of about one every three years.

Influence on the papacy by secular rulers also led to the suppression of the Jesuits in 1773. Suppression of the Jesuits meant that, at a time when the Church needed educated Catholics, many of the best colleges and universities worldwide were closed. At the time, the Jesuits ran 266 colleges and 103 seminaries. Interestingly, one of the few places that welcomed Jesuits was Russia, where Czarina Catherine the Great appreciated their contributions to knowledge.

FYI

The word *Gallicanism* comes from the ancient Roman name for French territory, *Gaul*.

FAITH ACTIVITY

Pope's Reign To put the idea of a new pope about every three years into perspective, look up the length of time each twentieth-century pope reigned. Who was pope for the longest time? Who had the shortest reign? Discounting the shortest, what was the average number of years a twentieth-century pope reigned?

The Impact of the French Revolution

The French Revolution was actually a series of events that happened over a period of time in the latter part of the eighteenth century. The Enlightenment serves as an important backdrop to the revolution because, as mentioned earlier, Enlightenment thinkers called into question all the institutions that had been held up as the pillars of society. On May 5, 1789, King Louis XVI called together the Estates General—the French parliament—because his treasury was depleted due to the cost of fighting recent wars.

This body, which had not met since 1614, was made up of representatives from the three estates: clergy, nobility, and common people. Almost from the beginning, the third estate, many clergy, and some nobles tried to steer the meeting into a movement demanding changes in the government. On June 17 many members of the Estates General gathered in a tennis court and proclaimed themselves a National Assembly, vowing not to leave until a constitution was approved.

On July 14, 1789, citizens of Paris attacked the Bastille prison and set its prisoners free. Because this act marked the beginning of the involvement of the common people in the process, this date is celebrated as the official beginning of the French Revolution. Over the next few years, stability in France deteriorated rapidly. In 1793, the king and his family were executed. During the next two years, tens of thousands of people were executed during the **Reign of Terror**. Church leaders, most of whom came from the noble class and sided with the nobility, went to the guillotine, as did many priests. In 1795 a group of leaders known as the Directory used the army to restore order. Then, in 1799 the most popular of the French generals, Napoleon Bonaparte, declared himself leader of France.

To understand the impact of the French Revolution on the Catholic Church, it is important to recall that France became Christian in 496 under King Clovis and, therefore, saw itself as "the eldest daughter of the Church." The faith was strong on the eve of the revolution. While local clergy generally identified with the common people, most Church leaders were identified with the nobility and held much property in this time when food and other resources were scarce.

▼ *Notre Dame Cathedral.*

During the revolutionary period, monasteries were overtaken, and communities of monks and nuns were disbanded. Instead of the pope appointing bishops, the people voted for their bishops and priests. All members of the clergy had to swear allegiance to the state rather than to the pope. As part of the revolutionary agenda, French leaders during the Reign of Terror tried to eliminate all reminders of the way things used to be run. They even proposed a ten-day week so that there would no longer be a sabbath day for worship. In effect, the French Revolution was not simply anti-nobility; it was also anti-Church. For decades following the revolution, Church leaders were fearful of ideas and movements that reflected a revolutionary spirit.

Napoleon and the Concordat with the Pope Napoleon Bonaparte (1769–1821) crowned himself emperor in 1804 after a decade-long series of military conquests and virtual leadership of France. Before Napoleon gained power, French armies had invaded Italy and deported the pope to France. The college of cardinals was disbanded, and many people thought that the papacy had come to an end. However, when Napoleon came to power, he realized that the majority of the common people throughout Europe clung to their Catholic faith. If he were to create the empire that he wanted, his task would be easier *with* Catholicism rather than against it. Napoleon, therefore, signed a **concordat** with the new pope, Pius VII, in 1801. According to the concordat, Napoleon would appoint bishops, but the pope would approve the appointments. By making this agreement directly with the pope, Napoleon validated the pope as the spiritual head of the Church, even in France. However, the spiritual authority or power given to the pope by Christ is constant despite historical circumstances and their effects on his temporal authority. The spiritual authority of the pope does not wax and wane because of either politics or war.

This acceptance of the pope's authority signaled a move away from Gallicanism to **Ultramontanism**. *Ultramontanism*, a Latin phrase meaning "beyond the mountains," meant that control of the French Church was in the hands of the pope, who resided beyond the mountains rather than in France. As European Catholics soured of the revolution and Napoleon, more and more of them looked to the pope as a symbol of an alternate system. Generally, Ultramontanists sided with those forces who wanted to restore the prerevolutionary order of things, often in an exaggerated way. Thus the fate of the Catholic Church in France during most of the nineteenth century rose or fell in conjunction with the fortunes of the nobility.

Since the time of Emperor Constantine, there had been a history of involvement of secular rulers in Church affairs. After Napoleon, popes found it necessary and beneficial to make concordats with many of the European countries ruled by Catholic monarchs. These concordats aimed at a balance of power between pope and ruler. As the nineteenth century progressed and democratically elected leaders governed European nations, concordats were either dismissed or ignored. By the time of Pius IX, who was pope from 1846 to 1878, the pope had little political power, but there was no question that the pope was the supreme and sole head of the Catholic Church.

> ## GROUP TALK
>
> Some Catholic thinkers of the time considered the themes of the French Revolution—freedom, equality, fraternity—reflective of the spirit of the early Church. Debate the following statement: Even though the French Revolution went in directions that were clearly unchristian, its original spirit embodied true Christian ideals.

A Closer Look

Cardinal Ercole Consalvi

The Church had a talented diplomat in Cardinal Ercole Consalvi (1757–1824), son of a noble family from Pisa, Italy. Cardinal Consalvi served as Vatican Secretary of State during the difficult years of Napoleon's rule. Consalvi brought a number of laypeople into the government of the Papal States and advised the pope to insist on making a concordat with Napoleon so that Church interests would be protected. In 1809, Consalvi and twelve other cardinals refused to recognize Napoleon's marriage to Marie Louise of Austria. Napoleon first ordered them to be shot but then instead ordered that they were to be deprived of their property and forbidden to wear any sign that they were cardinals. These thirteen cardinals came to be known as the *black cardinals* since they couldn't wear the red robes that other cardinals did. When Napoleon was defeated, Consalvi was reinstated as Vatican Secretary of State and negotiated restoration of the Papal States at the Congress of Vienna in 1814–1815.

Blessed Pope Pius IX—The First Modern Pope

After the chaos of the Napoleonic era, the leaders of Europe came together at the Congress of Vienna in 1814–1815. During this gathering they redrew the map of Europe. Through the efforts of its main architect, Prince Metternich of Austria, all royal monarchs were restored to their thrones. Metternich took particular pains to prevent any one country from becoming a "super nation" dominating all others. Metternich totally opposed democracy and predicted that the "American experiment" would never see a second generation. He also restored the Papal States to the pope. Metternich's reactionary views so dominated Europe until 1858 that this period is often called "the age of Metternich."

Church leaders of the time felt as most of Europe did—that it was time to return to the stability of the pre-Napoleonic days. The three popes elected during this period were good persons and encouraged much good work. They also expressed the conservative views toward politics common among the European monarchs of the time. The Papal States restored a feudal system. Jews were restricted to living apart from Christians in ghettos.

In 1846, the cardinals chose as pope someone identified with a more open viewpoint. He took the name Pope Pius IX and led the Church for thirty-two years, the longest reigning pope in history. The new pope began by taking steps that pleased the liberals of Europe. He offered amnesty to all political prisoners in the Papal States, instituted a representative form of government, and did away with censorship of ideas.

However, when, in 1848, a revolution forced Pius IX to flee to Naples and a republic was established in Rome, he quickly turned against liberalism and democracy. With the help of French troops, he regained control of the Papal States. But, republican forces continued to take control of more and more portions of papal territory. Then, in 1870, French troops withdrew to participate in a war in which France was engaged at the time. This allowed the Italian general Garibaldi to storm Rome. He declared Rome capital of a united Italy under King Victor Emmanuel.

Pope Pius IX refused to accept any terms under which he would give up his claims to the Papal States. He would not even sign a document that said he could "continue to enjoy the area of the Vatican and the papal apartments." He said that "enjoy" meant that he was there as a courtesy from the Italian government and could be told to vacate it if his "landlord" wanted it for other purposes. The pope announced instead that he would continue to live there as "the prisoner of the Vatican."

As he was losing temporal power, Pope Pius IX emphasized his role as pastor of the universal Church. For instance, in 1854 he proclaimed the dogma of the Immaculate Conception, which states that God favored Mary by preserving her from original sin from the first moment of her conception and that she remained free from personal sin throughout her life. Most earlier statements of official Church teachings came from Church councils. He also issued the *Syllabus of Errors*, a list of eighty errors that he regarded as being incompatible with Catholicism. In 1869, Pius IX called for a council, Vatican Council I, which proclaimed the doctrine of infallibility. Interestingly, as the council was voting on this teaching, Italian forces were overtaking Rome. Vatican Council I, along with the end of the Papal States, signaled a change in the role of the pope. From now on, popes would exercise their authority mainly as spiritual and moral leaders. In 1929, Italy recognized Vatican City-state as being under the civil rule of the pope. Thus, Pius IX was the first of the modern popes.

▼ *Pope Pius IX* by Antoine Chatelain.

Catholicism in England and Ireland

As mentioned in the last chapter, after King Henry VIII, England adopted a state-controlled religion that tended to be Catholic in theology and practice but was not aligned with the universal Church centered in Rome. For over a century after Henry, the Church of England contended with Catholics on the one hand and, on the other, with groups who wanted a reformed expression of Protestantism. Under Henry's daughter, Queen Elizabeth I, England enacted many anti-Catholic laws and moved closer to the Protestant camp. However, over the course of the eighteenth century, anti-Catholic laws came to be ignored. England perceived itself to be an enlightened, tolerant nation that didn't need to resort to old-fashioned persecution of religious dissenters to maintain stability. Finally, in 1829 England officially eliminated its anti-Catholic laws. During the period of the French Revolution, many French clergy made their way to England to avoid persecution at the hands of the revolutionary forces in France.

In the 1830s, a number of Anglican priests and bishops wanted the Church of England to become more Catholic. Some of the brightest churchmen in England joined this movement, called the *Oxford Movement* since a number of its members were associated with Oxford University. One of these Anglican priests, John Henry Newman, studied the early Church and concluded that the true Church should be centered around the bishop of Rome. Newman joined the Catholic Church in 1845. After Newman, a number of other influential English people joined the Catholic Church. These English Catholics advocated strong, centralized authority of the pope in spiritual matters.

Ireland never entertained Protestantism. When Henry VIII broke with Catholicism, the Irish in large measure remained staunchly Catholic. Protestantism gained a foothold in Ireland only when Scottish Presbyterians and some English Protestants settled in a section of Northern Ireland. In 1688, the English forced the reigning king, James II—who openly professed himself to be Catholic—out of England. In what the English call the Glorious Revolution, William and Mary, the Protestant daughter of James II, were given the English throne. The ousted James II attempted to regain control of England, using Ireland as a base. However, his forces were defeated by those of the new king, William of Orange. To this day Protestants in Northern Ireland are known as *Orangemen*, and Catholicism in Ireland and Northern Ireland is linked to anti-English resistance.

FAITH ACTIVITY

Conflict in Ireland What is the state of Protestant-Catholic relations in Northern Ireland today? Research the role that religion has played in English-Irish relations.

Three Leaders of the Church in England

Three men played an important role in the resurgence of Catholicism in England during the nineteenth century.

Nicholas Wiseman was actually born in Spain in 1802 but moved to Ireland as a child. He studied in Rome and was ordained a bishop. In 1840, Wiseman moved to England. He spent ten years traveling throughout the British Isles, getting a sense of the needs of the Catholic people, preaching, and developing contacts with all segments of English society. The pope appointed him Archbishop of Westminster in 1850. Because of the strong anti-Catholic reaction to this appointment, Wiseman wrote a pastoral letter called "Appeal to Reason and Good Feeling of the English People on the Subject of the Catholic Hierarchy." His eloquence and bold public appearances quieted antipapal activities in England. Wiseman became England's first cardinal since the time of Queen Elizabeth I, and he supported the Oxford Movement that made Catholicism an intellectual force in the country.

Henry Edward Manning was born into a wealthy and distinguished English family in 1808. He chose to become a college professor and a deacon in the Anglican Church. Manning became involved in the Oxford Movement where he became friends with John Henry Newman. In 1851, he was ordained a Catholic priest and went to study in Rome. When Cardinal Wiseman died in 1865, Manning was named the second Archbishop of Westminster and later a cardinal. He participated in Vatican Council I and was a leading proponent of the Church's support for working class people, becoming especially involved in the London dock strike of 1889.

John Henry Newman was born in 1801 in London. He received a classical education, coming into contact with Enlightenment thinkers such as Voltaire and Hume, whereupon he announced that he was an atheist. Convinced by a teacher to read the works of John Calvin, Newman converted to Anglicanism and was ordained a priest. He served as vicar at St. Mary's in Oxford and led the Oxford Movement. Initially, he attempted to show that Anglicanism was a middle ground between Romanism (centered on papal authority) and Protestantism (centered on individual judgment). Newman was a popular speaker and wrote many pamphlets on religious subjects. In one essay he argued that the thirty-nine articles of the Anglican Church were in line with the reforms of the Council of Trent.

Members of the Oxford Movement began to enter the Catholic Church, but Newman hoped for reconciliation between his religion and his questions. He articulated his search in a hymn called "Lead, Kindly Light." Finally Newman joined the Catholic Church. Two years later he was ordained and received permission from the pope to join the Oratory, a religious community founded by Saint Philip Neri. He continued to be a great influence on the scholarly communities of the Church and was named a cardinal in 1877.

Cardinal John Henry Newman. ▶

A Changing World

The Age of Enlightenment certainly did not bring about a world that was free of strife and guided by rational principles as promised. Common people suffered and often looked to the Catholic Church for comfort and meaning. While the leaders of Church and state argued over control of the Church at its higher levels, at the lower levels of society, in response to their Christian faith, heroic men and women gave their lives helping people in need. Also, as doors opened to lands where people had never encountered Christianity, other Catholics set out to spread the Good News of Christ to the people who lived there. In other words, the Christian message flourished even in the midst of the great changes taking place worldwide. Here are some of the major expressions of how the Gospel was lived out during the age of Enlightenment.

▼ *Baldacchino of St. Peter's Basilica by Gian Lorenzo Bernini.*

The Baroque in Art and Worship

In French the word *baroque* means "odd." **Baroque** art, architecture, music, style of worship, and even theological reflection were very popular in Catholic communities following the Reformation and throughout the Enlightenment period. The baroque style certainly was unusual, given the currents associated with Protestantism and the Enlightenment. While Reformed Protestants were removing statues from churches and simplifying their services, baroque churches were very ornate, and worship services were like grand theatrical productions. Baroque religious expression appealed to the senses. Religious expression was emotional, with joyful and exuberant art and music.

Although the baroque style appears to emphasize sensual and surface expressions of religion rather than depth, it certainly had its appeal, especially among ordinary Catholics. The Jesuit mother church in Rome, known as the *Gesu*, represents the baroque style of architecture. The baroque emphasized the humanity of Jesus and the tender, motherly qualities of Mary.

Varieties of Spiritual Life

Service to People Who Are Poor The seventeenth and eighteenth centuries offer a vast array of ways that people found to live the spiritual life. Two saints who deserve special mention are Vincent de Paul (1581–1660) and Louise de Marillac (1591–1660). Vincent was born into a peasant family but pursued the priesthood as a way to escape the poverty of his family. He used his charm to become a chaplain to the wealthiest families of Paris, including the queen herself. One day his father, who was dressed in shabby farmer's clothes, came to visit Vincent, and Vincent refused to acknowledge him. Vincent had a dramatic change of heart when a peasant on the estate of a wealthy family was near death and asked Vincent to hear his confession. After the confession the man thanked Vincent and remarked that if it were not for him, he might have died without benefit of confessing his sins.

This experience led Vincent to realize what a wonderful gift his priesthood was and that he should use it to be of service to those in need. The first thing he did was to train and organize priests for work in the French countryside, where the clergy were notoriously unprepared. Then he used his contacts among the wealthy to fund a variety of charitable projects. Vincent even convinced a number of wealthy women to dedicate part of their time to working among people who were poor and destitute. One woman, Louise de Marillac, realized that part-time workers were not sufficient to meet the needs of those suffering in and around Paris. Under Vincent's guidance, Louise founded the Daughters of Charity. The women chose not to live in convents as nuns. Instead they lived among people who were poor and served their needs. This was a radical idea. People who were poor were not to be brought to the convent; rather, the convent was to go out to them. Vincent admonished his workers to treat those who were poor as if they were dealing with their own children, or rather with God, since God is present in those who are poor.

Vincent de Paul and Louise de Marillac succeeded in creating organizations that we today might label forms of social work. They also stretched the understanding of the kinds of work that women could undertake. Vincent is the patron saint of charitable societies. In 1960 Pope John XXIII proclaimed Louise de Marillac patron of all Christian social work.

Everyday Spirituality Because of his outstanding writings on the spiritual life, Saint Francis de Sales (1567–1622) is patron of writers and the press. However, his message about how to live the spiritual life has something for everyone. After becoming a lawyer, Francis decided to pursue his dream of becoming a priest, and he worked in Geneva, Switzerland. If you recall from the last chapter, Geneva was at the time a hotbed of Calvinism. Francis was taking his life in his hands by speaking out for Catholicism there. However, his holiness impressed so many people that a number of Calvinists brought their families back to Catholicism. In his spiritual writings, Francis suggested that people should be motivated by love to practice internal and external self-mortification. He also pointed out that the spiritual life is different, depending on a person's vocation in life. A student can practice devotion as much as a teacher or a priest can; the experience will simply be different because of the difference in circumstances. For Francis a key was for people to develop good habits in their everyday lives, habits that lead them to be aware of God and to act out of love of God.

FAITH ACTIVITY

Personal Spiritual Life List three habits that you personally could develop that would help you in your spiritual life. Explain why these habits would be particularly beneficial for you.

The Holy Vagabond Does the idea of traveling around and living off of the land or on the streets have any appeal to you? A young Frenchman named Benedict Joseph Labre (1748–1783) attempted to enter a number of religious orders but was always turned down. He decided that his vocation was to live in the world as simply as he could, visiting shrines and praying as he traveled. He eventually arrived in Rome where he lived on the streets and never bathed or changed his clothes. Needless to say, people kept their distance from him. He did frequent the various churches of the city, however, and some people began to think that perhaps he wasn't just a homeless derelict but indeed a holy man. At the age of thirty-five, he collapsed on the steps of a church and died. Children began calling out, "The saint is dead, the saint is dead!" From there his reputation as a holy man grew, and he was canonized one hundred years later.

Teaching Children Who Are Poor In the seventeenth century, schooling was almost exclusively a privilege of the rich who could afford tutors for their children. The Frenchman, John Baptist de la Salle (1651–1719), patron saint of teachers, felt that men should be trained specifically to teach boys who were poor in order to help them out of poverty. La Salle introduced a number of innovations that have since become standard practice in teaching. Subjects were taught in the language of the students rather than in Latin. Teaching took place in groups rather than one-on-one. Also, subjects were taught according to a set schedule. La Salle did not want priests for this work but men dedicated exclusively to teaching. To that end he founded a community of religious brothers called the Brothers of the Christian Schools or simply the Christian Brothers. Today, members of the order he founded administer many educational institutions, and all teachers owe a debt to him.

A number of women also began communities dedicated to teaching and service to those who were poor. For instance, the French woman Julie Billiart (1751–1816) helped found a community of women known as the Institute of Notre Dame de Namur. When aristocrats and clergy were being executed in Paris, Julie risked her own life to hide priests who were being pursued by revolutionary forces. Even though she suffered from physical ailments for most of her life, Julie managed to establish many convents and to expand the work of her community.

Catholic Missionaries to Foreign Lands

Current Catholic teaching emphasizes that members of other religions are searching for God. In a sense, it is equally accurate to say that "God is searching for them." Catholic missionary activity reflects the Church's desire to bring the whole of humanity into the unity and salvation offered by Christ. Therefore, the Gospels clearly state that the followers of Jesus are to spread his message to every nation. The period of the Reformation was an age of exploration for European adventurers. Sailors, particularly under the flags of Portugal and Spain, made their way to parts of the world that only a few Europeans had previously visited. While sailors and political figures were most likely motivated by trade and conquest, the missionaries on these sea voyages saw an opportunity to introduce the Gospel message to new populations. Since Portugal and Spain were Catholic countries, the missionaries who traveled to these new lands were also Catholic, mostly Franciscans and Jesuits.

As happened in earlier periods in Church history, the missionaries who went to far-away lands knew that their lives were in danger, and yet many priests eagerly joined the missionary effort. Similarly, the first converts in these lands also were likely to suffer, either through the strain of rejection from their countrymen or through torture and death at the hands of those who felt threatened by a new religion and culture.

We will hold off discussion of missionary activity in the Americas until the next chapter. Northern Africa had a Christian population from the beginning period of Christianity, and, in a later chapter, we will examine more recent trends in African Catholicism. The story of Catholicism in Australia is linked to the story of Catholic—mostly Irish—prisoners sent there in exile. The story of Christianity's encounter with Southeast Asia and India demonstrates the appeal of the faith and its flexibility.

Christianity in China and Its Neighbors

China possessed an ancient and highly developed culture before it encountered Christianity. The first known presence of Christianity in China is traced to the year 635. A group of Christians called Nestorians traveled east from Persia and settled in China, but their descendants did not survive into the modern period.

After 1500, European missionaries in the Far East used two approaches to bring about conversion to Christianity. Missionaries from the mendicant orders—the Franciscans and Dominicans—worked among the common people and tried to make inroads there. Jesuits, on the other hand, engaged the most educated members of society and tried to make a case for Christianity in terms of the most exalted ideas of the native culture. For the most part, Jesuits were open to **accommodation**. For instance, in China Jesuits determined that Confucius was revered as a great sage and not a god, therefore the Chinese did not need to reject all of his teachings to be Christian. Some of his teachings were compatible with Christianity. The Jesuit missionaries also concluded that the great respect the Chinese had for their ancestors was compatible with Christianity.

◀ The Great Wall of China.

The most famous advocate of an accommodationist approach to missionary activity in China was the Jesuit Matteo Ricci (1521–1610). Ricci mastered the Chinese language and literature. He made a case for Christianity in terms of ancient Chinese writings. Ricci also tried to convince Chinese scholars that Europeans were not uncultured people. To do this he adopted upper class Chinese manners in dress, eating habits, and behavior. Some missionaries working among the poorer classes criticized this accommodationist approach and asked the pope to rule on the matter. In 1715, Pope Clement XI pronounced that excessive accommodation to local cultures as some Jesuits were doing was unacceptable. As a result, Christianity was presented unconformed to non-Christian aspects of Asian culture and came to be perceived by most as foreign and as a threat to Chinese and Japanese culture. Persecution of Christians set in. The struggle regarding inculturation in the Asian church continues to this day.

Two countries in Southeast Asia where Christianity made strong inroads were the Philippines and Vietnam. Korea encountered Christianity later than other countries, but Christianity—both Catholicism and Protestantism—has developed a strong presence there.

The Thien Mu Pagoda in Vietnam. ▶

Saint Paul Miki and Companions (d. 1597)

Saint Francis Xavier first introduced Christianity to Japan in 1549. By the end of the century, tens of thousands of Japanese had joined the Christian community. Paul Miki not only became Christian, he also joined the Jesuits and was renowned for his preaching. Japanese rulers began to fear the influence of this religion from a European culture and forbade Christian missionary activity.

When some Christians violated this law, the Japanese emperor decided to execute a group of known Christians. In 1597 he condemned twenty-six Christians to death by crucifixion. Soon after the death of Paul Miki and his companions, Japanese authorities began an active campaign to ferret out all Christians and put them to death. Many Christians were crucified. To identify Christians, Japanese authorities would place images of Christ or Mary on the ground and require everyone to stamp on them. Punishment for those who refused to do so was death for themselves and their families.

After such stringent persecution, Christianity apparently died out in Japan until 1854 when Japan's isolation from the West ended. A French priest arrived in 1860 to serve the French Catholic community in Nagasaki. In 1865, a group of Japanese citizens approached the priest and cautiously told him that they were Christians. Even after two hundred years without a priest or contact from other Christians, thousands of Japanese had continued to practice their Catholicism in secret and had handed the faith down to their children.

Missionaries to India Discover an Ancient Christian Community Portuguese missionaries first arrived in India in 1498. When they arrived they discovered an unexpected phenomenon—a small community of Christians already living there! These Christians claimed to be descendants of a Christian community founded by the Apostle Thomas in the first century. They had the equivalent of bishops and priests, practiced Christian rites, and possessed Christian writings including a composite of the Gospels.

At first these **Christians of Saint Thomas** welcomed the Portuguese as fellow Christians, and the missionaries were glad to see a Christian presence already in India. However, in time the two groups ran into conflict. For instance, the Saint Thomas Christians did not use images in their places of worship, their priests married, and they used both water and oil in Baptism. The Hindus of India had many sacred images. Therefore, to distinguish themselves from their Hindu neighbors, Saint Thomas Christians didn't use images. The Saint Thomas Christians were disturbed by certain Portuguese practices such as their use of images, their meat-eating habits, and their referring to Mary as "Mother of God" instead of "Mother of Christ."

Appeals to the pope from both sides attempted to resolve the conflict between the two groups. The two groups still remain in India today: Catholics who trace their lineage to the Portuguese missionaries, and a number of Christian groups who see themselves as descendants of Thomas and first-century Indian Christians.

GROUP TALK

Debate the following statements and explain your answers.

1. Missionaries who want to introduce people to the faith should spend their time with the leaders of a country rather than with the common folk.

2. Christianity is not the same as European culture; it should be expressed in terms of the culture in which it finds itself.

3. All Catholics who take their faith seriously should do what they can to bring others to the faith.

4. The Catholic Church today does not do enough to bring people into the Church.

Portuguese missionaries did manage to gain converts among a portion of the population of India that was not already Christian. The first group to convert to Christianity were lower-caste fishermen living along the seacoast. Entire clans of fishermen accepted Christianity, along with their wives and children. When the Spanish Jesuit Francis Xavier (1506–1552) arrived in India in 1542, he realized that these converts knew very little about Christian beliefs. Therefore, he wrote basic prayers and the creed in simple rhymes that were easy to remember and recite. Indian children would follow him around and recite the Lord's Prayer and other prayers with him. Through Francis Xavier, Catholicism gained a firm foothold in India. Pope Pius X declared Francis Xavier patron saint of Christian missions. He is also known as "the Apostle to India" and as "the Apostle to Japan," since he, at a later time, also traveled to that country.

The Italian Jesuit Roberto de Nobili added an entirely different dimension when he arrived in India in 1606. He realized that the religious scholars and holy men of the country were the **Brahmins**. In the Indian caste system, Brahmins dressed differently from others and would not eat or socialize with lower-caste persons. De Nobili decided that he would learn the ways of the Brahmins. He mastered their beliefs, joined in their austere practices, and even began to dress like them. He also disassociated himself from the meat-eating Portuguese Christians whom the Brahmins disdained. De Nobili concluded that he could become a Brahmin without denouncing Christianity and that Brahmins could become Christian without giving up their social caste, their distinctive dress, or their learning. Within three years, he converted fifty Brahmins to the faith. He also was accused of heresy by the Portuguese Christians. Nonetheless, de Nobili lived in India as the "Roman Brahmin" for fifty years and added to the Christian tradition there.

>Age to Age

New Religious Communities

The Holy Spirit led many holy women and men of this period to form religious communities to serve the needs of people of their time. The Holy Spirit has not stopped working within the Church in this way. Even in the past few decades new religious communities have begun to address the current needs of people. In 1950, Mother Teresa of India formally began the Missionaries of Charity, which has grown into a community of women dedicated to serving "the poorest of the poor." The Brotherhood of Hope, founded in 1980, is a community of vowed men who work with Catholics no longer actively involved in the Church to bring them back in the practice of their faith. Since 1982, the Franciscan Friars of the Renewal live and work in shelters for people who are homeless. The Sisters of Life (1991) work in many areas of support related to a culture of life, especially post-abortion counseling and support for older people. The Daughters of Mary, Mother of the Eucharist, is a Nigerian foundation of sisters who came to America in 2000 to work especially with immigrants from Nigeria.

Communities of lay people have also formed in recent decades to carry on unique work in the Church. Miles Jesu (1964) is a group of lay people whose goal is "to Christianize the secular world" by prayer and example. Later in this book we'll meet Jean Vanier, who in 1964 began a group where the poor and rejected of society, in particular persons with a disability, could find a home. The Catholic Corps began in 1975 as a community of lay persons who profess vows and live and work in everyday jobs to be a "Catholic presence" in American society.

Praying with Saint Vincent de Paul

Leader: Let us pray. Good Saint Vincent, help us always to remember your words that, "In serving the poor, you serve Jesus Christ . . . . You serve Christ in the person of the poor." In your day, you found Christ in the sick, the prisoner, the slave, the abandoned child, and those ravaged by war. Inspire us as we seek to serve Christ in the poor of our day. Amen.

Quoted in Robert P. Maloney, C.M., *The Way of Vincent de Paul*, pp. 26–27

Let us contemplate the practices laid out by Saint Vincent for the members of his congregation:

Be poor in spirit . . . . Listen humbly and well to all. Allow yourself to be evangelized by the poor . . . .

Learn to see all life as a gift. Share that gift generously with others . . . .

Be poor in fact. Accept some of the privations that poor people experience . . . .

Eat what is put before you. Do not complain about food. Drink moderately . . . .

Develop a simple life-style . . . .

Give generously to the poor

Often examine conscientiously how you live and work . . . .

Be sparing in the things you acquire . . . .

Be willing to labor hard . . . . Develop a "servant's attitude". . . .

The Way of Vincent de Paul, p. 119

All: Let us no longer say: it is I who have done this good work; for every good thing ought to be done in the name of our Lord Jesus Christ . . . . Be very much on your guard against attributing anything to yourself. By doing so you would commit robbery and do injury to God, who alone is the author of every good thing.

The Way of Vincent de Paul, p. 40

Review

1. What three reasons did the Inquisition give for condemning Galileo's position?
2. What perspective on truth seeking did Descartes and Bacon advocate?
3. What position on Christianity did most Enlightenment thinkers hold?
4. What is rationalism? How did the Church respond to it?
5. What is Gallicanism? What was the Church's response to it?
6. What effect did the French Revolution have on the Catholic Church?
7. Why did Napoleon's concordat with the pope support Ultramontanism?
8. What event occurred in 1870 that led Pope Pius IX to declare himself to be "the prisoner of the Vatican"? What was he protesting by taking this title?
9. Why is Pope Pius IX considered to be the first modern pope?
10. What was the Oxford Movement?
11. John Henry Newman concluded that the true Church should be centered upon what institution?
12. What effect did the Glorious Revolution have on English-Irish relations?
13. What experience led Vincent de Paul to become involved in service to people who were poor?
14. What did Francis de Sales emphasize in his spirituality?
15. What changes did John Baptist de La Salle introduce into education?

Key Words

accommodation (p. 245) The practice of aligning beliefs and practices from local cultures with Christianity.

baroque (p. 241) A style of art, architecture, and spirituality that emphasizes feelings and sentimentality.

Brahmins (p. 249) Members of the highest-ranking social class in the traditional Indian caste system.

Christians of Saint Thomas (p. 248) Indian Christians who trace their origins to the first century.

concordat (p. 235) An agreement between the pope and a head of state identifying the role that each would play in Church governance in that country.

deism (p. 225) Belief that God created the world and then left it to run according to natural laws.

Enlightenment (p. 220) The seventeenth- and eighteenth-century movement in Europe during which reason and science grew in importance as sources of truth.

Gallicanism (p. 233) A movement originating among the French Catholic clergy based on national rulers having authority for Church governance in their country.

geocentric (p. 221) Belief that the sun revolves around the earth.

heliocentric (p. 221) Belief that the earth and other planets revolve around the sun.

infallible (p. 228) Incapable of error in defining doctrines involving faith or morals.

monarch (p. 230) Head of a nation-state who claims to have complete authority in its governance.

rationalism (p. 225) A theory that nothing is true unless founded on scientifically demonstrable proofs based solely on reason and the five senses; condemned by the First Vatican Council.

Reign of Terror (p. 234) Period during the French Revolution when nobility and many clergy were executed by French revolutionary leaders.

scholasticism (p. 222) A method of intellectual inquiry dominant in western Christian civilization from the Middle Ages until the seventeenth century, and into the twentieth century among Catholic scholars.

Thirty Years' War (p. 231) War over religious, dynastic, and territorial issues; it involved most European nations but was fought mainly in Germany.

Ultramontanism (p. 235) Belief, often in an exaggerated form, that the pope alone has ultimate authority for Church governance in all countries.

>Yesterday and Today

The Catholic Church underwent a major transformation during the period of the Enlightenment, the age of discovery, and the time of intense political change in Europe. The sixteenth century had ended with a divided Christianity in the West. Following this jarring experience, Catholicism had to deal with thinkers who looked to radically new sources of truth. Some of these thinkers rejected or at least questioned core Christian beliefs. Catholics made major contributions to what would become the modern world. Men and women we now recognize as saints instituted modern approaches to social work, hospital care, and education. Catholic missionaries spread out across the globe and made Catholicism a religion that now has a home in practically every country and culture. The papacy also underwent change during this era of transformations. By the middle of the nineteenth century, the pope no longer served as both a head of state and the spiritual leader of the Church. Flowing from these changes, both the pope and the Church emerged in the modern world as a sacred presence in an increasingly secularized world.

▼ *First Baptism of the Indians by the Dominicans, Mexican School.*

TIMELINE

A.D. 1565
Spanish founding of St. Augustine, Florida

A.D. 1492
European exploration of the Americas begins

A.D. 1493
Pope grants power to Portugal and Spain to evangelize the Americas

A.D. 1531
Our Lady of Guadalupe appears to Juan Diego

A.D. 1609
Reductions established in South America

MOSAIC OF UNITY AND DIVERSITY

CHAPTER 9

THE CHURCH IN THE AMERICAS

A.D. 1492–1875

CHAPTER GOALS

In this chapter you will:

★ discover how Spanish explorers and settlers created a Catholic New Spain extending from southern South America to Northern California.

★ learn how French missionaries converted northern Native Americans to Catholicism.

★ see how first generation Catholics of the United States attempted to express their Catholicism in a predominantly Protestant society and in a new kind of political environment.

★ explore the cultural aspects of the Immigrant Church and the beginning of Catholic schools in the United States.

A.D. 1620
Pilgrims land in Massachusetts

A.D. 1634
Colony tolerating religious freedom established in Maryland

A.D. 1680
Death of Kateri Tekakwitha

A.D. 1682
Pennsylvania grants religious toleration

A.D. 1769
Junipero Serra founds California missions

A.D. 1776
Declaration of Independence

A.D. 1789
John Carroll elected first U.S. Catholic bishop

A.D. 1787
U.S. Constitution declares separation of Church and state

A.D. 1809
Mother Seton establishes a Catholic school

A.D. 1844
Nativist riots in Philadelphia

A.D. 1875
James Healy becomes first African American Catholic bishop in the U.S.

A Collision of Cultures

FIRST THOUGHTS

The American Catholic Church is a "mosaic of unity and diversity."

★ Find statistics about the makeup of the Catholic Church in the Americas.

★ Create a visual or audio representation of the Catholic Church of the Americas.

If you had to move to another country, would you try very hard to hold onto your old ways or decide to blend into the ways of your new culture? Can you imagine ever feeling "at home" some place else? Today, "being Catholic" and "being American" do not seem contradictory in any way. Indeed, according to the 2002 U.S. Census, more than twenty-six percent of the population of the United States is Catholic. However, that has not always been the case. Catholicism first came to the New World along with the conquering Spanish, Portuguese, and French explorers and traders. The English colonies were less hospitable to Catholics. One of the great tests of the freedom of religion clause in the U.S. Constitution came when waves of immigrants greatly increased the nation's Catholic population.

The story of Catholicism in the Americas began in 1492 with the arrival of Europeans. Since then, Catholicism has added greatly to the identity of the American continents, both North and South. While tensions between North and South American standards and the values of the Catholic Church have always existed, the Americas have done much to reshape Catholicism. Eventually, the success of the American experiment helped the Catholic Church become less fearful of and more open to the modern world.

Catholicism in Spanish America

In 1492, Christopher Columbus reached an island of the Americas, believing that he had landed on the eastern side of Asia. Although an Italian, Columbus sailed for the country of Spain, the most powerful European country of the sixteenth century and one that had avoided the turmoil of the Reformation. In 1493, the pope granted to Spain and Portugal total responsibility for evangelizing—that is, spreading the Gospel message—to all the new lands discovered by these two countries. Thus, European involvement in the Americas was intimately connected with the religious situation in Europe from the beginning. For the first decade or so, "America" meant the islands of the Caribbean. The Spanish established a capital city on Hispaniola and called it Santo Domingo. In 1504, just twelve years after the arrival of the first Spaniards, the Spanish Church established the diocese of Santo Domingo. In 1515, **conquistadors** took control of Cuba. Then, in 1519, they invaded the North American mainland, and New Spain began.

Mistreatment of the Native Americans Everyone familiar with the story of Europe's conquest of the Americas knows that the native populations were devastated by it. Within forty years, no "Indians," as the Spanish called the native people, were living on Hispaniola. Columbus had reported a thriving population on the island when he first arrived there. Diseases introduced by the Spanish, destruction of the Native American social systems, and direct killing combined to decrease the native population on the mainland as well. Estimates vary, but perhaps less than twenty-five percent of the Native American people survived. This decimation was not intended by the Spanish government and certainly was fought against by most representatives of the Catholic Church. Catholic Church leaders saw converts in these new lands as a sign of the health and well-being of Catholicism at a time when the reformers were questioning Catholicism.

In 1511, a Dominican priest who had recently arrived in Hispaniola denounced the Spanish from the pulpit for their mistreatment of the Native Americans:

> Are they not men? . . . You are all in a state of mortal sin . . . because of the cruelty and the tyranny you are inflicting on these innocent victims.
>
> Quoted in Adrian Hastings, *A World History of Christianity*, p. 332

Another Dominican, Antonio Valdivieso, went back to Spain to complain to King Charles V personally about the terrible treatment Native Americans were receiving. The king appointed Valdivieso bishop of Nicaragua. When he returned to Central America, Valdivieso realized that local Spanish leaders did not want to hear his message of justice for the natives and that his life was in danger if he continued preaching it. Nonetheless, Valdivieso made his way to the capital of Nicaragua and used the pulpit of the cathedral to defend the Native Americans. In 1550, the governor's son and several accomplices stabbed Valdivieso and two other Dominicans to death.

FAITH ACTIVITY

Native Americans Research and give an oral report or PowerPoint® presentation on one of the Native American groups of the Americas. Include in your report a description of religious beliefs or practices.

The Conquistadors Finding new sources of wealth, opening new trade routes to the East, and spreading the Christian message to new lands were the three reasons for Spain's active involvement in the conquest of the Americas. The conquistadors—the Spanish soldiers who led the takeover of Latin America—reduced these goals to one: finding wealth. The two major civilizations of Latin America were centered in Mexico and in Peru. The capital cities of the Aztecs (in Mexico) and Incas (in Peru) did possess signs of splendor and wealth. However, the conquistadors found little silver and gold in the territory they initially conquered. They therefore looked to another source of wealth—enslavement of the native people.

INTERPRET THE ART

Changing Styles Recall for a moment how art changed from the Dark Ages to the Renaissance. How do you think art—and the life, religious practices, and social structures that inspire art—changed for Native Americans in the years following Spanish and Portuguese colonization of the Americas?

An Incan drinking vessel depicting a warrior with a club and a feather-work shield, 1532.

Even though the rulers of Spain had forbidden making slaves of any people under their rule, the conquistadors and later Spanish settlers forced Native Americans to labor in mines and fields. The rulers of Spain faced a dilemma regarding slavery. On the one hand, they were morally opposed to it. On the other hand, they were becoming increasingly dependent on the wealth coming from the Americas—wealth gained from slave labor. The Native Americans, suffering from diseases and the total disruption of their social life, proved to be very unproductive as slaves. Most of those subjected to slavery died. In 1542, the Spanish crown ordered that all Native American slaves be freed. The crown further ordered the institution of reforms aimed at improving conditions for the native people. However, much damage had already been done; to further complicate matters, the settlers in New Spain did not always follow the orders coming from Spain.

The Missionaries The only voices speaking out for the Native Americans were the missionaries. Mexicans adopted Catholicism with much enthusiasm. One perspective on this phenomenon is that when their social and political world collapsed, so did their religious world. This collapse left a vacuum. The king of Spain replaced their ruler, Montezuma, and Catholicism replaced the worship of the sun. Mexicans built many churches and participated with particular fervor in the penitential processions of Good Friday. The first arch–bishop of Mexico established a college, hoping to educate some of the Mexicans for the priesthood. However, no priestly vocations came of this enterprise.

The Native Americans of Peru accepted Catholicism more slowly than the Mexicans did, and with less enthusiasm. Missionary Church leaders allowed Peruvian Native Americans only the Sacraments of Baptism, Penance, and Marriage. They didn't permit natives to receive the Eucharist since they felt that they were incapable of understanding it.

Not every missionary spoke out against the horrible conditions imposed on the Native Americans. A few proposed that despite the disruption and destruction the European invasion caused the Native Americans, introducing them to Christianity and providing them with Baptism justified the harsh measures. Some missionaries built churches and provided for the religious needs of the Native Americans, but did little to address broader issues of justice.

However, other missionaries attempted to improve conditions for Native Americans. The greatest defender of the Native Americans was Bartolome de Las Casas (1484–1566). Las Casas left Spain for the New World in 1502 at the age of eighteen. His father and uncle had sailed with Columbus on his second voyage, and Las Casas had heard about their adventures. He lived as a settler for a number of years and then was ordained a priest. Las Casas joined the conquistadors who landed in Cuba. There, he took Native American slaves, whom he put to work in a mine. In 1514, Dominican priests convinced Las Casas that his use of slave labor was wrong. Las Casas freed his slaves, joined the Dominicans, and returned to Spain where for the rest of his fifty-one years, he became the leading advocate for the Native Americans, doing everything possible to have the Spanish government pass laws in their favor.

Native American Catholicism

One stark reality of the European conquest of the Americas was that a European presence there could not be reversed. Church and government leaders, European settlers, and Native Americans—and a growing number of multiracial people—now living in either a Spanish- or Portuguese-controlled land had to deal with the tremendous transformation that had so rapidly taken place in America. Spanish and Portuguese settlers tended to try to create a world like the one they had left back home, including their practice of Catholicism. Meanwhile, people of Native American ancestry devised ways to express their Catholic faith that also incorporated their traditional Native American view.

GROUP TALK

The native population of Hispaniola was devastated by the Spanish explorers who landed there. Describe a current-day situation in which the same type of decimation wipes out whole groups of people. How has the Church responded to that situation? In what ways can Catholics your age be a voice for these people?

FYI

Members of a third order are neither priests, nor religious sisters or brothers, but lay people—a third order—associated with a religious community such as the Franciscans, Dominicans, and so on.

Saint Rose of Lima One saint who lived all of her life in the New World but who exhibited a spirituality of an earlier European era was Rose of Lima (1586–1617). The daughter of Spanish settlers in Peru, Rose's family was not making ends meet in the mines that were the family business. Her parents hoped that Rose, who was stunningly beautiful, would marry someone who could help the family financially. However, Rose felt called to the religious life, specifically to a life of prayer and self-sacrifice. She purposely disfigured her face so that she would be less attractive and joined the Third Order of the Dominicans. Rose helped her family by gardening and working on various crafts while living alone in a hut near her house. Eventually, she also worked among those who were poor in Lima, especially the Native Americans and slaves. During her life, Rose experienced much physical and spiritual suffering, which led to her death at the age of thirty-one. Canonized in 1671, Rose is the first American declared a saint. She is the patron saint of South America.

Our Lady of Guadalupe

On December 9, 1531, barely ten years after the Spanish conquest of Mexico, a native named Juan Diego was making his way to Mass in Mexico City. On the way he passed a hill that had been the site of a shrine to a Native American goddess. Juan Diego heard a woman call his name, and looking up he saw a woman speaking to him. The woman told Juan Diego that she was the Mother of God. She spoke to him of love, compassion, and hospitality. She instructed Juan Diego to tell the bishop to build a chapel on the hill in her honor. Juan Diego did as he was told. Not surprisingly, the bishop ignored him.

Two more times Juan Diego encountered the woman. The third time Mary appeared to him was in December. In spite of the cold, roses were growing at her feet. She instructed Juan Diego to gather the roses in his cape and present himself to the bishop. When he opened his cape before the bishop, the picture of the Virgin Mary was imprinted on it. The bishop built the chapel, and placed Juan Diego's cape on display within it. **Our Lady of Guadalupe** has been the object of great devotion ever since.

The story of Our Lady of Guadalupe is remarkable for a number of reasons. So much about it would have been unacceptable to the Spanish coming to power in Mexico, and yet devotion to Our Lady of Guadalupe has gained universal recognition in the Church. The event took place at a time when Franciscan missionaries were destroying temples dedicated to the Aztec gods upon whom Mexican religion centered. Mary appeared on the spot where a temple to a Native American goddess had stood. She appeared not to one of the Spanish settlers, but to a Native American. She left not words, as she typically did in Europe, but a visible image of herself. She identified not with those in control, but with those who were poor and oppressed.

The image of Our Lady of Guadalupe is neither of a Native American goddess nor a European Madonna. Her dress is European but with Native American decorations. Her face is *mestizo*, reflecting both European and Native American ancestry. Devotion to Our Lady of Guadalupe has sustained and given hope to Latin American and Native American people for more than four hundred years. As one author states:

The image of Guadalupe continues to hold a special meaning for the humble and oppressed peoples of the Americas. For others she is a potent symbol of the Church...that celebrates diversity, empowers the poor, and speaks with the voice of compassion. Where such a church lives, roses bloom in December.

Robert Ellsberg, *All Saints*, p. 538

FAITH ACTIVITY

Message for Today Name specific ways that Our Lady of Guadalupe's message of love, compassion, and hospitality can be applied to the world today.

The *Reductions* of Paraguay In working with the Native Americans, Jesuit missionaries tended to follow a strategy different from that of the Dominicans and Franciscans. Rather than concentrating on the two highly developed Aztec and Inca peoples, Jesuits went out into the frontiers and worked with the many Native American groups clustered in small villages apart from other tribes.

Following an approach advocated by Las Casas, the Jesuits introduced Christianity and European farming methods and craft work to the Native Americans. They transformed groups of Native Americans into self-sufficient farming communities who celebrated the Catholic feasts with much singing and ritual flare. Often the Jesuits would bring together tribes who previously did not speak to one another. These communities were known as *reductions*. All indications are that they did function well, blending together European and native cultures. They faced two problems, however. For one, Native Americans in the *reductions* faced attacks from Portuguese slave traders. The Jesuits in Paraguay received permission to train some of the Native Americans in the use of firearms so that they could serve as a police force protecting the community from harm. Second, leadership in these communities remained in the hands of the Jesuits. By 1767, the Jesuits were being suppressed in the area. Even though some priests continued the *reductions* as best they could, the lack of native priests and native leaders led eventually to the disintegration of this system.

Spanish Catholicism Moves North

We tend to think of the history of the Church in North America in terms of the thirteen English colonies. However, Christianity first entered what was to become the United States by way of Spanish explorers and missionaries, and later the French. Both Spain and Portugal understood the spread of Catholicism to be their God-given responsibility. A map of Mexico, or New Spain, from the seventeenth and eighteenth centuries reveals that it included a large portion of what later was the United States. In fact, only a small portion of the Americas was English.

In 1513, Ponce de Leon, searching for a "fountain of youth" that was spoken of in legends, arrived on the east coast of the North American mainland and called the area Florida. The Spanish established a permanent settlement in 1565 at a place they called St. Augustine. Missionaries built a church and mission there called *Nombre de Dios*. The mission still exists. It claims to be the oldest parish in continual use in the United States. In 1598, a statue of Our Lady of La Leche, depicting Mary feeding the baby Jesus at her breast, was brought to the mission. Devotion to Our Lady under this title still exists at the mission today.

Spanish explorers arrived in California as early as 1542. By 1772, missions designed to work with Native Americans dotted the California coast from the San Diego mission to the mission of San Francisco. Missionaries also served Spanish communities in other parts of the Southwest. By 1630, mission records document that more than five thousand Baptisms of native people took place in the area that is now New Mexico.

Juan de Padilla Many brave men and women brought the message of Christ to the native peoples who lived north of the Rio Grande River. Many of them lost their lives for their efforts. Franciscan friar Juan de Padilla came to Mexico in 1528. He learned the language of the Native Americans and worked on their behalf. When Francisco de Coronado announced his intention to lead an expedition into what is today New Mexico, Juan asked to join him. Over the next two years, de Padilla visited the pueblos of the Hopi Native Americans and other tribes. In 1542, Coronado decided to return to New Spain since he had not achieved his intended goal of finding the legendary cities of gold. De Padilla stayed behind in New Mexico and continued his missionary journeys. With the help of some members of the Wichita Nation, he traveled into and began a mission in what is now Kansas. In time, de Padilla decided to visit another Native American group, one that was the enemy of the people among whom he was then working. To prevent him from making this journey, one of the men in the group in which he was living killed him. Thus, Juan de Padilla became the first Christian martyr in what was to become the United States.

EXPLORE THE LAND

Early European Explorers and Missionaries The five main countries of origin for exploration of the new world were Portugal, Spain, France, England, and the Netherlands. Looking at the North American continent, choose one exploring country and write a one-page report on how it influenced the region or regions of North America in culture and religion.

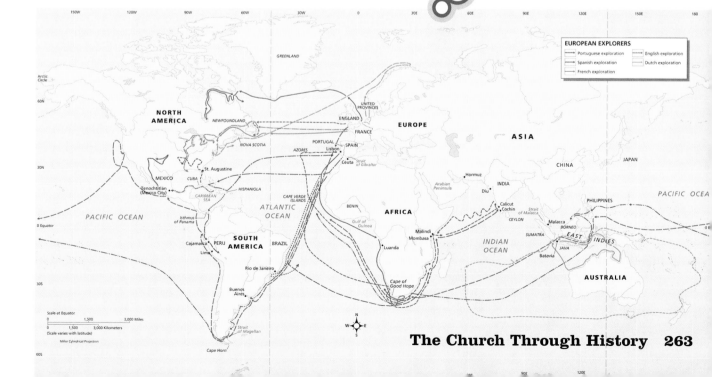

The Church Through History 263

Eusebio Francisco Kino Another early missionary to what is now the U.S. Southwest was Eusebio Francisco Kino. The only son of German noble parents, Kino joined the Jesuits in gratitude to God after recovering from a serious illness. He was ordained in 1678 and requested to go to the Philippines, hoping eventually to enter China. Instead, his Jesuit superiors sent him to New Spain. From there Kino went to work in California, learning the Piman language, which he always spoke with a German accent. As he traveled around northwest Mexico, including present-day Arizona, Kino used his knowledge of science to develop maps of the area.

Because he was a personal friend of King Carlos II of Spain, Kino secured a decree dispensing all Native Americans who converted to Christianity from working in the mines for twenty years. This made him a hated man among mine owners. They requested that another Jesuit be sent to investigate Kino's work, hoping that Kino would be removed. Instead, his fellow Jesuit who examined his efforts with the Native Americans found Kino's work to be worthy of high praise. Kino went on to discover the overland route to California and opened missions in California without the assistance of the military. To do this, he received financial support from generous benefactors. Using his missions as a base, Kino explored and mapped out most of the northwestern Mexican territory, which included portions of what is now the U.S. Southwest. He wrote a thesis demonstrating that Baja, or lower, California was a peninsula, not an island as previously thought.

Mission San Diego de Alcala, founded by Junipero Serra in 1769. ▼

Junipero Serra and the California Missions

Born on the island of Majorca in 1713, Miguel Jose Serra joined the Franciscans at the age of sixteen and took the name Junipero. An excellent student, Serra was assigned to teach at the university but longed to go to the missions. In 1750, he was released from his teaching responsibilities and permitted to go to New Spain. Once he arrived in Mexico City, he was again assigned to teaching and only occasionally sent to do mission work. On one of his missionary journeys, Serra was bitten by an insect that caused sores and swelling on his left leg and for the rest of his life it was painful for him to ride horseback.

When the pope suppressed the Jesuits, they had to abandon their California missions. Serra quickly volunteered to go to California to take up the work the Jesuits had begun there. Serra devised a plan to establish a series of missions along the coast. He eventually founded twenty-one missions, each one a day's walk from the previous mission.

On July 1, 1784, Father Junipero Serra reported on life at the Mission of San Carlos de Monterey:

> The Christians living at the mission pray twice daily with the priest in the church. More than one hundred twenty of them confess in Spanish and many who have died used to do it as well. The others confess as best they can. They work at all kinds of mission labor, such as farm hands, herdsmen, cowboys, shepherds, milkers, diggers, gardeners, carpenters, farmers, irrigators, reapers, blacksmiths, sacristans, and they do everything else that comes along for their corporal and spiritual welfare.

Quoted in John Tracy Ellis, ed., *Documents of American Catholic History*, p. 44

Father Serra mastered the Otomi language so that he could effectively communicate with the Pames. He was a strong advocate for the natives against the brutality of many obstinate white leaders. Father Serra made sure that Native Americans at the missions were taught agricultural and academic subjects.

By the time of Father Serra's death in 1784, more than 6,700 Baptisms were recorded and more than 4,600 Christian Native Americans were living in the missions.

FAITH ACTIVITY

What's in a Name List six cities in the western or southwestern United States whose names in Spanish have religious significance. Translate the names into English. For one of these cities, write a prayer based on its religious name.

Images of the Church

A Pilgrim People

> The one people of God is accordingly present in all the nations of the earth, and takes its citizens from all nations, for a kingdom which is not earthly in character but heavenly. All the faithful scattered throughout the world are in communion with each other in the holy Spirit so that 'he who dwells in Rome knows the Indians to be his members.'[1]

Documents of Vatican II, "Dogmatic Constitution on the Church," #13

From the beginning of the Church, Christians have been a Pilgrim People. Indeed, at the end of the Gospel according to Matthew, Jesus tells his followers to spread the message to the people of all nations. This image of the Church as a Pilgrim People is evident in the Americas. Today, the largest concentration of Catholics on any continent is in South America. The Church is at home in lands far from its starting point because, despite external differences, all people share a common home through their Baptism into the one Body of Christ.

The French Presence

FAITH ACTIVITY

Native American Spirituality One aspect of Native American spirituality that has become important to some people of the United States is the Native Americans' respect for the earth. Create and celebrate a class prayer service using some passages and themes from Christian and Native American customs.

French intentions upon arriving in Canada in 1534 appear to have been less grandiose than those of the Spanish. French explorers set out to find a Northwest Passage—a waterway through the northern part of America that would lead from the Atlantic Ocean to the Pacific Ocean—to the Far East and to search for silver and gold. Not until seven years later, in 1541, did the French attempt to establish a settlement in the New World, near Quebec. When they found no precious metals in the region, they abandoned this settlement. In time, the French did find wealth in the area, but it came in the form of fish off the Grand Banks of Newfoundland, and then in furs gained from trading with Native Americans or from trapping. Finally, in 1608, Samuel de Champlain tried to make Canada more than a trading post. Even his attempts were modest in comparison to those of the Spanish colonization.

Jesuit Work among the Northern Native Americans

The real impetus for colonizing New France came from the Jesuits. Beginning in 1632, Church leaders in France saw the French presence in the New World as an opportunity to engage in missionary activity. Remember that this was a period of great religious fervor in France, when Louise de Marillac, Vincent de Paul, and many others worked among those who were poor. The Jesuits in particular took on this task. They believed, at least initially, that the Native Americans would need to adopt a European lifestyle if conversion to Christianity was to be truly effective. A number of French men and women, both religious and lay people, caught the missionary spirit. Mademoiselle Jeanne Mance founded the Hospital of Saint Joseph in Montreal, and a noblewoman named Madame de la Peltrie convinced Ursuline nuns to establish a school for Native American girls. Other schools and hospitals followed.

Saint Isaac Jogues One of the first Jesuits to take on the task of working among the Native Americans of North America was Isaac Jogues. He arrived in New France in 1636. The Hurons were the first tribe friendly to the **Black Robes**, as they called the Jesuits. Jogues and the other Jesuits quickly discovered that the Native Americans had a deep spirituality. They decided that, rather than impose European civilization upon the Native Americans, they should learn and build upon the civilization and spirituality already present among them.

A problem the Jesuits had to deal with was that the various Native American tribes were constantly at war with one another. Identifying with one tribe invariably meant animosity from another. Thus while living with the Hurons, Jogues and his companions witnessed the torture of several Iroquois prisoners. In 1642, Mohawks—part of the Iroquois Confederation—captured Jogues and a few of his companions. Although he underwent extreme torture, Jogues was kept alive as a slave for a Mohawk woman.

Jogues, now a worn down, skeleton of a man, managed to escape and returned to France. However, Jogues felt his work with the Native Americans was not finished. So he returned to New France and took part in negotiations aimed at bringing peace among warring tribes. At the age of forty-nine, Jogues was killed by an Iroquois warrior who superstitiously thought Jogues was the cause of an outbreak of illness and crop failure. Jogues and seven companions were canonized in 1930, and were proclaimed patron saints of Canada in 1940.

Blessed Kateri Tekakwitha (1656–1680)

Kateri Tekakwitha (1656–1680) was born of a Mohawk chief and an Algonquin Christian woman in the very village where Isaac Jogues was martyred. Kateri's parents died from smallpox, and she became partially blind and had a disfigured face from the illness. Nonetheless, Kateri continued to be raised as a princess. When a priest visited the village, Kateri asked for Baptism, which she received. Her conversion to Christianity and her refusal to marry led the other members of her tribe to mock her. Kateri fled her village and made her way to a Christian Native American community near Montreal. There, she received her first Holy Communion and took a vow dedicating herself to Christ. Soon after, both French and Native Americans in the area noticed that she seemed to have mystical powers. The people around her began to treat her with great reverence. When she died, her face was cleared of the blemishes and disfigurement that she had had since a child. Even after her death, a number of priests and Native Americans reported that Kateri appeared to them, and miracles were reported through her intercession. Kateri was declared Blessed on June 22, 1980, by Pope John Paul II. Her feast day is July 14.

"Lord God, You called the virgin Blessed Kateri Tekakwitha to shine among the American Indian people as an example of innocence of life. Through her intercession, may all peoples of every tribe, tongue and nation, having been gathered into Your Church, proclaim Your greatness in one song of praise. We ask this through Our Lord Jesus Christ, Your Son, Who lives and reigns with You and the Holy Spirit, one God, forever and ever. Amen."

The Collect of the Mass celebrated in honor of Blessed Kateri Tekakwitha

Père Jacques Marquette Jacques Marquette was born in France in 1637, was educated by Jesuits in Rheims, and was ordained in 1666. He went to Montreal and studied the Algonquian dialects for two years. He then joined a mission near present-day Sault Sainte Marie, Michigan—1,500 miles west of Montreal. From there he moved even farther west to an area near Lake Superior. Eventually, he founded the mission of Saint Ignace on Mackinac Island in northern Michigan. Around this time, he met Louis Jolliet, who was trading with Native Americans in the same area. In 1672, Jolliet was named leader of an expedition that would explore the northern part of the Mississippi River the following year. Jolliet asked Father Marquette to be the chaplain of this group. The two, along with five other men, set out by canoe along the northern shore of Lake Michigan. They traveled the Fox River, Wisconsin River, and Mississippi River. Jolliet kept journals and created maps, which provided much information for later explorers.

The first Native Americans the group encountered were the friendly Illinois. Father Marquette promised to return to work with the people. In 1675, he traveled back to live among the Illinois, establishing the Kaskaskia Mission among them. Recognizing that his health was failing, Marquette decided to return to a mission in the north, but died before reaching his destination.

FAITH ACTIVITY

Missionary Story Research and tell the story of a French missionary to Canada or the United States in poetry, drama, or a PowerPoint® presentation.

Differences in Conversions in New Spain and New France
1. Compared to the Spanish, few French people wanted to immigrate to the New World.
2. When the Jesuits were disbanded they were hard to replace in the mission fields.
3. The fading spiritual fervor of the post-Reformation era in France meant fewer people were willing to be missionaries.

How Successful Were the Missionaries?

Despite the stories of heroic efforts on the part of French missionaries, the Native Americans of the northern regions of America did not become Catholic in the numbers that the Native Americans among the Spanish did. One French missionary reported baptizing numerous Native Americans but that these Native Americans would return to their old ways "at the drop of a hatchet." The French Catholic presence in Canada survived the takeover of the region by the English. However, Catholicism did not become the dominant religion of the North American Native Americans.

Catholicism in the Colonies

The tenor of the Catholic experience in the English colonies was very different from that in New Spain and in New France. The colonies were Protestant territory. Even in Maryland, chartered to the Catholic Calvert family, Catholicism was the Church of the governing elite but not of all the colonists. Also, Maryland was surrounded by colonies where the great majority of people were Protestants and suspicious of Catholics. In 1633 Cecil Calvert, the second Lord Baltimore, said to his fellow Catholics making their way to Maryland:

" . . .no scandal nor offence [is] to be given to any of the Protestants . . . all Acts of Romane Catholique Religion [are] to be done as privately as may be. And . . . all the Romane Catholiques [are] to be silent upon all occasions of discourse concerning matters of Religion. "

Quoted in *Documents of American Catholic History*, p. 98

▼ **Portrait of Cecil Calvert by Florence Mackubin.**

Maryland—A Safe Haven for Catholics

People from England founded all thirteen colonies along the eastern coast of North America. Members of the established Church of England governed in Virginia, the original English colony. However, religious dissidents of one sort or another founded most of the other colonies. They came to America seeking the freedom to practice their religion without interference. Puritans settled in Massachusetts. Roger Williams, who broke with the Puritans, founded Rhode Island. Much later, in 1681, William Penn began his "holy experiment" in Pennsylvania. He envisioned a place where Quakers could practice their religion but also, in a rare gesture for the time, welcomed members of other faiths to live together in peace and harmony.

Maryland began as a safe haven for Catholics but was not founded as a Catholic colony. In 1624 George Calvert, a member of Parliament and the first Lord Baltimore, became a Catholic. Because he was a favorite of King James I, Calvert's joining the Catholic Church did not negatively affect his position in society. He asked permission to begin a colony in the New World and tried first in Newfoundland, but the harsh weather discouraged him. He considered Virginia but soon realized that Catholics would not be welcome there. He therefore sought a charter to establish a colony north of Virginia. When Calvert died, his son Cecil received the charter and arranged for two ships to carry settlers to the new colony. Calvert's second son Leonard became Maryland's first governor. In 1649, the colonial government passed the **Act of Toleration** granting freedom of religion in Maryland, the only colony at the time to do so. Unfortunately, in time Puritans took over the colony and deprived Catholics of the right to vote, to worship publicly, or to run schools. This situation remained in force until just before the American Revolution.

Only about twenty of the two hundred people who originally set sail for Maryland were Catholic. One of those was a Jesuit priest, Father Andrew White. Father White had been banished to Belgium for serving the Catholic community in England during persecution there. When the two ships, the Ark and the Dove, sailed up Chesapeake Bay and landed on an island, Father White celebrated Mass on what settlers later named St. Clement. As the settlers cleared land, Father White built a mission he named St. Inigoes in honor of Ignatius Loyola, founder of the Jesuits. Father White moved among the Native Americans in the area and learned their language. He wrote a dictionary, a grammar book, and a catechism in the Algonquian language.

When the town of St. Mary's was established as the capital of Maryland, Father White built a church there. Lord Baltimore had insisted that religious toleration should be extended to all Christians in the colony. This system worked until 1645, when a Puritan ship stole into St. Mary's harbor and the crew overthrew Lord Baltimore's officials, destroying all Catholic chapels and arresting Father White and another Jesuit. The two priests were sent back to England in chains where they remained in prison for three years until they were acquitted, but again banished. Father White moved to southern England where under an assumed name, he ministered to Catholics in the area until his death in 1656. He is known as the "Apostle of Maryland."

John Carroll of Maryland, the Nation's First Bishop

The predominant figure in colonial Catholicism was clearly John Carroll. Born in Maryland in 1735, John and his cousin Charles left for Europe to study at a Jesuit school in Saint Omer, France. Upon graduation, Charles returned home to Maryland. John went on to become a Jesuit priest and taught in Europe. He traveled throughout the continent as a tutor, getting a sense of the many countries of Europe. In 1773, when the Jesuits were suppressed by the pope, Father Carroll returned to his mother's home in Rock Creek, Maryland. From there he served the spiritual needs of people in the surrounding area.

FAITH ACTIVITY

History of Catholics Write a report on the history of Catholics in one colony of the United States or in one province of Canada.

In 1776, John Carroll was asked to join his cousin Charles and the great American diplomat Benjamin Franklin in seeking Canadian support for the colonies' rebellion against England. French Canadians in particular were suspicious of anti-Catholic attitudes in the colonies, and the delegation failed to gain the support of Canada for the rebellion. Nonetheless, Franklin and Father Carroll developed a close friendship that endured through the years.

In 1782, there were twenty-one former Jesuits in what was by then called the United States. Father Carroll organized the men and wrote the pope a letter requesting that one of their number, Father John Lewis, be appointed superior of all U.S. clergy. They begged the pope not to appoint a bishop at that time, since they feared that American Protestants would view a Catholic bishop as an extension of bad experiences they had had with Catholic Church leaders in Europe. They especially did not want a bishop appointed from Europe, for fear that he would not understand the new U.S. experiment of separation of Church and state.

The pope agreed to appoint one of the former Jesuits as their superior. The pope discussed the appointment with various clergymen and ambassadors, among them the U.S. ambassador to France at the time, Benjamin Franklin. All agreed that Father Carroll should be the superior of the U.S. clergy and the official contact between the U.S. Church and Rome. Six years later Father Carroll requested that the U.S. priests be allowed to elect their first bishop. Again, the pope heard their request. The U.S. clergy met in 1789 and elected John Carroll the first Catholic bishop of the United States.

Bishop Carroll was appointed bishop of Baltimore, but his diocese included all the thirteen colonies. In 1791, with the help of Sulpician priests from France, he established Saint Mary's in Baltimore as the first U.S. seminary for the training of priests. In 1808, the Sulpicians opened Mount St. Mary's College in Emmitsburg, Maryland. Bishop Carroll also helped develop Georgetown College, now Georgetown University in Washington, D.C. In 1803, when President Thomas Jefferson purchased the Louisiana Territory, Bishop Carroll's diocese doubled in size. Bishop Carroll therefore arranged for four new dioceses to be created. He died in 1815.

When the Declaration of Independence had been signed in 1776, Catholics numbered 30,000—one percent of the American population. By Bishop Carroll's death in 1815, there were 200,000 Catholics in the United States. Catholics gained acceptance in the early days of the republic for two primary reasons. First, their numbers were so small that they were not perceived as a threat. Second, Bishop Carroll demonstrated such support for and sensitivity toward the new system of government that he convinced others that members of the Church could be both Catholic and American.

!FYI

John Carroll was the only U.S. Catholic bishop ever to be elected by the clergy, rather than appointed by the pope.

Religious Freedom   One of the reasons Maryland granted religious freedom to its colonists probably was that, although Catholics governed the colony from the beginning, they were a distinct minority. Conversely, William Penn, the founder of Pennsylvania, granted religious toleration on more strictly religious grounds. Penn was a member of the Religious Society of Friends, or Quakers, a religious group that had emerged in England late in the Reformation period. The Quakers in England had experienced persecution for their beliefs firsthand. Because of Pennsylvania's policy of religious toleration, a number of Catholics—mostly of German descent—settled there. At the time of independence, most American Catholics lived in either Maryland or Pennsylvania.

Catholics generally kept a low profile during the colonial period. However, there were exceptions. Charles Carroll, the wealthiest man in the colonies, represented Maryland at the Continental Congress and boldly signed his name to the Declaration of Independence. During the Revolutionary War, Charles Carroll served in Congress along with his cousin Daniel, and Thomas Fitzsimons—also a Catholic—represented Pennsylvania. Another exception to the rule was Thomas Dongan, a Catholic who served as New York's governor for six years. Many prominent Catholics came from Europe to join the fight for independence. John Barry is known as the father of the American navy. His statue stands in front of Independence Hall in Philadelphia.

FYI

In 1733, the Catholic community of Philadelphia built St. Joseph's Church. At one point, this church marked the only place in the entire British Empire where Mass could be legally celebrated. In 1763, another church, St. Mary's, was built nearby. These two churches survived periods of strong anti-Catholic activity and, today, continue to serve thriving Catholic communities particularly in the old colonial section of Philadelphia.

◄ Old St. Mary's Church in Philadelphia, photographed by Michael Reed.

The U.S. System

After independence from England, U.S. Catholics lived in a new kind of political system. Recall that in Europe the first half of the nineteenth century was the "age of Metternich," when the rulers of Europe, including the pope, returned with great determination to the old order. In the United States, on the other hand, people elected their own leaders. At least in theory, religion was to be completely separate from politics. People were free to practice the religion of their choice, and they had the right of free speech. No wonder that Metternich saw no future in the American system. It represented something novel and untried, and it certainly did not reflect the commonly accepted view of governance sweeping Europe at the time.

Should the U.S. system carry over into the area of Church governance? For many U.S. Catholics in the beginning of the nineteenth century, the answer was yes. For some, electing governing bodies on the parish level was both the American way and also the way of the early Church. This system, known as **lay trusteeism**, meant that a parish board of lay people controlled the buying and selling of land and property. Theoretically, this elected body could also choose the parish priest since it controlled parish finances.

Bishop Carroll recognized that lay trustees posed a problem. If members of a parish could hire or fire their priests, what would prevent them from choosing priests who did and said what they wanted rather than what was faithful to universal Catholicism? Also, canon law, the official law of the Catholic Church, stated that only bishops could assign responsibility for a parish church to a priest. Nonetheless, Bishop Carroll allowed the trustee system to continue. Keep in mind that no one at the time was entirely sure how to blend together being Catholic and being American in the U.S. sense. The U.S. system was as new for Catholics as it was for other religious groups. In addition, since priests had been scarce during the colonial period, Catholic lay people were accustomed to running their own religious affairs.

Trusteeism was an internal affair not supported by all Catholics in the United States. Conflicts between ethnic groups added to the controversy. Often a parish could find itself with a pastor of a different nationality and with a different understanding of Church from that of the majority of the parishioners. For instance, the U.S. Catholic population was becoming more and more Irish while most bishops were French or German. When some Irish American Catholics complained, the pope appointed a young Irish priest as bishop of the small, newly established diocese of Charleston, South Carolina. Bishop John England was only thirty-two at the time, but he was recognized as one of the brightest churchmen in Ireland. When he came to the United States, he soon took a strong leadership role in the Church. He also spoke regularly to non-Catholic groups, explaining to them that being Catholic and being American were not inconsistent. He even addressed the U.S. Congress on the matter. In his own diocese, Bishop England wrote up a constitution, whereby representatives of clergy and lay people would meet annually to look over Church affairs of the diocese and recommend changes. The constitution worked well but didn't survive after the death of Bishop England.

On the national level, the U.S. Catholic bishops held a series of councils during which they addressed common concerns. The 1837 Provincial Council, at which Bishop England played an important role, tried to relay to the country that no one had anything to fear from Catholics. They pointed out, for one thing, that:

> We are indeed comparatively few amongst the millions of our fellow-citizens; the greater portion of our flocks are in the humble, laborious, but useful occupations of life; we do not aspire to power, we do not calculate by what process we should be able, at some future day, to control the councils of the republic. . . .

Pastoral Letter of the Third Provincial Council of Baltimore, #18

The bishops also insisted, contrary to what many believed, that:

> We do not detract from the allegiance to which the temporal governments are plainly entitled, and which we cheerfully give; nor do we acknowledge any civil or political supremacy, or power over us in any foreign potentate or power, though that potentate might be the chief pastor of our church.

Pastoral Letter of the Third Provincial Council of Baltimore, #18

In other words, the bishops were stating that Catholics owed spiritual fidelity to the pope but that this fidelity in no way interfered with their ability to participate freely in the political system of the United States.

GROUP TALK

1. Among the parishes to which members of your class belong, describe the types of activities in which lay people are involved. Explain why there may be different opportunities available.

2. Discuss your views on papal and U.S. flags being displayed in church sanctuaries. Why do you think some communities choose to do this?

Democracy in America In 1835, a Frenchman named Alexis de Tocqueville published a book about what he observed while traveling about the United States. His *Democracy in America* offered an insightful report about the state of U.S. social and political life at the time. De Tocqueville made the following startling observations about U.S. Catholics:

> These Catholics are faithful to the observances of their religion; they are fervent and zealous in the belief of their doctrines. Yet they constitute the most republican and the most democratic class in the United States. This fact may surprise the observer at first, but the cause of it may easily be discovered upon reflection.
>
> I think that the Catholic religion has erroneously been regarded as the natural enemy of democracy. Among the various sects of Christians, Catholicism seems to be, on the contrary, . . . one of the most favorable to equality of condition among men. In the Catholic Church the religious community is composed of only two elements, the priest and the people. The priest alone rises above the rank of his flock, and all below him are equal.
>
> On doctrinal points the Catholic faith places all human capacities upon the same level; it subjects the wise and ignorant, the man of genius and the vulgar crowd, to the details of the same creed; it imposes the same observances upon the rich and the needy, it inflicts the same austerities upon the strong and the weak; it listens to no compromise with mortal man, but reducing all the human race to the same standard, it confounds all the distinctions of society at the foot of the same altar.

Quoted in *Documents of American Catholic History*, pp. 233–34.

GROUP TALK

1 Upon what basis does de Tocqueville claim that Catholicism lends itself to democracy? Do you agree or disagree with his assessment? Explain why or why not.

2 Do you think that being Catholic today supports developing democratic attitudes? Why or why not?

The Immigrant Church

The main characteristic of the Catholic Church in the United States from early in the nineteenth to around the middle of the twentieth century was the sheer volume of Catholic immigrants entering the country. The first major wave of immigrants were Irish, who tended to cluster together in the major cities of the East Coast. Later, German Catholics arrived in large numbers and typically made their way to the Midwest where they took up farming and related occupations. Still later, Italians and people from Eastern Europe entered the country. Estimates are that between 1790 and 1850, more than a million Catholics immigrated to the United States, causing Catholics to become the largest single religious denomination. A steady stream of Catholic immigrants continued until 1924, when the government enacted immigration laws, at least partially intended to reduce the influx of Catholics entering the country.

Immigrants arriving at Ellis Island in New York▼

This long period of immigration caused a strong negative reaction from many native-born, white, Anglo-Saxon Protestants. This group began a violent anti-religious movement known as **Nativism**. In 1834, Nativists burned down a convent in Massachusetts. Ten years later, rioters burned down two churches in Philadelphia. During the riots, thirteen people were killed, and more than fifty people were wounded. At times Nativism expressed itself in specific political parties, such as the **Know Nothing Party**, an anti-foreign, anti-Catholic political organization that flourished in the United States between 1852 and 1856.

Causes of Nativism

Fear of foreigners and their languages.

Protestants' fears of a Catholic takeover of Protestant-dominated land.

Fear of a return to the medieval world of superstitions and absolute monarchs.

Threats to the social landscape of the new nation.

Supplanting the position of native-born workers because Irish and German immigrants willingly worked for less money.

Bishop John Hughes (1797–1864)

Irish-born John Joseph Hughes immigrated to the United States at the age of twenty, and found work constructing bridges and roads in Pennsylvania and Maryland. While working on the farm at Mount St. Mary's Seminary in Emmitsburg, Maryland, he requested acceptance into the priesthood. The rector in charge thought that Hughes was too headstrong to make a good priest and put him off. Hughes sought help from a woman named Mother Elizabeth Seton who ran a school nearby. With her recommendation, the rector accepted Hughes into the seminary program where he was a fine student and exhibited great powers of persuasion with his speaking skills.

Upon ordination Father Hughes was sent to Philadelphia where he successfully defended the Catholic Church's position against lay trusteeism. He also faced the anti-Catholic propaganda that was leading to acts of violence against Catholics and Catholic Church property. In 1838, Father Hughes was named the bishop of New York and became the leading spokesman for the Catholic Church in the United States.

In New York, Bishop Hughes continued to take on Nativism and also defended immigrants. When New York Nativists threatened to imitate the violence that took place in Philadelphia, Bishop Hughes took a strong stand against them, and no major anti-Catholic incidents occurred in his city. To make a lasting public statement that Catholicism was here to stay in America, Bishop Hughes announced the building of a cathedral in Manhattan dedicated to Saint Patrick. Today, St. Patrick's Cathedral is one of the best-known landmarks in New York City.

! FYI

John McCloskey succeeded Bishop Hughes as bishop of New York. When he was born in 1810, the diocese of New York was two years old and had two churches and six priests. At his death in 1885, the New York diocese had 139 parishes and 279 priests. The growth that took place in Catholicism in New York City mirrors the growth that occurred throughout the Catholic Church in the United States. In 1875 the pope named John McCloskey a cardinal, the first U.S. priest so honored.

Sisters of Our Lady of Mercy One way that Catholicism gained respect among the rest of the U.S. population was through the good works performed by women religious. For instance, during the yellow fever epidemics that hit Charleston, South Carolina, in the 1850s, the Sisters of Mercy set aside their teaching duties and cared for those who were sick regardless of their religious background. One of the sisters wrote the following account of their work:

> During these years the Sisters had no hospital, but went about from street to street, through lanes and alleys, wherever the sick might be found, carrying baskets filled with the necessities of life and medicine, as these were needed. They worked heroically, all through the periods of disease, and all classes of citizens recognized the debt of gratitude due to these noble women. . . . When the troubles were over, our Sisters quickly returned to their schoolrooms and seemed to have forgotten what no one who had seen them could ever forget, that they had but a short time before been active amid the dark scenes of death from yellow fever haunting the entire community.

> Quoted in Rosemary Radford Reuther and Rosemary Skinner Keller, ed., *In Our Own Voices*, p. 41

Preserving the Catholic Faith of Immigrants

Until the mid-1800s, most Catholic children, if they attended school, went to a public school in their town. Almost exclusively, Protestants sat on school boards, and despite the laws separating Church and state, public schools were Protestant-biased institutions. For instance, all students studied the *King James Bible*, which was a Protestant version, and were required to recite Protestant prayers or attend Protestant services. Texts would often show white, Anglo-Saxon Protestants as hard-working, productive members of society. On the other hand texts portrayed immigrants, such as newly arrived Irish and Italian Catholics, in a negative light.

In 1844, a number of bishops attempted to get public schools to become more Catholic-friendly institutions. Bishop Francis Kenrick's appeal to the school board of Philadelphia set off the anti-Catholic riots in that city. The bishops feared that Catholic children, especially of newly arrived immigrants, were in danger of losing their faith in a school atmosphere hostile to Catholicism. Even though it would entail great expense, the bishops called for creation of Catholic schools to accompany all parishes throughout the country. Catholic schools were so successful that the Council of Baltimore, held in 1884, ruled that within two years every parish had to have a Catholic grade school.

At this same council, the bishops commissioned a priest to write in simple question-and-answer format a catechism that could be used with Catholic school children. The result, called the *Baltimore Catechism*, served as the standard text used in religious education until the 1960s.

Saint Elizabeth Ann Seton (1774–1821)

Elizabeth Ann Bayley was born into a prominent New York Episcopalian family in 1774. Elizabeth's mother died when she was three, but her father soon remarried. Elizabeth received a fine education and became fluent in French. She also became a fine musician. She married William Seton whose family ran a successful shipping company. In 1797, the shipping business went bankrupt. William's health suffered, and a doctor suggested a sea voyage to restore his health. Elizabeth sold the last of their possessions so that she and their children could accompany her husband on the journey. Together, they sailed to Italy to visit old friends. While there, William died.

While Elizabeth made arrangements to return to the family home, she began to attend a Catholic Church where she discovered that she was particularly drawn to the belief in the Real Presence of Christ in the Eucharist. She returned her family to New York, and in 1805 she became a Catholic.

In 1809, Bishop John Carroll gave Elizabeth some property in Emmitsburg, Maryland, on which she opened a school. Elizabeth, her daughters, and her sisters-in-law began the U.S. foundation of the Sisters of Charity. Although the order experienced long periods of near poverty and much illness that took the lives of three of the original sisters, the community survived and finally prospered. Mother Seton, as she came to be known, died in 1821, and, in 1975, was named the first native-born U.S. saint. We celebrate her feast day on January 4th.

African American Catholics

African American Catholics are often overlooked in the history of American Catholicism. Actually, some Africans living in the area of the Congo converted to Catholicism in the fifteenth century, and some of these Catholics entered the New World as slaves. Other slaves in Spanish territories became Catholic, as did slaves who worked for Jesuits in Maryland and Louisiana. There are also isolated stories of African Americans who were not slaves and who held onto their Catholicism despite discrimination from white Catholics.

One interesting family stands out during this time. An Irish immigrant named Michael Healy living in Macon, Georgia, had five children with his slave wife. One of their sons, James Augustine Healy, wanted to become a priest. Because of his African American ancestry he had to attend seminary in Montreal and Paris. He was ordained in 1854 for the Boston archdiocese, and he served as rector of the cathedral and then as chancellor of the diocese. In 1875, he was named bishop of Portland, Maine. He died in 1900. Two of Bishop Healy's brothers became priests and two of his sisters entered religious life. His brother Patrick, a Jesuit, served as president of Georgetown University.

The first native-born African American priest was Augustus Tolton, who was born to Catholic slaves in Missouri in 1854. During the Civil War, he and his mother escaped to Quincy, Illinois, where he attended the Catholic school. He inquired about becoming a priest, and since no American seminary accepted black students at the time, he was sent to Rome to study. After ordination, in 1886, Father Tolton became a pastor in Quincy. Other priests and his bishop did not support him when some people made racial comments about him. Discouraged, Father Tolton received permission to transfer to Chicago where he built St. Monica's church, which became a thriving Catholic parish.

FAITH ACTIVITY

U.S. Ethnic Makeup Find statistics describing the current ethnic make-up of Catholics in the United States. Were you surprised by your findings? What do you think this says about the Church in the U.S.?

Mother Mary Lange and the Oblate Sisters of Providence

On July 2, 1829, four black women met in a row house in Baltimore to pronounce simple vows. When the ceremony was over, a new order of nuns was born, the Oblate Sisters of Providence. This was the first canonically recognized order of black sisters in the Church. The leader of the group, Elizabeth Lange, had come to Baltimore after living as a refugee following a slave revolt in her native Santo Domingo in 1791 (modern-day Haiti and the Dominican Republic). Elizabeth took the name Mother Mary Lange. She had four obstacles to face in the Baltimore of her day: she was black in a slave-holding state, a woman in a male-dominated society, a Catholic when it was not popular to be Catholic, and French-speaking in an English-speaking city. But she was also a very spiritual and spirited woman.

At the time, Baltimore was home to many refugees from Santo Domingo. Seeing the lack of educational opportunities available for young black women, Elizabeth took action. With the financial support of some friends and benefactors, she established a school for black girls, began an orphanage and a school for religious education, took in elderly women in need of shelter, and helped black patients at the Baltimore almshouse during the 1832 cholera epidemic.

Mother Mary Lange was a spiritual and cultured person who valued education. She included the study of music, the classics, and fine arts in the curriculum of her school. As her accounting system for her order and its projects indicates, she also had an excellent business sense. She experienced many hardships and setbacks in her work. When her financial backers left Baltimore, her order was left destitute. She took in washing and ironing to support her sisters and the orphanage.

◄ Nuns clap their hands at World Youth Day 2005 in Cologne, Germany.

Seeing their poverty, the Archbishop of Baltimore, who came from a slave-owning family, recommended that the sisters disband. He suggested that they instead do housekeeping at the seminary. Elizabeth refused. Although it was unheard of that a black Catholic woman would say no to a white archbishop, he did not use his power to dissolve the community. The Oblates continued to provide education, spiritual direction, and shelter to the black community of Baltimore. They conducted a night school where adults could learn to read and write. After the Civil War, Mother Lange's order began a new era of working with the many destitute black children who flooded into Baltimore.

The sisters were physically threatened on a number of occasions, and in the 1860s Oblate sisters teaching in Philadelphia were repeatedly forced from walking on the sidewalks with white people. But Mother Mary chose the name of her order well. She had determination, never despaired, and always placed her cares in the hands of Divine Providence.

American Catholics and Slavery In 1839, Pope Gregory XVI condemned the slave trade. However, this pronouncement did not identify slavery as an evil in itself. In the earliest days of the English colonies, there were both black and white slaves; however, slavery soon came to be restricted exclusively to people of African descent. Slaves were viewed as property of their owners. Many Catholics owned slaves, including the Jesuits in southern Maryland and the Ursuline sisters in Louisiana.

Theological speculation seemed to suggest that as long as slaves had an opportunity to practice their religion, then Catholic teaching had no basis on which to condemn the institution of slavery itself. To complicate matters, many of those calling for the abolition of slavery also spoke out against immigration. Some Irish immigrants complained that while blacks were slaves in the South, the Irish of the North were "wage slaves" living in conditions not much better than black slaves experienced.

During the Civil War Catholics fought on both sides. General Beauregard of Louisiana was a Catholic and a renowned Southern leader. On the Union side, General Sherman was Catholic. Though Catholic leaders generally tried to remain neutral and work for reconciliation, one Southern bishop wrote a widely circulated sermon calling for secession from the Union and urging Catholics to fight for the South. He also reminded slave owners that they had an obligation to treat their slaves justly. Bishop Hughes of New York flew the American flag over the cathedral and recruited troops for the Union side. Midwestern bishops tended to support the war so that Nativists would not doubt Catholic patriotism, among other reasons.

FAITH ACTIVITY

African American Bishops Research how many African American bishops currently serve the Catholic Church in the United States. Find out who they are, where they serve, and what their stories can teach us about the Church today.

Most average Catholics seemed to follow the beliefs of their neighbors. Many based their decisions on what was economically best for their families. Especially in the South, devastation from the war was great. Heroic actions by Catholic chaplains and religious sisters convinced many people of the virtue and loyalty of Catholics.

The Church's position on slavery is quite clear: the enslavement of humans for commercial or political purposes, and any actions that promote or lead up to enslavement, are morally wrong. All people possess God-given dignity, and this equal dignity makes it morally wrong to buy, sell, or exchange humans as if they are merchandise, treating them as things not people.

GROUP TALK

As a group, list the religious arguments you would use to point out the evil of slavery to a person who advocates slavery.

>Age to Age

A Multicultural Church

The United States grew out of thirteen English-speaking colonies. In time, new states were added where languages other than English were spoken. Great waves of European immigrants also made the United States a multicultural, multilingual nation. American Catholics have always found a way to treasure and preserve their cultural heritage in their religious life. Even when the Mass and sacraments were celebrated in Latin, succeeding generations of ethnic Catholics held onto their native Catholic heritage. In many large cities, ethnic churches could be found within blocks of one another. Catholics spoke with pride of attending St. Cyril's Polish, St. Patrick's Irish, or St. Jean's French Catholic church. Slowly, as second and third generations moved to suburbs and away from their cultural enclaves in the cities, the need for churches serving specific ethnic groups diminished.

Today, with the arrival of many new immigrants from South and Central America, from Haiti and other Caribbean islands, from Asia and Africa, and from Eastern Europe, once again the U.S. Catholic Church is attempting to provide a familiar context for their worship. Parishes may offer liturgies in Spanish, Portuguese, French, Vietnamese, Korean, Igbo, and Tagalog, as well as for the hearing impaired. Some parishioners may take it upon themselves to learn enough of a new language to be able to welcome new members to the parish from foreign lands. All of this outreach is a continuation of the Gospel command to spread the Good News to all nations.

▲Hispanic Parishioners attending a church service at the Basilica of Our Lady of San Juan de Valle in Texas.

Praying with Saint Martin de Porres

Leader: No saint is more honored in Latin America than Martin de Porres, a son of a freed African slave who went on to give his life helping people who were poor as a humble Dominican lay brother. Let us reflect on one of the "little stories" told about this holy man:

"And around noon, about the time to eat, [Martin] went to the refectory and took a cup and a bowl to collect any food left from the religious who ate by his side. If he saw any poor at the door of the refectory his impatience was notable until he was able to bring them food, and in having met their need, he calmed down and ate but bread and water so that through his great abstinence more could be fed, a sign of his great charity. And after having finished eating he took his bowl and his cup full of food and went to the kitchen of the infirmary where he waited on sick and impoverished Spanish, Blacks, Indians and the poor from the neighborhood and dogs and cats which at that hour waited for sustenance from the hand of the said servant of God. And before distributing the food he would give them a blessing saying: 'May God increase it through his infinite mercy.' And it seems that that is what happened, that God increased the food through [St. Martin's] hand for all ate and their bowls were filled outside and all were contented, even the dogs and cats."

As told in Alex Garcia-Rivera, *St. Martin de Porres*, p. 93

All: Let us pray that, inspired by Saint Martin, we will be impatient until all those who are hungry in the world receive their fill. May our bowl and our cup overflow with generosity so that, through Christ Jesus, the miracle of feeding the multitude can be duplicated again and again among us. Amen.

>Review

1. What responsibility did the pope give the governments of Spain and Portugal in 1493?
2. Who were the conquistadors?
3. What three factors led to the decrease of the Native American populations who had contact with the Spanish?
4. Who is the first American declared a saint?
5. What Franciscan founded a series of missions along the California coast?
6. What two reasons led French explorers to go to Canada? What two sources of wealth did the French find there?
7. What obstacle did the Jesuits face in their attempts to convert the Native Americans they encountered?
8. Why were the French missions less successful in bringing about conversions among the Native Americans than the Spanish missions were?
9. In what sense was the Catholic experience different in the English colonies compared to that in the Spanish and French colonies?
10. What was the Act of Toleration?
11. Who was the first American Catholic bishop? How was he chosen?
12. What religious group controlled colonial Pennsylvania? What policy did they espouse toward other religions?
13. Define lay trusteeism.
14. What is Nativism and why did it flourish?
15. Why did the U.S. Catholic bishops call for creation of Catholic schools?

>Key Words

Act of Toleration (p. 271) The 1649 decree by the government of Maryland granting freedom of religion there.

Black Robes (p. 267) Term northern Native Americans used for the Jesuits because of the Jesuit's distinctive garb.

conquistadors (p. 257) Spanish word for "conquerors"; the Spanish men who first came to the Americas especially in search of wealth.

Know Nothing Party (p. 278) Anti-foreign, anti-Catholic political organization that flourished in the United States between 1852 and 1856.

lay trusteeism (p. 274) Control of parish funds and resources by an elected body of lay people.

mestizo **(p. 261)** A person of both European and Native American ancestry.

Nativism (p. 278) Anti-Catholic and anti-immigrant movement.

Our Lady of Guadalupe (p. 261) Considered the patron saint of the Americas.

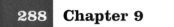

❯Yesterday and Today

In the United States the "American way," with its religious tolerance, its separation of Church and state, and its democratic principles, was something new for the Catholic Church. The pope was accustomed to consulting with the heads of state before appointing bishops. The U.S. president would have no part of this! Through the experiences in North and South America, the Church discovered that she could not only survive but thrive in the new world of democratic republics. By the end of the nineteenth century, the Catholic Church in the United States had grown into one of the most vibrant centers of Catholicism in the entire world. At the same time, the United States gained much from Catholicism. North America became the most culturally diverse continent in the world. Much of that diversity stems from northern European, southern European, Slavic, Hispanic, Asian, and African Catholics bringing their rich cultural heritages to the New World. The mosaic of unity and diversity that is the United States owes much to its Catholic population and to the Catholic Church.

▼*The Healing of the Lepers* by James Jacques Joseph Tissot.

TIMELINE

A.D. 1891
Rerum Novarum
written

A.D. 1871
Kulturkampf in Germany

A.D. 1878
Pope Leo XIII
elected

A.D. 1897
Catholic University of
America begins

A.D. 1903
Pope Pius X
elected

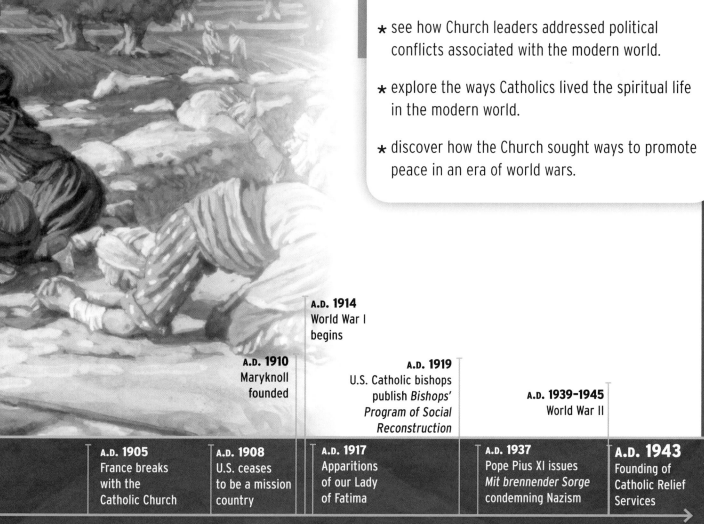

A SPIRITUAL AND MORAL PRESENCE

CHAPTER 10

THE CHURCH IN THE MODERN WORLD
1870-1950

CHAPTER GOALS

In this chapter you will:

* learn how Pope Leo XIII began modern Catholic social teaching, making the Church a leading voice for justice.

* see how Church leaders addressed political conflicts associated with the modern world.

* explore the ways Catholics lived the spiritual life in the modern world.

* discover how the Church sought ways to promote peace in an era of world wars.

A.D. 1914
World War I
begins

A.D. 1910
Maryknoll
founded

A.D. 1919
U.S. Catholic bishops
publish *Bishops'
Program of Social
Reconstruction*

A.D. 1939-1945
World War II

A.D. 1905
France breaks
with the
Catholic Church

A.D. 1908
U.S. ceases
to be a mission
country

A.D. 1917
Apparitions
of our Lady
of Fatima

A.D. 1937
Pope Pius XI issues
Mit brennender Sorge
condemning Nazism

A.D. 1943
Founding of
Catholic Relief
Services

How would you describe the "modern times" to someone from a previous era? Create your own image of "modern times." Then address the following questions.

★ What does your image have to say about the challenges the modern world presents to people trying to live a life of faith?

★ What role would you like the Church to have in the modern world?

★ Do you believe that balancing a life of faith with living in the modern world is more or less difficult than in past historical periods we have studied? Why or why not?

To whom do you turn when you are seeking guidance? The world is more complex than the one your parents, guardians, or even older sisters and brothers grew up in. That leaves you facing problems that no one, except your peers, has had to deal with. Is there nowhere to turn for answers and wisdom? In times of change, the Catholic Church has stepped forth to offer both.

More than one hundred years ago, the Catholic Church entered the modern world, carrying with it the life and teachings of Christ, which it offered people struggling to make sense of modern industry, modern warfare, and modern life. Stripped of its earthly kingdom in 1870, the Church was freed to become a universal spiritual and moral presence in the increasingly secularized world. The Church offered the wisdom it received from Christ, such as: Remember that you are made in the image and likeness of God; you are the light of the world and can share with people the hope of new life and life forever with God; you are part of a community that you need and that needs you; always respect the dignity and equality of others, for everyone is worthy of having their basic needs and rights met; treat all people, even people whom you don't like, with loving concern; be particularly attentive to the needs of those who are poor and suffering; and war is not glorious but tragic.

This chapter examines how the Church stayed the course as the world continued to identify itself less and less with ancient sources of wisdom such as those offered by the Church. During this period while an intense drama played itself out between the Church and the modern world, the Church offered invaluable resources that the world desperately needed, then as now.

Industry Flourishes

In the nineteenth century, Europe underwent a revolution that was every bit as jarring as the French Revolution. What the French Revolution did to European politics, the Industrial Revolution did to European social and economic life. Factories manufactured a staggering array of new products, making them available to more and more people. However, the factory system also transformed the relationship between workers and the products they made. As workers converted from being craftsmen to production line members, the whole mentality of being a worker changed. Rather than working to make a product, men and women now worked to make money.

Prior to the Industrial Revolution, a person learning a skill served first as an apprentice, then as a journeyman working for someone else, and finally as a master craftsperson. After the Industrial Revolution most factory workers were reduced to serving as lifelong apprentices, performing unskilled labor for someone else's profit. Workers came to be viewed as parts of a huge machine. They had no say in their working conditions, the amount of time they were required to work, the pay they would receive for their work, or how long they would have a job.

The Response Two positions surfaced as the way to respond to the increased industrialization sweeping the continent. One position was *laissez-faire* **capitalism**; the other was **socialism**. Capitalism advocated a "hands-off" approach by the government and workers (the French term *laissez faire* means "allow to do"). Invisible, unwritten laws of the marketplace would ensure that the entire capitalist system worked for the benefit of all. For example, if a factory is not run efficiently or products are not of high quality, then someone else will do better and force the original factory to close. Outside interference in the system, such as government regulations, only creates problems.

Socialism, on the other hand, called for a great deal of regulation of industry. In fact, Karl Marx—the leading advocate of socialism—wanted to do away with individual owners altogether. He felt that if workers owned and ran the factories themselves through the government, then the benefits of industry would be evenly distributed. Everyone would share in responsibility, work, material rewards, and leisure time. Governments should be instruments of, for, and by workers. Therefore, while the *laissez-faire* approach advocated keeping government out of industry, socialism insisted on government-controlled industry.

Catholic leaders addressed the problems created by the Industrial Revolution by steering a middle-of-the-road course between these positions. They criticized capitalist thinkers who proposed that private property was an absolute right allowing them to do whatever they wanted with what they owned. This mindset had led to ruthless individualism among many early capitalists and to workers being treated like mere commodities. Church leaders also criticized socialism for rejecting the right of private property.

> The Church has rejected the totalitarian and atheistic ideologies associated in modern times with 'communism' or 'socialism.' She has likewise refused to accept, in the practice of 'capitalism,' individualism and the absolute primacy of the law of the marketplace over human labor. [1]
>
> *Catechism of the Catholic Church*, #2425

In addition to entering into theoretical debates about what an industrialized society should be like, Church leaders offered specific recommendations about how to make the factory system more humane. For instance, near the end of 1869, Archbishop Wilhelm Ketteler of Germany, a leading voice for improving conditions for workers, asked his fellow German bishops to work for the enactment of the following laws:

> 1. The prohibition of child labor in factories;
> 2. the limitation of working hours for factory workers;
> 3. the separation of the sexes in the workshops;
> 4. the closing of unsanitary workshops;
> 5. Sunday rest;
> 6. the obligation to care for workers who are temporarily or permanently disabled;
> 7. the appointment by the state of factory inspectors.
>
> Marvin L. Krier Mich,
> *Catholic Social Teaching and Movements*, p. 7

Looking at the list, we get a sense of conditions associated with factory work at the time.

Pope Leo XIII Speaks Out for Workers

Pope Leo XIII, elected pope after Pius IX in 1878, was most responsible for formulating a Catholic position on problems associated with industrialization. Pope Leo knew the horrible conditions that existed for many workers both in Europe and in the United States. He believed that the Church could and should provide moral guidance in this important area. He also knew that in Europe many workers were turning to socialism and the atheistic perspective of Marx. Marx condemned religion for encouraging workers to accept their sufferings, arguing that religion's focus was on life after death and not on this life. Pope Leo feared that workers were thus cutting themselves off from the graces available through the Church. Finally, Pope Leo did not want the Church to be untouched by and uninvolved in the plight of workers. Catholic workers were children of the Church; as the head of the Church he felt it necessary to address their needs and help them see the value and dignity of their work.

In addition to a growing number of European Catholic leaders concerned about the plight of workers, the U.S. Church also petitioned the pope to speak out on this issue. In the United States, the vast majority of factory workers were Catholic. Many bishops and priests typically came from working families.

So in 1891, Pope Leo issued an encyclical called *Rerum Novarum* (its title literally means "of new things"). It is commonly referred to as *On the Condition of Workers*, which was the relatively new thing that the pope wanted to address. Many of those who spearheaded the movement for unionizing workers were Catholics who were motivated by their Church's call for justice in this document.

Rerum Novarum
1.   served notice to wealthy industrialists that they could not abuse workers for their own gain
2.   urged governments to step in when problems arose within industry
3.   declared that workers have a right to a living wage, thus ensuring basic rights for all citizens
4.   taught that workers have a right to form unions

Rerum Novarum was a groundbreaking document. That the pope would take on such a controversial issue that did not directly affect the political life of the Church was unusual. Pope Leo addressed the issue of workers' rights from a strictly moral standpoint. Until this time, people generally perceived the Church to be on the side of the old order and against the liberties advocated since the French Revolution. With his encyclical, Pope Leo announced to the world that the Church would engage in issues related to the problems and the freedoms associated with the modern world.

Rerum Novarum added to the legitimacy of the union movement. We may take it for granted that workers have unions and that management and workers together agree on contracts between them. However, in the late 1800s unions still represented a radical movement. Many people saw unions as an affront to charity and to private property. That is, owners were supposed to take care of their workers, but workers were not to *demand* anything of the owners. To do so took away an owner's opportunity to be charitable to workers. If workers required a factory to be shut down on Sundays, it violated an owner's private property rights. Now with Pope Leo's encyclical, workers could appeal to a document of the Catholic Church and demand their right to unionize.

The Lasting Impact of *Rerum Novarum* *Rerum Novarum* officially began what became an ongoing examination of issues of justice by Church leaders and members of the Church. A series of encyclicals written by popes over the last one hundred years have offered Catholics a source of

FAITH ACTIVITY

Right of Private Property Catholic social teaching says that private property is not an "absolute right" because the goods of creation (and what we produce with them) are intended for the use of all. What does this mean? Give three examples to illustrate this teaching.

guidance as they seek to live their faith in the midst of the changes that have marked the modern world. The encyclicals are a voice for people suffering from injustice throughout the world. Modern Catholic social teaching echoes the teachings of Jesus and the Fathers of the Church that the Church has *preferential love* for those who are oppressed by poverty.

Beginning with *Rerum Novarum*, Pope Leo offered one way by which the Church is involved in the modern world. In the words of the *Catechism of the Catholic Church*: "The Church's social teaching proposes principles for reflection; it provides criteria for judgment; it gives guidelines for action" (*CCC*, #2423). The Church offers these guidelines in response to difficult social problems people face today.

GROUP TALK

Laborem Exercens (On Human Work), an encyclical written by Pope John Paul II in 1981, contains comments about technological, economic, and political developments that influence the world of work.

1 How do you think the world of work has changed in the past few decades?

2 What messages would you like the Church to offer the world today regarding the world of work?

U.S. Contributions to Catholic Social Teaching

Leaders of the Catholic Church in the United States came to be actively involved in the labor movement for a very practical reason—that's where the vast majority of the country's Catholic people were. One of the first labor unions in the United States was the Knights of Labor, which functioned as a secret society to protect itself from outside interference. The majority of its leaders and members were Catholics.

In 1884, at the request of the archbishop of Quebec, Pope Leo XIII condemned the Knights of Labor in Canada. In Europe, people typically joined secret societies as an alternative to the Church. Cardinal James Gibbons of Baltimore knew that the Knights of Labor was not a secret society like the ones in Europe. He also knew that the Knights of Labor provided a valuable service to U.S. workers. Cardinal Gibbons traveled to Rome in 1887 to make the case that it would be a grave mistake for the pope to condemn the Knights of Labor in the United States. He appealed to the pope that since "the great questions of the future are not those of war, of commerce or finance, but the social questions, the questions which concern the improvement of the condition of the great masses of people, and especially of the working people, it is evidently of supreme importance that the Church should always be found on the side of humanity, of justice toward the multitudes who compose the body of the human family" (John Ellis, ed., *Documents of American Catholic History*, p. 448). The pope did not condemn the Knights of Labor in the United States. A few years later he wrote *Rerum Novarum*.

Following World War I, many people in the United States saw the end of the war as an opportunity to establish a new economic and social agenda. Father John A. Ryan, who taught at Catholic University of America, wrote *The Living Wage*—his vision of a social agenda for postwar United States. When the U.S. bishops adopted his plan and published it in 1919 as the "Bishops' Catholic Program of Social Reconstruction," many people accused the bishops of advocating socialism. Nevertheless, many proposals they made have become accepted policies in the United States.

Bishops' Economic Agenda Proposals
initiate a minimum wage
create and maintain high rates of wages
originate a government-mandated social security insurance for all workers
advocate worker participation in the management of industry

Documents of American Catholic History, p. 601

The year 1919 was neither the first nor the last time that American bishops were labeled socialists because of their strong stand on behalf of workers. In 1894, an interviewer asked Bishop John Ireland how he responded to those who called him "the Socialist Bishop." Bishop Ireland answered in a way similar to how many Church leaders since then have answered that accusation:

> If by Socialists you understand those who are preoccupied by social necessities and miseries, who desire to improve the state of society, and who ask, in view of this improvement, not only action of individuals and influence of voluntary associations, but also a reasonable intervention of the civil power, yes, I am a Socialist. But if by 'Socialist' you understand those who share the theories of Marx, of Benoit Malon, of Greef, and others—theories which consist in denying the rightfulness of private property in land and in instruments of labor—no, I am not a Socialist.

Documents of American Catholic History, pp. 486–87

Mother Jones
(1830–1930)

One of the most outspoken members of the U.S. labor movement was Mary Harris Jones, who was known throughout most of her life as "Mother Jones." Born into a Catholic family, Mary taught in a convent school. She married, but her husband and four children died in the yellow fever epidemic in Memphis in 1867. She moved to Chicago and became a seamstress. One evening she wandered into a meeting of the Knights of Labor, one of the few labor organizations of the time to accept women equally with men. At the age of fifty, she immersed herself in the labor movement. Her outlook on religion was fairly simple: "Pray for the dead and fight like hell for the living."

For the next fifty years, Mother Jones appeared wherever workers were fighting for better conditions. She especially deplored child labor. In Mother Jones' autobiography, she catalogued some of the ways that life for workers improved over her lifetime, most of which she herself helped to bring about:

> In spite of oppressors, in spite of false leaders, in spite of labor's own lack of understanding of its needs, the cause of the worker continues onward. Slowly his hours are shortened, giving him leisure to read and to think. Slowly his standard of living rises to include some of the good and beautiful things of this world. Slowly the cause of his children becomes the cause of all. His boy is taken from the breaker, his girl from the mill. Slowly those who create the wealth of the world are permitted to share it.
>
> Quoted in Marvin L. Krier Mich, *Catholic Social Teaching and Movements*, p. 39

Mother Jones died in 1930, seven months after her one-hundredth birthday. Many dignitaries attended her funeral Mass at St. Gabriel's Church in Washington. Another funeral service followed in Illinois where a choir made up of miners sang the parts of the Mass.

▲ Mary Harris Jones, c. 1907.

FAITH ACTIVITY

Social Reformers One expression of Catholicism that addressed the problems of workers in the United States was the Catholic Worker Movement, founded by Peter Maurin and Dorothy Day. Research the movement and write a report, poem, or play on it—its principles, its founders, and its work today. Propose a way that students in your school can help workers in need today.

The Catholic Worker Movement

Many groups in the past two centuries have called for social reform. One such group was small in numbers but widespread in its influence. In 1932, a recent convert to Catholicism named Dorothy Day met a homespun philosopher and visionary named Peter Maurin. Maurin convinced Day that any program of social change needed to be based on spirituality, hospitality, mutual cooperation, and community. He believed that Catholicism offered the best foundation for a future in which people would share goods and care for one another. In 1933, Day began *The Catholic Worker* newspaper. She and Maurin opened a house of hospitality in New York City and a farming commune in upstate New York. Maurin believed that these three projects were models for the social change called for in Catholic social teaching. He wanted every parish to be a "house of hospitality" as well as a place of spirituality.

Some members of the Catholic Worker movement have been pacifists and have voiced their opposition to all the wars of the past decades. Often people associated with the movement have been jailed for acts of protest against racism, unfair labor practices, and war. Catholic Worker houses currently operate in a number of U.S. cities, and the *Catholic Worker* newspaper is still published and available for sale at its original price—a penny a copy.

Rose Cohn, Dorothy Day, and ▶ Charlotte Margolies, 1917.

Political Controversies

The Catholic Church transcends all nations. During the last decades of the nineteenth century, however, the countries of Europe continued the march toward increasing their power as separate nations. This created tensions with the Catholic Church. In Germany, for instance, the powerful Prussian Prime Minister, Otto von Bismarck, waged a *Kulturkampf* ("culture war") against the Catholic Church. Beginning in 1873, Bismarck enacted laws limiting the power of Church leaders in Germany. He wanted to strengthen German identity by removing Catholicism from the daily life of the German people. He expelled religious communities and placed the schools they ran under the control of the state. He arrested members of the clergy, including cardinals, who resisted his decrees.

Some German citizens were enraged at this persecution of the Catholic Church. Many of those who opposed Bismarck's *Kulturkampf* policies formed a political party called the *Centrum*. When the party became a threat to Bismarck's plans, he sought a way to back down from his anti-Catholic stand without losing face. With the election of a new pope, Leo XIII, in 1878, Bismarck used the occasion to push for a concordat with the Church. The concordat restored the Church to its traditional place in German society.

FAITH ACTIVITY

Catholic Identity Name three symbols or practices associated with Catholicism. Choose one of these and with a story, a poem, a painting, a play, or another medium, illustrate for people who are not Catholic why the symbol or practice is important for Catholics.

France began a Third Republic in 1875. When Leo XIII became pope, he attempted to improve the relationship between the French leaders of the republic and Catholic Church leaders. Intellectuals in the French government, however, still perceived Catholicism as being opposed to liberty. In 1905, the French government suppressed all forms of the Catholic religion, closed more than 13,000 schools, and expelled or secularized all religious communities.

In England, the Catholic Church restored its leadership in 1859 when Cardinal Nicholas Wiseman was named Archbishop of Westminster. After centuries of tension between Catholicism and Anglicanism, the Oxford Movement and the restoration of the hierarchy gave English Catholics hope that a rebirth of the Church in England would follow. However, the Church and the state merely settled into a peaceful coexistence. This condition lasted until 1896, when Pope Leo announced that Anglican orders were not valid. In other words, he declared that Anglican priests and bishops since about the time of King Edward were not validly ordained and did not possess orders in line with apostolic succession. This papal proclamation was perceived as an insult to the members of the Church of England and led to a resurgence of anti-Catholic feelings in the country.

◀ Canterbury Cathedral.

The Church in Mexico

Mexico has had a confusing relationship with the Church. At times, priests actually ran the government there. At other times, Mexican rulers excluded Church leaders from participation in the government. The constitution of 1917 was particularly anti-Catholic. It declared that:

1. there could be no criticism of the government

2. only Mexicans could be clergy

3. the Church could not own property

4. privileges of the Church were revoked and the papal ambassador was expelled from the country

During this period, the head of the Mexican government launched a wave of persecutions against Catholics. A Mexican young man named Miguel Pro went to Europe where he was ordained a Jesuit priest. He returned to Mexico and used a variety of disguises and accents to visit the underground Catholic community. One day he posed as a garbage man, another as a college professor. He celebrated the sacraments for people as often as possible at a time when performing even one Baptism would have earned him the death penalty.

A group of Mexicans, driving a car owned by one of Miguel Pro's brothers, attempted to assassinate a former president. After the attempt failed, police gathered all the Catholic leaders they could find. They captured Miguel and his brother Humberto and, although they found no evidence that the two were involved in the plot, incarcerated them without a trial. In 1927, at the age of thirty-six, Miguel was taken before a police firing squad where reporters were invited to witness the death of this "traitor." Miguel held out his arms in the form of a cross and proclaimed, "Viva Cristo Rey!"—a Spanish phrase for "Long live Christ the King." A photograph of Miguel Pro with arms extended became a holy card seen throughout the world. "Viva Cristo Rey!" became the motto of the underground Church in Mexico. On September 25, 1988, Father Pro was beatified by Pope John Paul II.

The Americanist Controversy

In the United States, tension between identifying with one's nation and identifying with one's faith expressed itself within the Catholic community. Key to the problem was the question of **assimilation**. For instance, should German Catholics and Italian Catholics become absorbed into the great melting pot of U.S. culture, or should they hold onto their differences? Some immigrant Catholics wanted to establish separate schools and maintain as much as possible a separate identity as Catholics and as members of their ethnic group. Other Catholics wanted to assimilate into the mainstream of U.S. life. They felt that no fundamental conflict existed between Catholicism and U.S. culture. They wanted Catholics and the Catholic Church to exhibit an easy blending of Catholic faith and U.S. culture. In the late 1800s, Archbishop Michael Corrigan of New York represented the position that Catholics should remain separate. Archbishop John Ireland of St. Paul, Minnesota, led those advocating an assimilationist position.

The controversy over Catholicism and U.S. culture became an international issue when a short biography of a U.S. priest named Isaac Hecker was translated from English into French. Hecker, who had been active in New England intellectual circles, became a Catholic as an adult. In 1858, he received permission from Pope Pius IX to begin a new order of priests, called the Paulists, dedicated to bringing Protestants into the Catholic Church. He proposed to accomplish this by preaching in ways that would appeal to Protestants and by meeting intellectual challenges on their own ground. In a sense, Father Hecker wanted to "Catholicize" the United States by "Americanizing" Catholicism. That is, he believed that only a truly American Church would succeed in making the United States more Catholic. To him, the separation of Church and state created an ideal environment for the unhindered spreading of the Catholic message. Father Hecker attracted a number of well-educated men to Catholicism and to the Paulists. Paulists even preached in Protestant churches during an era when merely entering a Protestant church was frowned upon for Catholics. These priests engaged in what later would be an important aspect of Church life: **ecumenism**—joining together with members of other religions for discussion and shared prayer.

In 1891, a Paulist priest published a biography of Isaac Hecker that included a preface by Archbishop Ireland. A French priest translated the biography in 1897 and then went about hailing Father Hecker as a model for spreading the Catholic faith everywhere. He praised Father Hecker's democratic spirit and his openness to modern culture. Some members of the French Church, who held onto traditional French Catholicism, challenged certain ideas that they associated with Father Hecker, such as the separation of Church and state, and asked Pope Leo XIII to address their concerns. They referred to the ideas to which they objected as *Americanism*, implying that the liberalism that had swept across Europe and had earlier been condemned by Pope Pius IX now found a home in the Catholicism of the United States.

In 1899, Pope Leo sent a letter to James Cardinal Gibbons, Archbishop of Baltimore, condemning "what some have called Americanism." The pope carefully did not accuse any U.S. bishops or other members of the Church with holding these ideas, but he warned U.S. Catholics that such ideas were erroneous. For example, one belief condemned as

FYI

Pope Leo XIII was the first pope to call non-Catholic Christians "separated brethren."

Americanism was exalting the natural over the supernatural order. Both liberal and conservative U.S. Catholic bishops felt affirmed by the pope's letter, since no one knew any Catholics who held positions condemned in it. Nonetheless, it caused American theologians to be cautious when offering theological opinions for fear that they would slip into positions that would fall under the category of Americanism.

A few years later, in 1902, the U.S. bishops sent Pope Leo a letter congratulating him on his twenty-fifth anniversary as pope. In his response to their letter, the pope revealed his feelings toward the great progress that U.S. Catholicism had made:

> While the changes and tendencies of nearly all the nations which were Catholic for many centuries give cause for sorrow, the state of your churches, in their flourishing youthfulness, cheers Our heart and fills it with delight.

Pope Leo XIII's "Congratulations to the Church of the United States," April 15, 1902, in John Tracy Ellis, *Documents of American Catholic History*, p. 544

GROUP TALK

1. Do you believe that assimilation is an issue for any groups in the United States today? If so, who are those groups?

2. If your family recently immigrated to the U.S., or if you know any immigrants or children of immigrants, how do they approach the issue of assimilation?

3. What advice would you give children of immigrants regarding assimilation?

James Cardinal Gibbons
(1834–1921)

At the turn of the nineteenth century, the U.S. Church was blessed by the leadership of James Cardinal Gibbons. He was the leader of the Church in the United States who most forcefully took on the causes of workers and of Catholic assimilation into U.S. culture.

Born in Baltimore in 1834, Gibbons was baptized in its cathedral, where he would later serve as archbishop. As a child he returned to Ireland with his family until 1853. He and his family then moved to New Orleans, where he decided to enter the seminary in Baltimore. In 1861, he was ordained. In 1872, he was appointed bishop of Richmond and became the young-

est bishop to attend Vatican Council I. In 1877, he was named Archbishop of Baltimore and served in that capacity until his death in 1921.

During his years as archbishop, Cardinal Gibbons served as the leading spokesman for U.S. Catholicism. The pope chose him to preside over the Third Plenary Council of Baltimore held in 1884. This council did much to set the direction for U.S. Catholicism far into the twentieth century. It mandated parish schools and called for the writing of the *Baltimore Catechism*. It proposed establishing the Catholic University of America, which opened in Washington, D.C., in 1887.

Until his death at the age of 87, Cardinal Gibbons took on the many difficult issues facing U.S. Catholics. He particularly addressed the concerns of workers, calling for strict regulation of sweatshops, where many Catholics worked. He took the controversial stand of supporting the entrance of the United States into World War I. Finally, he helped to organize all U.S. bishops into a national conference, which provided a forum by which the U.S. Church has addressed important issues ever since.

◄ **Cardinal James Gibbons.**

The Modernist Controversy

Over the course of the nineteenth century, leaders of the Catholic Church felt that the influence and authority of the Church in the world were being diminished. In the eyes of most Church leaders, without Christ and his Church to lead the way, the modern world was heading into treacherous waters. Certain viewpoints that seemed to go against Catholicism came to be lumped together and were labeled *modernism*. By the end of the nineteenth century, even some priests and perhaps some bishops were perceived as advocating some dangerous teachings.

Modernism was not a specifically identifiable school of thought. One position associated with modernism was denying that people could determine the existence of God through the use of reason, as Saint Thomas Aquinas proposed in his "proofs for the existence of God." Some Catholics also believed modernism was proposing that the Church and Church practices developed over time in response to human need, as opposed to being divinely instituted by Christ.

In 1907, Pope Pius X, who followed Pope Leo XIII, decided to address what he considered the errors of modernism in an encyclical, *Pascendi Dominici Gregis*, which is Latin for "Feeding the Lord's Flock." A number of priests were excommunicated for teaching modernism, and in 1910 the pope required all priests to take an oath against modernism. Although the next pope, Benedict XV, took immediate steps to ease tensions among Catholics who held different positions, the oath against modernism remained a requirement for priesthood until 1967.

The campaign against modernism set Catholic intellectual life on a course separate from the path that many other scholars were taking at the time. It would be decades before Catholic scholars realized that the condemnation of modernism did not rule out approaches to scripture study and other areas of theology that other scholars were using. Eventually scholars reasserted a more traditional Catholic position, that theology—faith seeking understanding—finds the use of reason and intellectual inquiry to be totally compatible with the life of faith. Thanks to the leadership of Pope Pius XII and others, in time scientific study of the Bible by Catholic scholars achieved a level of depth and sophistication rivaling that of other scholars.

FAITH ACTIVITY

Influencing the Modern World
Three men who greatly influenced the modern world were Karl Marx, Charles Darwin, and Sigmund Freud. Describe the basic teachings of one and explain the impact the teachings might have had on religion. Provide a Catholic response to each of the main teachings.

Pope Saint Pius X
(1835–1914)

The man who became Pius X, Giuseppe Sarto, came from humble beginnings in northern Italy. Father Sarto was a parish priest for twenty years before being chosen to be spiritual director and rector of a seminary. Later, he became bishop of Mantua, a diocese that had been part of the Papal States but was then in disrepair. As the people grew to love their new pastor, Bishop Sarto revitalized the Church in the area. In recognition of his work, the pope named him a cardinal in 1894 and appointed him patriarch of Venice.

When Pope Leo XIII died, Cardinal Sarto bought a round-trip train ticket for Rome, sure that he would never be considered for pope. Once the conclave began, however, an old privilege that the Church had extended to a secular ruler came into play. The emperor of Austria vetoed the election of a certain cardinal who appeared to be the front-runner for the papacy. A number of cardinals then began to look to Cardinal Sarto as a worthy candidate because of his reputation for holiness and pastoral care. He reluctantly accepted the papacy, taking the name Pius X.

Pope Pius made his mark particularly in the area of liturgical reform. He encouraged daily reception of Communion and lowered the age at which children could first receive Communion to seven, allowing them to receive the Eucharist before Confirmation. He also supported the Catholic Action movement, which was an attempt to get lay people more involved in the Church. Pope Pius served as pope during the period just before the outbreak of World War I. He spoke out strongly against building up armies and about the uselessness of war. He died just weeks before the start of the war. Pope Pius was proclaimed a saint just forty years after his death, the first pope in more than 300 years to be so honored.

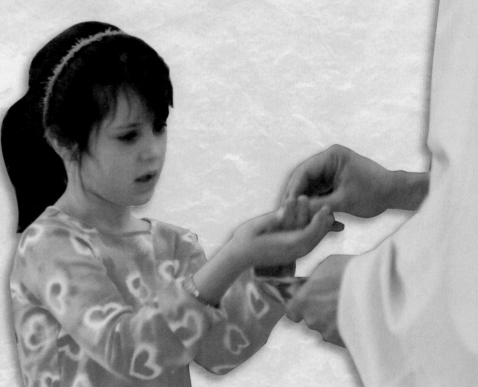

Catholic Spiritual Life

Increased secularization characterized the modern era. That is, it focused more on worldly concerns divorced from a life of faith and the message of salvation offered by Christ. It focused on material progress to a greater degree than interior, spiritual progress. Against the backdrop of increased secularization, Catholics found a variety of ways to live their spiritual life.

One of the principal expressions of spirituality during this period can be characterized as **devotional Catholicism**. Devotional Catholicism refers to practicing popular devotions similar to those from the Baroque period, such as devotion to the Sacred Heart. For example, recitation of the rosary was a popular Catholic devotion throughout the modern period. Also, in 1830, a French nun in her mid-twenties, Catherine Laboure, reported to her confessor that she had received a vision of the Blessed Mother who asked to have a medal made to honor her Immaculate Conception. From that time on, many Catholics worldwide wore what came to be known as the Miraculous Medal. Also known as *popular piety*, these customs and practices continue to be an important expression of faith for many people today. And, in connection to the liturgy of the Church, a number of preachers, and eventually the pope, encouraged more frequent reception of the Sacraments of Penance and Reconciliation and of Communion. These two recommendations were and remain among the Precepts of the Church.

The Precepts of the Church

The **precepts of the Church** are laws or commandments that name specific actions Catholics need to take with regard to moral life and worship. These basic laws existed in some form well before the sixteenth century. In the United States, the precepts were prescribed in 1886 following the Third Plenary Council of Baltimore. Overall, the precepts are meant to help us connect the way we worship and pray (liturgical life) with the choices we make and the way we live our faith in everyday circumstances (moral life). The celebration of the sacraments and participation in the Church's worship strengthen and nourish us to lead moral lives.

1. Attend Mass on Sundays and on holy days of obligation, and avoid unnecessary work.

2. Confess your sins at least once a year.

3. Receive Holy Communion at least once in the Easter Season.

4. Observe the prescribed days of fasting and abstinence.

5. Provide for the material welfare of the Church, based upon one's ability.

A series of apparitions of Mary took place in towns throughout Europe. At first authorities discouraged devotions related to these apparitions, but later the Church formally approved a number of them as having content consonant with public revelation. Besides Our Lady of Lourdes mentioned earlier, one of the most famous apparitions took place in Fatima, Portugal, in 1917, when three young children had visions of the Blessed Mother.

Living Out the Gospel Message

Devotional practices sustained many Catholics during the modern period. As has always been true, there were also people living out the Gospel message in saintly, heroic ways. Their stories tell of a Catholic faith that continued to inspire good works and compassion for others.

Saint Damien—The Leper Priest As a youth in Belgium, Joseph de Veuster was muscular but soft-spoken. He wanted to become a priest, but many people thought that he was not intellectually up to the challenge. His older brother, himself a priest, tutored Joseph until he was accepted by the Sacred Heart Fathers, where he took the name Damien. The Sacred Heart Fathers sent Father Damien to their mission in Hawaii to serve a parish covering 2,000 square miles.

Father Damien loved his work. However, he discovered that leprosy was rampant on the islands. As soon as anyone contracted leprosy, by law he or she had to report it to the authorities, who would send the person to the island of Molokai. Molokai had no visitors and no laws. Children with the disease were sent to Molokai just like anyone else, to survive as best they could.

In 1873, the local bishop asked if any priest would volunteer to go to Molokai to serve the people there for a short time. Damien volunteered but insisted that he be sent there permanently. He was thirty-three at the time. When the bishop arrived with Father Damien on Molokai, he told the people, "I have brought you someone who will be a father to you." His words turned out to be true. Father Damien immediately began his work. He needed his physical strength to build chapels and houses on the island. Unfortunately, he also had to build coffins—more than 2,000 in the first few months he was there. Before his arrival, death was so commonplace that there was no attempt at proper burials. Father Damien made sure that every person who died was buried with dignity. He introduced hygienic practices as best he could, but in his work Father Damien couldn't avoid contact with the deteriorating disease. At Mass one day in 1885, he began his sermon with the words, "We lepers . . . " His people knew then that he, too, had contracted the disease.

Father Damien was able to continue his work for a few more years and died peacefully in 1889. He was buried in the "garden of the dead" on Molokai, which he had transformed into a place where the dead would be respected. However, in 1936 the Belgian government returned his body to his native land so that the people of Belgium could honor him."

Saint Thérèse of Lisieux—"The Little Flower" Seven years after Father Damien's death, a young Carmelite nun died in a convent in Lisieux, France. Despite the fact that her only claim to fame was doing little things well and that she died when she was only twenty-four, this young woman, born Thérèse Martin, became one of the most popular saints of all time. Her appeal with so many people actually stems from what she herself would call her "littleness."

As a child, Thérèse wanted to join her two older sisters who were nuns in the Carmelite monastery. When she was fourteen, she and her father, along with a group of pilgrims, had an opportunity to meet the pope. Everyone was told not to say anything when introduced to the pope, but Thérèse daringly said: "Holy Father, in honor of your anniversary, please allow me to enter Carmel although I am not of the age required." Touched by her faith, Pope Leo XIII assured her that if God wanted it, she would be in Carmel soon. The next year, her bishop allowed Thérèse to enter the convent.

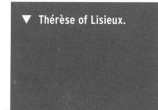

▼ Thérèse of Lisieux.

Recognizing her talent for writing, Thérèse's superior asked her to write her life story, which was published after her death as *The Story of a Soul*. In it she describes her approach to spirituality: "Do little things well, recognizing that our most insignificant actions are a response to the love of Jesus." One challenge that Thérèse faced about which she writes was her being stricken with tuberculosis, which was a deadly illness at the time. After her death in 1897, Thérèse's life and spirituality sparked interest worldwide. She became known as "the Saint of the Little Way." Most people are not destined to achieve great accomplishments. Saint Thérèse's life reminds us that saintliness involves doing ordinary things with the right spirit—saying hello to a stranger in a supermarket, being nice to someone we don't like, cleaning dishes after a meal, or changing a child's diapers. Even though she never left her hometown except for her one trip to Rome, Thérèse (along with Francis Xavier) was declared a patroness of foreign missions. Her feast day is October 1.

Saints Frances Cabrini and Katharine Drexel Two women who did much for the U.S. Church are Frances Cabrini and Katharine Drexel. The thirteenth child of an Italian farm family, Cabrini became a nun and worked with orphans. Pope Leo XIII asked her to go to the United States to continue her work. She asked for advice and support from the Italian community in New York, and an orphanage was built. Mother Cabrini returned to Italy to bring more sisters to the United States. She founded Columbus Hospital in New York and eventually opened more than fifty institutions in eight countries. She became a U.S. citizen in 1909.

Katharine Drexel was born into a wealthy Philadelphia Catholic family in 1858. The Drexels taught their children that wealth was a responsibility. When Katharine and her sister inherited the family fortune in 1885, Katharine decided that her share should be used to assist Native Americans and African Americans. She asked the pope to send missionaries to the United States for this work, but the pope instead challenged Katharine to become a missionary herself.

Katharine accepted the pope's challenge and formed the religious order of the Sisters of the Blessed Sacrament for Indians and Colored People. She founded many educational institutions, including Xavier University in New Orleans, Louisiana, the only Catholic university dedicated to the education of African Americans.

Missionaries and Monasteries

In recent decades the Church in the United States has sent many missionaries to other lands. In 1906, less than one hundred U.S. missionary sisters, priests, and brothers served the Church outside the country. Then, in 1911 two diocesan priests, Father James Walsh and Father Thomas F. Price, founded the Catholic Foreign Mission Society of America. They set up headquarters near Ossining, New York, and called it Maryknoll. Today, Maryknoll encompasses men and women religious and lay volunteers who perform missionary work throughout the world.

The contemplative life, which involved living apart from the world in monasteries as monks or as cloistered nuns, did not initially draw many U.S. Catholics. However, in 1790 some Carmelites began a monastery in Port Tobacco, Maryland. The cool reception they received led them to move to Baltimore in the early 1800s. In 1848, Trappist monks founded the Abbey of Gethsemani in Kentucky, and in 1849 other Trappists settled near Dubuque, Iowa. Both monasteries thrived and continue to exist today.

Thomas Merton is perhaps the most famous U.S. monk. Merton's parents died when he was young, leaving him a trust fund. Merton traveled around the world, experiencing and enjoying life. He finally entered Columbia University in New York to seek a serious career. Through his studies and extensive reading, Merton found himself drawn to Catholicism. He joined the Church in 1938 and three years later entered Gethsemani monastery, where he lived the rest of his life.

Merton's abbot recognized the writing talent that the new monk possessed. He asked him to write the story of his spiritual journey. When it was published in 1948, *The Seven Storey Mountain* was the year's best-selling book. Even though Merton lived his life in his Kentucky monastery, he actively followed the critical issues facing the world and wrote about many of them. In 1968, on one of the rare occasions when he left Gethsemani, Merton died as the result of an accident while attending a conference on monasticism in Thailand.

Called "the Great War" because it involved all of the world's great powers, World War I resulted in unparalleled devastation and loss of life. Catholics fought on both sides in the war. The papacy put its energy into trying to bring about an end to hostilities. Failing that, it used its resources to provide aid to the injured and support to people displaced by the conflict.

Politically, Pope Benedict XV remained neutral during the war. Both sides, therefore, accused him of favoring the enemy. The Germans called him "the French pope"; the Allies called him "the German pope." When the war ended, Pope Benedict encouraged the victors to avoid retaliation against those who were defeated and to restore order as much as possible.

At his election as pope, Pius XI stated his desire to resolve the relationship between the Vatican and the country of Italy. In 1922, Mussolini became dictator of Italy. His fascist party was in complete control. He sought the complete support of the people and realized that he needed to settle the "Roman Question," as the status of the Vatican was called. In a 1929 agreement called the *Lateran Treaty*, the pope gave up all claims to the former Papal States. The pope accepted a financial settlement for the lost properties and was given complete control and ownership of Vatican City and certain other properties in and around Rome.

EXPLORE THE LAND

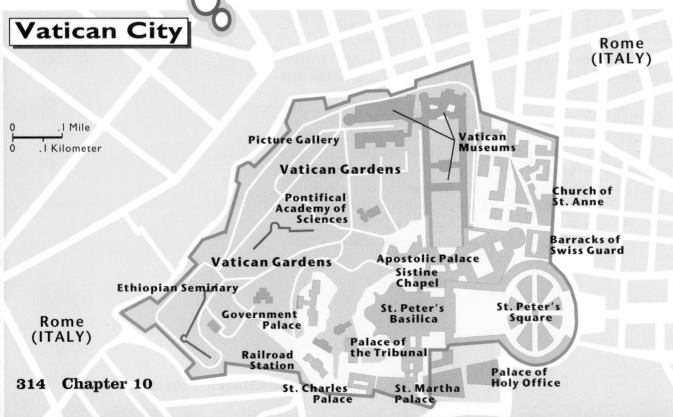

Vatican City

Rome (ITALY)

0   .1 Mile
0   .1 Kilometer

Picture Gallery

Vatican Museums

Vatican Gardens

Pontifical Academy of Sciences

Church of St. Anne

Vatican Gardens

Apostolic Palace
Sistine Chapel

Barracks of Swiss Guard

Ethiopian Seminary

St. Peter's Basilica

St. Peter's Square

Government Palace

Rome (ITALY)

Railroad Station

Palace of the Tribunal

Palace of Holy Office

St. Charles Palace

St. Martha Palace

There was also a concordat between the Vatican and the Italian government that dealt with religious practices and rights. However, Mussolini failed to live up to the concordat, and in 1931, the pope issued "On Catholic Action in Italy," an encyclical against fascism.

Finding himself in a similar situation in 1937, Pope Pius XI wrote an encyclical condemning Hitler after he violated a concordat between the Vatican and the Nazi government. To avoid having it suppressed by Mussolini, Hitler's ally, the pope had the encyclical smuggled out of Rome in the suitcase of a young U.S. priest—the future cardinal archbishop of New York, Francis Cardinal Spellman.

Images of the Church

Temple of the Holy Spirit

People living during the first half of the twentieth century experienced many dark times. Two world wars raised death by violence to an unprecedented level. The Great Depression of the 1930s caused economic hardship throughout the world. Through all these hardships, the Church stood as a beacon proclaiming that people are greater than their shortcomings and encompass more than their earthly lives. Human beings have a transcendent character; they are temples of the Holy Spirit just as the Church itself is the Temple of the Holy Spirit, always drawing people to Christ despite forces tugging in other directions. He gives us hope. He teaches us to pray, providing new expression to the various forms of prayer—blessing, petition, intercession, thanksgiving, and praise. The Holy Spirit is the soul of the Body of Christ, the Church. He is the source of the Church's life, unity, and richness of gifts, talents, and diversity.

Developments Between the Wars

Catholic-Protestant Relations Catholics and Protestants fought on both sides during World War I. Immediately following the war, Catholic and Protestant organizations worked together to aid the victims of the war. Therefore, much of the fear and distrust that had marked the relationship between the two groups disappeared. Scholars from both traditions tried working together on common projects, especially in the area of scripture study. From 1921 to 1925, Catholics—with Vatican approval—and Anglicans held informal talks between themselves. Positive relations among various Christian groups in the 1920s and '30s paved the way for the spirit of ecumenism and for the intensive interreligious dialogue that took place following Vatican Council II.

Native Clergy As French and German forces took over opposing territory, they expelled in large numbers missionaries from enemy nations. Because there were few native clergy in these mission lands, this left many Catholics without the sacraments. The popes who served after World War I regretted that the Church had not done more to foster vocations in the mission lands. In 1923, Pope Pius XI appointed an Indian Jesuit as a bishop in India. In 1926, the pope personally ordained six native Chinese bishops. He later appointed a Japanese bishop for Nagasaki, a Vietnamese bishop, and in 1939 the first black African bishop. By the Second World War there were native bishops in forty-eight former mission countries.

Lay Involvement Vatican Council II increased Catholic awareness that all members of the Church share a "universal call to holiness" by virtue of our Baptism and Confirmation. Along with clergy and vowed religious, Catholic lay people are to be witnesses to Christ within whatever circumstances they find themselves. This concept of the prophetic mission of lay people became popular early in the twentieth century under Pope Pius X. The pope called upon lay people to get involved in what he called **Catholic Action**—small groups of Catholics meeting with a priest and trying to become more informed about the faith.

In the United States, one organization that took the pope's message to heart was the Extension Society. This group of lay Catholics dedicated themselves to building churches, rectories, and schools in isolated areas of the country. Pope Pius X was so pleased with the work of Extension that he named it a pontifical institute, placing it under the direct supervision of the Vatican. In 1921 in Holland, the Grail movement promoted Christian values among women employed in social work, in medical fields, or in religious formation. The Catholic Students Mission Crusade involved young people in supporting the work of the missions. A number of groups formed for married couples to provide mutual support. Under Pope Pius XII groups of lay people formed a variety of institutes engaged in ministries from running soup kitchens to houses of prayer.

Liturgical Renewal Some Catholics were calling for liturgical renewal. They wanted a clearer, more direct connection between the Mass and the Christian life. If that was to happen, the assembly needed to be more than passive observers of the liturgy.

A Benedictine monk at St. John's Abbey in Minnesota, Virgil Michel (1890–1938), was an early advocate of liturgical renewal. He pointed out that "the entire life of the true Christian must be a reflection and a further expression of his life at the altar of God. If he is predominantly a passive Christian there, can we expect him to be an active Christian in his daily life out in the world?" (Quoted in Robert Ellsberg, *All Saints*, p. 276).

The Church and Communism The communist takeover of Russia was a great blow to the Church. Communism was stridently antireligious, and it proposed taking over the world. When Joseph Stalin succeeded Lenin in 1924, he began a series of persecutions against Lutherans, Baptists, and Catholics. Thousands of men and women religious were either imprisoned or killed. In the 1930s, Pope Pius XI condemned communism and asked for worldwide prayers for Russian Christians.

World War II

Eugenio Pacelli became Pope Pius XII in 1939, as the world was entering another devastating war. Pope Pius was a good choice to lead the Church during this difficult time. He came from Roman nobility, had served in the Vatican diplomatic corps—including a period as the pope's ambassador to the Nazi government in Germany—and had traveled extensively while he was Vatican Secretary of State.

During World War II, Pope Pius XII was placed in an intolerable position. Surrounded by Italy, one of the Axis powers, whatever the pope did might well have failed. In his first address, he pleaded for peace, and his first encyclical called upon all humanity to restore God to his rightful place in society. Some have questioned whether the pope might have done more to confront Hitler and a prevailing anti-Semitism. Most historians propose that, given the political realities in which he found himself, he did what he could without endangering lives in Germany and elsewhere. In 1939, he wrote what can only be interpreted as a condemnation of the Nazi regime, but he feared that continued confrontation with Hitler would actually lead to loss of more innocent lives.

Around six million Jews died in the Holocaust. Millions of Catholics, including priests and nuns, also died under the Nazis. Pope Pius and many Catholics in Europe did what they could to alleviate suffering. The pope arranged that churches, convents, and other Church properties should offer security and safety to Jewish refugees. More than 15,000 Jews were hidden in the papal summer residence, Castel Gandolfo, alone.

FAITH ACTIVITY

Christian Witness Three Christian witnesses who died during World War II were Maximilian Kolbe, Edith Stein, and Franz Jagerstatter. Research one of these people's lives, or that of another Christian who died during the Holocaust, and present a written, oral, or electronic slide presentation based on your research.

In 1943, Nazis ordered Roman Jews to pay a large ransom or be shipped to a concentration camp. The pope ordered that sacred vessels should be melted down to help pay the ransom. He also instructed members of the Vatican diplomatic corps to use their resources to aid the safe passage of Jews from areas of danger. In Bulgaria his representative filled out 5,000 fake baptismal certificates for Jewish children to save them from deportation. The pope believed that Hitler might kidnap him and take him to Germany. He therefore wrote a letter of resignation that would go into effect the moment he crossed the border of the Vatican. The cardinals would then be free to elect a new pope.

When peace was finally restored in 1945, Pope Pius XII addressed himself to the needs of refugees. Vatican resources helped in the search for more than eleven million displaced persons.

After the War Another of the pope's major political concerns in the postwar era, however, was communism. Communist governments controlled the Soviet Union and most of Eastern Europe and later spread to China. In 1949, the pope declared that any Catholic who joined the communist party was excommunicated from the Church.

After World War II, Pope Pius XII named many new cardinals, a number from non-European countries. Before native clergy achieved leadership positions in these countries, Catholicism was perceived as a foreign entity. With the appointments of native Church leaders, the faithful were better able to identify themselves as Catholics connected to a broader Church. Over the course of the twentieth century, the Catholic Church lived out its universal character through the diversity of cultures in which she existed.

After World War II, Pope Pius XII made a number of changes in the rules concerning the liturgy. In 1953 he issued an apostolic constitution which allowed evening Masses and reduced the amount of time required for fasting before receiving Communion. Following Vatican Council II in the 1960s, liturgical renewal would become one of the most apparent changes that took place in the Church.

>Age to Age

Catholic Relief Services

"The fundamental motivating force in all activities of CRS is the Gospel of Jesus Christ as it pertains to the alleviation of human suffering, the development of people and the fostering of charity and justice in the world. CRS provides direct aid to the poor, and involves people in their own development, helping them to realize their potential. And CRS educates the people of the United States to fulfill their moral responsibilities toward our brothers and sisters around the world by helping the poor, working to remove the causes of poverty, and promoting social justice."

Catholic Relief Services (CRS) is an organization that operates under the direction of the U.S. Catholic Bishops, and has as its goal addressing the social problems that plague the world. The bishops founded CRS in 1943 to assist people in need outside of the United States. At the time, the world was suffering under the ravages of war. CRS continues to be one of the most effective organizations in the war against poverty worldwide.

A CRS program with which you may be familiar is Operation Rice Bowl, a Lenten program that raises money for projects related to food issues. Operation Rice Bowl invites people to make a contribution to alleviating hunger by combining prayer, fasting, learning, and giving during the Lenten season. Sometimes schools adopt special programs to help in the effort, such as the food service company for the Philadelphia Catholic high schools which donates twenty-five cents for every slice of pizza sold on a particular day.

CRS has numerous other programs in which youth and young adults can participate, such as Food Fast, School Connectivity, and Work of Human Hands.

Praying with the Church, Past and Present

(All quotes from Dorothy Day, in *Solutions to Violence*, Colman McCarthy ed.)

Reader 1: One of the greatest evils of the day is the sense of futility. Young people say, "What can one person do? What is the sense of our small effort?" They cannot see that we can only lay one brick at a time, take one step at a time; we can be responsible only for the one action of the present moment. But we can beg for an increase of love in our hearts that will vitalize and transform these actions, and know that God will take them and multiply them, as Jesus multiplied the loaves and fishes (p. 30).

All: We shall never pray until we feel more deeply, and we shall never feel deeply enough until we envisage what is actually happening in the world (p. 27).

Reader 2: What we would like to do is change the world— make it a little simpler for people to feed, clothe, and shelter themselves as God intended them to do. And to a certain extent, by fighting for better con- ditions, by crying out unceasingly for the rights of the workers, of the poor, of the destitute—the rights of the worthy and the unworthy poor, in other words—we can . . . change the world; we can work for the oasis, the little cell of joy and peace in a har- ried world. We can throw our pebble in the pond and be confident that its ever-widening circle will reach around the world (p. 19).

All: No one has the right to sit down and feel hopeless. There's too much work to do (p. 18a).

All: Blessed Jesus, as Dorothy Day learned the impor- tance of every little action from Saint Thérèse of Lisieux, "The Little Flower," may we recognize that we make a difference in all that we do. Help us to contribute to the betterment of our world little by little. Amen.

▶Review

1. What is the difference between *laissez-faire* capitalism and socialism? What position did Catholic Church leaders take toward capitalism and socialism?
2. What contribution did Pope Leo XIII make to Catholic social teaching in 1891?
3. What four principles did Pope Leo XIII propose that helped workers?
4. Who were Mother Jones, Peter Maurin, and Dorothy Day?
5. Why did Otto von Bismarck initiate his *Kulturkampf?*
6. How did many French intellectuals at the end of the 1800s view Catholicism?
7. What is assimilation? What two positions did U.S. Catholic leaders take toward assimilation?

8. In his 1902 response to the U.S. bishops, how did Pope Leo XIII view the U.S. Church?
9. Name two positions associated with modernism.
10. Give two examples of Catholic devotional practices.
11. Describe Saint Thérèse of Lisieux's approach to the spiritual life.
12. What type of work do members of Maryknoll perform?
13. What political position did Pope Benedict XV take during World War I?
14. What steps did Pope Pius XI take to strengthen the Church in former mission countries?
15. What is Catholic Action? Give two examples of organizations that promoted Catholic Action.

▶Key Words

assimilation (p. 303) Members of minority groups adopting the values and characteristics of the dominant culture in which they live.

Catholic Action (p. 317) The movement calling for active involvement of lay people in the Church.

devotional Catholicism (p. 309) Practices of religious popular piety among Catholics.

ecumenism (p. 304) Actions aimed at dialogue and the restoration of unity among Christians.

laissez-faire capitalism (p. 293) Economic system that advocates that people with money (capital) can use their money as they wish without restrictions from governments or other sources.

precepts of the Church (p. 309) A list of laws put forth by leaders of the Church which help the faithful grow in love with God and others, pray an "indispensible minimum" amount, and grow in moral effort. (See *CCC*, Glossary.)

socialism (p. 293) Economic system that advocates government control of all instruments of production, such as farms and factories.

Yesterday and Today

Major challenges faced the Church as it entered the modern world. The concept that civil governments should be totally separate from the Church went against longstanding Catholic practice, even though it seemed to be working in the United States. People in Europe and the United States had adopted new ways of making a living. Industrialization held out promise of improving lives, but it was causing a great deal of suffering in the process. Thus Church leaders were called upon to address social and economic issues. Finally, the first half of the twentieth century saw unparalleled devastation due to war and hatred. After tremendous transformations, and after two world wars, the Church remained strong and vital. In the late 1940s Church leaders decided that it would be a good time to take stock of the Church and of its place in this modern world. It would take a new pope, John XXIII, and another decade before the Church would call a council that would usher in changes rivaling those taking place in the world around it.

A.D. 1960
Election of
John Kennedy, first
Catholic U.S. president

TIMELINE

A.D. 1958
Election of Pope John XXIII

A.D. 1959
Pope John XXIII announces that there will be a council

A.D. 1962
Beginning of Vatican Council II

A.D. 1963
Death of Pope John XXIII; election of Pope Paul VI

THE CHURCH OF VATICAN COUNCIL II

1950-1977

CHAPTER GOALS

In this chapter you will:

★ explore how the Church offered direction and comfort to a world torn apart by war.

★ see why Pope John XXIII called for a council to renew and update the Catholic Church.

★ explore the message and clarification of Church teachings that came from the council.

★ understand the role of Pope Paul VI in continuing the council and implementing changes following Vatican II.

A.D. 1974
Vatican Declaration on Procured Abortion

A.D. 1965
Vatican Council II ends; Pope Paul VI addresses the United Nations

A.D. 1968
Latin American bishops meet and set agenda for the work of justice

A.D. 1971
Publication of *Justice in the World*

A.D. 1973
Roe v. *Wade*. U.S. Supreme Court decision legalizes abortion

A.D. 1975
Fall of Saigon, ending Vietnam War

FIRST THOUGHTS

Imagine that you have been invited to Rome to participate in a meeting to establish an agenda for the Catholic Church today and in the future—Vatican Council III. Write up a list of recommendations.

The Call for Renewal

Did you ever feel as though you needed to step back and take stock of yourself? Perhaps you began high school with grand plans, but somewhere along the way you became sidetracked. At such times, looking back and looking forward are important. The ancient philosophers were right: The unexamined life is not worth living.

In the early 1960s, the Catholic Church decided to take stock of herself and her place in the world. She did so at a three-year event known as Vatican Council II. The immediate impetus for the council was the election of a new pope, John XXIII—a kindly, unassuming Italian who had worked in many of the world's trouble spots during his career as a diplomat and a bishop. His call for a council was by itself a sign of the Holy Spirit's continued presence in the Church, guiding her to be faithful to Christ's mandate to make and nurture disciples in the ever-changing circumstances of the world around her.

This chapter will look closely at the council and then at the post-Vatican II Church to see how the Church identified and fostered a message of truth and hope in response to "the signs of the times," much as she had done throughout history.

A Spiritual and Moral World Crisis

During the first half of the twentieth century, two world wars devastated Europe. Besides the deaths and physical destruction, they also left a spiritual and moral vacuum. For instance, during World War II a group of well-educated, at least formerly Christian German men decided that the most efficient way to address the "Jewish problem" was to annihilate all Jews. How could men who had a Christian upbringing decide that children, women, and men should be killed indiscriminately simply because they were identified as belonging to a different religion or a different ethnic group? When word reached the press outside of Germany that the Nazi government was systematically killing all those who were Jewish, the announcement did not even make the front page of the *New York Times.* The Holocaust and circumstances surrounding it indicated that the world faced a serious spiritual and moral crisis.

However, the Catholic Church showed signs of health after the war. The Church had a strong European base, but she was growing in other parts of the world as well. Before there was a United Nations, the Church was an international body made up of people from every nationality and ethnic group. The Church was a voice for spiritual and moral concern. The case can certainly be made that by far the Church did more to protect victims than any other non-governmental organization.

Church leaders realized that in this difficult post-war era the Church had much to offer the world—indeed, that the message she bore was essential for the struggling world community. However, if the Church was to use the gifts of her founder and provide direction and hope to a despairing world, she would have to enter into serious dialogue with people from the world's many nations and religions. The Church would need to address expressions of contemporary culture. She would rely on and follow the guidance of the Holy Spirit in her mission of bringing Christ to the world.

The Post-War World and the Pre-Vatican II Church

Nuclear Weapons In addition to the senseless destruction of World War II and the morally bankrupt murder of Holocaust victims, other events signaled the need for a re-examination of purpose by all factions of the world community. Near the end of the war, the United States unleashed a weapon of unprecedented destructive capacity. The atomic bomb annihilated two Japanese cities—Hiroshima and Nagasaki, the center of Japanese Catholicism. The atomic bomb loomed as a specter overshadowing everything else in the post-war world. Nuclear weapons demanded that people learn how to live together peacefully or else die together. The term "nuclear holocaust" frightened the world community from the late 1940s into the 1980s. When the bishops met at Vatican Council II, they recognized that peacemaking had to silence the guns of war: "All these factors force us to undertake a completely fresh appraisal of war"[1] (*Documents of Vatican II*, "Pastoral Constitution of the Church in the Modern World," #80). As we will see time and time again, the bishops saw their task as applying the unchanging, core fundamental truths of the faith to new situations that had never before existed. The articulation of these beliefs

People wave glowsticks in front of ▶ gutted A-Bomb dome building in Hiroshima.

FAITH ACTIVITY

Rise of Communism Research the origins of communism. What Catholic principles can be used as an argument against communism? Describe in a short paragraph the effects of the fall of communism in recent years.

needed to be rethought so that the Church could most effectively bring the light of Christ to bear on the life of all people.

Communism The war ended fascism in Italy and Germany. However, the atheistic principles of communism adopted by the Soviet Union earlier in the twentieth century spread into Asia and controlled most of Eastern Europe. Advocates of communism seemed to be everywhere. Communism was not simply an alternative form of government; it proposed absolute control of all aspects of life. The Church and communism were not compatible. Pope Pius XII staunchly opposed communism and spoke out against it often during the 1940s and '50s. At Vatican Council II, Church leaders called for establishment of a world order based on principles of justice and cooperation in order to avoid the destructiveness to the human spirit accompanying communism. At the same time, the popes of the council attempted to open communication with communist leaders.

Global Community During the council, in 1963, Pope John XXIII took time to write an encyclical called *Peace on Earth (Pacem in Terris)*. In it he pointed out, "we are confronted in this modern age with a form of society which is evolving on entirely new social and political lines. Since all peoples have either attained political independence or are on the way to attaining it, soon no nation will rule over another and none will be subject to an alien power" (#42). In other words, the pope was praising the end of **colonialism**.

In the aftermath of World War II, the creation of the United Nations indicated that the people of the world wanted to establish a mechanism that would help prevent wars in the future. The United Nations also embodied the hope for a global community. In 1965, Pope Paul VI endorsed the United Nations and its efforts by stating:

> Our message is meant to be first of all a solemn moral ratification of this lofty Institution, and it comes from Our experience of history. It is as an 'expert on mankind' that We bring this Organization the support and approval of Our recent predecessors, that of the Catholic hierarchy and Our own, convinced as We are that this Organization represents the path that has to be taken for modern civilization and for world peace.

Pope Paul VI, "Address to the United Nations General Assembly," October 4, 1965

Liberation Movements World War II was primarily a conflict among industrialized nations and the middle-class people who dominated them. Beginning in the 1950s, new conflicts began to emerge on the world scene. Besides the "First World" of Western democracies and the "Second World" of communist nations, a "Third World" of nations and peoples not aligned with either group also existed. These nations and groups of people cried out for recognition and equality.

In response to inequalities and injustice, various groups formed liberation movements that would flourish, especially in the later 1960s. In Europe and in the United States, university students in particular started calling for radical changes in the way power and economic prosperity were divided in the world. Even before the term "women's liberation movement" became popular, Pope John XXIII observed in 1963: "the part that women are now playing in political life is everywhere evident. . . . Women are gaining an increasing awareness of their natural dignity. Far from being content with a purely passive role or allowing themselves to be regarded as a kind of instrument, they are demanding both in domestic and in public life the rights and duties which belong to them as human persons" (*Peace on Earth*, #41). Another liberation movement that had a significant effect on the Church was the one initiated by and on behalf of people who are poor in Latin America.

FYI

In the mid-1950s, the terms *First World*, *Second World*, and *Third World* began to be used to distinguish among Western industrialized countries, the communist bloc of countries, and the economically undeveloped countries of the world. Today the term *developing countries* is often used.

FAITH ACTIVITY

Role of Women Research and report on women in the workplace, in society, and in the Church today compared to fifty years ago.

◄ Women marching for equal rights

Pope John XXIII

Angelo Roncalli was born in 1881 to a family of peasant farmers in northern Italy, the third of thirteen children. Although he entered the seminary at age twelve and was ordained when he was twenty-three, Roncalli never lost touch with his peasant background. He studied in Rome, taught Church history, and published books on the subject. During World War I, Roncalli served as a chaplain in the army medical corps. After the war he was named an archbishop and represented the pope in Bulgaria, Greece, and Turkey. In these assignments he spent time with members of the Eastern Churches, other religions, and minority groups. Through these assignments he grew comfortable interacting with people of different faiths and ethnic backgrounds and learned more about the suffering of others. When World War II began, he managed to use his international contacts to secure safe passage for thousands of Jews fleeing Europe.

When the war ended, Archbishop Roncalli expected to settle into a less stressful position. However, the war had created a problem for the Catholic Church in France. During the war, a pro-German government had controlled France. After the war, General Charles de Gaulle led France in identifying those who had collaborated with the Nazis. De Gaulle insisted that thirty-three bishops had to be removed for collaborating with the Nazi regime during the war. The pope needed Archbishop Roncalli's skill as a diplomat and his personal charm to help resolve the problem. Archbishop Roncalli was able to convince de Gaulle to allow all but three of the bishops to remain in their positions. He also averted other crises in France during his time there. When the pope named Archbishop Roncalli a cardinal in 1953, President Vincent Auriol of France claimed the ancient privilege of French monarchs and presented him with the cardinal's red hat. Cardinal Roncalli was also invested into the French Legion of Honor.

Once again, Cardinal Roncalli expected that he would return to Rome and work in the Vatican offices. Instead, the pope named him Patriarch of Venice. For five years he served the people of Venice, who quickly came to love him. His kindly demeanor, coupled with his rotund shape, reminded many of his people of a favorite great-uncle or a grandfather.

In October 1958, Pope Pius XII died. Cardinal Roncalli, seventy-six at the time, left Venice for Rome, expecting to return shortly. However, Pope Pius had suffered through a lengthy illness and consequently had let the number of cardinals dwindle. Only fifty-one cardinals came to the conclave to elect a new pope and nineteen of them were over seventy-eight years old. After three days, no one person emerged as a favorite. The cardinals looked for a compromise candidate, perhaps someone who would serve as pope for a short time. Then additional cardinals could be named so that a clearer choice for a longer reigning pope could be made later. On the fourth day of the conclave, the cardinals elected Cardinal Roncalli pope. Even he referred to himself as *papa de passagio*—a transitional pope.

A Pope from and of the People Pope John XXIII surprised many people when he quickly named twenty-three new cardinals. This broke a longstanding tradition that there be no more than seventy cardinals at any given time. For the first time, cardinals were named from the Philippines, Japan, Mexico, and Africa. Pope John's personal style and pastoral spirit were also a big surprise to those used to the previous formality of the Vatican structure. During the first few months of his pontificate, the pope visited orphanages and hospitals. He discontinued the tradition of the pope dining alone, often inviting one or more people to join him for meals. He dropped in on Vatican offices to meet the staff, learn their names, and talk with them. His greatest surprise, however, came on January 25, 1959, when he announced to a few cardinals that there was soon to be an ecumenical council of the Church.

Vatican II—Christ's Presence

A pivotal event in the history of the Church took place around the year a.d. 50. Members of the Christian community were struggling with the question of what to do about non-Jews who wanted to join them. Recalling the words of Jesus that "where two or three are gathered in my name, there I am there among them" (*Matthew 18:20*), the Church held its first council—the Council of Jerusalem. That gathering at Jerusalem began a pattern that became more formal later on when, from time to time, Church leaders came together to deal with issues facing the Church.

However, in the 500 years before Vatican II there had been only two councils. The Council of Trent (1545–1563) followed on the heels of the Protestant Reformation. Vatican Council I (1869–1870), which defined papal infallibility, ended abruptly because of the overthrow of the Papal States. Since Trent, the Vatican had become an intricate bureaucracy. Vatican offices were in place to run the Church and to decide on important matters. Under Pope Pius XII, many non-Europeans worked in Vatican offices as representatives from throughout the world.

When Pope John XXIII announced that he wanted to hold a council, he received an unexpected response. Many officials in the Vatican opposed it. They felt that after the First Vatican Council the Church no longer needed councils since the position of the pope and the Vatican had been strengthened and clarified. However, Pope John with his outgoing personality, courage, and foresight saw things differently. He said that the Church is not a museum. Rather, she is a loving mother who has much to share with her children. He desired to throw open the windows of the Vatican to allow fresh air into its corridors. Since historically a council was the instrument the Church had used to bring about thoughtful response to situations within and outside of the Church, Pope John took the risk of calling for a council. He set a date for the opening session and told those responsible to get materials together in time.

The council began on October 11, 1962, when 2,500 bishops from all over the world walked in procession for two hours through Saint Peter's square into the largest church in the world. Their faces represented all the colors and continents of the world. Among the bishops were more than 500 from South America, 118 from Africa, and 126 from Asia. At the end of the procession, John was carried aloft for all to see. Tears accompanied his smiles, as he was overjoyed that his council had finally begun.

During his sermon at the liturgy beginning the council, the pope first warned against the "prophets of doom" who could see only the "darkness burdening the face of the earth." He said that such people were acting as if they had learned nothing from history, the great teacher of life. He then went on to set out his intentions for the council. It was not to define new doctrines or dogmas. Instead, the Church needed to "bring herself up to date where required." He desired *aggiornamento* in the Church, an Italian word meaning "to make things ready for today"—today's needs, today's times, today's people. He wished the council fathers to express the substance of ancient doctrine in new ways. As part of its agenda, he wanted the council to condemn no one, saying that: "Nowadays . . . the Spouse of Christ [the Church] prefers to make use of the medicine of mercy rather than that of severity." After his opening remarks, the pope left the council fathers alone to their own deliberations and did not return until the closing ceremony of the first session two months later.

As the council was getting under way, Pope John's doctors informed him that he had stomach cancer. He felt certain that Giovanni Cardinal Montini, the first man he named a cardinal, would succeed him as pope and that the council would be in good hands.

> Pope John XXIII intended the Council to be both the occasion and the means for renewing the Church. He spoke of the paradoxes by which the Church is 'always living and always young.' She 'feels the rhythm of the times' and, therefore, in a marvelous manner 'radiates new light, achieves new conquests, while remaining identical with herself, faithful to the divine image impressed on her countenance by her Spouse, Who loves her and protects her, Christ Jesus.'

National Conference of Catholic Bishops, *The Church in Our Day* (1967), #11

Pope John XXIII Sets the Tone for the Council

Many people thought the world's bishops would quickly ratify the documents prepared by various commissions before the council began. As it turned out, the bishops overwhelmingly rejected such a scenario. In fact, the very first meeting ended after fifteen minutes because two cardinals asked for time to consult with other bishops about membership on the commissions. When presented with opportunities to vote on prepared documents, the vast majority of bishops voted against the documents presented to them. As a result, everyone involved went scrambling to study matters anew. Bishops attended evening gatherings at which leading theologians explained recent developments in liturgical studies, biblical studies, and theologies in the Church.

John stayed away from the council and assured the bishops that they should discuss issues in a free and open atmosphere. Watching the proceedings on closed-circuit television, John enjoyed seeing the lively exchange of ideas that was taking place and the way bishops were now working together and even challenging one another. Although only Catholic bishops could speak during the formal sessions, representatives from Christian denominations and other religions attended the council as observers. Some bishops noted that, at the council, exchanges during coffee breaks were often as fruitful as the formal presentations.

Fifteen women were chosen to be official *auditors* (listeners) at the council. The women auditors received some of the best seats at the council. One woman auditor later reported that while she was to be a listener at formal sessions, she was encouraged to be an active participant in commissions and other working groups of the council. By the third session of the council, the women auditors were placed on committees working on the documents. Through this committee work, their views were included in the vision of the Church that came out of the council.

Bishop Peter Cule of Mostar The following incident demonstrates how Pope John's style set the tone for the council. A month into the first session, Yugoslavian bishop, Bishop Peter Cule of Mostar, addressed the members about his belief that the name of Saint Joseph should be added to the canon of the Mass. All speeches were to be delivered in Latin and limited to a certain amount of time. The Yugoslavian bishop spoke haltingly and in a nervous manner, continuing on past his allotted time. He was hard to understand, and the bishops were losing patience with his ramblings. The president of the council finally interrupted him and said, "Complete your holy and eloquent speech. We all love Saint Joseph." Soon after, the president turned off the microphone, and Bishop Cule returned to his seat with his speech unfinished.

Pope John, who was watching these proceedings, knew the bishop personally. He knew that the bishop's speech problem resulted from four years spent in a concentration camp and from his torture at the hands of communists. One time the bishop had even been put on a train that was deliberately crashed, with the intention of killing everyone on board. The bishop survived with two broken hips. Although he was in poor health, he had come to the council specifically to make his plea on behalf of Saint Joseph. Three days after Bishop Cule's speech, Pope John announced to the world that he had made a decision. Effective December 8, 1962, the name of Saint Joseph was to be inserted in the canon of the Mass.

The Death of Pope John XXIII

When the first session of the council ended, some people pronounced it a failure, since the bishops had agreed on no decrees. Pope John, however, gave a closing address in which he expressed how pleased he was at the work accomplished. He pointed out that starting slowly afforded the bishops an opportunity to get to know each other. Disagreements were an important step in the council's process. Meanwhile, the Church had to use all of her resources to bring Christ to the world. The council was to begin again in September of 1963. However, Pope John's health continued to deteriorate over the early part of the year. Surrounded by his family and friends, "good Pope John" died on June 3, 1963, at the age of eighty-one. Whether the council continued would be the decision of his successor.

GROUP TALK

Name three developments that have taken place in the past century that the Church has benefited from and three developments over the same time period that the Church should criticize. Give reasons for each of your selections.

The Impact of Vatican II

The bishop's work of renewal during the Second Vatican Council was preceeded by years of study and research. The council continued this work, and renewal has continued to take place in the Church up to the present time.

As Pope John expected and hoped, Giovanni Montini was the next cardinal elected pope. In June 1963, Pope Paul VI immediately announced that he would continue the council and the direction that the Church had taken under Pope John. The council reconvened in September of 1963. In his opening address Pope Paul laid out his understanding of the council's four principal aims:

- first, the Church must impart to herself and to the world a new awareness of her inner nature

- second, there must be a renewal and reform of the Church

- third, the Church should work to bring about Christian unity

- fourth, the Church should be in dialogue with today's world

These aims resonate through many of the council's documents and continue to resonate through the Church today.

The Council Was More than Its Documents

An amazing gift of the Church is that she has remained faithful to the message of Christ and core fundamental teachings of her Tradition throughout her history. While the council produced sixteen documents, the impact of the council cannot be reduced to those documents alone. The council carried with it a spirit of inquiry and self-reflection, an attitude of dialogue, and an openness to change that went beyond the walls of St. Peter's Basilica where the bishops met. As word leaked out about discussions taking place within St. Peter's, Catholics in many parts of the world were buzzing about topics related to their religion that they had taken for granted a few years earlier. Lively discussion and anticipation were the order of the day. It was an exciting time to be Catholic.

Catholics worldwide generally knew and loved the fundamental beliefs and practices of their faith. However, no one knew where the Holy Spirit would lead the Church in interpreting these truths of faith for modern times. When the bishops voted on a particular statement or called for further debate on how to respond to a controversial social issue, they were never completely certain what all the consequences would be. Realizing that they did not have time to discuss all matters, the bishops designated commissions to study various aspects of Church life. For instance, commissions were formed to implement the liturgical reforms called for. The efforts of these commissions would bring about changes in the aspects of how the sacraments were celebrated while maintaining their theology and meaning. For example, the three rites of the revised Sacrament of Penance and Reconciliation emphasized the communal nature and scriptural basis of the sacrament, harkening back to early Church practice. As a result of these adjustments to the way the sacrament was celebrated, Catholics in different eras had different experiences of the same sacrament. These differences do not take away from the effect or meaning of the sacraments. They are intended to help Catholics enter more deeply into the grace received in the sacraments.

The Documents

A plaque near the entrance to St. Peter's Basilica in Rome names the bishops who participated in Vatican Council II. They were proud of their work. The documents of the council deserve close attention. People seeking to understand Catholicism and to live as Catholics would find worth pondering passages such as the following from "The Pastoral Constitution on the Church in the Modern World."

GROUP TALK

One result of Vatican II was the change to the three rites of the Sacrament of Penance and Reconciliation. What other sacraments have had changes in the way in which they are celebrated since Vatican II? How do these changes affect the experience of the sacraments?

Images of the Church

The People of God

The central term used for the Church by Vatican Council II is "the people of God." The phrase originally referred to God's Chosen People, our ancestors in faith, the Israelites with whom God made a covenant. By Jesus' death and Resurrection, a new and everlasting covenant was established between God and all people. Belonging to God's People did not require being born into the community by race or culture, but being born by faith in Christ and Baptism. By the power of the Holy Spirit, Christ established his Church, "a chosen race, a royal priesthood, a holy nation, God's own people. . . . Once you were not a people, but now you are God's people" (1 Peter 2:9-10). No matter where you live, what role you play in the Church, we are one united people. Everyone is needed; everyone is important.

A major development since Vatican Council II has been the increased involvement of lay people in all aspects of Church life. Since the council, many more of the people involved in this Church work are lay people serving as administrators in Catholic schools, hospitals, and social service agencies. The increased involvement of lay people in the Church–

in service, worship, and parish life–does not take away from the unique roles that ordained and religious life have. Rather, it clarifies that Church members have different gifts and functions, and all members are the people of God. Through their Baptism and Confirmation, all Catholics are meant to be living witnesses to Christ, as priest, prophet, and king.

The Documents

A plaque near the entrance to St. Peter's Basilica in Rome names the bishops who participated in Vatican Council II. They were proud of their work. The documents of the council deserve close attention. People seeking to understand Catholicism and to live as Catholics would find worth pondering passages such as the following from "The Pastoral Constitution on the Church in the Modern World."

The joys and hopes, the grief and anguish of the people of our time, especially of those who are poor or afflicted, are the joys and the hopes, the grief and anguish of the followers of Christ as well. Nothing that is genuinely human fails to find an echo in their hearts (#1).

Yet it happens rather frequently, and legitimately so, that some of the faithful, with no less sincerity, will see the problem quite differently. . . . Let them, then, try to guide each other by sincere dialogue in a spirit of mutual charity and with a genuine concern for the common good above all (#43).

Theological research, while it deepens knowledge of revealed truth, should not lose contact with its own times, so that experts in various fields may be led to a deeper knowledge of the faith (#62).

Austin Flannery, *Vatican Council II* (Collegeville, MN: Liturgical Press, 1977)

The Documents of Vatican Council II—Major Themes and Implications

Titles	Major Themes	Major Implications
Constitution on the Sacred Liturgy	expresses principles for liturgical renewal that laid the groundwork for the many liturgical reforms that have followed the council	• Revisions are made to the rituals of the Mass and the sacraments. • The language of the people was allowed to be used at times instead of Latin in rites for the sacraments and liturgy, one way of encouraging the role of the assembly in worship. • Official liturgy and sacraments are emphasized over sacramentals. • Church art, architecture, and decorations focus on the liturgy. • Liturgy becomes an impetus for ecumenism.
Decree on the Media of Social Communication	discusses the importance of communications for continuing human progress and the contribution that Catholics in particular might make	Church leaders more clearly recognize the power of the media.
Dogmatic Constitution on the Church	promotes an understanding of the Church that highlights mystery, ecumenism, shared authority, the laity, and the need for reform and renewal	• Increased participation of lay people in the Church. • An increased respect for those not of the Catholic faith, and an understanding that those non-Catholics who have been baptized are in certain, but not perfect, communion with the Church. • An increase in sensitivity that those who have not heard the Gospel but who seek God and follow his will as they know it through their conscience, that they, too, can have eternal salvation.

Pope John Paul II with ▶ representatives of 12 world religions during a World Day of Prayer for Peace.

The Documents of Vatican Council II—Major Themes and Implications

Titles	Major Themes	Major Implications
Decree on the Catholic Churches of the Eastern Rite	praises the theological and liturgical heritage of those Churches in the East that have remained united with Rome	There is greater recognition that "Catholicism" is more than just "Roman Catholicism."
Decree on Ecumenism	acknowledges responsibility on all sides for the controversies underlying divisions among Christians; seeks dialogue and unity with "our separated brethren"	Catholics on all levels engage more strongly in inter-faith dialogue.
Decree Concerning the Pastoral Office of Bishops	defines the authority and duties of bishops in their own dioceses, in their regional gatherings, and in the Church as a whole	The collegial role of bishops receives greater clarification and increased.
Decree on the Adaptation and Renewal of Religious Life	calls for reforms in institutional structures and regulations, but sees the key to renewal as the practice of the vows of poverty, chastity, and obedience	Members of religious orders are encouraged to study original spirit of their founder.

The Documents of Vatican Council II—Major Themes and Implications

Titles	Major Themes	Major Implications
Decree on Priestly Training	calls for sound formation of priests, including particular attention to high standards in academic, spiritual, and pastoral training	The unity of priests and people is emphasized.
Declaration on Christian Education	affirms the importance of Christian education in home, school, and church and calls for an updating of methods in line with the social sciences	* Greater numbers of lay people and non-ordained religious receive professional theological training. * Parishes increase religious education opportunities for adults. * Religious education on all levels experiment with various techniques.
Declaration on the Relation of the Church to Non-Christian Religions	calls for openness toward and cooperation with the major religions of the world	* Respect and dialogue replace fear of and hostility toward other religions. * An increased awareness of the important relationship with the Jewish people and their lack of responsibility for the death of Jesus.
Dogmatic Constitution on Divine Revelation	defines how Scripture and Tradition function as the primary expressions of Christian revelation; notable for its acceptance of up-to-date methods in Scripture study and in theology	* There is deepened appreciation for nature and the non-human world as good. * There is recognition that all people can come to know God. * Scripture and Tradition are reaffirmed as twin sources of truth. * Scientific analysis of Scripture is increased.
Decree on the Apostolate of the Laity	encourages the laity to live a spiritual life and to proclaim the gospel through family, work, and social action	The involvement of the laity in the Church is encouraged and welcomed.

The Documents of Vatican Council II—Major Themes and Implications

Titles	Major Themes	Major Implications
Declaration on Religious Freedom	argues that the basic dignity of human beings demands freedom from coercion in matters of religion; all people should be free to worship according to their own conscience	• Human dignity, freedom, and primacy of conscience become more visibly associated with Catholicism. • Church teaching advocates freedom of religion.
Decree on the Missionary Activity of the Church	stresses the importance of the missionary outreach of the Church, particularly through the formation of community in local churches	New styles of missionary activity that are more accepting of and respectful toward local cultures are developed.
Decree on the Ministry and Life of Priests	clarifies the duties of priests and their relations with bishops and lay people	• All priests reflect the priesthood of Jesus. • Priests should foster greater involvement of lay people in the life of the Church.
Pastoral Constitution on the Church in the Modern World	portrays the Church as being in service to the world; presents in particular the Church's positions concerning family, culture, economics, politics, and peace	• The Church is recognized as a voice of challenge and hope. • The Church endorses certain characteristics associated with the modern world, such as freedom, tolerance, and the use of science. • Married life is emphasized as a fundamental form of spirituality. • The Church speaks out more forcefully about justice and peace.

Theme column information from Dennis M. Doyle,
The Church Emerging from Vatican II, pp. 18–19

Pope Paul VI

An Advocate of Ecumenism

As Pope Paul announced the goal of Christian unity, he turned to face the area where observer-delegates from other Christian communities were seated. He said that their presence at the council stirred great hope in his heart, as well as a feeling of sadness at their separation. "If we are to blame in any way for that separation," he said to them, "we humbly beg God's forgiveness, and ask pardon, too, of our brethren who feel themselves to have been injured by us." His statement shocked those who insisted that the Church has no stain or blemish, but was greeted by the majority of those listening with great joy. It was one of the more important moments of the council.

Throughout his papacy Pope Paul preached that non-Catholic Christians who believed in Christ and were baptized are in communion, albeit imperfectly, with the Catholic Church. Pope Paul became the most traveled pope up to his time. Many of his journeys included meetings with leaders of other religions. In 1964, he traveled to the Holy Land where he met with the Orthodox Patriarch of Constantinople. It was at this historic meeting that the two leaders removed the mutual excommunications that had been in place since 1054, the year of the East-West Schism. In 1969, Pope Paul addressed the World Council of Churches, the largest body representing Christians in the world. He also continued to seek open exchanges with communist leaders as Pope John had done before him. To improve relations between the Church and the communist governments in Eastern Europe he took a more open stance toward them, called *ostpolitik*. In this way he hoped to gain some religious freedom for Christians living under communism.

The Pope of Social Justice

Pope Paul VI's mother and father had been heavily involved in charitable work and in politics. His father was co-founder of the Italian Popular Party and was one of the first Catholics allowed to run for public office after the pope permitted Catholics to participate in Italian politics. Even as a child, Pope Paul heard about problems facing workers who were poor. When he became archbishop of Milan, he dedicated himself to the workers of the city, celebrating Mass with them in factories and holding meetings where the Church's teachings on social justice could receive a fair hearing.

Pope Paul composed a number of documents that contain some of the Church's hardest-hitting statements about justice and concern for those who are poor. In 1968, Pope Paul traveled to Bogota, Colombia, where he delivered his message about the needs of those who are poor. Later that same year, the bishops of Latin America met in Colombia to discuss how Vatican Council II could be applied to their area. They began where Pope John XXIII began—by attempting to "read the signs of the times" in light of the Gospels. The bishops were

FAITH ACTIVITY

Vision of Justice Read one of the following documents that reflect Pope Paul VI's vision of justice. Select one passage from the document and create a collage, a drawing, or a poem that would reflect its message.

* *On the Development of Peoples (Popularum Progessio)*

* *A Call to Action: Letter on the Eightieth Anniversary of Rerum Novarum*

* *Justice in the World (Justicia in Mundo)*

▼ Pope Paul VI in Uganda

shown a slide presentation outlining the massive amount of poverty that plagued Latin America. They realized that the great gulf between the few who were extremely rich and the many who were extremely poor was the "sign of the times" that they needed to address throughout their countries.

These Latin American bishops realized that the Gospel message could not be separated from the work of justice; the Good News of Christ had to be Good News for people who were poor in their specific social and economic circumstances. Second, people who are poor need to develop a sense of their own dignity and grow in power. This conclusion meant that Church leaders needed to begin working directly with those who are poor rather than trying to coerce rich people and government officials to offer charity to those who are poor. Some Church leaders who took this stance came to be viewed as enemies of the state or of wealthy landowners. Over the next few decades, Catholics involved with those who were poor were martyred for the work they were doing. The bishops also realized that poverty in Latin America was tied to a broad system that created wealth for some but that kept large numbers of people poor. Thus, the bishops started looking at economic systems and social structures such as North American companies that owned large tracts of land in South America. These companies used cheap labor to produce coffee, sugar, and fruit to be shipped to North American markets. The bishops realized that any program for helping people who are poor needed to analyze how economic systems operated.

GROUP TALK

Vatican Council II endorsed the movement among lay people known as Catholic Action. Catholic Action followed what it called the Observe-Judge-Act approach to problems. Identify a problem facing the Church today and apply this three-step approach to it.

The Pope of Liturgical Reform

For most Catholics of the 1960s and 1970s, liturgical renewal was the most evident sign that the Church was reaching out to her members in different ways. The Mass and the other sacraments were celebrated in the language of the people as well as in Latin. The altar looked like and served the function of a table around which the community gathered, rather than being exclusively a place of sacrifice. The role of the assembly was encouraged, and those gathered could recite responses, offer intercessions, and greet one another during the sign of peace. Liturgies began to include more congregational singing led by choirs or a cantor.

One significant change in the liturgy that reflected a renewed emphasis within Catholicism was the emphasis placed on the Scripture readings. The Church switched from a one-year cycle of two readings to a three-year cycle of three scripture readings—all proclaimed in the language of the people. Therefore, Catholics were exposed to the richness of the Scriptures as they never had been before.

Pope Paul also restored the ministry of **permanent deacons** for Church service. Since early in Church history, being a deacon was a step toward being ordained as a priest. With the changes directed by Pope Paul, men—including married men—could be ordained as permanent deacons.

The Church tapped into the beauty of the liturgy as it had been celebrated for centuries, and refreshed practices aimed at the spiritual participation of all gathered. However, what we celebrate did not change, neither did Christ's presence in the Eucharist nor the Holy Spirit's work in the liturgy.

FAITH ACTIVITY

Church Practices Interview someone over age sixty and ask the person to describe the Church and Church practices that existed before the changes brought about by Vatican Council II. Compare them to Church practices today.

▼ Altar servers lead the recessional from Mass.

>Age to Age

The Rite of Christian Initiation of Adults

In 1868 Charles Lavigerie, the first archbishop and later cardinal of Algiers, founded a missionary society known as the White Fathers to work in Uganda. He had seen in his native France that many baptized Catholics didn't practice the faith due to a lack of education. He instructed his new order not to baptize those who wished to join the Church until after a four-year process of formation and education. Then the newly baptized were to continue receiving religious instruction while part of the Christian community. A 1909 report from his society indicates that Uganda had 135,000 newly baptized and 151,480 people preparing for Baptism.

At Vatican II, African missionary bishops reported on the success they had with this restoration of the catechumenate, or preparation period leading up to Baptism. You may remember reading about the lengthy process involved in joining the Church that existed during the third century. Becoming Christian meant a sharp break with previous friends and lifestyles. Entering the Church meant choosing new life with Christ and a new community of faith; it required a permanent commitment and often meant great trials. In today's world, faith also demands a commitment because Christian beliefs are often in tension with those of society.

Following Vatican II, the Church restored the Rite of Christian Initiation of Adults, or RCIA. Participating in the RCIA means much more than going to classes. It involves conversion to new life in Christ. Although doctrinal instruction is part of the process, the formation of disciples is more like an apprenticeship. One "journeys" with Christ as the disciples journeyed with Jesus in the Gospels, learning more and more over time. Companions—members of the Church community already baptized—"walk the journey of faith" with those considering joining. Rites and blessings are held during parish liturgies so that the larger community can be a prayerful support to those on the journey. At some point all the catechumens of a diocese assemble in the cathedral before the bishop and have their names inscribed in the Book of the Elect. On Holy Saturday at the Easter Vigil, the catechumens are baptized, confirmed, and receive the Eucharist for the first time. In the United States on Holy Saturday 2004, more than 110,000 new members joined the Catholic Church. RCIA continues to renew the Church by welcoming those who want to journey with Jesus.

Prayer

Praying with Thomas Merton

Leader: Hear the words of the American monk Thomas Merton. Ponder their meaning for your own life.

Reader 1: In Louisville, at the corner of Fourth and Walnut, in the center of the shopping district, I was suddenly overwhelmed with the realization that I loved all those people, that they were mine and I theirs, that we could not be alien to one another even though we were total strangers. It was like waking from a dream of separateness, of spurious self-isolation.

Love and Living, pp. 24–25

Reader 2: But the question of love is one that cannot be evaded. Whether or not you claim to be interested in it, from the moment you are alive you are bound to be concerned with love, because love is not just something that happens to you: *it is a certain special way of being alive.*

Love is, in fact, an intensification of life, a completeness, a fullness, a wholeness of life. We do not live merely in order to vegetate through our days until we die. Nor do we live merely in order to take part in the routines of work and amusement that go on around us. . . . It is for this that we came into the world—this communion and self-transcendence. We do not become fully human until we give ourselves to each other in love.

Love and Living, pp. 24–25

All: My Lord God, I have no idea where I am going. I do not see the road ahead of me. I cannot know for certain where it will end. Nor do I really know myself, and the fact that I think I am following your will does not mean that I am actually doing so. But I believe that the desire to please you does in fact please you. And I hope I have that desire in all that I am doing. I hope that I will never do anything apart from that desire. And I know that if I do this you will lead me by the right road, though I may know nothing about it. Therefore, I will trust you always though I may seem to be lost and in the shadow of death. I will not fear, for you are ever with me, and you will never leave me to face my perils alone. Amen.

Thoughts in Solitude, p. 81

❭Review

1. What event associated with World War II led Church leaders to realize that the world faced a moral and spiritual vacuum?
2. What change in perspective did the Church need to make if it was to address the problems facing the world following World War II?
3. What four developments in the post-war world led the Church to examine its role in the world?
4. Name two assignments served by Pope John XXIII that helped prepare him for the papacy during a time of change. Explain.
5. What does it mean to say Pope John XXIII was initially thought to be a *papa de passagio*?
6. What is the meaning of *aggiornamento*?
7. What type of direct involvement did Pope John XXIII make in deliberations of Vatican Council II? What effect did this have on council deliberations?
8. How did Pope John XXIII respond to the work of the first session?
9. In what sense was Vatican Council II greater than the documents it produced?
10. What changes continued to occur in the Church for years following the council?
11. Name some of the themes addressed by the various commissions of the council.
12. What four aims for the council did Pope Paul VI identify?
13. What was Pope Paul VI's stance toward the Orthodox Patriarch of Constantinople and the communist governments of Eastern Europe?
14. What three conclusions did the Latin American bishops arrive at that reshaped Catholic social teaching?
15. Name three changes in the liturgy that occurred during the papacy of Pope Paul VI.

❭Key Words

aggiornamento (p. 335) The spirit of updating the Church that Pope John XXIII wanted for Vatican Council II.

colonialism (p. 330) The rule of one country by another.

permanent deacons (p. 349) Men ordained to assist the bishop and priests in various pastoral duties and ministries of hospitality and charity.

>Yesterday and Today

Inspired by the Holy Spirit, the bishops of Vatican Council II ushered in monumental changes for the Church. When calling for a council, Pope John XXIII trusted in God's grace and the guidance of the Holy Spirit. He believed that a council would produce great enlightenment and necessary renewal for the Church. Since the council, the Church has helped bring about positive change for herself and for the people of the world. Every pope since the council has dedicated himself to continuing and implementing the vision of Church identified at the council. While only a few thousand bishops directly participated in the council, every participating Catholic was involved in what can rightly be called the "Vatican II Church." The work of the Church following the council continues the work of the Church commissioned by Jesus 2,000 years ago—to bring the light of Christ to the world.

TIMELINE

A.D. 1983
U.S. Catholic bishops
publish *The Challenge
of Peace*

A.D. 1978
Election and death of
Pope John Paul I; elec-
tion of Pope John Paul II

A.D. 1979
Mother Teresa of
Calcutta receives
Nobel Peace Prize

A.D. 1981
Assassination
attempt on
Pope John Paul II

A.D. 1986
U.S. Catholic bishops
publish *Economic
Justice for All*

THE GOSPEL OF LIFE

1978-PRESENT

A.D. 1995
Pope John Paul II writes *The Gospel of Life*

A.D. 2002
Religious leaders meeting in Assisi condemn terrorism

A.D. 1989
Fall of the Iron Curtain

A.D. 2000
The worldwide Church celebrates Jubilee Year 2000

A.D. 2001
Coordinated terrorist attacks in the United States

A.D. 2003
Pope John Paul II speaks out against military action in Iraq

A.D. 2005
Death of Pope John Paul II; election of Pope Benedict XVI

If you have Internet service in your home, determine the greatest distance to which you have had instant access. Do you think of countries in other parts of the world as "distant lands" or as places easily seen and connected to as part of a "global village"? Fifty years ago, if you had left home on a trip to many parts of the world, you would have been out of touch with family and friends for weeks. Now you can travel almost anywhere and be in constant contact with people back home. As the clock turned from 1999 to 2000 around the world, you may have watched on television how people in every time zone celebrated the event. The world of recent decades is a different place from what it was even 50 years ago.

The Catholic Church has not stood frozen in time in response to recent changes. Our Church leaders pay close attention to current world developments. They continue to voice their concerns about matters of world interest. Political and religious leaders of all types meet to discuss and solve major and minor problems. The Church proclaims the Gospel of Life to a world community undergoing rapid change but still desperately in need of the counsel and consolation that come from faith in Christ.

For the latter part of the twentieth century, the Church was blessed with the strong leadership of Pope John Paul II. During this period the makeup of the Church as a worldwide community became even more evident. In fact, the Church experienced its greatest growth in Africa and parts of Asia, away from the traditional European and North American strongholds of Christianity. Under Pope John Paul II, the papacy was an active voice in the major moral, social, and political issues of the day.

Pope John Paul I— The "Smiling Pope"

After the death of Pope Paul VI in 1978, on the very first day of balloting, the cardinals elected as pope Albino Luciani, Patriarch of Venice. To honor his recent predecessors, the new pope was the first in history to take two names—Pope John Paul I. The son of a migrant worker and sometimes socialist, John Paul I was the first pope born in the twentieth century.

▲ Pope John Paul I smiling at
a crowd, from a window at
Vatican City.

He immediately broke tradition by refusing to be crowned
with the papal tiara. Instead, he chose to be installed as "the
Universal Pastor of the Church."

Pope John Paul I died on September 28, 1978, after serving
as pope for only thirty-three days. During his time as pope,
he endeared people with his wonderful sense of humor and
his gentleness of spirit. He gained the nickname "the smiling pope" because of his way of dealing with people. He
often brought children up to his throne during official audiences and spoke with them directly. Earlier, when he was an
archbishop, John Paul I wrote a series of letters to fictional
characters or people from history explaining Catholic teaching in simple language. These letters were published in a book
entitled *Illustrissimi*. The following passage is characteristic of
the compassionate spirit of John Paul I:

> How wrong, dear Peguy, are those who do not have hope! . . . it is never
> too late. God is not merely called Father. He is the Father of the prodi-
> gal son, and sees us when we are still far off, and is moved and, run-
> ning, comes to throw His arms around us and kiss us tenderly.
>
> *Letters from John Paul I, p. 25*

The Church Through History   357

Pope John Paul II: A New Pope for a New Time

Karol Wojtyla of Poland, Pope John Paul II, was the first non-Italian pope since the sixteenth century. He was fifty-eight when elected, which was young compared to other popes. He was from a communist country and spoke many languages proficiently. He had been an actor, a poet, and a philosopher. For recreation he enjoyed mountain climbing and skiing. He soon became the most widely traveled pope in history. Overall he visited nearly 130 countries. On numerous occasions, he visited Asia and Africa where the Catholic Church was experiencing great growth. In 1998, he made history by visiting Cuba and meeting with its communist leader, Fidel Castro. In March of 2000, he visited the Holy Land, stopping to pray at the Western Wall. In 2001, Pope John Paul II became the first pope in more than a thousand years to visit Greece, taking an important step toward continuing dialogue with the Orthodox Churches. In the same year, he became the first pope to enter a Muslim mosque. Earlier he had also visited a Jewish synagogue.

Pope John Paul II published more than thirteen encyclicals and many other writings. Under his direction, the Church adopted a revised code of Canon Law, regulating Church practices. In 1985, bishops who were gathered in Rome decided that it was time to put together a new official catechism for the Catholic Church, as there had not been an official catechism since the one written immediately after the Council of Trent in the sixteenth century. Pope John Paul agreed to appoint a commission to write a new catechism, and he named Joseph Cardinal Ratzinger to head up the Interdicasterial Commission for the *Catechism of the Catholic Church*. Originally written in French, an English translation of the *Catechism of the Catholic Church* appeared in 1994. It has become a sure and authentic reference book for theologians, scholars, pastors, seminarians, diocesan and parish staff, and Catholic religious education in need of a systematic and reliable account of the "precious deposit of Christian doctrine," which is the Apostolic faith.

Besides his travels and his writings, another aspect of Church life in which Pope John Paul made a great contribution was his naming of saints. He declared 1,338 people "blessed" and 482 people "saints." Catholics from around the globe now have officially recognized saints from their own cultures.

Every pope since Vatican Council II has dedicated his papacy to continuing its work. In 2001, Pope John Paul continued this tradition by stating:

> With the passing of the years, the council documents have lost nothing of their value or brilliance . . . Now that the Jubilee has ended, I feel more than ever in duty bound to point to the Council as the great grace bestowed on the Church in the 20th century: There we find a sure compass by which to take our bearings in the century now beginning.
>
> "Apostolic Letter *Novo Millenio Ineunte* for the Closing of the Jubilee of the Year 2000," #57

Pope John Paul II and the Fall of Communism The contribution to the modern world for which Pope John Paul II received greatest recognition is also one of the most important events of the twentieth century—the end of communism in the former Soviet Union and in Eastern Europe in the 1990s. Certainly, people in these countries rejected communism for a variety of reasons: workers felt violated and not treated with dignity; communism proved to be economically inefficient; and because of its strident atheistic stance, communism left a spiritual void.

In Pope John Paul's native country of Poland, a peculiar state of affairs existed. While the government officially endorsed atheism, the people were over ninety-five percent Catholic. Catholic leaders were the foremost proponents of an alternative to communism in Poland. Pope John Paul II worked publicly and behind the scenes to bring about a loosening of control by communist leaders. Eventually, communism lost its hold on Poland, then on the rest of Eastern Europe and Russia.

Pope John Paul II at the ▶ Beatification Ceremony of Mother Teresa of Calcutta.

Life of Pope John Paul II Present a report, poem, video, or electronic slide presentation on the life of Pope John Paul II or describe key points made in one of his writings.

A Voice for Life From the beginning of his papacy, Pope John Paul was aware that Christianity would soon be celebrating 2,000 years of existence. He wanted to lead the Catholic Church into the new millennium as a vibrant community, one ever faithful to Christ. He possessed a wonderful, Catholic sense of the universal Church as a people in unity through the unity of the Father, the Son, and the Holy Spirit. As he had led the Polish Church against communism, he also intended to lead the universal Church to be a voice for life, love, and hope wherever there was what he called a "culture of death." In recent decades, many Catholics have been inspired by Pope John Paul II to proclaim the Christian message of life, equal human dignity, justice, and peace against the forces of death and violence. Never before have more Catholics realized that social and economic inequalities oppose the equal human dignity we all share, and that action must be taken. John Paul II was a voice for this change.

Pope John Paul had been the victim of a violent attack. On May 13, 1981, while riding in St. Peter's plaza during his Wednesday audience, he was shot by a man named Mehmet Ali Agca. The exact motive for the shooting was never clear. The pope was rushed to a local hospital, the first time a pope had ever gone to a hospital, and was operated on to remove the bullet. After his recovery, the pope visited the man who had tried to kill him in his prison cell, praying with him and forgiving him for his act.

Pope John Paul II in ▶ Mehmet Ali Agca's cell, forgiving him.

The End of an Era Pope John Paul II, suffering in particular from Parkinson's disease, died on April 2, 2005. As the two hundred and sixty-fourth pope, he reigned for twenty-six years, the third longest papacy after that of Saint Peter (reported to have been from a.d. 33–67) and that of Blessed Pius IX (1846–1878). With his travels to other countries and his visits with pilgrims from all parts of the world, he was the most visible pope in history. For Catholics under the age of thirty, he had been the only pope they had ever known.

In the days before his funeral, more than a million people viewed his body. Some stood in line for twenty-four hours to see him. Three-hundred thousand mourners attended his funeral in St. Peter's Square, including U.S. President George W. Bush and two former U.S. presidents. It was the first time that a U.S. president attended the funeral of a pope. The funeral rites were broadcast by television to billions of people throughout the world. The then Joseph Cardinal Ratzinger, prefect for the Congregation for the Doctrine of the Faith and close confidant of the pope, presided at his funeral liturgy.

Pope Benedict XVI Begins His Reign

On April 18, 2005, during the second day of balloting, the cardinals of the Church elected Joseph Cardinal Ratzinger as the new pope. He chose the name Benedict XVI and is the first German pope since Hadrian VI in 1523 and the oldest person elected pope since Alexander VIII in 1689. During his installation ceremony, Pope Benedict followed the tradition of his two predecessors and was not crowned but instead was invested with a cloth called a pallium symbolizing that he was the universal pastor or shepherd of the Church. He also did not include the tiara, or crown, in his coat of arms, but replaced it with a bishop's miter. He did put in his coat of arms a symbol from his native Germany, a bear.

Continuing the Work of His Predecessors Almost immediately, Pope Benedict made it clear that he would continue the work of his recent predecessors. He quoted Pope John Paul II saying that Vatican Council II was to be the guidepost for the Church as it enters the twenty-first century. Pope Benedict had been a *peritus,* or "expert," at the council and knew it well. He quickly touched on themes that Vatican II had emphasized as the agenda for the Church. He especially declared his concern for ecumenism, working toward union with other Christian groups such as Orthodox Christians and toward ongoing dialogue with non-Christian religions. Following a theme of Pope John Paul II, Pope Benedict ended his inaugural homily by appealing to young people:

> If we let Christ into our lives, we lose nothing, nothing, absolutely nothing of what makes life free, beautiful and great. No! Only in this friendship are the doors of life opened wide. Only in this friendship is the great potential of human existence truly revealed. Only in this friendship do we experience beauty and liberation. And so, today, with great strength and great conviction, on the basis of long personal experience of life, I say to you, dear young people: Do not be afraid of Christ! He takes nothing away, and he gives you everything. When we give ourselves to him, we receive a hundredfold in return. Yes, open, open wide the doors to Christ—and you will find true life. Amen.
>
> Pope Benedict XVI, Inaugural Homily, April 24, 2005

Images of the Church

The Light of Christ

The bishops of Vatican Council II chose the name *Lumen Gentium* for their document on the Church. It means "light of the world" or "light of humanity." Jesus Christ is the light of the world; the Church brings that light to all people. Soon after Pope John Paul II died, a new pope was elected; this reminded people that the Catholic Church is connected to Christ not just in spiritual ways but in a concrete, historical way as well. The light of Christ continues to shine in the Catholic Church through the Scriptures, the sacraments, her Tradition, her visible leaders, and the community of people who pray together and carry on the work of Christ.

The Church in the World

The Church in El Salvador

The largest concentration of Catholics in the world today is in Latin America. In recent decades, the Latin American Church has had more than its share of martyrs. Perhaps the continent's most well-known martyr was the archbishop of San Salvador, Oscar Romero, who died a martyr's death on March 24, 1980.

At the beginning of his ministry, Romero was not a likely candidate for martyrdom. As a priest, he believed that his role was to live a life of personal holiness. He condemned priests who became involved in social issues, calling such actions "the politicization of the priesthood." When named bishop of Santiago de Maria in 1972, he had Jesuits removed from the national seminary because they spoke out on economic and social issues. Thus, government officials saw him as docile and unthreatening. Romero was named archbishop of San Salvador, capital of El Salvador, in 1977. The very week that Romero was installed as archbishop, government troops began a series of massacres. Archbishop Romero protested the killings, but meekly and respectfully. He urged charity on the part of the government and restraint on the part of the clergy.

Archbishop Romero's attitude changed radically when a priest friend, Father Rutilio Grande, was killed during one of the massacres and his body was dumped on top of the garbage heap where the government dumped their victims to warn others about the consequences of rebellion. Archbishop Romero knew Father Grande was a good and committed priest who was balanced and sensible in his work with those who were poor. After Father Grande's death, Archbishop Romero became an active voice for those who were poor and oppressed in El Salvador. He personally went daily to the dump and gathered the bodies of those killed. He announced on the radio the names of the victims and begged the army to stop the killings. He suspended Mass everywhere in the archdiocese but in the cathedral so that people could assemble together. He preached regularly about the commitment of the Church to be with those who were oppressed.

GROUP TALK

The Church is, by definition, a community. List some historical circumstances when the community dimension of the Church was strongly manifested.

His fellow bishops urged him to go slowly in his condemnation of violence and injustice, but he insisted that it was his duty as bishop to serve the people. He stopped attending government functions to express his rejection of its policies. Archbishop Romero spent more and more time with the people, saying that, "With this people, it is not hard to be a good shepherd." He wrote the president of the United States to ask him to stop providing military assistance to the Salvadoran government. In his radio address on March 23, 1980, Archbishop Romero directly addressed the soldiers in the army:

> 'We are your people. The peasants you kill are your own brothers and sisters. When you hear the voice of the man commanding you to kill, remember instead the voice of God. Thou Shalt not Kill. . . . In the name of God, in the name of our tormented people whose cries rise up to heaven, I beseech you, I beg you, I command you, *stop the repression.*'

> The next day, while celebrating Mass in the chapel of the hospital where he lived, he was shot through the heart, dying within minutes. He was the first bishop to be killed at the altar since Saint Thomas Becket in the twelfth century. Romero had spoken of his death in an interview two weeks before the event: 'I have frequently been threatened by death. I must tell you, as a Christian, I do not believe in death without resurrection. If I am killed, I shall arise in the Salvadoran people.'

> Story adapted from and quote taken from Robert Ellsberg, *All Saints*, 1997

Women Martyrs in El Salvador Four women from the United States—Sister Ita Ford mm, Sister Dorothy Kazel osu, Sister Maura Clarke mm, and Jean Donovan—were so deeply touched by people of El Salvador who were caught up in the crossfire of political conflicts and economic hardships that they chose to live among them and help them in whatever way they could. The lay person in the group, Jean Donovan, grew up in Connecticut and learned courage and compassion from her brother, Michael, who suffered from Hodgkin's disease.

Donovan moved to Cleveland for work and served as a volunteer in the diocesan youth ministry program. When she heard about a mission project in El Salvador sponsored by the diocese, she felt called to go there and to spend some time helping people whose lives were marked by so much suffering. She joined a group dedicated to helping refugees—people who had lost home and livelihood due to the violent exchanges that constantly occurred between government and rebel forces. Mainly, she cared for the children who were wounded or who had lost their families in the conflict. Because she used her natural sense of humor to lighten their lives, her co-workers called her "Saint Jean the Playful."

Donovan steered clear of any involvement in political issues. Most of her time was spent with Sister Kazel. They transported those who were sick and brought food and medical supplies to people in areas not otherwise easily accessed. Donovan and Sister Kazel also trained catechists who taught others about the Catholic faith. They helped prepare people for celebrating the sacraments. She wrote home that she often thought about returning to the United States but didn't want to leave the children whom she called "the poor, bruised victims of this insanity."

The murder of Archbishop Romero in March 1980 did not deter Donovan from continuing her work. She had personally witnessed the death of Salvadorans with whom she worked. These atrocities actually strengthened her resolve to stay with the people she had come to love. She assured her friends back home who feared for her safety that "they don't kill blond-haired, blue-eyed North Americans."

On December 2, 1980, members of the Salvadoran National Guard stopped the women at a roadblock and took them to an isolated location where they were abused and shot. The soldiers buried their bodies in a shallow grave by the side of the road.

These brave and dedicated women knew the danger they were in because of their continuing work with people who sought safety and to have their basic needs met. Archbishop Romero had earlier said: "One who is committed to the poor must risk the same fate as the poor. And in El Salvador we know what the fate of the poor signifies: to disappear, to be tortured, to be captive, and to be found dead."

The Church in India

The last few decades of the twentieth century produced a number of saintly Christians who carried on the work of the Church throughout the world. None received greater international recognition than Agnes Bojaxhiu of Albania, known to the world as Mother Teresa. At seventeen she entered the Sisters of Loreto and set sail for Calcutta, India, where she taught in a school for wealthy girls. At the age of thirty-six, while traveling on a train through the Himalayan mountains, Sister Teresa received what she described as "a call within a call." She felt that God wanted more of her, namely, he wanted her "to be poor with the poor and to love him in the distressing disguise of the poorest of the poor."

Sister Teresa asked permission to give up teaching and to devote herself to caring for the people of Calcutta who were poor. Instead of her religious habit, she wore a simple Indian-style sari. She went barefoot through the slums of the city tending those on the streets who were sick and dying. She also taught children who lived in these poor sections. By 1948, enough women joined her in her work that she sought permission to form a new religious community, the Missionaries of Charity. Mother Teresa and her sisters performed a simple act of charity: they took people dying in the gutters and cared for them, letting them know that someone loved them and valued them as children of God. The sisters found God in the faces of the people who had nothing and were dying.

As her work became better known, the Indian government awarded Mother Teresa the "Lord of the Lotus," an honor given to those who have aided the people of India. She received the first Pope John XXIII Peace Prize from the Vatican. In 1979, she was awarded the Nobel Peace Prize. She traveled throughout the world and spoke about the need to relieve both physical and spiritual poverty. By the time she died in 1999—viewed by many as a saint of our day—her sisters had missions in more than thirty countries. Mother Teresa was beatified by Pope John Paul II on October 19, 2003.

The Church in Canada

Jean Vanier was born in 1928 to a family of wealth and privilege. By his early twenties he was an officer in both the Canadian and British navies. His life changed in the 1960s after he visited a home for men with mental disabilities. Vanier was deeply moved by how each of the men seemed starved for simple friendship, attention, and affection. Vanier began visiting a series of such institutions, and in each one he found people who felt unwanted and unnecessary. He also discovered that when treated with kindness, these same people would beam with joy.

In August, 1964, Vanier founded L'Arche. In a farmhouse in France, people both with and without mental handicaps lived in community. For Vanier, Christian virtues such as mercy and loving-kindness remain abstractions except in a community context. He felt that regardless of class or state in life, no one should be left out of experiencing life in community. According to its charter, L'Arche intended to be a new type of family or community where the strong help the weak, and the weak help the strong. In time, L'Arche grew to more than one hundred communities in twenty-six countries. There are also non-residential communities in which people meet to "share their sufferings, their joys, to celebrate together and to pray."

Jean Vanier's message is particularly important today. We have made great advances in so many areas of life—technology, medicine, scientific knowledge. And yet so many people feel lonely; so many people continue to feel starved for basic community. Vanier decided that he would focus on persons with mental disabilities as the basis for forming community. However, true friendships and community can happen in any setting.

> **!FYI**
>
> The name of the L'Arche movement was derived from Noah's Ark by members of the first community. *L'Arche* is French for "the ark."

GROUP TALK

1. In what ways do you seek to meet the need for community relationships in your own life?

2. Based on your experiences with friendships, do you believe that community is a basic human need? Explain.

3. What qualities does a healthy community possess? What role does the Church play as the basis for community in your life?

The Church in Africa

Pope John Paul II made numerous visits to the continent of Africa, where Catholics enthusiastically greeted the messages of Vatican II. In 1939, Masaka, Uganda, had become the first Catholic diocese entirely staffed by African clergy under its bishop, Joseph Kiwanuka. African Catholics welcomed the "world Church" that Vatican II and Pope Paul VI had called for. The Africans didn't want "being Catholic" to mean "being European." Even before the council, elements of African culture had been introduced into the liturgy in Africa. The approval by the council of using the language of the people in the liturgy opened up new and exciting possibilities for African Catholicism. Africa is a pluralistic continent with tribal, linguistic, and religious diversity. The spirit of Vatican II helped guide African Catholics in meeting the challenges of their diverse culture. Finally, the Vatican II Church took a stand against colonialism at the very time that many African nations were gaining independence from colonial rule. Vatican II's emphasis on social justice gave Africans, suffering oppression left over from their colonial past, a sense of hope that the world recognized their problems and wanted to help.

While Africa has experienced a great deal of turmoil and bloodshed, the AIDS crisis, and natural disasters such as droughts in recent decades, African Catholicism has continued to thrive since the time of the council. In recent years, however, Catholics have been both the perpetrators and the victims of violence between ethnic groups. For instance, over the last four decades of the twentieth century, more than two hundred African priests were murdered. Sisters of religious orders have related tales of armed youths entering convents and killing everyone they can find. Unfortunately, sometimes those doing the killing have been Catholics themselves. The Church's teachings on peace, justice, acceptance of diversity, and faith in God are needed tools for helping Africans shape their future.

Catholic Priest in ▶
Africa, helping locals.

The Church in Europe

After the great devastation of two world wars, Europe needed rebuilding—not only its physical structures and infrastructures, but its spirit as well. Following World War II, church attendance dropped off significantly, and a sharp decline in religious vocations occurred. Vatican II did much to reinvigorate religious fervor among Catholics, especially in its promotion of ecumenism.

Leading up to Jubilee Year 2000, the Catholic Church held six regional assemblies in the 1990s to address concerns and identify signs of hope for particular areas. There was one for Africa in 1994, for America in 1997, for Asia in the spring of 1998, and for Oceania in the fall of that year. The European Church held regional assemblies in 1991 and in 1999. At these European synods, the bishops of the continent addressed the collapse of communism in Eastern Europe and expressed hope for the newly developing democratic governments replacing communist regimes there. They also raised concern about problems for family life and society that can accompany quick prosperity, and they issued a call for justice in the treatment of new immigrants. The 1999 synod specified ten signs of hope for European Catholicism and for all citizens of Europe. These signs of hope suggest that Christian values and Catholics themselves will continue to play an important role in European life of the third millennium.

FAITH ACTIVITY

Areas of Agreement Research and write a report on the areas of agreements that were reached between the Lutherans and Catholics in the "Joint Declaration on the Doctrine of Justification."

Signs of Hope for the European Church

1. the Christian martyrs of the twentieth century

2. the holiness exhibited by many Christians

3. the "rediscovered freedom" of Churches in Eastern Europe

4. the Catholic Church's increased focus on its mission to spread Christ's message

5. new religious movements and communities

6. renewed interest in traditional religious institutions and expressions of faith

7. increased awareness of the co-responsibility shared by all Christians

8. the growing involvement of women in the Church

9. the great progress experienced in the area of ecumenism, especially the Lutheran-Catholic "Joint Declaration on the Doctrine of Justification"

10. growing interaction between the Churches of the East and the Church of the West

The St. Egidio Community Signs of life in the European Church can be found in the many new forms of religious communities there, especially among the young. One such community is the St. Egidio community of Rome.

The St. Egidio community was founded in Rome in the late 1960s by a layman, Andrea Ricciardi. It is a "new movement," having been founded after Vatican II. There are approximately 40,000 members, most of whom are lay people (predominantly male), in about 60 different countries.

The St. Egidio community has three main objectives: to serve the poor, to stimulate ecumenical activity, and to pray and spread the Gospel. Members are not all Catholic. Many are from other denominations, but they all meet regularly for community prayer. The community in Rome gathers daily for prayer at the historic church of Santa Maria in Trastevere. They also operate a soup kitchen that can accommodate nearly 1,500 people on a daily basis.

Following in the spirit of Pope John Paul II, the St. Egidio community has organized annual interfaith meetings. In 1986, Pope John Paul II invited many religious leaders of different faith backgrounds to Assisi to pray for world peace. The St. Egidio community has also shown success in mediating international disputes, particularly in Africa.

Representatives of ▶ different religions march for peace in Lisbon at a conference organized by the St. Egidio Community.

The Church in the United States

As the world moved into the middle of the twentieth century, U.S. Catholics were moving into a new phase. Up until World War II, they belonged to what we described earlier as the immigrant Church. Even into the 1950s, many priests serving parishes in the United States were from Ireland. The event that most clearly demonstrated that Catholics had finally "made it" in the United States was the 1960 election of John Kennedy, the first—and to date, the only—Catholic president in the nation's history.

Remember that anti-Catholic and anti-immigrant prejudice had a strong history in the United States. Therefore, Catholic leaders hesitated to say anything negative about the way of life in the United States. Beginning in the 1960s, the U.S. Catholic bishops became more vocal in criticizing some policies and values dominant in U.S. culture. For instance, during the Vietnam War the U.S. bishops stated that young people protesting the war were often motivated by principles consistent with Catholic principles (See Pastoral Letter of the U.S. Catholic Bishops on "Peace and Vietnam," #9). They declared that a young man had a right to register as a **conscientious objector** and also a right to **selective conscientious objection** (refusing in conscience to participate in one particular war that he believed to be immoral). Selective conscientious objection was a controversial position at the time since many young people were opposed to the Vietnam War but not necessarily to all warfare.

In the 1970s, the U.S. Catholic bishops addressed many right to life issues, such as abortion, euthanasia, and capital punishment. In the 1980s, the bishops produced two pastoral letters that proved to be highly controversial. The first, *The Challenge of Peace: God's Promise and Our Response*, written in 1983, focused on war and nuclear weapons. The second, *Economic Justice for All*, written in 1986, focused on the U.S. economy and on fair distribution of wealth and resources.

A number of Catholics felt as though the bishops had gone too far in their criticisms of the country in these two letters. However, these letters signaled that Catholic leaders were going to speak out against policies, practices, and values that they believed to be contrary to Gospel values and harmful to people. The letters led to serious discussion within and outside the Church and influenced statements by other churches and political policies.

Beginning in the 1960s, individual Catholics, often motivated by their religious beliefs, also took strong stands about timely social issues. Besides those that chose conscientious objector status, many Catholics were active in the civil rights movement. In addition, large numbers of Catholics participated in the movement to unionize migrant farm workers. César Chávez, who led the movement, was personally inspired by Catholic teachings on justice. Catholics have also been leaders in pro-life movements.

FAITH ACTIVITY

Nonviolent Protest César Chávez spearheaded the drive to unionize migrant farm workers using nonviolent protest techniques to win support for his cause. Formation of the United Farm Workers represents a remarkable story of people who are working with people who are not poor to bring about change. Research the role César Chávez played in the UFW union and report on it to the class.

GROUP TALK

Discuss in groups the following statements. Decide whether you agree or disagree and tell why.

1. The United States should increase the amount of economic aid it provides countries where there are many people who are poor.

2. The Catholic Church in the United States should send priests, religious, and committed lay people to work in less developed such as areas, some parts of Latin America.

3. In countries where they believe oppression exists, Church leaders should publicly criticize oppressive government policies.

César Chávez ▶

Sister Thea Bowman—A Dancing Prophet

In 1989, an African American woman from Mississippi who was a granddaughter of slaves was invited to address the U.S. Catholic bishops' conference on Black Catholics. Following her spirited presentation on what being black and Catholic meant in the Church of the '90s, she asked the bishops to stand and clap their hands and praise God with their voices and with their bodies. With gusto, they joined her in singing, "We Shall Overcome."

Who was this woman who could challenge the bishops to give blacks a greater voice in the modern Church, and who could coax the bishops to join her in singing and dancing? Her name was Bertha Bowman. Bertha was born in Yazoo City, Mississippi, in 1937. Although Baptist, she attended a Catholic school run by Franciscan sisters. Bertha decided that she wanted to become a Catholic and a nun. At the age of fifteen, she left Mississippi for Wisconsin to finish her education and become a Franciscan sister—the only black woman in the entire order. She took Thea as her religious name in honor of her father. After college, Sister Thea attended Catholic University in Washington, D.C., where she encountered the African American style of Catholic worship that she missed while living in LaCrosse, Wisconsin. The gospel hymns, the spirituals, the dancing, and the testifying that made up black Church services reflected the message of deliverance from sin and slavery and entrance into freedom and life. This message spoke to the black experience in America.

After her studies at Catholic University, Sister Thea went on to help found the Institute of Black Catholic Studies at Xavier University in New Orleans. From this base, Sister Thea traveled throughout the country, combining musical performance, preaching, and story-telling. Her message was, "If we speak the word that is Christ in love and faith, with patience and prayer and perseverance, it will take root. It does have power to save us. Call one another! Testify! Teach! Act on the Word! Witness!" She would always have her audience on their feet, clapping their hands in songs of praise.

In her forties, Sister Thea was diagnosed with breast cancer. The prayers and hymns that she offered for other people, she now needed to sustain herself. She prayed, "Lord, let me live until I die." She continued her work, sometimes giving presentations from a wheelchair and wrapping her almost bald head in a bright turban. Sister Thea died in 1990, having touched the hearts of thousands of U.S. Catholics through her spirited worship of our loving God.

Story is adapted and quotes taken from Phyllis Zagano, *Twentieth-Century Apostles*

Signs of Hope in the U.S. Church

Today in Catholic parishes throughout the United States, teenagers and adults assist at liturgies and volunteer their time to run sports programs and tutor children. Parishes often coordinate clothing drives and food preparation for homeless shelters. In some parishes English, Spanish, Vietnamese, and other cultural elements are integrated into the Mass and other services. Baptisms, weddings, and funerals crowd parish schedules so that people can celebrate within a Church context their most important events. Parishes provide time and space for visits before the Blessed Sacrament and for quiet prayer. Bible groups meet to pray and study the Scriptures together, and a variety of Lenten services help Catholics make that season spiritually rich. Within the Rite of Christian Initiation of Adults (RCIA), people prepare for reception of the Sacraments of Initiation, guided by committed volunteers who serve as their catechists and sponsors. In other words, the Church in the United States continues to provide the way for Catholics to encounter Christ and to manifest Christ in the world.

Present and Future

Do you feel as though you have something special to offer the world? What gifts, talents, or personality traits do you share with others? How do you bring happiness to family, friends, acquaintances, and strangers? History is, by definition, about the past. The Church, however, is a living organism. She has a past, a present, and a future. God's presence in the world is never an abstract concept. Instead, it is channeled through the Church and her people.

Many people today have taken up the banner of being the Church in the world; saintly people are not just figures from the past. Followers of Christ are making history now. The part that you play in that history is up to you.

The Church—Christ Present in the World

"From the beginning of his public life Jesus chose certain men, twelve in number, to be with him and to participate in his mission. . . . through them he directs the Church" (*Catechism of the Catholic Church*, #551). What Christ entrusted to his Apostles they in turn, under the inspiration of the Holy Spirit, handed on to all generations until Christ returns in glory. In other words, the Church is historical. It began with a small group of Jesus' followers and continues today as the community of his followers guided and led by the Holy Spirit. Christ, who gave his all to heal the sick and bring peace through forgiveness of sins, is present today in his Church. Christ, who made sure that the little ones of his time were never left out, is present today in his Church. Christ, who nourished his chosen ones with his very Body and Blood at the first Eucharist, is present today in his Church. Christ, who died and rose from the dead to assure us that eternal life awaits us, is present today in his Church. The Church's history reveals the mystery of Christ present in the world. That mystery is ongoing in the Church today.

> Everyone who breathes, high and low, educated and ignorant, young and old, man and woman, has a mission, has a work. We are not sent into this world for nothing; we are not born at random; we are not here, that we may go to bed at night, and get up in the morning, toil for bread, eat and drink, laugh and joke, sin when we have a mind, and reform when we are tired of sinning, rear a family and die. God sees every one of us; he creates every soul . . . for a purpose. He needs, he deigns to need, every one of us. He has an end for each of us; we are all equal in his sight, and we are placed in our different ranks and stations, not to get what we can out of them for ourselves, but to labor in them for him. As Christ has his work, we too have ours; as he rejoiced to do his work, we must rejoice in ours also.

John Henry Cardinal Newman, "God's Will the End of Life," from *Discourses Addressed to Mixed Congregations*, 1849

The Communion of Saints In some Catholic elementary schools, it is customary for students to learn about a particular saint, memorize a few lines about his or her life, and dress up like that saint for a presentation to the rest of the school. Some high school students can still remember the speech they memorized about the saint many years earlier. The presentation often ends with one teacher's saying something like "We hope you have learned something about the saints and the good they did. Now it is our turn. You and I are the saints of the twenty-first century. We can model Jesus in our day just as these earlier saints did in their day."

The "communion of saints" expresses something of the wonderful mystery of the Church as the reign of God manifest on earth and awaited with joy in the fullness of time. Too often saints are thought of as the exceptional ones, as people who couldn't possibly have lived normal lives. The saints mentioned in this text have sometimes been heroic witnesses to faith, and led active lives during which they initiated new groups or programs. Others have lived their lives in very ordinary, commonplace ways. However, there is one thing all saints have in common—all of them have experienced the wonder of God's presence in their lives. All Christians *believe* in God, but saints have a *love relationship* with God. You may come to recognize that the wonder of life is a gift from a loving God in which you will want to participate as much as you can—even though many forces may seem to be holding you back. Your attempts to live life to the fullest, a life that is not yours alone but is shared with everyone else on earth, is a call to holiness and sainthood.

However, the invitation is not without its struggles. The Church is a communion of sinners as well as a communion of saints. Our study of history has revealed that to us. Today we share our strengths and our weaknesses, just as people of the past did. However, we must not overlook the goodness that surrounds us simply because it is manifest in flesh and blood people rather than in characters described in a book. Families seek ways to live Christian values. In schools and hospitals, in parishes and houses of hospitality, people pray together, try to be kind to one another, and help one another out. They search for ways to be of service to people in need in their communities. They dedicate themselves to working for justice and peace, and they study Scripture and Church history in order to know God's will better. These people are the saints of today.

In his inaugural homily Pope Benedict XVI reminded Catholics that they are members of the communion of saints in these words: "Indeed, the communion of Saints consists not only of the great men and women who went before us and whose names we know. All of us belong to the communion of Saints, we who have been baptized in the name of the Father, and the Son and the Holy Spirit, we who draw life from the gift of Christ's Body and Blood, through which he transforms us and makes us like himself" (April 24, 2005).

A Beginning, Not an End

"Awaiting you are tasks and goals which can appear out of proportion to human strengths. Do not be discouraged! Being Christian has never been easy, nor is it today. Following Christ requires the courage to make radical decisions, often against the current."

Pope John Paul II (Jubilee Mass Dedicated to the Laity, November 26, 2000)

Our study of Church history has introduced us to a community attempting to be faithful to God, facing sacrifices asked to be made, grateful for blessings received, and confident in the life to come because of Christ Jesus. The Church we have studied is the work of the Holy Spirit. The Church of the future will be the Holy Spirit working through all of us who accept the challenge of bearing Christ in our lives and our world. A Church history course is not an end. It is just the beginning.

FAITH ACTIVITY

Turning Things Around Write a short story or present a visual depiction describing how a fault or a weakness ends up being the means by which someone helps others.

>Age to Age

The Gospel of Life

Pope John Paul II wrote many encyclicals on important issues facing the world today. One of his most powerful encyclicals was *The Gospel of Life*, written in 1995. A glance at any news program today reminds us of the many situations in which life itself is threatened. In 1973, the U.S. Supreme Court decreed that a woman has a constitutional right to have an abortion. Assisted suicide laws and other policies related to terminally ill persons call into question the value that we place on those who are vulnerable in our society. At times cloning and stem cell experimentation are discussed or advocated without concern for the fundamental respect due human life. Pope John Paul II's encyclical attests to the fact that the Catholic Church has been at the forefront in promoting a culture of life and challenging a "culture of death." Many Catholics are active in pro-life organizations; you may be familiar with some such organizations in your area. Here are a few national pro-life groups:

- First, Do No Harm, an association of members of the medical profession committed to the protection of life;

- Human Life International, an organization that serves as a clearinghouse for information on anti-life issues surfacing around the globe;

- American Life League, a group committed to helping their fellow citizens learn about threats to the sanctity of life in the United States;

- Africa 2000, an organization that helps inform Americans about policies and procedures of U.S. agencies in dealing with the people of Africa related to foreign aid, population information, and life issues.

❯Prayer

Praying with Mother Teresa of Calcutta

Opening Prayer:

Make us worthy, Lord, to serve our neighbors
throughout the world
who live and die in poverty and hunger.
Give them, through our hands, this day
their daily bread, and by our understanding love,
give peace and joy. ("Through Our Hands" p. 136)

Reading:

O God, we pray for all those in our world who are suffering from injustice: for those who are discriminated against because of their race, color, or religion; for those imprisoned for working for the relief of oppression; for those who are hounded for speaking the inconvenient truth; for those tempted to violence as a cry against overwhelming hardship; for those deprived of reasonable health and education; for those suffering from hunger and famine; for those too weak to help themselves and who have no one else to help them; for the unemployed who cry out for work, but do not find it.

We pray for anyone of our acquaintance who is personally affected by injustice. Forgive us, Lord, if we unwittingly share in the conditions or in a system that perpetuates injustice.

Show us how we can serve your children and make love practical by washing their feet. ("Making Love Practical" p. 68)

Closing Prayer:
Lead me from death to life,
from lies to truth.
Lead me from despair to hope,
from fear to trust.
Lead me from hatred to love,
from war to peace.
Let peace fill our hearts, our world,
our universe . . . . peace, peace, peace. Amen.
("Lead Me" p. 9)

(in *A World on Its Knees*, compiled by Madonna Therese Ratliff, FSP)

>Review

1. What approach did Pope John Paul I use in *Illustrissimi*?

2. Name three characteristics that made Pope John Paul II unique among modern popes.

3. List four ways that Pope John Paul II contributed to the modern world.

4. Who is Pope Benedict XVI and what is one theme of his papacy to date?

5. How did Archbishop Oscar Romero's stance on political involvement change after the death of Father Rutilio Grande?

6. In what ways did Jean Donovan serve the people of El Salvador?

7. For what type of work is Mother Teresa noted?

8. What is the name of the religious order founded by Mother Teresa?

9. Name four reasons why African Catholics welcomed the changes encouraged by Vatican Council II.

10. In what types of activity are members of the St. Egidio community involved?

11. Name two signs of hope for the European Church.

12. How did the place of Catholics in U.S. society change from the late 1940s to the '60s?

13. Give three examples of how Catholic leaders, beginning in the late 1960s, became critical of U.S. society.

14. What two controversial issues did the U.S. bishops write pastoral letters about during the 1980s?

15. Give three examples of signs of life in the U.S. Catholic Church.

>Key Words

conscientious objector (p. 371) One who refuses in conscience to participate in all wars.

selective conscientious objection (p. 371) Refusing in conscience to participate in one particular war that a person believes to be immoral.

>Yesterday and Today

One day in 1999, two older priests watched as the church building where they had served for many years was being torn down. One remarked to the other that their church would soon be gone. They both realized that "the church" to which they referred was not only a building. Rather, "the Church" they had known and in which they had grown up was now externally transformed into something quite different. The Church entering the new millennium was in many ways a new and different entity from what they had known during their youth. Nonetheless, they also realized that it still proclaimed Christ Jesus, the Gospel, and Christ's presence in history and throughout the world, as it had always done.

Pope John Paul II, Pope Benedict XVI, and other leaders have guided the Catholic Church into a new millennium. Many Catholics have demonstrated that Christ's presence in the Church continues through their lives of active participation in the Church, service, and prayer. As in the past, the Church of tomorrow will be the work of the Holy Spirit made visible through its people and its divinely chosen leaders. Think about your role as Church leaders of the present and the future. How will your presence make a difference in the Church and in the world?

Glossary

accommodation—The practice of aligning beliefs and practices from local cultures with Christianity. (*245*)

Act of Toleration—The 1649 decree by the government of Maryland granting freedom of religion there. (*271*)

Acts of the Apostles—The book of the New Testament that tells the story of the early Christian community. (*12*)

aggiornamento—The spirit of updating the Church that Pope John XXIII wanted for Vatican Council II. (*335*)

anti-pope—Someone who falsely claims to be pope. (*165*)

apologists—Christian thinkers who defended and explained Christian beliefs. (*44*)

Apostolic See—A term used for the papacy, identifying the pope as successor to the Apostle Peter; also called the "Holy See." (*75*)

Arianism—A heresy denying that Jesus is truly God. (*68*)

Ascension—The Risen Christ enters into heavenly glory. (*13*)

assimilation—Members of minority groups adopting the values and characteristics of the dominant culture in which they live. (*303*)

atheism—The denial that God exists. (*38*)

Babylonian Captivity—Period from 587 to 539 b.c. when the Jewish nation did not exist and Jewish leaders were exiled to Babylon. (*9*)

Babylonian Captivity of the Papacy—Period during which the pope resided in Avignon in the Kingdom of Naples. (*160*)

baptistery—The place where Baptisms are celebrated; originally a separate building and now typically a section of a church. (*101*)

baroque—A style of art, architecture, and spirituality that emphasizes feelings and sentimentality. (*241*)

basilica—A Greek word meaning "king's hall"; currently the term is used to designate a certain church of historical significance that continues to play an important part in the religious life of a particular region. (*102*)

bishops—Means "overseers"; ordained Church leaders who are successors of the Apostles and have received the fullness of the Sacrament of Holy Orders. (*55*)

Black Death—Popular name for the bubonic plague, so named because body parts turned black from lack of blood. (*158*)

Black Robes—Term northern Native Americans used for the Jesuits because of the Jesuit's distinctive garb. (*267*)

Brahmins—Members of the highest-ranking social class in the traditional Indian caste system. (*249*)

canon—The Church's complete list of sacred books of the Bible. (*47*)

catechumens—Unbaptized persons preparing for membership in the Church. A person becomes a catechumen after celebrating the Rite of Acceptance into the order of catechumens. (*52*)

Catholic Action—The movement calling for active involvement of lay people in the Church. (*317*)

celibacy—"The state or condition of those who have chosen to remain unmarried for the sake of the kingdom of heaven in order to give themselves entirely to God and to the service of his people" (*CCC*, Glossary). (*102, 128*)

Charlemagne—King of the Franks who was crowned Roman Emperor by the pope in 800. (*112*)

Christendom—Christian-dominated Western Europe of the Middle Ages. (*120*)

Christians of Saint Thomas—Indian Christians who trace their origins to the first century. (*248*)

cloistered—Literally, "behind walls"; women and men religious who choose to live within monasteries. (*85*)

colonialism—The rule of one country by another. (*330*)

communion of saints—All the faithful Church members on earth, in heaven, and in purgatory. (*189*)

conciliarism—Belief that Church councils have greater authority than the pope. (*164*)

conclave—A meeting of cardinals to elect a pope. (*130*)

concordat—An agreement between the pope and a head of state identifying the role that each would play in Church governance in that country. (*235*)

conquistadors—Spanish word for "conquerors"; the Spanish men who first came to the Americas especially in search of wealth. (*257*)

conscientious objector—One who refuses in conscience to participate in all wars. (*371*)

convents—The residences of religious women who are bound together by vows to a religious life. (*85*)

conversion—A radical reorientation of one's whole life away from sin and evil and toward God. (*11*)

conversos—Jews and Muslims who converted to Christianity, either willingly or unwillingly, following the Christian takeover of Spain. (*174*)

Council of Jerusalem—The first Church council, which was called to resolve the growing controversy over whether or not Gentile Christians would have to observe Jewish law. (*27*)

Council of Nicaea—Meeting of bishops in 325 that condemned Arianism and formulated the Nicene Creed. (*69*)

Council of Trent—Post-Reformation meeting of the world's Catholic bishops to reform the Church and clarify Catholic teaching. (*205*)

covenant—Originally an agreement or contract between two parties. Came to be applied exclusively to the promise God made to the Jewish people and then through Christ to the Church. (*6*)

deacons—Third degree of the Sacrament of Holy Orders; the man is ordained to assist the bishop and priests in a variety of ways; in the early Church, someone appointed to serve those who were poor or otherwise needy in the community. (*35*)

deism—Belief that God created the world and then left it to run according to natural laws. (*225*)

desert fathers—Christian men who lived alone in desert territories of northern Africa and the Middle East in order to sacrifice their lives to Christ. Some women also choose this lifestyle. (*83*)

devotional Catholicism—Practices of religious popular piety among Catholics. (*309*)

diaspora—Scattering of the Jewish people from their homeland. (*9*)

Diet of Worms—Meeting of the leadership of the Holy Roman Empire during which Luther refused to recant his beliefs. (*190*)

Donation of Pepin—King Pepin's designation of the central part of Italy to be governed by the pope. (*112*)

Eastern Orthodox Churches—Christian Churches with origins in the Eastern Roman Empire that are not in union with the pope and Church centered in Rome. (*136*)

Eastern Rite Catholic Churches—Catholic Churches whose origins were in the Eastern Roman Empire that are in union with the pope and Church centered in Rome. (*136*)

East-West Schism—The official separation of the Eastern (Orthodox) Church and the Western Church; also referred to as the Great Schism. (*134*)

ecumenical council—A meeting to which all bishops of the world are invited to exercise their authority in union with the pope, the successor of Peter, in addressing concerns facing the worldwide Church. (*69*)

ecumenism—Actions aimed at dialogue and the restoration of unity among Christians. (*304*)

Edict of Milan—Declaration allowing religious freedom in the Roman Empire. (*41*)

Edict of Nantes—Document granting some rights to Huguenots. (*194*)

Enlightenment—The seventeenth- and eighteenth-century movement in Europe during which reason and science grew in importance as sources of truth. (*220*)

excommunication—A severe ecclesiastical penalty that excludes the offender from taking part in the Eucharist or other sacraments. (*134*)

Exodus—God's saving intervention in history, as narrated in the Book of Exodus, by which he liberated the Hebrew people from slavery in Egypt and brought them into the Promised Land. (*8*)

Exsurge Domine* and *Decet Romanum Pontificem—Papal decrees excommunicating Martin Luther. (*190*)

Fathers of the Church—A designation for Church leaders during the early centuries of Christianity whose teachings collectively helped to formulate Christian doctrine and practices. (*77*)

filioque—Latin term meaning "and from the Son." (*134*)

Gallicanism—A movement originating among the French Catholic clergy based on national rulers having authority for Church governance in their country. (*233*)

Gentiles—Persons of non-Jewish faith or origin. (*23*)

geocentric—Belief that the sun revolves around the earth. (*221*)

Gospels—The four accounts of the life of Jesus in the New Testament. The word "Gospel" means "good news." (*11*)

grace—Our participation in the life of God. "Grace is *favor,* the *free and undeserved help* that God gives us to respond to his call to become children of God, adoptive sons, partakers of the divine nature and of eternal life."[1] (*CCC,* #1996). (*99*)

Great Western Schism—The period from 1378 to 1417 during which two and then three rival people claimed papal authority. (*163*)

Gregorian chant—Follows a simple melody. It is is chanted in monophonic ritualistic pattern in plainsong. (*102*)

Gregorian Reforms—A series of Church reforms under Pope Gregory VII. (*130*)

Hagia Sophia—Church of the Holy Wisdom built in Constantinople and currently serving as a museum in Istanbul, Turkey. (*93*)

Hebrew—The tribe of Abraham, later to be known as Israelites and then Jews. (*5*)

heliocentric—Belief that the earth and other planets revolve around the sun. (*221*)

Hellenization— The spread of Greek culture, begun during the time of Alexander the Great. (*9*)

heresy—A belief, attitude, or teaching that is contrary to revealed truth and to the Church's doctrine of faith. (*45*)

heretic—Someone baptized a Christian who obstinately holds a position on an article of faith that conflicts with officially defined Church teachings. (*45*)

hijrah—The flight of Muslims from Mecca to Medina in 622; event marks the beginning of the Muslim calendar. (*97*)

Huguenots—Members of the French Reformed community. (*193*)

humanism—During the Renaissance, an emphasis on the human in intellectual and artistic activity. (*175*)

Huns—A tribe originating in China; one of the last barbarian groups to invade Western Europe. (*74*)

iconoclast controversy—Conflict caused by the Eastern emperor's decision to condemn the use of icons in worship. (*134*)

Incarnation—The truth that the second Person of the Blessed Trinity, while remaining God, assumed a human nature and became man. (*45*)

indulgences—The remission of temporal punishment resulting from sin for oneself and also for the souls in purgatory. (*186*)

infallible—Incapable of error in defining doctrines involving faith or morals. (*228*)

Inquisition—Trials established to help curb the spread of heretical doctrines. (*151*)

interdict—Prohibition against celebrating sacraments in a particular area. (*177*)

Islam—A monotheistic religion based on submission to God's will, believed to have been revealed to Muhammad in the early seventh century. (*97*)

J–L

jubilee year—A special year of prayer and pilgrimage in the Catholic Church that takes place every fifty years; also called a holy year. (*158*)

justification by faith—God's gracious act of rendering a sinful human to be holy and endowed with grace (in Catholic and Orthodox doctrines) or as acceptable to God (Lutheran). (*200*)

Know Nothing Party—Anti-foreign, anti-Catholic political organization that flourished in the United States between 1852 and 1856. (*278*)

La Pietà—Michelangelo's statue of Mary holding the crucified Jesus. (*176*)

laissez-faire **capitalism**—Economic system that advocates that people with money (capital) can use their money as they wish without restrictions from governments or other sources. (*293*)

laity—Baptized Catholics who share in Jesus' mission and continue his work on earth but are not ordained. (*56*)

lay investiture—The practice of lay persons (such as kings) appointing bishops, priests, abbots, and abbesses. (*128*)

lay trusteeism—Control of parish funds and resources by an elected body of lay people. (*274*)

liturgical calendar—Seasons and feasts of the Church year to mark events in the life and Paschal Mystery of Christ as well as the lives of Mary and the saints. (*100*)

M–O

Manicheans—A religious cult that viewed reality as a constant struggle between spirit (good) and matter (evil). (*80*)

marks of the Church—There are four marks of the Church: the Church is one, holy, catholic, and apostolic. These are mentioned in the Nicene Creed. (*18*)

martyrs—Persons who witness to the truth of the faith by enduring death to be faithful to Christ. (*34*)

mendicant—Religious communities whose members live among people and rely on the charity of others. (*147*)

mestizo—A person of both European and Native American ancestry. (*261*)

missionaries—People who spread the Christian message to other people, usually in other lands. (*106*)

monarch—Head of a nation-state who claims to have complete authority in its governance. (*230*)

monk—A person who lives the monastic life, engaging in prayer, meditation, and solitude. (*83*)

Monophysitism—Belief that Jesus has only one nature, instead of the traditional Christian teaching that Jesus has two natures—human and divine. (*70*)

Muhammad—Founder of the Islamic religion. (*97*)

Muslims—Members of the religion of Islam. (*97*)

mysticism—Knowledge of God through experience; an intense experience of communion with God. (*168*)

Nativism—Anti-Catholic and anti-immigrant movement. (*278*)

negative theology—Belief that God can never be known by the intellect alone. (*169*)

Nicene Creed—Summary of essential Christian beliefs written and approved at the Councils of Nicaea (325) and Constantinople (381). (*69*)

ninety-five theses—Martin Luther's statement of principles regarding penance and the abuse of indulgences. (*185*)

orthodoxy—A doctrine, belief, attitude, or teaching that is consistent with revealed truth and with the Church's doctrine of faith. (*45*)

Our Lady of Guadalupe—Considered the patron saint of the Americas. (*261*)

papal bull—A formal decree by a pope sealed with a round leaden seal (in Latin, *bulla*). (*159*)

Papal States—Part of Italy the pope ruled until 1870. (*112*)

Paschal Mystery—The mystery of, and events involved in, our redemption: Jesus' suffering, death, Resurrection, and Ascension. (*8*)

Passover—Jewish feast commemorating the deliverance of the Jewish people from death by the blood of the lamb sprinkled on their doorposts in Egypt. (*8*)

patriarch—A Christian bishop of the early Church in certain major cities of the Roman Empire. This title is still in use in Eastern Churches today. (*94*)

Peace of Augsburg—Allowed each prince to decide the religion of his subjects. (*192*)

Peasants' Revolt—A series of uprisings by German peasants against their landowners. (*191*)

Pentecost—The "fiftieth" day after Easter when the Holy Spirit was manifested, given, and communicated to the followers of Jesus, beginning the new "age of the Church," when Christ lives and acts in and through his Church. (*13*)

permanent deacons—Men ordained to assist the bishop and priests in various pastoral duties and ministries of hospitality and charity. (*349*)

Pontifex Maximus—The term means "the greatest bridge-builder"; title for emperors and, later, the pope. (*65*)

precepts of the Church—A list of laws put forth by leaders of the Church which help the faithful grow in love with God and others, pray an "indispensible minimum" amount, and grow in moral effort. (See *CCC*, Glossary.) (*309*)

predestination—Belief that God has selected some people for hell and others for heaven regardless of any personal actions or merit. (*198*)

Presbyterian—A Protestant Christian religion characterized by governance by a group of elders and traditionally Calvinistic in doctrine. (*197*)

presbyters—Another name for elders or priests; in the early Church, presbyters were closely associated with the bishop in the exercising of leadership in some faith communities. (*55*)

rationalism—A theory that nothing is true unless founded on scientifically demonstrable proofs based solely on reason and the five senses; condemned by the First Vatican Council. (*225*)

Reformation—A series of political and religious events beginning in the sixteenth century that resulted in the division of Western Christianity into Catholic and Protestant communities. (*185*)

reign of God—Also known as the kingdom of God or kingdom of heaven, God's presence in the world through Christ. The Church "is the Reign of Christ already present in mystery" (*CCC*, #763). (*11*)

Reign of Terror—Period during the French Revolution when nobility and many clergy were executed by French revolutionary leaders. (*234*)

Resurrection—"The bodily rising of Jesus from the dead on the third day after his death on the cross and burial in the tomb" (*CCC*, Glossary). (*13*)

Rogation Days—Three days of prayer and penance before the Solemnity of the Ascension to ask God's blessing on the harvest. (*100*)

Sacrament of Reconciliation—One of the Church's Sacraments of Healing and Forgiveness; the sacrament through which those who sin are reconciled with God and the Church. (*103*)

sacraments—Effective signs of grace, instituted by Christ and entrusted to the Church, by which we share in divine life through the work of the Holy Spirit. (*49*)

scholasticism—A method of intellectual inquiry dominant in western Christian civilization from the Middle Ages until the seventeenth century, and into the twentieth century among Catholic scholars. (222)

selective conscientious objection—Refusing in conscience to participate in one particular war that a person believes to be immoral. (371)

showings—Julian of Norwich's term for her mystical encounters with Christ. (170)

simony—The payment of money to be appointed to a Church office. (128)

socialism—Economic system that advocates government control of all instruments of production, such as farms and factories. (293)

sola scriptura—Belief that the Bible is the sole source of religious truth. (199)

Spanish Inquisition—The process in Spain for identifying and punishing suspicious non-Christians and those said to be heretics. (173)

spiritual exercises—A thirty-day program of spiritual practices developed by Saint Ignatius Loyola. (209)

Summa Theologica—Saint Thomas Aquinas's comprehensive systematic examination of Christian theology. (141)

theocracy—Form of government in which religious leaders are the secular leaders as well. (197)

Thirty Years' War—War over religious, dynastic, and territorial issues; it involved most European nations but was fought mainly in Germany. (231)

Tradition—The living and authentic transmission of the teachings of Jesus in the Church. (48)

Truce of God—A rule enacted by the medieval Church forbidding warfare during certain holy days of the year. (130)

Ultramontanism—Belief, often in an exaggerated form, that the pope alone has ultimate authority for Church governance in all countries. (235)

Union of Florence—A short-lived agreement between leaders of Eastern and Western Christianity on certain doctrines of faith. (172)

Vandals—One of the most destructive nomadic tribes; adopted Arianism when they converted to Christianity. (74)

Visigoths—A Germanic tribe who settled primarily in Spain; the first such group to lay siege to Rome. (74)

Vulgate—Saint Jerome's Latin translation of the Bible; the word vulgate is derived from the same Latin root as vulgar, which originally simply meant "of the common people." (81)

Endnotes:

Introduction
1. St. Augustine, *In Jo. Ev.* 21, 8: PL 35, 1568.
2. *LG* 8 § 3; cf. *UR* 3; 6; *Heb* 2:17; 7:26; *2 Cor* 5:21.
3. Cf. *1 Jn.* 1:8–10.
4. Cf. *Mt* 13:24–30.
5. See Leo XIII, Encyclical *Sapientiae Christianae*, 10 Jan. 1890: ASS 22 (1889–90) p. 392. Idem Encyclical *Satis Cognitum*, 29 June 1896: ASS 28 (1895–96) pp. 710 and 724 ff. Pius XII, Encyclical *Mystici Corporis*, loc. Cit., pp. 199–200.

Chapter 3
1. Council of Chalcedon: DS 302.

Chapter 4
1. *1 Tim* 2:4.
2. *AG* 9.
3. Cf. *Jn* 1:12–18; 17:3; *Rom* 8:14–17; *2 Pet* 1:3–4.

Chapter 5
1. *LG* 8.

Chapter 7
1. *Indulgentiarum doctrina*, 5.
2. Cf. *SC* 33N; *LG* 10.

Chapter 8
1. *LG* 12.
2. *Acts* 9:13; *1 Cor* 6:1; 16:1.

Chapter 9
1. See St John Chrysostom, *In Io.* Homily 65, 1: PG 59, 361.

Chapter 10
1. Cf. CA 10; 13; 44.

Chapter 11
1. See Vatican II, Dogmatic Constitution on the Church, *Lumen gentium*, ch 3, n. 22.

Glossary
1. Cf. *Jn* 1:12–18; 17:3; *Rom* 8:14–17; *2 Pet* 1:3–4.

Photo Credits

Alamy 4, 6, 178, 253, 378; AP Wideworld 19, 24, 55, 130, 136, 158, 261, 277, 282, 357, 359; Art Resource 23, 34, 38, 43, 47, 65, 68, 74, 78, 98, 105, 108, 120, 124, 146, 186, 214, 226, 232, 238, 241, 278; Bishop Moore Catholic High School ix, 31, 61, 72, 99, 117, 179, 222, 323, 351, 379, 381; Bridgeman 12, 14, 16, 76, 84, 112, 164, 175, 176, 188, 192, 195, 210, 228, 258; Corbis 24, 40, 57, 58, 82, 93, 96, 114, 217, 138, 160, 172, 299, 300, 306, 360, 368; Getty 184, 215; Mapquest 9, 122; Masterfile 29; MD Archive 270; Michael Reed 273; PhotoEdit 92, 103, 286, 295, 317; Photos.com 23, 27, 42, 84, 126, 129, 256, 289.

Index

A–C

a.c. (*ante Christum*), 101
a.d. (*anno Domini*), 101
abbess, 125
abbot, 125
Abraham, 5–8, 35; *see also* Genesis
accommodation, 245
Act of Toleration, 271
Acts 1:20, 54
Acts 2:2–4; *Acts 2:17–18*, 15
Acts 2:38, 51
Acts 6:1, 35
Acts 9:3–6, 24
Acts of the Apostles, 12, 15–16, 19–21, 54
    and Christianity, 15
    and Gentiles, 25, 26
    and Holy Spirit, 15–16
Adels, Jill Haack, 83, 226
Africa, and Church, 333, 334, 356, 358, 368, 369
African American Catholic, 282–285, 312, 373
aggiornamento, 335
Albigensianism, 150–151
    and *believers*, 150
    and *perfects*, 150
Alexander the Great, 9
All Saints, 261, 318, 364
American colonies
    and Catholicism, 270–273
    and religious freedom, 273
Americanism, 304
anti-pope, 165
apologists, 44–45
Apology, The, 40; *see also* Tertullian; Deacon Lawrence
Apostle to India, 249; *see also* Xavier, Francis
Apostle to Japan, 249; *see also* Xavier, Francis
Apostle to the Gentiles, 24; *see also* Paul
Apostolic See, 75
Apostolic Succession, 18
apparitions of Mary, 261
Archbishop Michael Corrigan, 304
Archbishop Ketteler, and working conditions, 295
Arian controversy, 70, 79
Arianism, 68, 74–75, 79
    and Saint Ambrose of Milan, 78
Arius, 68–69
Ascension, 13
assimilation, 303–305
atheism, 38, 330
Attila, 74; *see also* Huns
auditors, 336
Avignon papacy, 160
    advantages of, 161
    and Black Death, 158, 166

and Great Western Schism, 163
Aztecs, and Catholicism, 258
b.c. (before Christ), 101
Babylonian Captivity of the Papacy, 160–161
Bacon, Francis, 223, 227
Baltimore Catechism, 281, 306
Baptism
    and baptistery, 101
    beginnings of, 51
    buildings for, 101
    and Christianity and Judaism separation, and Gentiles, 25–26
    literal and spiritual meaning, 51
baptistery, 101
barbarian, original meaning, 74
baroque, 241
basilica, 102
Battle of Tours, 98, 112
Bayley, Elizabeth Ann; *see* Saint Elizabeth Ann Seton
Benedict XIII, 164; *see* Great Western Schism; Roger of Geneva
Benedict Joseph Labre, 243
Bible
    and Acts of the Apostles, 12, 15–16, 19–21, 54
    Hebrew, 5
birthday of the Church, 6; *see also* Pentecost
bishops, 55, 121, 205, 274
bishop of Rome, 75
    as Emperor of West, 75
    as pope, 75
Bismark, Otto von, 301
Black Death, 158, 166
    Church impact of, 166–168
    Jews spreading of, 167
    and monasteries, 167
Black Robes, 267
Bojaxhiu, Agnes; *see* Mother Teresa
Bonaparte, Napoleon, 235
    concordat with pope, 235
    future role of the pope, 235–236
Book of Kells, 125
Bowman, Sister Thea, story of, 373
Brahmins, 249
Brother Sun, 148
bubonic plague; *see* Black Death
Byzantium, 65, 133
1 Corinthians 11:20, 21, 50
Cabrini, Frances, and modern spiritual life, 312
calendar
    Christian, 101
    liturgical, 100
Calvert, George, 270
Calvin, John, 197–198
Canada, and Church, 367
canon, 47
    defined, 382

    and New Testament, 47
    setting of, 47–48
canon law, 274
    and Pope John Paul II, 358
Canterbury Tales, The, 139
    Wife of Bath, 139
Cardinal Ercole Conslavi, story of, 236
Cardinal Humbert, and Sicily, 136
Carmelite, 312
    and John of the Cross, 212–213
    and Teresa of Avila, 212–213
Carroll, John, 271–272, 281
Catechism of the Council of Trent, 206
catechumens, 52
cathedral, 121, 140
Catherine of Aragon, 194–195
catholic, meaning of, 106
Catholic Action, 317
Catholic Foreign Mission Society of America, 312
Catholic Heritage, The, 139, 140
Catholic schools, pioneer of, 141
Catholic Social Teaching Movements, 294, 297, 299
Catholic Source Book, The, 100
Catholic Students Mission Crusade, 317
Catholicism
    and American colonies, 270–273
    Church of England, 195
    and Council of Trent, 205, 206, 334
    and culture assimilation, 303–305
    devotional, 309
    differences with Protestantism, 184–192, 273, 280
    and Industrial Revolution, 292–300, 303, 314
    and Ireland, 85, 106, 107
    and modernism, 307
    mysticism, 168–170
    Native Americans, 259–260, 267, 269
    new age of science, 223–225
    Popular Devotions, 227–228
    and rationalism, and deism, 225–227
    reformation of, 184–192
    sacramental religion, 49–53
    and scholasticism, 141, 222, 227
    and Thirty Years' War, 231
    U.S. system, 274–276
    and World Wars, 314–321, 328–329
Catholic-Protestant Relations, between World Wars, 316
celibacy, 102, 128
    and Council of Trent, 205
    and Eastern Church, 102
    and First Lateran Council, 102
    and Western Church, 102
Centrum, 301
Charles the Great; *see* Charlemagne
Charlemagne, 112, 122–125, 127
    as Christian Emperor, 113
    uniformity of Christianity, 113

Charles V, Emperor, 205, 258
Chaucer, Geoffrey, 139
Children's Crusade, 145
China, and Christianity, 246
Christendom, 120, 122
Christian calendar, 101
    and Dionysius Exiguus, 101
Christian Church, and Jewish roots, 9–16
Christian God versus other gods, 38–39
Christian practices, 45
Christianity, 360; *see also* Church; Eastern
    Church; Reformation era; Western
    Church
        and Abraham, 5–8, 35
        and Acts of the Apostles, 12, 15–16,
            19–21, 26, 54
        and Baptism, 11
        causes of reformation, 185–189
        and China, 246
        and Constantine, 64–65, 69
        conversion to Islam, 98
        and crusades, 136, 144–145
        East and West, 41, 92, 133
        England conversion, 106, 108–109,
            111
        and Enlightenment, 220
        and Gentiles, 25
        and Hellenistic Jewish Christians,
            23, 35
        and icons, 134–135, 248
        and India, 248–249
        Ireland conversion, 85, 106, 107
        and Jews, 9, 21, 23, 120, 167, 173–174
        and Judaism, 21, 23, 120
        and Middle Ages, 41, 92, 120, 126,
            129, 138–139, 144–151, 168, 170,
            212–213
        and monotheism, 6, 7
        persecution of, 34, 36–38, 40, 41, 66,
            93
        and Roman Empire, 10, 13, 66, 74, 93
        and Roman gods, 51
        and Scandinavia, 177
        separation from Judaism, 21–23
        susceptibility to persecution, 36
        and Union of Florence, 172
Christians; *see* Christianity
Christians of Saint Thomas, 248
Christina, Queen of Sweden, story of, 232
Church, *see also* Christianity; Church
    practice; Eastern Church; Fathers of the
    Church; Reformation era; Tradition of
    the Church; Western Church
        and Africa, 333, 334, 356, 358, 368,
            369
        and Black Death, 158, 166
        buying and selling of indulgences,
            186, 188
        Canada, 367
        and communism, 318
    Eastern and Western differences,
        133–137
        and Europe, 369–370

        and feudalism, 126
        and heliocentric theory, 221
        and Holy Spirit, 13, 15, 18, 19, 72, 77
        and immigrants, 277, 280
        and India, 366
        and Middle Ages problems, 127–137
        and science, 220–225
        and Thirty Years' War, 231
        and Union of Florence, 172
        and women, 331
Church in Our Day, The, 335
Church of England, 195
        Manning, Henry Edward, 240
        Manning, John Henry, 240
        and Puritans, 195
        Queen Elizabeth I, 195, 239
        and Virginia, 270
        Wiseman, Nicholas, 240, 302
Cicero, 80
City of God, 79, 80
Clarke, Sister Maura, and El Salvador,
    364–365
cloistered, 312
Cluny, 129; *see also* monasticism
        and Duke William of Acquitaine, 129
colonialism, 330
*Colllect of the Mass celebrated in honor of
    Blessed Kateri Tekakwitha, The*, 268
Columbus, Christopher, 174, 257
Comby, Jean, 67, 207
communion of saints, 189, 376–377
        and indulgences, 189
communion of sinners, 377
communism, 321, 330, 369
        and Church, 318
        fall of, 359
conciliarism, 164
conclave and Pope Nicholas II, 130
concordat, 235–236, 301, 314–315
Concordat of Worms, 131
Confessions, 80
Congregation for Divine Worship and the
    Discipline of Sacraments, 100, 114
Congress of Vienna, 237
conquistadores, 257–258, 260
conscientious objector, 371
Constantine, 64–65; *see also* Christianity;
    Edict of Milan; Roman Empire
        and Byzantine Church, 133
        and Council of Nicaea, 69, 134
Constantinople, 65, 69, 135, 381; *see also*
    Byzantium
        fall of, 172
convents, 85
conversion, 11, 19, 173
        of England, 106, 108–109, 111
        of Europe, 111
        of Ireland, 85, 106, 107
conversos, 174
Council of Chalcedon, 70
Council of Constantinople, 69, 381
Council of Jerusalem, 27
Council of Nicaea, 69, 134–135
        and Constantine, 69

        defined, 69
        and Trinity, 134
Council of Trent, 164, 205, 206, 334
crociati, 144
crucifixion, 13, 17
Crusades, 136, 143–145
cuius region, 192
Cule, Bishop Peter, 337
Cunningham, Lawrence, and pilgrimage,
    139–140
Cyrus, King of Persia, 9

da Vinci, Leonardo, 176
Dark Ages (dark period), 74
Day, Dorothy, and *The Catholic Worker*,
    300, 323
Daughters of Charity, 242; *see also* Louise
    de Marillac, Vincent de Paul
de Las Casas, Bartolome, story of, 259,
    262
de Leon, Ponce, 262
de Marillac, Louise, 242
de Nobili, Roberto, 249
de Padilla, Juan, 263
de Paul, Vincent, 242
de Tocqueville, Alexis, and *Democracy in
    America*, 276
de Veuster, Joseph; *see* Saint Damien
deacons, 35
Deacon Laurence, legend of, 40; *see also*
    Tertullian; *The Apology*
deacon, Stephen, 24, 27, 35
Decet Romanum Pontificem, 190
Declaration of Independence, 272
deism and Catholicism, 225
Descartes, René, 223, 227
desert fathers, 83
Deus vult, 144
devotional Catholicism, 309
diaspora, 9–10, 23
Diego, Juan
        and Our Lady of Guadalupe, 261
Diet of Speyer, 191
Diet of Worms, 190
Dillenberger, John, 188
dioceses, 41
Diocletian, 41; *see also* persecution
Directory on popular piety and the
    liturgy; Principles and guidelines, 100,
    114
Documents of American Catholic History,
    265, 270, 276, 298, 305
Documents of Vatican II, xi, xii, xiii, 8, 329
Dodaro, Robert, OSA, 87
Dogmatic Constitution on the Church, 265
Dominican, 169, 258, 260
Donation of Pepin, 112
Donovan, Jean, and El Salvador, 364–365
Doors to the Sacred, 78
Drexel, Katherine, and modern spiritual
    life, 312

Duke William of Aquitaine, 129
Eastern Christianity; *see* Christianity; Church; Eastern Church; Eastern Orthodox
Eastern Church
    and celibacy, 102
    development of, 92–93
    differences with Western, 133–137
    and excommunication, 134
    and Greek language, 133
    and icons, 133–135
    language difficulties, 136
    and patriarch, 135
    and Sicily, 135
    and split from Western Church, 133–134
    and Trinity, 134
    Union of Florence, 172
Eastern Europe; *see* Christianity; Church; Eastern Church, Roman Empire, Western Church
Eastern Orthodox Churches, 57, 133, 136, 358, and Trinity, 69; *see also* Eastern Church
Eastern Rite Catholic Churches, 136
East-West Schism, 133–137
Ecclesiastical History of the English People, 109
Eckhart, Meister, and mysticism, 169
    ecumenism, and negative theology, 169
ecumenical council, 69, 333
    and Pope Paul VI, 346
ecumenism, 304
    Decree of, 343, 369
Edict of Milan, 41, 66
Edict of Nantes, 194
Edict of Worms, 190
Education, and Catholicism in America, 280–281
Egypt, 8
eius religio, 192
El Salvador, 363
    and Oscar Romero, 363
    women martyrs, 364–365
Ellis, John Tracy, 265, 270, 276, 298, 305
Ellsberg, Robert, 261, 318, 364
Emperor Domitian
    and persecution, 38
    and Roman gods, 51
Emperor Justinian, 93
England
    anti-Catholic laws, 239
    conversion to Christianity, 106, 108–109, 111
    Oxford movement, 239
    state-controlled religion, 239
England, Bishop John, and American system, 274–275
Enlightenment, 220
    art and worship, 176–177
    baroque, 241
    missionaries to foreign lands, 259
    spiritual life, 225

Entrenchment of Scholasticism, 227
Erasmus, 139
Eucharist, 21, 43
    beginnings of, 50
    buildings for, 101
    liturgy and spiritual meaning, 51
Europe
    and Church, 369–370
    conversion to Christianity, 234
Eutyches, and Monophysitism, 70
ex cathedra, 229
excommunication, 134
    and Cardinal Humbert, 136
    of Greek Church, 135
    and Patriarch Michael Cerularius, 135–136
    and Pope Leo IX, 136
Exiguus, Dionysius, and Christian calendar, 101
Exodus, 8
    and Christians, 8
    and Jews, 8
Exsurge Domine, 190
Extension Society, 317
faith, Protestantism and Catholicism, 280
Fascist party, 330
Fathers of the Church, 77, 104, 383
Festival of Weeks, 13
feudalism, 120, 126
    and the Church, 120
filioque, 134–135, 172
fire and wind, 15; *see also* Spirit of God; symbols
First Lantern Council, and celibacy, 102
Flannery, Austin, 329, 341
foederati, 111
food sharing of, 21
Ford, Sister Ita, and El Salvador, 364–365
fountain of youth, 262
Four Gallican Articles, 233
France
    Four Gallican Articles, 233
    and Industrial Revolution, 293
    and Louis XIV, 233
    and North America, 266–269
    and pope, 233, 314
    and Protestantism, 193
    Archbishop Angelo Roncalli, 332
    Revolution, 234–235
Franciscans, 244, 264; *see also* Saint Francis of Assisi
Franciscans and Dominicans, 245; *see also* mendicant; mendicant orders; Saint Francis of Assisi, 146–148
Franks, and Europe conversion, 111
French Revolution, 234, 239
    and concordat, 235
    Reign of Terror, 234
Friars Minor, 148; *see also* Saint Francis of Assisi

G–I

Galilee, 11

Galilei, Galileo, 220–223
    heliocentric theory, 221
    inductive reasoning, 222
Gallicanism, 233
Gamaliel, 19; *see also* Sanhedrin
Genesis 12:2–3, 22:17, 6
Gentiles, 23, 25, 35
    and Acts of the Apostles, 12, 15–16, 19–21, 54
    and Apostle to, 24
    and Baptism, 26
    and Paul, 24, 27
    and God-fearers, 23
geocentric, 221
Georgetown University, 272
Germany, and Industrial Revolution, 314
Gesu, 241
Gibbons, James Cardinal, 304
    story of, 306
global community, 330
Glorious Revolution, 239
God's Will the End of Life, 376
God-fearers, 23
Good Friday, 13
Gospels, 11, 12
    development of, 46–48
    life and teaching of Jesus, 11–13
    oral tradition, 46
    written, 46
Gospel according to Luke, 5, 12
Gothic,
    architecture and cathedral, 140–141
grace, 99
Great Humanist, 196; *see also* Erasmus
Great Persecution, 41; *see also* persecution
Great War, 314
Great Western Schism, 163
    and Avignon Papacy, 163
    and conciliarism, 164
    council at Constance, 164
    and John XXIII, 164
    and Pope Urban VI, 163
    recognized popes, 163
    resolving of, 164
    and Roger of Geneva, 163
Greek Church, 44, 133; *see also* Eastern Church
Greek culture, and God, 9, 133
Green, Vivian, 111
Gregorian chant, 102
Gregorian Reforms, 130
Gregorian University, 267
Haack, Jill, 83
Hagia, Sophia, 93, 133, 136, 172
Hastings, Adrian, 257
Healy, James Augustine, 282
Healy, Michael, 282
Healy, Patrick, 282
Hebrew, 5
Hecker, Isaac, 304
heliocentric, 221
Hellenistic Jewish Christians, 35
Hellenistic Jews, 9, 35; *see also* Jews and Greek culture, 9

Hellenization, 9–10
Henry IV, 193
Henry VIII, 194–195, 239
hermit, 83
heresy, 45
heretic, 45
hijrah, 97
Hindus of India, 248
Hippolytus, 165
Hiroshima, 329
History Needs to Include Women's Contributions, see L'Osservatore Romano
History of the Christian Tradition, A, 138
Holy Spirit
    and Acts of the Apostles, 15–16
    and Church inspiration, 19
    guidance of, 72
    and Pentecost, 13, 18, 27
How to Read Church History, Vol. 1, 67, 111
How to Read Church History, Vol. 2, 207
Hughes, Bishop John, story of, 279
Huguenots, 193
humanism, 175
Huns, and Attila, 74
Hus, John, 177
icons, 134–135, 248; *see also* images
    and Leo the Isaurian, 135
    and Pope Gregory II, 135
iconoclast controversy, 134–135
idolatry, 134–135, 248
images,
    and Christianity, 134
    and Islam, 134
    and Judiasm, 134
Immaculate Conception, 238
immigrants
    and Church, 277
    and education, 280
    preserving Catholic faith, 280
In Our Own Voices, 280
Inaugural Homily, 362, 377
Incarnation, 45
Incas, and Catholicism, 258
India
    and Christianity, 248
    and Church, 366
indulgences, 186, 188
    and Archbishop Albrecht, 187
    and Sacrament of Penance and
        Reconciliation, 186
    selling of, 188–189
    treasury of merit, 189
Industrial Revolution, 292–300
    and France, 293
    and Germany, 314
    and Mexico, 303
    and modern spiritual life, 292
    and Pope Leo XIII, 295–297
    and *Rerum Novarum*, 296–297
    and socialism, 293–294
    and United States social teaching,
        297
    and worker conditions, 293, 295
infallible, 228

Inquisition, 151, 221
interdict, 177
Iraq, 6
Ireland
    Bishop John, 298, 304
    and Catholicism, 239
    Christian conversion, 85, 106, 107
Isaac, 5–7
Islam, 97
    and Abraham, 5–8, 35
    and Battle of Tours, 98, 112
    Christian conversion to, 98
    and Crusades, 144–145
    and images, 134
    and monotheism, 7
    and Spanish Inquisition, 173
Israel, 8
Israeli Jews, 35; *see also* Jews
Italy, and Renaissance, 175–176

J–L

1 John 4:7–8, 29
James, 2:14–17, 29
James II, 239
Japan, and Christianity, 247, 333
Jesuits, 209–210, 233, 244, 249, 262, 264,
    269
    Black Robes, 267
    and Gregorian University, 267
    and Northern Native Americans, 267
    Spiritual exercises, 209–210
    suppression of, 363
Jesus
    human and divine, 11–13
    Jewishness of, 11
    as Messiah, 5–6, 15, 21, 99
    as Son of God, 6, 13
    and women, 56
Jews
    and Babylonian Captivity, 9
    and Baptism, 11, 26, 25, 174
    and Black Death, 158, 166, 167
    brief history of, 6–9
    and Christian, 21, 23, 36
    and *conversos*, 174
    and Crusades, 35
    and Greek culture influence, 9
    Hellenistic, 9–10, 35
    Israel, 8–9
    Roman periods, 36
    and Spanish Inquisition, 173–174
    and World War II, 319, 328–329
Joan of Arc, story of, 170
John 3:3–5, x, 14
John 18:36, 14
John, and Sanhedrin, 20
John of the Cross, 212–213
John XXIII; *see* Great Western Schism
Jones, Mary Harris, story of, 299
Joshua 10:12–13, 223
jubilee year, 158, 359
Jubilee Mass dedicated to the Laity, 377
Judaism; *see also* Jews

and Abraham, 5–8, 35
    belief in God, 7
    and Christian relations, 9
    and Christianity, 21, 23, 120
    and Crusades, 144
    of diaspora, 9
    and images, 134
    and monotheism, 6–7
    Palestine practice, 8–10
    and Spanish Inquisition, 173–174
    and Roman Empire, 10, 13, 36, 74
    separation from Christianity, 21, 23,
        25–27
Jude 1:20–21, 29
Julian of Norwich, 170, and mysticism,
    168–169
justification by faith, 200
Kant, Immanuel, 224
Kazel, Sister Dorothy, 364–365
Keith, Dr. Kent M., 59
Kennedy, John, 371
Kerrick, Francis Bishop, 280
King Clovis, Europe conversion, 112, 234
King Ferdinand, 173
King Louis XVI, and French Revolution,
    234–235
Kino, Eusebio Francisco, 264
Kiwanuka, Joseph, and Uganda, 368
Klein, Rev. Peter, 100
knight, 120, 121, 143
Knights of Labor, 297, 299
    and Cardinal Gibbons, 297–298
Know Nothing Party, 278
Korea, Catholicism and Protestantism,
    246
Krier, Marvin L., 294, 297, 299
Kulturkampf, 301; *see also* Otto von
    Bismark
La Pietà, 176
Laboure, Catherine, 309
laissez-faire capitalism, 293–294
laity, 56
Lange, Mother Mary, 283; *see also* Oblate
    Sisters of Providence
languages, difficulties with Churches, 136
Lateran Treaty, 314
Latin Church, 75, 316, 321, 331; *see also*
    Western Church
Lawyers, patron saint of, 196; *see also*
    Thomas More
lay investiture, 128
lay trusteeism, 274
lay people, 317
Leo the Isaurian, and icon, 135
Leper Priest, The; *see* Saint Damien
Letters from John Paul I, 357
*Letter of Pliny, Roman Governor, to Emperor
    Trajan*, 39
liberation movements, 331
Lily of the Mohawks, 268; *see also* Tekak-
    witha, Kateri
Little Flower, The, and modern spiri-
    tual life, 311; *see also* Saint Thérèse of
    Lisieux

liturgical calendar, 100
liturgical reform, 318, 338, 339, 348–349
liturgical renewal, 319, 321
Living Wage, The, 298
L'Osservatore Romano, 57
Luciani, Albino; *see* Pope John Paul I
Luke 4:18–21, 5
Lumen Gentium, xii, xiii, 362
Luther, Martin, 139, 188, 190–191
    excommunication of, 190
    and indulgences, 188
    and ninety-five theses, 188

Magyars, 125
Manicheans, 80
Manning, Henry Edward, story of, 240
Margaret of Scotland, story of, 132
Mark 1:14, 13
marks of the Church, 18
Marquette, Père Jacques, 269
Martel, Charles, 98, 112
Martin Luther: Selections from His Writings,
    188
Martos, Joseph, 78
martyrs, 34, 66
    Deacon Laurence, 40
    Justin, 93
    Romero, Oscar, 363
    Perpetua and Felicity, 37
    Stephen, 24, 27, 35
    women, 364–365
Martys of Conscience, 196; *see also*
    Thomas, More
Marx, Karl, 294–295
Mary, and Mother of the Church, 22
Mary Harris Jones, *see* Mother Jones
Maryland, 270–271
    and Act of Toleration, 271
    and Father Andrew White, 271
    John Carroll, 271
Massachusetts, and Puritans, 270
Matthew 16:13–17, 17
Matthew 18:20, 334
Maurin, Peter, *see* Dorothy Day
McGonigle, Thomas D., 138
medieval, 138; *see also* Middle Ages
Melody of Theology, The, 224
mendicant, 147
mendicant orders, 146–147, 245
    founders of, 147
    Saint Dominic, 150, 152
    Saint Francis of Assisi, 146–148
Merovingian dynasty, 112
Merton, Thomas, 313
Messiah, 17, 35; *see also* Jesus; Son of God
mestizo, 261
Metternich, 237, 274
Mexico
    and Industrial Revolution, 303
    and Miguel Pro, 303
Michel, Virgil, 318

Michelangelo, 176
    and Sistine Chapel, 176
Middle Ages; *see also* medieval
    cathedral, 140
    and Christendom, 120–122
    and Cluny, 129
    crusaders and reformers, 144–151
    East and West, 41, 92
    and feudalism, 126
    knight, 120, 121, 143
    and mysticism, 168, 170, 212–213
    pilgrimage, 138–139
    Pope Gregory VII, 131
    and serfs, 121, 126
    theologian, 141
    and vassals, 126
Miraculous Medal, 309
missionaries, 66, 106, 259, 262, 316
    and U.S. Church, 312
    success of, 259–265, 269
Missionaries of Charity, 366
modern spiritual life,
    Cabrini, Frances, 312
    and Drexel, Katharine, 313
    and Saint Damien, 310
    Saint Thérèse of Lisieux, 311
modernism, 307
Moments of Crisis in Jewish Christian
    Relations, 96
monarch, 230
monasteries
    and U.S. Church, 312–313
    and Vikings, 125
monasticism,
    and Black Death, 158, 166
    and Cluny, 129
    and convent, 85
    and Duke William of Aquitaine, 129
    reform of, 129
monastic movement, 83, 85; *see also* mo-
    nasticism 83, 85
monk, 83; *see also* Saint Anthony
Monophysitism, 70
monotheism, 6, 7
More, Thomas, story of, 196
Moses, 8, 35
Mother Jones, 299
Mother Teresa, 359, 366
    and Missionaries of Charity, 366
Muhammed, 97
Muslims, 97, 98
    and *conversos,* 174
    and Crusades, 144–146
    and Franciscans and Dominicans,
    146
    and Spanish Inquisition, 174
Mussolini, 314–315
mysterion, 50
mysterium, 50
mysticism, 168, 170, 212–213
    and Catholicism, 168
    and Echart, Meister, 169
    and Julian of Norwich, 170
Nagasaki, 247, 316, 329

nationalism, and Reformation era, 187
National Conference of Catholic Bishops,
    335
Native Americans
    and Catholicism, 259–260, 267, 269,
       312
    mistreatment of, 257–260
Nativism, 278
    and Bishop John Hughes, 279
    causes of, 277–278
negative theology, 169
Nero, 17, 38; *see also* persecution
    and Roman persecution, 36
Nestorians, 245
New History of Christianity, A, 111
New Testament
    and canon, 47
    and Gospels, 11, 12
Newman, John Henry, 239, 240, 376
    recognition of writings for, 47
Nicene Creed, 69, 73
    Councils of Nicaea, 134–135
    Constantinople, 69, 381
Niceno-Constantinopolitan Creed, 69; *see*
    also Nicene Creed
Nombre de Dios, 262
North America
    and Catholicism, 257, 262, 277–280
    and de Padilla, Juan, 263
    and de Leon, Ponce, 262
    and Kino, Eusebio Francisco, 264
    French presence, 266–269
    and Serra, Junipero, 264
Northern Ireland,
    and Orangemen, 239
    and Protestants, 239
Novo Millenio Ineunte, 359
nuclear weapons, 329
nun, 83, 312
Oblate Sisters of Providence, 283; *see also*
    Mother Mary Lange
O'Connell, Rev. Maurice V., xiv
On Condition of the Workers; see Rerum
    Novarum
Order of Preachers, 150
orthodoxy, 45
Our Lady of Guadalupe, 261
Our Sunday Visitor's Encyclopedia of the
    Saints, 51
Oxford Movement, 239, 302

1 Peter 2:9, 29; 2:9–10, 340
Palestine, 8–10
papa de passagio, 333
papal bull, 159
Papal States, 112, 237, 334
    and Mussolini, 314–315
Paraguay, *reductions* of, 262
Pascendi Dominici Gregis, 307
Paschal Mystery, 8
Passover, 8,
patriarch, 94

Pastoral Constitution of the Church in the Modern World, The, 329, 349
Pastoral Letter of the Third Provincial Council of Baltimore, 275
Patriarch Michael Cerularius, and Sicily, 135–136
Patristic period, 78–82
patron of all Christian social work, 242; *see also* de Marillac, Louise
patron of lawyers, 196, *see also* More, Thomas
patron of the Americas, 261; *see also* Our Lady of Guadalupe
patron of writers and the press, 242; *see also* Saint Francis de Sales
patron saint of Christian missions, 260; *see also* Xavier, Francis
patron saint of South America, 311; *see also* Saint Rose of Lima
patron saints of Canada, 267; *see also* Saint Isaac Jogues
patroness of France, 170; *see also* Joan of Arc
Paul, 24, 75, 128
    Apostle to the Gentiles, 24, 27
    of Tarsus, 35
Paulists, 304
Peace and Vietnam, 371
Peace of Augsburg, 192
Peace on Earth (Pacem in Terris), 330, 331; *see also* Pope John XXIII
Peasants' Revolt, 191
Pelikan, Jaroslav, 224
Penance, *see* Sacrament of Reconciliation
Penn, William, and Pennsylvania, 273
Pentecost, 13, 15, 18, 19, 27, 72, 77
    and Holy Spirit, 13, 15, 18, 27
People's Crusade, 145
Pepin the Short, 112, 113
perfects, 150
peritus, 362
permanent deacons, 349
Perpetua and Felicity, 37; *see also* persecution
persecution
    age of, 34
    Christianity susceptibility to, 36
    and Diocletian, 41
    and Emperor Domitian, 38
    first Christian, 35
    the Great, 41
    legend of Deacon Laurence, 40
    and Nero, 38
    Perpetua and Felicity, 37
    Roman, 36, 66, 93
    timeline of, 34
Peter, 15, 17, 18, 75, 128
    and Gentiles, 25
    and *Matthew 16:13–17,* 17
    as pope, 165, 361
    called "rock," 17
    and Sanhedrin, 20
    and "Son of the living God," 17
Philippines, and Christianity, 246, 333

pilgrim, 138
pilgrimage, 138–139
    and The Canterbury Tales, 139
Pontifex Maximus, 65
Pope
    and bishop of Rome, 75
    and Gregorian Reforms, 130
    infallible, 228
    moral and spiritual authority of, 228
    and Napoleon, 235–237
    recognized during Western Schism, 163–165
    and Ultramontanism, 235
Pope Benedict XII, and Babylonian Captivity of the Papacy, 160–161
Pope Benedict XIII; *see* Great Western Schism; Roger of Geneva
Pope Benedict XV, neutrality during war, 307, 314
Pope Benedict XVI, 361–362, 377
Pope Boniface VIII
    and jubilee year, 158
    and papal bull, 159
Pope Clement XI, 246
Pope Gregory II, and icon, 135
Pope Gregory VII, 131
Pope Gregory XVI, and slavery, 284
Pope Gregory the Great, 114
    and conversion of England, 106, 108–109, 111
    and Gregorian chant, 102
Pope Innocent III, and Albigensians, 150
Pope Innocent IV, and torture, 151
Pope Innocent XI, Four Gallican Articles, 233
Pope John Paul I, 357, 362
Pope John Paul II, 137, 303, 357–361, 362, 366, 369, 370, 377, 378, 381
    and Canon Law, 358
    and Communism, 359
Pope John XXIII, 165, 328, 334, 353, 366; *see also* Great Western Schism
    death of, 337
    from and of the people, 333
    and global community, 330, 332–333, 347
    Peace on Earth (Pacem in Terris), 330, 331
    story of, 332–333
    women, 331
Pope Julius II, and Michelangelo, 176
Pope Leo I, 70
Pope Leo III, 112, 113, 127
    and Charlemagne, 113
Pope Leo IX, and Sicily, 135, 136
Pope Leo XIII, 312
    and Americanism, 304–305
    and England, 302
    and France, 302
    and Germany, 301
    and industrialization, 295
Pope Paul III, 205
Pope Paul VI, 338, 356–357, 368
    as advocate of ecumenism, 346

liturgical reform, 338, 348–349
social justice, 347
United Nations, 330
Pope Pius IX, 237–238, 304, 361
    and Immaculate Conception, 238
    infallibility, 228
    and Papal States, 237
    Syllabus of Errors, 238
Pope Pius X, 249, 307, 308, 310, 317
    and modernism, 307
    story of, 308
Pope Pius XI, and communism, 314–315, 318
Pope Pius XII, 307, 316
    and communism, 321, 330
    and liturgical renewal, 321
    and World War II, 319–320
Pope Urban VI, and Great Western Schism, 163
Popular Devotions, 309
popular piety, 309
Portugal, and Christianity, 248, 249
precepts of the Church, 309
predestination, 198
Presbyterian, 197
presbyters, 55
Price, Father Thomas F., 312
Priest and Council of Trent, 205
Prince Metternich, 237, 274
printing press, and Reformation era, 187
Pro, Miguel, 303
Promised Land, 8
Protestant Reformation, 184
    and Peasants' Revolt, 191
    Council of Trent, 334
Protestantism
    differences with Catholicism, 184–192, 273, 280
    and Northern Ireland, 239
    and *sola scriptura,* 199
Protestants, meaning of, 191
Provincial Council, 275
Puritans, 195
    and Maryland, 270–271
    and Massachusetts, 270
Quakers, 273
Queen Elizabeth, 195, 239
Queen Isabella, 173, 194
Quigley, James F., 135
Radical Tradition, The, 87
rationalism, 225, 227
Ratzinger, Joseph; *see* Pope Benedict XVI
RCIA; *see also* Rite of Christian Initiation of Adults
Readings in Western Religious Thought, 170
reductions, 262
Reformation, 164, 177, 185; era,
    buying of church offices, 185–186
    Catholicism, 190–192
    causes of, 185–189
    church leaders, 185–186, 190
    Church of England, 195
    Diet of Speyer, 191
    heroes of, 190, 197–198

and indulgences, 186
and King Henry VIII, 194–195
and Martin Luther, 185
and nationalism, 187
Peace of Augsburg, 192
Peasants' Revolt, 191
poorly trained clergy, 167
and Presbyterianism, 197
printing press, 187
Protestantism and Catholicism, 193–195
Queen Elizabeth I, 195, 239
and Reformed Christianity, 185
and Renaissance, 175–177
spirituality of lay people, 191
and spread of Protestantism, 193–198
and Switzerland, 197
and theocracy, 197
reign of God, 11, 18, 19
Reign of Terror, 234
Renaissance, 175–177
problems during, 177
and Reformation era, 185
Rerum Novarum, 296
impact of, 296–297
Reuther, Rosemary Radford, 280
Rhode Island, and Roger Williams, 270
Ricci, Matteo, and China, 246
Richard the Lionhearted of England, and crusades, 145
Rite of Christian Initiation of Adults (RCIA), 350, 374
Rite of Baptism of Children, 72
Rogation Days, 100
Roger of Geneva, and Great Western Schism, 163
Roman Empire; *see also* Eastern Church; Western Church
and Arianism, 68
and bishop of Rome, 75
and Charlemagne, 112, 113, 122–125
and Constantine, 64–65
East and West, 41, 92, 133
and Edict of Milan, 66, 69
fall of Western , 74, 172
and Jewish people, 10, 13, 36
and persecution, 34, 36–38, 40, 41, 66, 93
and Thirty Years' War, 231
Roman gods, 51
Romanesque, 140
Romans 12:4–5, 54
Romans 16:1–7, 56
Romero, Oscar, 363–365
Roncalli, Angelo; *see also* Pope John XXIII
rubrics, 207
Ruiz, Alphonese, 213
Russia, conversion to Christianity, 131, 233
Russian Orthodox Church, 172–173;
Ryan, Father John A., and social reconstruction, 298
Sacrament of Penance, 186, 189, 309
and Vatican II, 339; *see also* Sacrament of Reconciliation

Sacrament of Reconciliation, 103, 186, 189, 309, 339
and indulgences, 186
and Saint Columban, 103
sacraments, 49
Baptism, 51
beginnings of, 50, 52–53
Church initiation, 51
and Church practice, 50
development of, 50–51
Eucharist, 21, 43
sacramentum, 50
sacrilege and treason, 45
Saint Ambrose, bishop of Milan, 78–79, 80
and Arians, 68, 70
and Saint Augustine, 80
Saint Angela Merici, story of, 211
Saint Anselm, 141
Saint Anthony of Egypt, 83, story of, 84
Saint Athanasius, archbishop of Alexandria, 77, 84
Saint Augustine, bishop of Hippo, 79, 80
Saint Basil, archbishop of Caesarea, 83
and monasticism, 83
Saint Bernard of Clairvaux, and crusades, 145
Saint Boniface
Apostle to Germany, 111
and conversion of Europe, 111
Christian God versus other gods, 111
Saint Bridget of Sweden, 161
Saint Catherine of Siena, 161–163, story of, 162
Saint Charles Borromeo, story of, 208
Saint Clare of Assisi, story of, 149
Saint Columban, 103
Saint Damien, modern spiritual life, 310
Saint Dominic, 150, 152
Order of Preachers, 150
Saint Elizabeth Ann Seton, and Catholic schools, 281
Saint Francis de Sales, 242
Saint Francis of Assisi, 146–148
and Friars Minor, 148
Saint George, as knight, 143
Saint Gregory (I) the Great, pope, 111, 114
Saint Gregory of Nazianzus, bishop of Sasima, 82
Saint Helena, 82
Saint Hilda, Abbess of Whitby, story of, 110
Saint Ignatius of Loyola, 209, 271
Saint Isaac Jogues, and Northern Native Americans, 267
Saint Jerome, priest, 75, 80–81
and Vulgate, 81
and women, 81
Saint John Chyrsostom, patriarch of Constantinople, 50, 82
Saint Joseph, and Vatican II, 337
Saint Katherine Drexel, 313
Saint Leo the Great, story of, 76
Saint Louise de Marillac, 242
Saint Macrina, 202

Saint Margaret Clitherow, story of, 202
Saint Monica, 82
Saint Nonna, 82
Saint Paul Miki and companions, story of, 247
Saint Paula, 81
Saint Philip Neri, story of, 211
Saint Rose of Lima, 260
Saint Thérèse of Lisieux, modern spiritual life, 311
Saint Thomas Aquinas, 141, 222, 227, 307
existence of God, 227
Saint Vincent de Paul, 242
Sanhedrin, 20, 35
Gamaliel's, 19
and John, 20
and Peter, 20
Santo Domingo, 283
Saperstein, Marc, 96
Saracens, 113, 125
Sarah, 6
Sarai; *see also* Sarah
Sarto, Giuseppe; *see* Pope Pius X
Saul of Tarsus; *see* Paul
Saul; *see* Paul
Savonarola, 177
Scandinavia, and Christianity, 177
schism, 163
East-West Schism, 133–137
scholasticism, 141, 222, 227
science
and Church, 220–225
characteristics of, 223
Scotland, and Presbyterianism, 239
Scriptures
identification of, 11
Protestantism and Catholicism, 280
second Constantine, 123; *see also* Charlemagne
selective conscientious objection, 371
Septuagint, 10
serf, 121
Service Requesting Pardon, 144
Seven Storey Mountain, The, 313
sharing, and Christianity, 21
shavu'ot, 13; *see also* Festival of Weeks
shim'on, 17; *see* Peter; Simōn
showings, and Julian of Norwich, 170
Sicily
and Cardinal Humbert, 136
East-West, 135, 136
and Patriarch Michael Cerularius, 135–136
and Pope Leo IX, 9, 135, 136
Simōn; *see* Peter; Shim'on
simony, 128
Sister Moon, 148
Sistine Chapel, and Michelangelo, 176
slavery, and American Catholics, 284–285
"Smiling Pope", 356; *see also* Pope John Paul I
social structure, 45
socialism, 293, 294
Socialist Bishop, 298
Society of Jesus, 209; *see also* Jesuits

sola scriptura, 199
Solutions to Violence, 323
Son of God, 13; *see also* Jesus; Messiah
Spain
    Catholicism in North America,
      256–265
    and Christianity, 173–174
    conquest of the Americas, 257–259
    and mistreatment of Native
      Americans, 257–260
    and slavery, 260, 282, 283
    and Spanish Inquisition, 173, 194
    and spread of Protestantism, 194
Spanish Inquisition, 173, 194
Spirit of God, 15; *see also* fire and wind;
  symbols
spiritual exercises, 209
spiritual life, 309
    Saint Damien, 310
spiritual and moral crisis, 328
    the Holocaust, 319–320, 328
St. Augustine, 262
St. Peter's Basilica, 17, 176, 186–187, 339,
  341, 360
St. Monica's church, 283
Stephen, 24, 27, 35
stigmata, 148
Story of a Soul, The, 311
Story of the Church, The, 229
Sultan Malik-al-Kamil, 146
Summa Theologica, 141
Switzerland, 197
Syllabus of Errors, 238
symbols, Spirit of God, 15
synagogues, 21
Synod of Whitby, 109, 110

T–V

teachers, 1
Tekakwitha, Kateri, story of, 268
Teresa of Ávila, 212–213
Tertullian, 40; *see also The Apology*, Deacon
  Laurence
Thalia (The Banquet), 68
theocracy, 197
theologian, 141
Thirty Years' War, 231
    and peace at Westphalia, 231
Tolton, Augustus, 283
torture, 173
Tradition, 48
Tradition of the Church, and knowledge
  of Jesus, 13–14
Trappists, 312
Trinity, 80
    and Council of Nicaea, 134
    and Eastern Orthodox, 134
    and Western Church, 134
Truce of God, 130
Twentieth-Century Apostles, 373
U.S. Catholic Bishops Apostolic Letter
  Novo Millenio Ineunte, 359
    Challenge of Peace: God's Promise and

Our Response, The, 371
    Economic Justice for All, 371
    Jubilee Year 2000, summary points,
      369
    Peace, and Vietnam, 371
Ukraine
    and Vladimir of Rus, 133
    conversion to Christianity, 133
Ultramontanism, 235
Uman Sanctam, 159
Union of Florence, 172
United Nations, 328–330
United States, and Church, 274, 284,
  371–374
Ur, 6; *see also* Iraq
U.S. system
    Catholicism, 274–276
    and culture diversity, 289
Valdivieso, Antonio, bishop of
    Nicaragua, Native American
    mistreatment, 258
Vandals, 74
    and Arianism, 74
Vanier, Jean, 367
Vatican Council I, 334
Vatican Council II, 316–317, 321, 327–349,
  353, 359, 362, 369
    documents, 341–345
    impact of, 338–345, 368
    liturgical reform, 321, 339
    social justice, 347
    themes and implications, 342–345
Venerable Bede, 109
Vietnam, and Christianity, 246
Vikings, and monasteries, 125
Visigoths, 74
Vladimir of Rus, 133
Vulgate, 81

W–Z

Walsh, Father James, 312
Western Christianity; *see* Christianity;
  Church; Western Church
Western Church
    and celibacy, 102, 128
    and Charlemagne, 112, 113, 122–125
    development of, 69
    differences with Eastern, 69, 133–137
    and feudalism, 126
    and Gothic, 140–141
    and icons, 134–135, 248
    language difficulties, 136
    and Magyars, 125
    and mystery, 50, 53, 137
    and patriarch, 95, 133–137
    and Saint Augustine, bishop of
      Hippo, 79, 80
    and Saracens, 113, 125
    and Sicily, 9, 135
    and split from Eastern Churches,
      133–137
    and Trinity, 134
    uniformity and Charlemagne, 124

Union of Florence, 172
  union with Western Europe, 123
  and Vikings, 125
Western Europe, 64; *see also* Christianity;
  Church; Roman Empire
White, Andrew Father, 271
William of Orange, 239
Williams, Roger, and Rhode Island, 270
Wisdom of the Saints, The, 83, 226; *see*
  also Saint Basil; Adels, Jill Haak
Wiseman, Nicholas, story of, 240, 302
Wojtyla, Karol; *see* Pope John Paul II
women
    auditors at Vatican II, 336
    Bowman, Sister Thea, 373
    Cabrini, Frances, 312
    Christina, Queen of Sweden, 232
    Clarke, Sister Maura, 364–365
    and convent, 85
    Donovan, Jean, 364–365
    Drexel, Katherine, 312
    and early Church, 56–57
    Ford, Sister Ita, 364–365
    Jones, Mary Harris, 299
    Margaret of Scotland, 132
    martyrs in El Salvador, 363–365
    Mary, Mother of the Church, 22
    and monasteries, 83–85
    and monasticism, 85
    Mother Theresa, 359, 366
    Oblate Sisters of Providence, 283; *see*
      also Mother Mary Lange
    Romans 16:1–7, 56
    Rose of Lima, 260
    Saint Angela Merici, 211
    and Saint Jerome, 81
    Sisters of Our Lady of Mercy, 280
    Tekakwitha, Kateri, 268
women's liberation movement, 331
World History of Christianity, A, 257
World Wars, 314–321, 328–329
    Catholic-Protestant Relations, 316
    Catholicism, 314–321, 328–329, 369
    Church and communism, 318
    WW II to the Cold War, 329–330
    lay involvement, 317
    liturgical renewal, 318
    and Native Clergy, 316
written Gospel, 46
Wyclif, John, 177
Xavier, Francis, 249, 311
Zagano, 373
Zwingli, Ulrich, 197